Risk Taking

Risk Taking

A STUDY IN COGNITION AND PERSONALITY

Nathan Kogan | *Michael A. Wallach*

GREENWOOD PRESS, PUBLISHERS
WESTPORT, CONNECTICUT

Library of Congress Cataloging in Publication Data

Kogan, Nathan.
　Risk taking.

　Reprint. Originally published: New York : Holt, Rinehart and Winston, c1964.
　Bibliography: p.
　1. Risk-taking (Psychology)　2. Decision-making.
3. Cognitive styles.　I. Wallach, Michael A.　II. Title.
[BF637.R57K63　1983]　　　153.4　　　　83-12584
ISBN 0-313-23250-4 (lib. bdg.)

153.4
K78

Copyright © 1964 by Holt, Rinehart and Winston

All rights reserved

Reprinted with the permission of Holt, Rinehart and Winston

Reprinted in 1983 by Greenwood Press
A division of Congressional Information Service, Inc.
88 Post Road West, Westport, Connecticut 06881

Printed in the United States of America

10 9 8 7 6 5 4 3 2 1

Preface

Psychology's recent past has witnessed what may be interpreted as a growing discontent with certain traditional distinctions of fields and topics that can be found as the chapter headings of almost any introductory textbook. "Thinking" typically has been dealt with as one area of inquiry, "personality" as another. So also "opinions and attitudes," "aptitudes and abilities," and "motivation" usually may be found as distinct and separate rubrics. The origin of these particular categories within psychology has, we would submit, been more one of historical and professional convention than of conceptual analysis. Thus, for example, concern with intellective aptitudes and abilities arose on the part of persons interested in assessment and selection of individuals for applied goals, while workers studying thinking and problem solving were to be found within the confines of research laboratories. Both groups seemed, however, to be dealing with cognate substantive issues. Neither group had much to do with animal psychologists, whose studies of the effects of physiological needs on various animal behaviors formed the nucleus of materials referred to under the "motivation" topic, nor were members of any of these three professional specialties often found to fraternize with clinical psychologists, whose concern with the emotions and affect in humans came to be described as "personality" research. "Motivation" and "personality" research both seemed to involve affect, however, and affect certainly possessed a potential role in thinking and intellective performance. Work on intergroup attitudes, prejudice, ideologies, and opinions, in turn, was carried on by researchers who had little contact with, for example, work either in the aptitude-testing tradition or in the tradition of experiments on thinking and problem solving. Again, however, attitudes and opinions certainly were forms of thinking, and certainly could covary with intellective abilities.

Some of these traditional separations have, to be sure, been breaking down over the last years. Thus, psychometric sophistication, once almost the sole province of those concerned with ability and achievement tests, now also can be found among students of attitudes and opinions and of personality. Work on motivation in animals has come increasingly to be applied to problems of the emotions in man. Yet it required an intrusion of theory from another social science, economics, before the beginnings of some radical changes in orientation could be glimpsed within psychology concerning the traditional demarcations noted above. Economists had been concerned for some time with how people make decisions when the element of risk is present. Economic theories of choice had been formalized over the last decades by Knight, Shackle, Marschak, and Arrow, among others. These approaches analyzed the expected consequences of decisions into two parts: the desirabilities of expected alternative outcomes, and the respective probabilities of the outcomes in question. The economists' attempts to come to grips with decision making under conditions of risk seemed to possess implications for psychological work in all the traditional areas of inquiry described above. The process as a whole concerned thinking and problem solving. The presence of consequences or "payoffs" introduced issues of personality and motivation. Matters of ability or aptitude could bear upon one's knowledge of the alternatives being considered. Further, questions of ideologies and attitudes could influence the evaluation of potential outcomes and of their likelihoods.

In short, the economists' concern with risk taking invited, if psychologists were to accept the challenge, a fundamental reanalysis of the problem of how man thinks, broadly conceived. We first came upon the economists' work, and first felt the challenge it offered to psychology, in the days when both of us were graduate students in social psychology at Harvard University. There, in the Laboratory of Social Relations building on Bow Street, we were exposed to the work that led to the book, *A Study of Thinking*, by Jerome S. Bruner, Jacqueline J. Goodnow, and George A. Austin. The Harvard research basically was concerned with analyzing the process of concept attainment in terms of the kinds of strategies persons may use in evaluating potential instances of a concept, and these strategies were defined with reference to risk and conservatism in one's attempts to gain knowledge of the concept. Here was an analysis of conceptualizing activities in decision-making terms.

Excited by the possibilities of this approach, we undertook a series of empirical investigations of various aspects of the risk-taking concept. This work, supported by a grant (M-2269) from the National Institute of Mental Health, United States Public Health Service, is briefly referred to in the first chapter of the present volume. Although the results of our studies gave us more knowledge about certain aspects of cognitive processes and a better understanding of the behavior involved in risk taking, we obtained no direct evidence to the effect that elements of individual differences in risk taking entered into cognitive behaviors. We even found ourselves forced to conclude in one paper that ". . . attempts to conceptualize various judgmental and cognitive processes in decision and risk terms must be considered premature." At about the same time, however, evidence began accumulating, in the area of expressive behavior as well as that of risk taking, which suggested that an evaluation of whether two variables are related or not for an unselected sample of persons may be too simple an approach. If the sample under study were divided in terms of some theoretically relevant characteristic, such as degree of emotional disturbance, it could be found that a particular kind of relationship might hold for one of these subsamples but not for the other. Emotional disturbance under such circumstances could be described as a characteristic which "moderated" another relationship — that is, which influenced the form of this other relationship. This technique of inquiry in terms of moderator variables seemed to hold promise of casting new light on the problems of interest to us.

Consideration of relevant moderating variables constitutes the basis of the research that is reported in the present volume. The result has permitted us to investigate risk taking as it operates within a motivational context, to study the meaning of generality and specificity in risk-taking behavior, to examine relationships with cognitive-judgmental and intellective ability behaviors, to consider how different individuals react to the consequences their decisions generate, and to evaluate the influence of personality considerations in steering persons toward risk or conservatism. All of this work can be described as an attempt to learn what concepts drawn from the study of risk taking can teach us about the psychology of thinking in its broad outlines. The outcome is a conceptual vantage point that prevents us from making a complete return to such insulated textbook chapter headings as "attitudes and opinions," "intelligence," "personality," and "thinking." We feel that the moderator variable method has permitted us to come a few steps closer in our interpretations to the behavior of individuals, while still maintaining quantitative rigor. The method may well hold promise, too, for other areas of psychological inquiry in addition to the one of concern in this volume.

The research that we shall report was supported in part by a grant (G-17818) from the Division of Social Sciences, National Science Foundation. We are indebted to a number of people for substantial contributions to the present work. Susan E. Karp and Leighton A. Price served with high competence as research assistants. John R. Dilworth was responsible for speeding the tabulation of data, and Henrietta L. Gallagher supervised the statistical analysis with indispensable care and responsibility. Gerri

Asbury provided invaluable secretarial assistance, and her typing of the manuscript was outstanding in its speed and accuracy. Christine A. Holcombe, Maude R. Pritchard, and Marie Davis carefully proofread the manuscript. Ellen Anderson contributed to the research with her highly effective performance of secretarial duties, Pauline B. Voorhees carefully supervised various clerical activities connected with the research, and Sally B. Matlack facilitated the work by her careful attention to various administrative matters and by her preparation of the index.

We are grateful, finally, to the many individuals who have provided us with valuable aid and criticism as our work has progressed. Among those whom we wish to thank are Donald K. Adams, Irving E. Alexander, Daryl J. Bem, C. Alan Boneau, Jack W. Brehm, Roger Brown, Fred L. Damarin, Norman Frederiksen, Fritz Heider, Edward E. Jones, Frederic M. Lord, Peter Madison, Donald G. Marquis, Samuel Messick, Halbert B. Robinson, David L. Rosenhan, David R. Saunders, Harold Schiffman, Lawrence J. Stricker, Ronald Taft, Michael Wertheimer, and Karl Zener. In addition, we are indebted to Theodore M. Newcomb for his aid in the processing of the manuscript. Our wives, Edith and Lise, also deserve our gratitude for their patience and understanding.

Princeton, New Jersey N. K.
Durham, North Carolina M. A. W.
January 1964

Contents

Preface   v

1 | THE PROBLEM   1

    Risk Taking and Cognitive Processes   2
    Generality within the Decision-Making Domain   7
    The Role of Intellective Processes   10
    The Role of Personality Processes   12

2 | THE PLAN OF THE STUDY   21

    The Subjects of the Study   21
    Details of the Procedure   21
    Method of Analysis   32

3 | RELATIONSHIPS WITHIN THE DECISION-MAKING DOMAIN   38

    Decision Making in Hypothetical versus Payoff Contexts   38
    Decision Making in Different Payoff Contexts   47

4 | POSTDECISIONAL PROCESSES   70

    Decision-Making Strategies and Monetary Outcomes   70
    Monetary Outcomes and Postdecision Satisfaction   79
    Decision-Making Strategies and Postdecision Satisfaction   88
    Summary   92

5 | DECISION-MAKING AND INTELLECTIVE PROCESSES 94

Verbal Aptitude 94
Mathematical Aptitude 102
Analytic versus Global Functioning 111
Summary 120

6 | DECISION-MAKING AND COGNITIVE-JUDGMENTAL PROCESSES 124

Confidence of Judgment 124
Extremity of Judgment 132
Category Breadth 146
Extremity of Self-rating 151
Summary 155

7 | PERSONALITY CORRELATES OF DECISION MAKING 159

Relationships for Samples as a Whole 159
Examination of Moderator Effects 164
Summary 185

8 | CONCLUSIONS AND IMPLICATIONS 188

Implications for Method 188
Implications for Risk-Taking and Postdecisional Processes 190
Implications for Cognitive-Judgmental Processes 193
Implications for Intellective Abilities 199
Implications for Personality Correlates 202
Implications for the Study of Thinking 205
Implications for Decision Making on National and Military Issues 211

References 215

Appendixes 221

Index 271

1

The Problem

We begin with an observation the general validity of which has become, in the modern world, all too tragically apparent: Human thinking can be colored by, and indeed sometimes dominated by, motivational factors.

Reason and the emotions have been recognized to be adversaries from the very beginnings of Western thought. It was Freud's contribution to fathom something of the depths from which these unruly emotions take their origins. Psychologists as yet know little, however, of the particular ways in which human thinking can be subject to influence from emotional quarters or can remain independent of such influence, the particular aspects of thinking that can be so subject, and the particular kinds of individuals who are more or who are less likely to be open to such influence. Indeed, we have yet to arrive at a firm understanding of the psychological processes involved in thinking, and of the kinds of manifestations, in turn, that can be considered to reflect greater or lesser motivational involvement in thought's progress. The research reported in this volume was undertaken with the hope of adding to our knowledge of these matters. In particular, the work here reported was inspired by an attempt to look at human thinking and problem solving from the point of view of the risks, potential costs, and potential gains that may face the individual as he proceeds in his efforts. Little is yet known about risk taking and about its possible implications for thinking. One can hardly afford to neglect the role that risk and conservatism may play in thinking, however, because of the obvious fact that many of the forms of psychological activity that we customarily call "thinking" eventuate in some kind of decision making. Decision making, in turn, involves the weighing of alternatives in terms of their desirabilities and their likelihoods. Issues concerning the avoidance or acceptance of risks in arriving at decisions hence are likely to be important ingredients in thinking processes.

The authors felt that an exploration of this general area might hold the key to an increased understanding of the motivational involvement that so often, and with such painful consequences, influences man's thought. The authors also hoped that such an exploration would further our knowledge of the other side of the coin — how to describe and conceptualize the workings of more "motivation-free" processes in thinking. An inquiry that held any promise of answering these questions seemed especially demanding of pursuit in an age when motivationally controlled thinking, if not understood for what it is and held in check, can have dire consequences for mankind.

In this first chapter, we shall consider the reasoning and evidence that led to the present research. In particular, we shall explore the possible relationships that may exist between risk taking and judgmental or cognitive processes, the question of generality within the risk-taking or decision-making domain, the possible roles that may be played by intellective ability factors, and the possible influences that may be exerted by personality dispositions.

RISK TAKING AND COGNITIVE PROCESSES

Over the course of the past few years, we have witnessed a marked trend toward conceptualizing various cognitive processes in strategy or decision-making terms. These efforts have essentially represented an attempt to bridge the gap between two traditions of theory and research that, until quite recently, followed fairly independent paths of emergence and development. The impetus toward *rapprochement* came, in large part, from the work of Bruner, Goodnow, and Austin (1956). Proceeding within the framework of concept attainment, these investigators suggested that subjective probability and utility considerations might enter into categorizing activities.

Further studies in the foregoing tradition followed. In a perceptual judgment experiment, for example, Bruner and Tajfel (1961) distinguished broad and narrow categorizers in terms of a willingness to risk errors of inclusion and exclusion, respectively. Further, these researchers concluded that in reacting to environmental change, the "narrow categorizer appears to prefer the risk of *reacting* and possibly being wrong. The broad categorizer prefers the risk of *not reacting* to change and possibly being wrong" (p. 241).

Although the study showed breadth and narrowness of categorization both to involve risks, albeit of different types, it is worth noting that Wallach and Caron (1959) described narrow categorizers as binding concepts to most frequent or familiar instances, a process suggestive of *conceptual conservatism.* Such an interpretation seemed particularly appropriate in the light of obtained sex differences that showed women to be consistently more narrow in their categorizing than men (see also Pettigrew, 1958; Wallach & Kogan, 1959). Also relevant were observations (Klein, 1958; Hamilton, 1957) suggesting that narrow categorization might be associated with anxiety and uncertainty.[1] Bruner and Tajfel remarked that narrow categorizers "have a tendency to minimize risk of error by the nay-saying route, preferring the consequences of error that come from avoiding contact with threatening objects" (1961, p. 231).

In a recent monograph, however, Gardner and Schoen (1962) seriously called into question the Bruner-Tajfel risk-taking interpretation on the grounds of a number of statistical and methodological artifacts. Gardner and Schoen concluded by rejecting a strategy or risk-taking analysis of categorization behaviors as a theoretically unprofitable pursuit. Such a challenge could hardly go unheeded, of course, and the authors accordingly hope in the present volume to explore exhaustively the risk-taking implications of various cognitive-judgmental processes.

In previous research the authors of this book began to examine the risk-taking implications of certain cognitive functions, with particular emphasis upon judgmental confidence and extremity. Sex and age differences in confidence and extremity were observed that appeared congruent with an interpretation of these variables in terms of some kind of risk-taking or boldness construct. Thus, the authors (Wallach & Kogan, 1959) found that males exhibited greater confidence of judgment than females. Males, furthermore, were more extreme than females in their judgments at low and moderate confidence levels, but the reverse pattern obtained at high confidence levels. In interpreting these findings, the authors proposed that "feminine conservatism is learned through fear of punishment in subjectively ambiguous situations. On the other hand, when a situation is perceived as highly certain, a counterphobic release of boldness seems to occur" (p. 563). With regard to age differences in confidence, the authors (Wallach & Kogan, 1961) found that young men were significantly higher in confidence than old men, but that young and old women did not differ in this respect. Turning to age differences in extremity, the authors observed that for both sexes, older subjects were less extreme at high confidence levels than younger, suggesting that an important consequence of aging might be a greater unwillingness to "go out on a limb" even when one was highly confident of one's judgment. Confidence of judgment also proved to be related to ratings of risk-relevant concepts in a semantic dif-

---

[1] In an unpublished factor-analytic study of categorization behavior, Messick and Kogan obtained a factor for women containing an inventory measure of anxiety and two indexes of narrowness of categorization.

ferential procedure (Kogan & Wallach, 1960). Subjects high in confidence evaluated such concepts as "risk" and "stock market" more positively than subjects low in confidence.

Various lines of evidence indicated, therefore, the apparent appropriateness of conceptualizing judgmental variables in risk-taking or decision-making terms. Encouraged by such findings from their own investigations and those of others, the authors attempted to relate measures of judgmental extremity and confidence, on the one hand, to measures of utility and subjective probability on the other. Although judgmental extremity and confidence were significantly related to each other, however — and utility and subjective probability were also significantly related — the authors found no associations between the judgmental and decision-making indexes (Wallach & Kogan, 1961). More recently, Slovic (1962), using a variety of cognitive and decision tasks, failed to demonstrate more than a slight degree of relationship between these domains. Finally, Brim, Glass, Lavin, and Goodman (1962), in a factor-analytic study of decision processes, reported that the extremity and desirability (utility) components of a decision yielded separate factors. These results of the authors and of other investigators were especially perplexing in view of the array of other cognitive findings that seemed to require some sort of general risk-taking interpretation.

One objective of the present research was the resolution of this apparent discrepancy. The path toward such a resolution may be clearer if we pause to take a closer look at the concepts and measures employed in previous research. Consider first the cognitive-judgmental area. In terms of its possible strategy implications, category width — to choose one example — seemed to be a highly appropriate variable. A person's possession of broader or narrower category boundaries evidently involves a preference for errors of inclusion or exclusion. Some subjects prefer to take the risk of including a few instances not belonging to the category, rather than risk leaving out any instances perceived as warranting category membership. Other subjects prefer to leave a few "correct" instances outside of the category, rather than risk including any instances that might not belong. Evidently, each of the foregoing strategies reflects risk taking of a distinct kind. The analogy to Type I and Type II errors in tests of statistical hypotheses is apparent.

Despite this clear qualitative distinction between strategies in establishing category boundaries, however, investigators have been predisposed to convert the distinction into a single, continuous dimension of risk taking. In this framework a preference for errors of inclusion and hence for wider categories was considered a less conservative strategy. The evidence for such a conceptualization, however, was of an indirect sort — age and sex differences indicating that females and older persons were more narrow and less extreme in their judgments, for instance. Although such evidence might be suggestive of an association between category breadth and greater risk taking, a note of caution was necessary until more appropriate and rigorous tests were conducted. There was no necessary *logical* reason that a cognitive task offering a choice between two qualitatively distinct forms of risk should have been linearly related to explicit risk-taking variables, or even linearly related in the one direction proposed. Because, in fact, there was evidence indicating that classes defined in terms of the characteristics that warrant inclusion possess greater psychological value than classes defined in terms of the characteristics that determined exclusion (Wallach, 1959), it might even have been suggested that, at least under certain conditions, errors of inclusion (which maximize the class of greater value) should have been perceived as a lesser risk, and errors of exclusion (which minimize the class of greater value) should have been perceived as a greater risk. A basis existed, in other words, for expecting that narrow categorizing (risk-of-exclusion errors) might represent stronger risk taking than broad categorizing (risk-of-inclusion errors). One of the purposes of the present investigation, then, was the clarification of existing relations, if any, between cognitive-judgmental forms of risk and the type of risk inherent in decision making.

A critical distinguishing characteristic between the kinds of risk involved in cognitive processes and in decision making concerns their implicit and explicit natures, respectively. The cognitive-judgmental tasks we have considered ostensibly deal with problem-solving performance; the risk element is more or less covert, emerging *implicitly* in terms of the strategy the subject employs in meeting the overt task requirements. Actually, the subject often was not told whether he had been correct or incorrect. Thus, the risk element, if present at all, is based on the subject's assessment of his own tolerance limits for error. Decision-making procedures, by contrast, introduce risk *explicitly*, in terms of the subject's assessment of probabilities of success and failure and their corresponding utilities preparatory to making a choice. The risk element is clearly explicit whether the decisions occur in a hypothetical success-failure context or in a situation involving direct gain-loss consequences.

Let us turn next to the validity problem. In the case of the cognitive-judgmental procedures, the processes conceptualized were quite close to the tasks employed, suggesting a high degree of face validity. Take the Pettigrew (1958) category width test as an example. Labeling an individual as a "broad categorizer" implied nothing more than that he tended to judge extreme instances of a category as more distant from a central tendency value, relative to comparable judgments rendered by "narrow categorizers." Or consider the Wallach and Caron (1959) "poggles" task, in which a series of geometric figures, identical but for variation in a single criterial attribute of acuteness of angle, were to be judged as belonging or not belonging to the "poggle" class. The subjects had previously learned in a concept-attainment situation that the figures constituting the class of "poggles" all possessed a particular angle. The formal similarity of the latter procedure — a geometric category width task — to the Pettigrew test may be readily appreciated. In both tests, all of the essential characteristics of the processes being conceptualized were mirrored in aspects of the experimental tasks.

Such is not the case in the decision-making domain. Many studies carried out from the viewpoint of individual differences have confined themselves to decisions in hypothetical contexts, often on the assumption that these represented a simulation of what the subject would have done in a real decision situation. Thus, the investigations by Slovic (1962), Brim *et al.* (1962), and the authors (Wallach & Kogan, 1959; 1961) were based exclusively upon decisions of a hypothetical kind. The subjects in these studies did not experience positive or negative outcomes as a consequence of their decisions. Choices in these hypothetical decision contexts thus might not have related to choices under payoff conditions. Accordingly, the failure to find generality in risk taking across the cognitive and decision domains might have been directly attributable to the hypothetical character of the decision tasks employed. Subjects' ego-involvement in decisions of a hypothetical sort might have been quite weak. By using decision outcomes involving monetary payoffs in substantial amounts, on the other hand, the investigators might have ensured that subjects would experience the positive and negative consequences of their choices. For this reason, decisions made under payoff conditions might have yielded the kinds of relationships with cognitive-judgmental tasks that actual studies failed to uncover.

In the authors' earlier work, subjects were presented with a 12-item instrument (Appendix E) in which each item represented a choice dilemma between a risky and a safe course of action. The subject's selection of the probability level for the risky alternative's success that would make it sufficiently attractive to be chosen thus reflected the deterrence value of failure in a particular decision area. The procedure was of a semiprojective nature, the subject having been asked how he would advise others in the situation described. It was assumed, of course, that the subject's advice to others reflected his own regard for the desirability of success relative to the disutility of failure. This "dilemmas of choice" situation obviously represented decision making of a hypothetical sort. No relations were found between the level of risk inherent in these decisions and scores on the cognitive-judgmental tasks described previously (Wallach & Kogan, 1961). The general weight of evidence, then, was suggestive of a high degree of specificity with regard to the kinds of risks embodied in cognitive-judgmental and in decision tasks. One reason that the authors deemed it premature to abandon the search for generality across these two areas, however, was the restricted set of decision-making variables that had been employed in previous studies. Given the scanty evidence regarding the relation between decisions in a hypothetical situation and in a context involving specific payoff consequences, the authors decided to focus directly on the issue by devising a variety of decision-making procedures incorporating payoff conditions. Such a step was expected to provide a basis for an exhaustive analysis of relations between the cognitive and decision domains. The utilization of a wider variety of decision-making procedures raised still another question, however: What generality exists with regard to the decision-making domain in and of itself?

GENERALITY WITHIN THE DECISION-MAKING DOMAIN

The authors turned, then, to the various kinds of decisions in whose terms questions of overt risk taking could be formulated. Considering first the distinction between chance and skill situations, the authors reasoned that one might well find that the tendency toward risk or caution exhibited consistency across these two types of settings, applying both in the case of decisions where outcomes were beyond the subject's control and in the situation where the positive or negative consequences of a particular decision were contingent upon the performance of the subject. On the other hand, the analytic distinction between chance and skill might prove to be an empirical distinction as well. Relationships found by Atkinson, Bastian, Earl, and Litwin (1960) between need achievement and risk taking were stronger when the risks involved concerned questions of skill rather than chance. This finding tended to support the view that decisions in chance and skill situations are psychologically dissimilar. A more direct examination of the chance-skill distinction by Littig (1962) indicated that, when compared with a chance-oriented group, a skill-oriented group tended to prefer lower objective probabilities of winning (for larger potential rewards), as if the involvement of one's own skill had swelled the subjective probabilities of success. An exhaustive discussion of the chance-skill dichotomy has been provided by Cohen (1960).

A distinction was also drawn by the authors between decisions of the bet-preference type (for example, Coombs & Pruitt, 1960) and decisions of the information-seeking kind where costs and prizes were introduced (for example, Irwin & Smith, 1957). In the former, probabilities of winning and losing were combined with monetary utilities of varying magnitude to yield a set of possible bets. These bets often were presented in a paired comparisons arrangement, the subject specifying the member of the pair he preferred to select, with the understanding that he would later have the opportunity to "play" all or some of the bets for the prizes involved. The information-seeking procedures, by contrast, posed a problem to be solved. Successive items of information relevant to the problem's solution were made available to the subject one unit at a time. The subject could request as much information as he wanted before rendering a decision, but the more he asked for, the lower his prize for a correct decision. The prize was forfeited for an incorrect solution. Accordingly, the risk element entered as the subject decided, relative to the costs incurred, when it was "safe" to venture a decision.

As a final procedural variation within the decision-making domain, the authors considered the question of the psychological implication of decision outcomes. Let us spell out this notion in some detail. A complete simulation of the decision making that characterizes everyday life would require, in the realm of monetary decisions, that the subject invest his *own* funds in his decision-making endeavors. The imposition of such a requirement in recruiting subjects would, of course, drastically attenuate the available pool of volunteers. Accordingly, most investigators have been willing to settle for a procedure in which funds were made available to subjects along with the opportunity to increase those funds during the course of the decision-making sequence. In such a case, a person could not leave the experimental situation any poorer than he entered, especially so where the person was reimbursed at a specified hourly rate for his time.

If subjects were required to invest their own money in the decision-making tasks, one might anticipate radical changes in the utility functions, depending, of course, on the subjective utility of money for the subjects concerned. For some individuals, the experimental situation would assume a predominantly negative tone, with the likely consequence that there would be a refusal to bet on less than an almost sure thing.

The authors make no claims to success in getting subjects to use their own financial resources in a decision-making experiment. The authors felt it to be entirely feasible, however, to achieve an approximation of that goal by presenting a subject with a final decision-making task in which his accumulated winnings over a series of prior decision-making procedures could be used to enhance those winnings, or, alternatively, could be lost. One might argue that the foregoing procedure could not allow for a net loss to the subject relative to his financial status at the beginning of the experiment. However, if a monetary prize had truly assumed a "belongingness" character for a subject (Heider, 1958), it seemed reasonable to expect that its loss would be keenly felt, particularly where an option was available not to gamble at all with that prize.

One element that could not be overlooked in the present context was the magnitude of prior accumulated winnings, because there might well be a relation between that value and the degree of risk taking manifested. Accordingly, when exploring the extent of consistency in risk-conservatism under conditions where the subject's financial resources were not in jeopardy and under circumstances where the subject was investing his own newly acquired resources, it was necessary to control for the magnitude of the latter. Whether consistency would obtain in the two contexts cited was, of course, a matter for empirical test. The present study will later offer evidence relevant to this issue.

Another point of concern to the authors in connection with overt risk taking was the relation between the person's style of decision making and the extent of his satisfaction with postdecisional outcomes. So, too, the authors felt it necessary to explore relations between decision making and outcomes and between outcomes and postdecisional satisfaction. Satisfaction-dissatisfaction with postdecisional outcomes has been a major preoccupation of cognitive dissonance theory (Festinger, 1957; Brehm & Cohen, 1962). Most of the relevant experimental work carried out in that tradition has involved the study of postdecisional processes as these have been affected by various situational manipulations. There has been little or no emphasis on the relationship between decision strategies and postdecisional processes. Nor has there been much concern with how and why individuals differ in their tolerance of cognitive dissonance and in their preferred modes of dissonance reduction. One investigator (Rosen, 1961), working on the assumption that the retention of dissonant cognitions involves the risk of being wrong, reported a significant inverse relationship in males between dissonance reduction and a cognitive risk measure of category width. Broad categorizers apparently tolerated cognitive dissonance better than did narrow categorizers. Unfortunately, Rosen used an "intelligence test" set in administering the category width test, thus complicating the interpretation of his findings. The present study will offer manifold opportunities for further exploration of relations between aspects of cognitive dissonance and both implicit and explicit risk-taking dimensions.

Although all of these decision procedures assessed various aspects of risk taking, there was little evidence regarding the empirical generality of a risky or cautious decision-making style across those procedures. We did have evidence (Wallach & Kogan, 1961) that the person who was more cautious in the hypothetical dilemmas of choice situation (greater disutility of failure) also tended to attach lower probability estimates to predictions of how well he would do in a motor performance context (greater subjective probability of failure), but no payoffs were involved in the latter case. The finding indicated the existence of some generality across decision-making tasks, but it was nevertheless evident that we had barely scratched the surface of the problem.

What psychological meaning, furthermore, were we to attach to such generality if it was revealed? In all of the various decision-making tasks that have been sketched, one could contrast two broad classes of decision-making determinants. On the one hand were the idiosyncratic task requirements that differentiated one of these procedures from another, and the idiosyncratic experiences that each person encountered in these various situations. On the other hand were the elements that the procedures shared, the most broad-gauged of these elements being the fact that all of the tasks, in one way or another, involved considerations of risk taking. To the extent that generality could be found — in other words, that consistently risky or conservative orientations would emerge across the wide range of these diverse decision-making situations — it would be evident that idiosyncratic situational requirements, which varied from task to task, had been slighted in favor of motivational predispositions toward risk or conservatism. One of the purposes of the present research was to determine whether such a dominance of motivational predispositions could be observed. To push the matter yet another step, could one find, in turn, that such a dominance was more characteristic of certain kinds of people than of others? This question, too, was one of the authors' concerns.

THE ROLE OF INTELLECTIVE PROCESSES

Information regarding the intellective correlates of decision making has been quite sparse. In their factor-analytic study of decision processes, Brim *et al.* (1962) did include a verbal intelligence measure, which yielded substantial loadings on several of the decision-making factors in one or more samples. Unfortunately, these results were generally ignored in the theoretical interpretations that Brim and his colleagues provided for their factors. Scodel, Ratoosh, and Minas (1959) compared Wechsler vocabulary subtest scores with risk taking in a gambling context, but no significant correlations were obtained. A significant inverse relationship between verbal aptitude and variability in risk taking was observed, however. Scodel *et al.* interpreted this finding as suggestive of dependence on previous outcomes in the less intelligent and the formulation of stable strategies in the brighter subjects. Note should be taken, however, of a failure, in a study by Liverant and Scodel (1960), to replicate the finding.

In the present investigation, the authors were concerned with intellective processes both as a control and as variables of interest in their own right. With regard to the control function, there was evidence indicating that categorizing behavior is not entirely independent of various abilities (Gardner, Jackson, & Messick, 1960; Bruner & Tajfel, 1961; Messick & Kogan, 1963). Hence, it seemed to be necessary, when relating cognitive-judgmental and decision-making variables, to consider the influence of more strictly intellective processes.

There was the further possibility of a direct association between decision making and aptitude. In bet-preference and information-seeking tasks, there might possibly prove to be strategies that were optimal in the sense of maximizing a subject's winnings. The individual of higher intelligence might be more insightful with regard to optimizing than his less intelligent counterpart. A test of this hypothesis seemed quite possible in the context of the present investigation, given the actual payoffs subjects received when called upon to implement their decisions.

Another issue that had to be considered when dealing with traditional measures of verbal and mathematical aptitude concerned the penalty for guessing customarily included in the instructions to such tests. These tests thus might be influenced by risk-taking considerations. The gambling response set in test taking was first described by Cronbach (1946) and relevant empirical studies were subsequently carried out by a number of investigators (Sheriffs & Boomer, 1954; Coombs, Milholland, & Womer, 1956; Ziller, 1957; Messick & Hills, 1960; Quereshi, 1960; Slovic, 1962).

The measures of intellective processes incorporated in the present study were three in number. Verbal and mathematical aptitude tests were included so that we might further explore relations between decision making and the conventional indexes of intelligence. The authors also decided, however, to include, as an index of analytic functioning, an embedded figures procedure involving the ability to extract a form from a confusing context. Performance on this test was orthogonal to verbal and mathematical aptitude, but on the other hand was highly correlated with performance on spatial relations indexes (Gardner, Jackson, & Messick, 1960) and on various subtests from the "performance" section of the Wechsler intelligence scales for children and for adults (Witkin, Dyk, Faterson, Goodenough, & Karp, 1962). Of particular interest, for the authors' purposes, was the relation between embedded figures performance and the field-independence construct. A net of intellective, cognitive, and personality relationships had been shown to surround that construct (Witkin, Lewis, Hertzman, Machover, Meissner, & Wapner, 1954; Witkin et al., 1962), but the relationship between field-independence–field-dependence and decision-making variables had not been explored, though one might well have expected connections to exist on the basis of the personality structures presumed to characterize field-independent and field-dependent individuals. The results available in the literature were so far from clear, however, that it was quite difficult for the present authors to formulate directional hypotheses. Thus, Elliott (1961) reported that field-dependent persons tended to describe themselves as indecisive, practical, and conventional, qualities that one might expect to be associated with conservatism in decision making. At the level of defense mechanisms, however, Witkin et al. (1962) and Crutchfield and Starkweather (1953) found evidence suggesting that the field-dependent subject "undercontrols impulses," "acts with insufficient thinking and deliberation," is restless and impulsive in a childish manner. Field-independent persons, in contrast, were found to be "overcontrolled," "meticulous," "aloof," "overdefended against feeling." On these bases one would predict that the field-dependent individuals would be the greater risk-takers, feeling more free to indulge in bold, reckless adventures whereas with their carefulness and their control against impulsiveness, the field-independent persons would be the more conservative.

In short, a depth approach to personality seemed to generate a set of expectations with regard to field independence and decision making that was quite the reverse of a surface-trait approach. The authors expected the examination of relationships between decision-making indexes and embedded figures performance to prove quite enlightening with regard to the implications of the field-independence construct for risk and conservatism in various decision-making contexts.

THE ROLE OF PERSONALITY PROCESSES

Finally, the authors considered the role of personality. That the authors were concerned with the possible part played by anxiety in mediating categorization behavior has already been mentioned. One could cite, in addition, an array of studies exploring relationships between risk taking and a variety of personality dimensions. Atkinson (1957) offered a theoretical model relating need achievement and fear of failure (test anxiety) to risk taking in skill contexts, a model receiving empirical confirmation in a study by Atkinson and Litwin (1960). Scodel et al. (1959) reported that the Atkinson model also fits the case of risk taking in chance contexts (gambling behavior), and in addition they found value and social class differences between those who preferred high or low payoff bets. Again in a gambling context, Liverant and Scodel (1960) demonstrated a relationship between risk taking and extent of internal-versus-external control revealed by a forced-choice personality inventory (the general feeling that one is either more of an active, causal agent or more of a passive recipient of effects in dealings with one's environment). A penchant for internal control evidently contributed to lower levels of risk taking and to less variability in the choice of decision alternatives when the setting involved chance — in other words, when in fact no internal control was possible.

The present study proposed to employ personality variables in a markedly different way. Rather than confining themselves to a search for additional personality correlates of risk-taking behavior, the authors decided to cast personality variables into a moderator role.[2] It appeared possible that previously unsuccessful attempts to find relationships between cognitive-judgmental and decision indexes reflected the failure to use appropriate personality dimensions as moderator variables rather than the genuine absence of such relationships. The authors suspected that samples divided into high and low subgroups on a critical personality dimension might exhibit different patterns of correlations between cognitive and decision variables. In one or the other subsample, for instance, relations between these two domains might be strong and positive; in the other, relations might be weak but positive — or absent, weakly negative, or strongly negative. Because of this possibility of different correlational patterns, a negligible zero-order correlation in the sample as a whole might well obscure relationships of substantial magnitude in subsamples divided on the basis of a relevant moderator.

The authors had achieved a modicum of success in discovering moderator relationships in a related problem area. The authors (Kogan & Wallach, 1961) had demonstrated the moderating function of manifest anxiety in affecting the magnitude of relations between subjective age and risk taking in an older sample. The older those subjects low in anxiety felt, the less willing they were to expose themselves to risk. Highly anxious subjects, on the other hand, exhibited no relationship between these variables.

What were the most likely candidates to select as potential moderators in the present context? The authors felt that test anxiety and defensiveness offered the best leads. Atkinson (1957) had conceptualized test anxiety as a motive to avoid failure. On this basis, two possible outcomes were indicated when test anxiety was cast in the role of moderator between cognitive-judgmental and decision-making variables. First, it was conceivable that test anxious subjects would perceive and respond to cognitive-judgmental as well as to decision tasks in success-failure terms. This finding would obviously serve to increase the magnitude of relationships between the domains under consideration. On the same line of reasoning, subjects low in test anxiety would manifest a contrastingly greater independence between decision and cognitive-judgmental contexts, because such individuals would presumably be less sensitized to the potential success and failure implications of their performances in the cognitive-judgmental domain.

There was, however, an equally compelling antithetical possibility. One might reason that previous failures to obtain significant relations between cognitive-judgmental and decision-making variables were a direct outcome

---

[2]Statistical aspects of moderator variable analysis are described in Ghiselli (1956; 1960a; 1960b; 1963) and in Saunders (1956). The general relevance and potentialities of this form of analysis in personality and cognition research are discussed in Wallach (1962).

of the presence of highly test anxious individuals in the sample under study. According to this view, test anxiety might be a motivational disruptor the effect of which was to prevent the emergence of performance consistencies in the various cognitive-judgmental and decision tasks used in earlier investigations.

Consider next the variable that has been variously designated as "repression" and "denial" (S. Freud, 1925; A. Freud, 1946), "defensive inhibition" (White, 1956), and "defensiveness" (Rogers, 1959); we shall employ the last of these designations. Assuming that defensiveness implies an excessive concern with image maintenance, we might expect that risk or caution would comprise an integral part of the self-image, with the defensive individual adopting a risky or conservative posture consistent with the image. Such a defensive concentration upon image maintenance, the authors believed, would contribute toward a heightened consistency relative to the more casual approach of the nondefensive individual, who might be more sensitive to the particular properties of the various cognitive and decision tasks confronting him.[3]

The authors did not expect that the moderator functions of test anxiety and defensiveness would necessarily be confined to relations between cognitive-judgmental and decision-making behaviors. It was entirely conceivable that the relation of intellective performances to decision-making processes might also be susceptible to the moderator effects of test anxiety and defensiveness. Finally, such moderator influences might also be manifest within the decision-making domain itself. In both of the foregoing cases, the authors were again in no position to state specific hypotheses with regard to differences in the magnitude and sign of correlations in subsamples of subjects comprised in terms of test anxiety and defensiveness scores. There was no basis in previous theory and research for formulating monolithic predictions in the present problem area. One could merely point out some of the various possible alternatives, and then go on to discover which of them actually obtained.

With regard to aptitudes and decision making, it seemed reasonable to suppose that test anxiety and, possibly, defensiveness would affect the utilization of intelligence in a decision-making context. Excessive concern about failure or a strong need to impress another — an experimenter, in particular — with one's boldness in making decisions could hardly fail to

---

[3]The authors' choice of moderators was influenced not only by conceptual considerations, but also by the authors' success when employing similar moderators in other contexts (Kogan & Wallach, 1961; Wallach & Gahm, 1960; Wallach & Greenberg, 1960; Wallach, Green, Lipsitt, & Minehart, 1962). Given the directions suggested by this prior work, the authors felt it inadvisable at the present time to consider still other possible moderators such as need achievement.

interact with a subject's ability level to accentuate or depress levels of risk taking. Thus, the highly test anxious person of high intelligence might structure a decision task as one in which avoiding miscalculation and rash impulse would bring greater rewards, whereas the highly intelligent individual low in test anxiety might show the kind of imaginative flexibility that would permit greater risks in the pursuit of monetary reward. The latter type of subject might define the decision-making task as constituting a distinct challenge to range freely into high levels of risk.

Turning to relationships among the decision-making tasks themselves, the authors found various possibilities when moderator influences were taken into account. Considering, for example, the relation between bet strategies and information-seeking procedures, the authors noted the radical difference between the decision contexts in the two cases, and accordingly reasoned that any significant positive relationship that emerged between them would, of necessity, reflect a consistent mode of monetary risk regulation. Was such consistency more likely to emerge in subsamples low on the moderator variables under discussion? Or, on the other hand, would test anxiety and defensiveness prove to enhance motivational arousal and hence the salience of the success-failure aspects of these tasks, thereby contributing toward consistencies across explicit risk-taking procedures? The latter alternative appeared the more probable, for the reason that matters of explicit risk and conservatism might be expected to motivationally engage those persons ranking high on test anxiety and defensiveness to a stronger degree than individuals low in these personality dispositions. The reader will recall the earlier discussion of fear-of-failure implications of test anxiety and the image-maintenance aspects of defensiveness.

Other relationships within the decision-making domain also constituted likely candidates for moderator effects. Thus, there were the important associations that might exist among decision-making indexes, postdecision outcomes, and satisfaction. With regard to the relation of monetary outcomes to decision-making strategies in a context of skill, for example, there might prove to be possible debilitating effects of test anxiety on skilled performance in a success-failure situation. As a consequence, high and low test anxious subjects might employ identical risk-taking strategies in a decision task involving motor skill, yet the magnitude of the correlation of strategy indexes with actual monetary results might vary substantially.

Earlier in this introduction the authors spoke of the feasibility of making the risk implications of decisions in a laboratory context more lifelike by permitting a subject to accumulate a monetary prize and then providing him with the option of betting it in a subsequent decision task. Allusion was made to the necessity of controlling the magnitude of the prize in order to evaluate the extent of subsequent risk taking. The authors felt that the relationship between prior accumulated winnings and subsequent risk taking might well vary as a function of the moderator variables under study. Phrased very directly, the question was one of determining whether persons high or low in test anxiety and/or defensiveness would be more influenced by the size of the potential stake in arriving at a decision concerning the level of risk to assume in gambling with it.

The authors could conceive of a case where the prior winnings would be so very substantial that the utility of a further gamble would drop to zero. The magnitude of winnings in the present experiment could obviously not achieve such proportions. Still, as the authors have suggested, it could be expected that subjects would be more reluctant to gamble with larger sums of money. This "apparent" relationship — one based on purely rational monetary considerations — might well be aborted in the case of subjects for whom taking on or turning down a gamble had special emotional significance. It was not difficult to assess where such subjects might fall on dimensions of test anxiety and defensiveness.

The authors considered, finally, the possible moderator relationships that might operate in the case of postdecision satisfaction with outcomes. Again, if the meaning of winning and losing varied with test anxiety and defensiveness, the association between such monetary outcomes and the expression of dissatisfaction with one's prior bets could well assume different forms in the various moderator subgroups. The detailed specification of such functional relationships in personality subgroups would contribute substantially, the authors felt, to the study of individual differences in cognitive dissonance phenomena.

Thus far, the authors had speculated on the effects of moderator variables considered one at a time. An analysis at that level did not allow for the possibility that test anxiety and defensiveness might interact in distinctive ways to affect the magnitude and direction of relationships among the variables under study. The discovery of such moderator interaction effects would require a division of the sample of subjects on the basis of test anxiety and defensiveness considered simultaneously. If the degree of association between the moderators proved to be low, four subgroups with approximately equal numbers of subjects in each could be formed: low test anxiety–low defensiveness; high test anxiety–low defensiveness; low test anxiety–high defensiveness; and high test anxiety–high defensiveness.

The authors then attempted a psychological delineation of the kinds of persons one might find in each of the four subgroups produced by dividing samples on both moderators simultaneously. Subjects low in both test anxiety and defensiveness would appear to be the least disturbed. Their low level of defensiveness would suggest that they were also genuinely low in test anxiety. When test anxiety was high and defensiveness was low, the anxiety evidently would reach consciousness and could, in Atkinson's (1957) terms, enhance motivation to avoid failure. One would expect such subjects to be especially sensitive to the failure and monetary loss potential of the various procedures employed in the study. Subjects low in test anxiety and high in defensiveness might be described as "successful defenders." For these subjects, anxiety presumably would serve a "signal" function (S. Freud, 1936), which would distort and blunt the expression of psychically dangerous drives. Strict denial of shortcomings and weaknesses and overemphasis of positive qualities would characterize such persons. Finally, there would be the subjects high in both test anxiety and defensiveness. These individuals might be described as unsuccessful defenders. The defensive processes, which would work with overseverity in most spheres for such persons, would apparently be ineffective in the case of the stresses created in test and academic performance contexts. Fear of failure, in short, might appear to break through the defensive barriers erected to handle anxiety signals. In considering the four types of individuals described, one might be tempted to conceive of the highly test anxious and defensive person as the most conflicted and disturbed. It is necessary to note, however, that the powerful defensive structure characteristic of such persons strongly suggested that, relative to their highly test anxious but low defensive peers, they might be more adept at coping with the stress aroused in success-failure contexts.

In sum, then, the authors proposed to locate the subjects in one of four subgroups on the basis of the moderator variables of test anxiety and defensiveness. Within each subgroup, relations among the major variables of the study would be explored.

A word about sex differences is very much in order. Earlier in this introduction, the authors referred to differences between males and females in the general nature of their performances on cognitive-judgmental and decision-making tasks (Wallach & Caron, 1959; Wallach & Kogan, 1959). The effect of sex as a moderator variable has received little attention. In a related area, Gardner, Holzman, Klein, Linton, and Spence (1959) demonstrated that the direction and magnitude of interrelationships among cognitive control principles were sex-linked. The authors would have been quite surprised, then, if males and females did not yield a different pattern of correlations between variables in the domains under investigation here. There was every reason to suspect on intuitive grounds that the psychological meaning and implications of risk taking might differ in males and females. Such differences could be expected to affect patterns of relationships in the male and female samples as a whole; but it was of greater significance that the patterns of relationships that resulted from employing test anxiety and defensiveness as moderators might also be different for the two sexes. For this reason, the authors decided that results would be reported separately by sex throughout.

The authors turned finally to the issue of direct personality correlates of risk taking. This phase of the study of personality's role, although secondary in importance to consideration of the moderator function of personality variables, nevertheless held promise of contributing to our knowledge of risk-taking behavior. Furthermore, the present investigation provided an opportunity to explore some of the behavioral implications, if any, of various paper-and-pencil scales of self-described personality characteristics. Psychological literature has reported a number of personality scales the content of which would lead one to expect significant associations with actual risk-taking behavior. It was understood, of course, that failure to find such associations would not invalidate the scales employed, for the obvious reason that they had not been constructed for the purpose of predicting extent of risk taking. If, however, significant relationships with risk taking could be obtained, we would have learned a bit more about risk-taking behavior, and at the same time we would have gained a greater appreciation of what the personality scales in question might be measuring. In short, the authors were engaged in an exercise in construct validation (Cronbach & Meehl, 1955).

The authors might describe the particular scales used in their work for direct correlational purposes. Moderator variables have already been discussed and need not concern us further here. Content scales in the present phase of the study included manifest anxiety, rigidity, impulsiveness, self-sufficiency, and independence. It was the authors' expectation that manifest anxiety and rigidity would be inversely related to risk taking, whereas impulsiveness would be positively associated with risk taking. The basis for these expectations was a strictly intuitive one. It seemed reasonable to suppose that manifest anxiety and rigidity would inhibit boldness in decision making out of fear for negative consequences. Such consequences, it was felt, would exacerbate symptoms in the manifestly anxious, and would signify loss of control in the rigid individual. Conservative behavior in decision-making tasks would therefore prove a less threatening course for "anxious" and "rigid" individuals to pursue.

Impulsiveness, by contrast, was expected to enhance risk-taking tendencies. Persons scoring high on an impulsiveness scale were expected to pay less regard to future consequences of decisions than nonimpulsive individuals. The authors suspected that subjects who avoided a critical, reflective set on decision-making tasks might turn out to be greater risk takers. The assumption made here, of course, was that critical reflection and impulsiveness are incongruous psychological characteristics.

Self-sufficiency and independence, in turn, appealed to the authors as characteristics likely to be associated with intermediate levels of risk taking. Persons high on those characteristics, in the authors' view, would eschew both the conservative and risky extremes as nonoptimal, preferring instead more "rational" strategies entailing moderate risks and payoffs.

A number of scales tapping response styles were included both for control purposes and as variables of interest in their own right. With regard to the control aspect, the inclusion of social desirability and acquiescence scales might inform us whether any relationships between content scales and decision-making variables were partially attributable to systematic tendencies to respond in a socially desirable or agreement-prone manner, respectively. At the same time, evidence was accumulating that response styles were important personality variables in their own right (Jackson & Messick, 1958), though it was noted that attempts to relate response styles derived from personality inventories to nonverbal behavior on independent experimental tasks had not met with great success (McGee, 1962). The authors resolved, however, to pursue the matter further by examining the magnitude of relations between indexes of acquiescence and social desirability, on the one hand, and measures of risk-taking behavior on the other. A third response-style index could be derived from a personality inventory when the format permitted the subject to express on a rating scale the degree to which the statement was characteristic of him. We shall call this stylistic indicator a person's "extremity of self-rating." Peabody (1962) had recently demonstrated that extremity scores in bipolar scales were independent of content dimensions and showed wide generality across various content domains.

In the present context, an extremity score seemed to represent the degree of judgmental conviction a subject displayed in endorsing or rejecting various self-referent statements. A person with a high extremity of self-rating score evidently exuded a great deal of confidence in indicating the sort of person he was. If such self-confidence extended to judgments and decisions about external events, we might well find a greater willingness to take risks on the part of the more extreme individual, relative to the risk-taking behavior of the person who did not rate himself extremely.

How about moderator relationships in the case of the personality variables described? There was a special problem here, one that could be relatively ignored in the case of relationships in the ability, cognitive-judgmental, and decision-making domains. Personality variables derived from inventory scales tend to intercorrelate with one another. Hence, the authors could probably expect some statistically significant correlations between the personality dimensions selected as moderators — test anxiety and defensiveness — and some of the other personality indicators discussed. The statistical implication of such a correlation was rather serious in the present case, for restriction-of-range problems would arise if either of the variables in whose relationship the authors were interested was in turn significantly associated with either of the moderators. Nevertheless, it might well be that some of the personality variables in question were independent of both moderators. If such was the case, the exploration of possible moderator effects again became relevant. Of course, even in the case where the moderator was related to neither of the variables being correlated, moderator differences would not be affirmed unless we were assured that variances of measures in the moderator subgroups were reasonably comparable. Differential variability would, of course, lead to differences in the magnitude of correlations, quite apart from whatever psychological effects might be operative.

Summing up, the present study proposed to inquire into the following questions:

1. What relations exist among conservatism-risk of decisions made in a hypothetical context and in various payoff contexts?

2. What are the relationships among decision-making strategies, outcomes, and postdecisional satisfaction?

3. Do cognitive-judgmental processes have risk-taking implications?

4. Do the various intellective abilities affect conservatism-risk in decision making?

5. Can relationships be found between personality and decision-making variables that will contribute to a better understanding of both?

6. When test anxiety and defensiveness are cast into the role of moderator variables, do they influence the pattern of relationships among decision-making measures, and the pattern of relationships of these, in turn, to cognitive-judgmental, ability, and personality indexes?

In the chapters that follow, the authors will first describe the study's procedures; then report the findings and consider them in the light of the foregoing questions and of the other points that have been treated in the preceding pages; and finally, turn to the major conclusions that have been reached as a result of this research.

2

The Plan of the Study

THE SUBJECTS OF THE STUDY

A total of 114 male undergraduates and 103 female undergraduates comprised the subjects of the authors' research. These subjects attended two similar noncoeducational private colleges of superior scholastic reputation with student bodies predominantly middle class in socioeconomic background. The subjects were volunteers recruited on the basis of advertisements in the college newspaper and announcements in classes. Subjects were told that they would be paid at the rate of approximately $1.50 per hour, and in addition, they were informed that they would have the opportunity to earn more money on some of the experimental procedures employed in the investigation.

DETAILS OF THE PROCEDURE

Administration of the entire battery of procedures required approximately five hours. Two to three sessions were scheduled for each subject. The first session consisted of procedures adapted for group administration, and accordingly subjects were run in small groups ranging in size from approximately 10 to 15 during this phase of the study. Upon completion of the group-administered procedures, subjects were scheduled for one or two individual sessions devoted to those procedures requiring individual administration. For this phase of the study, a female experimenter was provided for the female sample, a male experimenter for the male sample.

The various procedures employed are classified and described as follows.

Cognitive-judgmental measures

The procedures in the cognitive-judgmental category were group-administered.

1. CATEGORY WIDTH TEST. A complete description of the category width test may be found in Pettigrew (1958). It is entitled "Estimation Questionnaire" and is introduced as being "designed to find out what types of estimates people make about a number of things." In brief, the test consists of 20 multiple-choice items, each listing the average value of a particular category or dimension and requiring the subject to select the largest and smallest members of the category. High scores on the test reflect broad categorization — selection of values deviating substantially from the average value provided. Pettigrew reported that the test yields two factors, one unrelated to and one significantly correlated with mathematical aptitude. Accordingly, two scores were obtained in the present study, based on the item factor loadings reported in the Pettigrew article.

2. JUDGMENT EXTREMITY-CONFIDENCE PROCEDURE (APPENDIX D). The judgment extremity-confidence instrument was adapted from a study by Brim (1955) and had been employed in earlier work by the authors (Wallach & Kogan, 1959; Wallach & Kogan, 1961). In brief, the test consists of 50 statements of the sort, "The chances that event X is so are about ——— in 100." Five confidence categories follow, with the subject requested to specify whether he is "very sure," "quite sure," "moderately sure," "slightly sure," or "not sure at all" of his judgment. These categories were weighted 5 to 1, respectively, so that higher scores would reflect greater confidence. With regard to extremity, judgments are more extreme as they deviate up or down from an estimate of 50 in 100. Higher scores thus reflect greater extremity.

For purposes of the present analysis, separate extremity scores were obtained at each of three levels of confidence. Judgments rendered at "very sure" and "quite sure" levels were combined to yield a score for extremity under high confidence. Correspondingly, probability estimates given under "slightly sure" and "not sure at all" conditions were combined to yield a score for extremity under low confidence. Judgments in the "moderately sure" category were not included in the present analysis, so that we might be able to make extremity comparisons under markedly different confidence conditions.

3. EXTREMITY OF SELF-RATING. The index of extremity of self-rating concerns the degree of intensity of accepting or rejecting personality statements as descriptive of oneself. This index as used in the present study was derived from personality-inventory materials that will be discussed in the

next section. The inventory, heterogeneous with respect to item content, employed a 6-point response format. Items were assigned values of 1, 2, and 3 for least, intermediate, and most extreme responses, respectively.

Personality measures

Measures of personality were obtained by means of two inventories in which items from various scales were randomly mixed. One of the inventories employed a "true-false" response format; the other made use of a 6-point Likert scale format. Many of the scales employed were balanced — half of the items were keyed in one direction, the remaining half in the opposite direction. Balanced scales have the clear advantage of reducing the contribution of acquiescent and nay-saying response styles to the content score derived from the scale.

In listing the various personality scales employed in the study, the authors will first cite those used as moderator variables, then proceed to scales proposed as direct correlates of risk taking, and conclude with scales included for control purposes.

As an index of the moderator variable of *test anxiety*, the anxiety scale developed by Alpert and Haber (1960) was used. This is a balanced 19-item instrument. Ten of the items are keyed in the test anxious direction (they are of the form, "Anxiety hinders my test performance — agree or disagree"), and the remaining nine are keyed in the opposite direction (they are of the form, "Anxiety facilitates my test performance — agree or disagree"). Also included in the inventory was the Sarason (1958) Test Anxiety Scale. The latter has 21 items of which 18 are keyed in the test anxious direction. The authors chose the Alpert-Haber in preference to the Sarason scale as a moderator chiefly because of the balanced property that makes the Alpert-Haber scale less susceptible to acquiescent and nay-saying response tendencies. The two scales do, however, correlate quite highly with each other ($r = .57$ for males, $r = .60$ for females). When the respective reliabilities of the scales are taken into account, (Appendix C), it is evident that both are tapping essentially the same construct.

We turn next to *defensiveness* as a moderator variable. Here, the authors chose to employ the scale devised by Crowne and Marlowe (1960). This is a 33-item balanced scale conceptualized by its authors as a measure of the "need for social approval." Item style and content indicate that the instrument has "lie scale" properties, and accordingly, it was used in the present investigation as a "defensiveness" index — an index of the tendency to deny personal traits that, although moderately undesirable, are possessed by virtually everyone and to accept traits that are highly desirable but possessed by virtually no one. Support for this analysis of the Marlowe-Crowne scale has been provided by Strickland and Crowne (1963), who found that high scorers on the scale terminate psychotherapy earlier than do low scorers. The inventory also contained 26 items that Sarason (1958) selected from the MMPI K Scale, also presumably related to defensiveness. Of the 26 items, all but two are keyed in the defensive direction. The authors' preference for the Marlowe-Crowne scale was again partially based on the fact of its balanced keying. It must be noted, however, that the r's between the Marlowe-Crowne and the K scales are .64 and .34 for males and females, respectively.

We turn next to those scales included as possible direct correlates of risk taking:

1. SELF-SUFFICIENCY SCALE. The self-sufficiency scale used was a balanced 10-item scale adapted from the Personality Research Inventory (Saunders, 1955). Properties of the revised scale were reported in Messick (1962).

2. INDEPENDENCE-YIELDING SCALE. The version of the independence-yielding scale used contained 14 items adapted from Barron (1953) and Crutchfield (1955). Seven items were keyed in each direction.

3. GOUGH-SANFORD RIGIDITY SCALE (ORIGINAL ITEMS LISTED IN ROKEACH [1960]). The Gough-Sanford Rigidity Scale comprises 24 items, balanced for rigidity-flexibility keying.

4. IMPULSIVENESS SCALE (BARRATT, 1959). Twenty-two items were selected to yield a balanced impulsiveness scale, with 11 items keyed in each direction.

5. MANIFEST ANXIETY SCALE. The short form of the Manifest Anxiety Scale (MAS) developed by Bendig (1956) was used. The scale contains 20 items, of which 16 are keyed in the anxious direction.

In addition to these content scales, two "response style" scales were included for control purposes and as measures of interest in their own right, as follows.

6. SOCIAL DESIRABILITY SCALE (EDWARDS, 1957). The Social Desirability Scale is a 39-item instrument on which extensive research findings have been reported. It is designed to assess the tendency to respond consistently in a socially acceptable manner.

7. ACQUIESCENCE. Couch and Keniston's (1960) Agreement Response Factor was used to test acquiescence. There are 18 items, of which 11 are keyed in the acquiescent direction. This scale measures the tendency to agree or disagree consistently, regardless of content, in answering inventory items.

A few comments about scoring are in order. Scores for each scale were derived by counting the number of keyed items endorsed. For this purpose, the inventory employing the 6-point response format was given dichotomous scoring in terms of the direction of response. The extremity information was retained for another purpose, however. Namely, the inventory in question was scored for *extremity of self-rating* as described previously.

Intellective ability measures

For all subjects, scores on the verbal and quantitative sections of the College Entrance Examination Board's Scholastic Aptitude Test (SAT) were available to serve a control function. These traditional indexes of verbal and mathematical aptitude are of additional interest in the present context because they incorporate a penalty for guessing — a characteristic that may leave them open to risk-taking influences. In the case of the female subjects, a seven-minute Advanced Vocabulary Test and a ten-minute Mathematics Aptitude Test were also administered. Both were selected from French's (1954) kit of aptitude and achievement tests. These tests differed from the SAT in two major respects: they did not incorporate penalties for guessing in their instructions, and they were administered under less stressful conditions because considerations of college admission were not involved. In sum, a context of greater permissiveness prevailed with these latter tests than with the SAT.

As a further control, a measure of analytical functioning (Witkin *et al.*, 1954; Witkin *et al.*, 1962) was included in the test battery. This variable is also of interest in its own right as an assessor of dispositions toward field dependence and field independence. A 30-minute multiple-choice embedded figures test (EFT) — an index of the ability to detect a geometric form in a confusing visual context — was group-administered to both male and female subjects. The group form, developed by Jackson, Messick, and Myers (1964), proved to be highly correlated with the individually administered Embedded Figures Test originally developed by the Witkin team.

Decision-making measures

Unlike the two preceding sets of procedures, some of the tasks in the decision-making battery required individual administration.

1. CHOICE DILEMMAS PROCEDURE. A detailed description of the group-administered choice dilemmas procedure instrument may be found in Appendix E. Earlier research with this procedure was reported in Wallach and Kogan (1959; 1961); Kogan and Wallach (1961); and Wallach, Kogan, and Bem (1962). Briefly, each item represents a choice dilemma

between a risky and a safe course of action. A subject's selection of the probability level for the risky alternative's success that would make it sufficiently attractive to be chosen thus reflects the *deterrence of failure* for him in a particular decision area. The instrument is of a semiprojective nature, the subject being asked how he would advise others in the situations described. It is assumed, of course, that an individual's advice to others reflects his own regard for the desirability of success relative to the disutility of failure. Probability levels provided for the success of the risky alternative are 1 in 10, 3 in 10, 5 in 10, 7 in 10, and 9 in 10. A subject may also refuse to gamble on the risky alternative, no matter what the probabilities. In that case, a score of 10 in 10 is assigned the item. It can be seen that higher scores are associated with greater conservatism.

2. CHANCE BETS INSTRUMENT. In the group-administered chance bets task, subjects were given pairs of dice bets varying in terms of probabilities of winning and losing, and the amounts of money to be won or lost. The individual chose, in each of 66 pairs, the bet he would prefer to play. The 66 randomly ordered pairs represented all possible combinations of four probabilities of winning (1/9, 1/4, 1/2, 3/4) and three stakes (15¢, 30¢, 60¢). All bets were of zero expected value. The subject was instructed to consider each bet pair independently. To involve the subject in the task and thereby insure that his choices were significant, the experimenter told the subject he would later have the opportunity to play the bets chosen in the dice game for the amounts of money described in the bets. The instructions further specified, "... be sure that you choose now the bets that you actually will want to play, because you will be held to them." To illustrate further the nature of the task, the first bet pair is given below. (See Appendix F for the complete instrument.)

1/9 to win $1.20   1/2 to win $.60
8/9 to lose $.15   1/2 to lose $.60

Five strategy indexes were derived, two based on selection of monetary amount or utilities (potential winnings and losses), two based on selection of probabilities, and the last based on a combination of probability and monetary value.

a. Maximization of gain (MG) — choice of that alternative with the larger potential winnings.

b. Minimization of loss (ML) — choice of that alternative with the smaller potential loss.

c. Long shot (LS) — choice of that alternative with the lower probability of winning.

d. Minimization of deviation from 1/2 (MD) — choice of that alternative with the probability of winning that is closer to 1/2.

e. Maximization of variance (MV) — choice of that alternative with the greater variance (Coombs & Pruitt, 1960). Variance = $pq\,(a - b)^2$, where a and b are monetary outcomes having probabilities of occurrence of p and q, respectively. The equation indicates that variance increases as probabilities of gain and loss approach 0.5 (maximum uncertainty), and as amounts of gain and/or loss increase. Edwards (1961) has recently noted that variance preferences are not independent of utilities in the case of two-alternative bets.

A separate scoring key was prepared for each of the foregoing strategies. For some of the item pairs, a particular strategy could not be scored because of ties (for example, a bet pair requiring a choice between two 50:50 bets with different monetary values could not be scored for LS and MD). The total number of bet pairs on which the strategy scores were based thus varied as follows: 66 for MG, 48 for ML, 54 for LS, 45 for MD, and 66 for MV. The subject's score on each strategy represented the number of times over all appropriate bet pairs that he selected the alternative keyed for the strategy in question. Hence, a score indicates degree of adherence to a particular strategy. It should be recognized, of course, that the five strategy measures are not independent.

3. SKILL BETS. A specially constructed shuffleboard was used for the purpose of obtaining strategy indexes under skill conditions. The apparatus consisted of a Formica-top board, 7 feet long and 1 foot wide, mounted on a wooden base 3 feet in height. A ledge was attached to one end of the shuffleboard as a backstop for the puck. Embedded in the ledge was an 8-inch ruler, with readings in units of $\frac{1}{16}$ of an inch from 0 at the geometrical center of the board to 4 inches at the extreme left and 4 inches at the extreme right. Two wooden posts were placed against the ledge on opposite sides of the 0 point and equidistant from it.

The experimenter provided the subject with a shuffleboard stick and a penny as a puck. The penny was placed inside a circle engraved in the Formica top at the subject's end of the board (opposite the end with the ledge). The subject's task was to shoot the penny from the circle to the area between the two wooden posts placed against the ledge without touching either of the posts. The distance between the posts could be narrowed or widened with the aid of the ledge ruler. Satisfying the success criterion could obviously be made progressively more difficult, by narrowing the distance between the posts. The experimenter requested that the subject release the penny from the stick before it crossed a line located $1\frac{1}{2}$ feet from the subject's end of the table.

Following the preliminary familiarization with the procedure, the experimenter remarked to each subject: "You'll have a chance to make some money at this game on a future occasion, but first I want to give you some preliminary practice at the game and then I want to see how good you are at it. I am going to set the posts at various distances from each other, and each time I want you to try to aim the penny so that it goes between the two posts without touching either of them."

The first 16 trials consisted of two successive attempts at each of eight between-post distances. These trials were intended to familiarize subjects with the motor aspects of the task, and hence the subject's performance was not recorded. The sequence of trials involved a progressively decreasing separation, starting at 7 inches and ending at 1½ inches, between the posts.

The actual practice series then followed. There were 16 blocks of eight trials each, each block being presented with 5, 2, 7, 4, 1½, 3, 6, and 2½ inches as the separation, in sequence, between posts. The experimenter recorded the number of successes out of 16 tries at each of the eight post separations (Appendix G-1). The eight distances chosen for the practice series permitted other distances to be interpolated between any two of the original ones, thus facilitating greater accuracy in setting up the required odds of success for each subject's payoff matrix. The experimenter selected the four between-post distances yielding the closest approximation to odds of 2 successes in 16, 4 in 16, 8 in 16, and 12 in 16. These probabilities — 1/8, 1/4, 1/2, and 3/4 for winning (associated with 7/8, 3/4, 1/2, and 1/4 for losing) — were selected by the authors in view of their close match to the probabilities used in the chance bet procedure. Recall that 1/9 was used there, whereas 1/8 is used in the present procedure; otherwise, the probabilities are identical. The expected monetary values were also identical in the chance and skill bet procedures. These correspondences between the two procedures were designed to permit analytic comparisons.

A dittoed sheet was prepared listing the four probabilities of winning and losing and the associated potential monetary winnings at each of three levels of stake (Appendix G-2). The experimenter filled in, for each subject, the between-post distances corresponding to the probabilities as based on the subject's prior performance. The probabilities of winning and losing hence were the same for all subjects, the requisite post separations for each person being dependent upon his own performance in the practice series. The derivation of the payoff matrix was explained by the experimenter in as much detail as necessary.

The experimenter then handed the subject a booklet containing pairs of shuffleboard bets. The booklet was similar in format to the chance bets booklet described previously. In fact, the ordering of the 66 bet pairs was identical in the two booklets. However, it was felt that the meaning of the shuffleboard bet pairs might not be as self-evident as the dice bets, and, accordingly, the experimenter put four sets of posts of different height and color at the end of the shuffleboard, with separations corresponding to the subject's success in getting the coin between the posts one eighth, one fourth, one half, or three fourths of the time. The experimenter assured the subject that the probability-distance relationship had been derived from his actual performance in the practice trials. The subject was told that he would later have the opportunity to play his bets on the shuffleboard for the amounts of money that he now chose. The experimenter further informed the subject that he would be held to his choices in the subsequent play of the bets.

The five strategy measures obtained in the dice bet procedure were also derived in the present case. Identical scoring keys were used for the chance and skill bet procedures.

4. NUMBER JUDGMENTS. Instructions for the number judgments procedure were adapted from Irwin and Smith (1956; 1957). In brief, subjects were shown 3- by 5-inch cards one at a time. Each card had a number stamped on it. The experimenter informed each subject that the pack contained 300 cards, shuffled to yield a random order. The subject was required to make a decision regarding the average of the numbers in the pack — namely, whether it was greater or less than 0. The instructions specified that the subject interrupt the experimenter's presentation of cards as soon as the subject had made up his mind about the plus or minus direction of the mean. Following the subject's decision, the experimenter presented him with a card containing five categories of confidence (identical to the confidence categories used in the judgment extremity-confidence test described previously). The subject expressed his degree of confidence in his decision.

There were five packs of cards in all, each containing 300 cards. Each pack was placed in a metal file box, from which the cards were drawn and in which they were replaced after exposure. The first pack of cards was a practice deck; no prize was offered and no costs were attached to the cards. For each of the remaining four packs, a maximum prize of 50¢ was offered for a correct decision, and the subject was charged 1¢ for each card that he saw. A subject won nothing for an incorrect decision. The experimenter continually informed the subject of the amount of money being spent for cards. In view of the prizes and costs involved, numbers were actually printed on only the first 50 cards in each pack of 300, although the subjects were given to understand that all had numbers on them. In the case of the practice pack, subjects who had not made a decision by the forty-fifth card were asked to come to a decision within the next five cards. These subjects were informed that the first series was a practice run, and hence did not warrant any further expenditure of time. The means and SD's (in parentheses) of the five packs were as follows: $+.5$ (2.0), $+1.0$ (7.5), $-.5$ (2.0), $-.5$ (7.5), $+1.0$ (2.0). Ten different numbers were used in each pack and these were randomized within blocks of ten. Each number, in other words, was represented in its respective pack a total of five times.

The subject was not informed regarding the correctness of his decision on each pack. Rather, he was informed of his total winnings on this particular procedure at the end of the experimental session.

The average number of cards drawn from the four experimental packs is the number judgments score of major interest. The larger this number, the more conservative is the strategy, in the sense that the subject prefers a smaller gain of which he is relatively sure to a potentially larger prize that may not materialize. An average confidence score across the four experimental packs was also obtained.

5. CLUES. In the clues task, subjects guessed the identity of four common objects on the basis of clues provided. The objects and clues were adapted from Worley (1960) and Roberts (1960). Twenty-six clues were available for each object. These were printed on 3- by 5-inch cards and exposed to subjects one at a time. Prizes were offered for a correct guess and costs were attached to each clue. An incorrect guess meant that the prize was forfeited. In these respects, the task was similar in format to the preceding number judgments procedure. The maximum possible prize for correctly identifying any one of the four objects was 50¢. In order to win this amount, a subject would be required to identify the object correctly on the first clue, which was provided free. All subsequent clues had costs attached. Clues 2 through 11 cost 1¢ each, clues 12 through 16 cost 2¢ each, and clues 17 through 26 cost 3¢ each. Each subject was provided with a cost sheet so that he might keep track of the amounts he spent for clues.

Subjects were not informed about the actual identities of the objects used in the task. Information about winnings was withheld until the end of the experimental session.

A single score — average number of clues desired over the four objects — was derived from the task. The greater the number of clues requested, the more conservative is the decision making.

6. CHANCE AND SKILL PLAYS. The instructions for chance and skill bets explicitly stated that an opportunity would be provided to play the bets selected. Time limitations on the authors' research precluded the playing of all 66 bets for both procedures. Accordingly, a sample of 22 — every third bet chosen — was played for the amounts stated in the chance and skill conditions; hence, there were 44 plays in all. Chance and skill bet preference booklets were returned to the subject so that he could be assured of playing the bets he had selected. Half of the subjects played their chance bets first, and the remaining half played their skill bets first.

Details of the Procedure | **31**

For chance bets, a chart was provided (Appendix H), showing what dice combinations correspond to the particular probabilities to which the subject had been exposed earlier. The chart indicated, for example, that a 1/9 bet would win only if a 9 were rolled, a 1/4 bet would win only if a 5 or 6 were rolled, and so on. The experimenter gave assurances that the chart was mathematically accurate.

For skill bets, the subject was again given a personal chart (Appendix G-2), this one showing the post distances corresponding to his probabilities of success and failure based on his past performance in the shuffleboard practice series.

The subjects began both the dice and shuffleboard plays with $4.00 provided by the experimenter. The instructions specified that, at the end of the series of 22 plays, subjects with $4.00 or less could keep 10 percent of that amount. Subjects accumulating more than $4.00 could keep $.40 (10 percent of $4.00) plus half of everything over $4.00. For example, a subject ending with $8.00 would show a $2.40 profit ($.40 + $2.00). Subjects losing all of the money provided and going into debt would have their debt cancelled.

In order to obtain some indication of the effect of bet outcomes on original bet selections, the experimenter asked the subject, prior to each play (except the first) in the dice and shuffleboard conditions, whether, if he were given the opportunity to choose again, he would stick with his original selection or choose the other member of the bet pair. For skill bets, the experimenter set up a second pair of posts so that the subject could more adequately gauge his satisfaction with his original choice relative to the other member of the bet pair. Of course, the subject was not permitted to alter his original selections. A "chance bet dissatisfaction" and a "skill bet dissatisfaction" score were computed for each subject, to reflect the number of times a subject stated a desire to shift to the other bet, if he had been permitted to do so.

7. FINAL BET. Following the chance and skill plays, a subject's overall winnings were computed. Information regarding amounts won on number judgments and clues was conveyed to the subject, and these sums were added to chance and skill play winnings to yield a total. At this point, the experimenter presented the subject with the final bet procedure. A verbatim account follows.

"Your total winnings, beyond your regular salary of $7.50, add up to $———. You are entitled, if you wish, to take all your money, total winnings as well as regular salary, and leave now. I am willing, however, to play one final game of chance with you. I shall give you the opportunity of winning up to six times your total winnings shown above. Of course, there is also the risk of losing all of your winnings. You keep your regular salary in any case. If you choose to play this game, a six-sided die will be used. I pledge to you that it is a completely fair die. You can bet that one, two, three, four, or five of the sides of this die will turn up on any single throw. The more sides you bet on, the less money you can win, but also the less the likelihood of your losing. Shown below are the five types of bets from which you can choose, the chances of your winning and losing on each, and the amounts that you get if you win. In every case, you lose your total winnings if you do not win.

Type of bet	One face	Two faces	Three faces	Four faces	Five faces
Chances of winning	1/6	1/3	1/2	2/3	5/6
Chances of losing	5/6	2/3	1/2	1/3	1/6
Total prize if you win	—	—	—	—	—

"Just to prove to you that this is completely fair, I am going to let you select the face or faces that would win for the bet that you make. I will also let you shake the die in the container yourself. Please shake it well before tossing."

The experimenter explained how the various prize values were derived by showing how the various numbers of faces corresponded to the probabilities. All amounts were filled in for the subject in the blank spaces provided. Total prizes for the five alternative bets indicated were obtained by multiplying total winnings prior to the final bet by a value of 6, 3, 2, 1½, and 1⅕, respectively, thus yielding bets of equal expected value. For example, if a person's previous winnings totaled $4.85, his prizes for the various bets ranged from $29.10 to $5.82. The amounts of money involved hence could be substantial, insofar as the college-student subjects were concerned.

A subject's score on the final bet consisted of the number of faces selected (1 to 5). A score of 6 was assigned if the subject refused to take the final bet. Hence, the larger the score, the more conservative is the subject's behavior.

METHOD OF ANALYSIS

With four broad classes of variables under investigation — cognitive-judgmental, intellective ability, personality, and decision-making — and with each subsuming several variables in turn, the usual strategy of analysis would involve the computation of a matrix of intercorrelations between all pairs of variables, followed by a factor analysis of that matrix. Factor analysis is based, of course, on assumptions of linearity of relationships over the entire score range of the variables included in the analysis. The expectation of moderator effects, however, necessarily implies a nonlinear model. Hence, if test anxiety and defensiveness should exert the kinds of moderator effects expected, the particular statistical method employed must do justice to the empirical results obtained. The standard factor-analytic model would obviously be inappropriate under the circumstances. It would be feasible, of course, to conduct separate factor analyses of the moderator subsamples. However, the reduced ratio of variables to subjects that would ensue would introduce certain practical problems regarding stability of factors. Furthermore, we are interested not only in the magnitude and direction of relationships within moderator subgroups, but also in the differences *between* those subgroups. The authors find it more reasonable at the present stage of theoretical development to examine differences between correlations than to become involved in the complexities of assessing differences between relatively unstable factor structures.

The present study will not attempt to explore all possible relationships among variables. Thus, interrelationships among cognitive, ability, and personality dimensions have been studied by Gardner *et al.* (1959), Gardner *et al.* (1960), Fillenbaum (1959), and Forehand (1962). It will be granted that the studies cited were not concerned with moderator effects. But bringing a moderator analysis to bear on the relationships in question, although of considerable interest, would take us well beyond the scope and purpose of the present investigation. We shall accordingly concentrate on the relationships between cognitive-judgmental, ability, and personality variables, on the one hand, and decision-making variables on the other. Further, we shall examine relationships among decision-making variables themselves, because little information is available in psychological literature concerning this important issue.

In reporting a relationship between a pair of variables, correlations[1] for the male and female samples as a whole will be cited in the text prior to the tabular presentation of the moderator results for that pair of variables. With respect to the moderator analysis, the procedure consisted of ordering all subjects within sex on the moderator, and then dividing the samples as close to the median as feasible into highs and lows. Where the size of the high and low subsamples differs by more than one case, it may be presumed that the authors dichotomized at a natural break in the distribution of scores on the moderator variable in question.

Each subject, then, has been classified as high or low on test anxiety and on defensiveness. Accordingly, in our analysis we can treat moderators one at a time or simultaneously. In the latter case, a fourfold classification of subjects is involved. It should be noted that the two moderators — test

---

[1] All correlations reported in the study are Pearson product-moment coefficients.

anxiety and defensiveness — are statistically independent in both males ($r = -.05$) and females ($r = .01$). Hence, variations across the four subgroups in frequency of cases will be quite small.

Table A

ILLUSTRATIVE MODERATOR VARIABLE TABLE FOR MALES: CORRELATIONS BETWEEN VARIABLE X AND VARIABLE Y FOR PERSONALITY SUBGROUPS

DEFENSIVENESS

		Low	High	Low + High
TEST ANXIETY	Low	r_{LL} $N = 30$	r_{LH} $N = 35$	r_{LL+LH} $\Sigma N = 65$
	High	r_{HL} $N = 27$	r_{HH} $N = 22$	r_{HL+HH} $\Sigma N = 49$
	Low + High	r_{LL+HL} $\Sigma N = 57$	r_{LH+HH} $\Sigma N = 57$	$z =$ $\Sigma\Sigma N = 114$

$z =$

In order that moderator effects not be obscured, the authors have organized the tables of results into small units. The relation between each pair of variables under consideration will be cast in the form of two-by-two tables as shown in Tables A and B. Sample sizes for males and females are respectively illustrated. These sample sizes apply in all of the analyses of the study. Entered in the model tables are correlations between a particular pair of variables under each of the moderator conditions. Within the cells of the table, the correlations apply to subsamples of subjects selected on the basis of the two moderator variables considered simultaneously. Thus, the upper left cell contains a correlation coefficient for subjects low in both test anxiety and defensiveness; the lower right cell shows the correlation for subjects high on both moderators; the upper right and lower left cells are assigned to low test anxious–high defensive subjects and high test anxious–low defensive subjects, respectively. The marginals of the table report the correlations for the moderators taken singly. The right-hand marginal is reserved for high and low test anxious subgroups; the lower marginal is given over to high and low defensive subgroups. Also listed in the marginals of the table are z values, the normal deviate statistic indi-

Table B

ILLUSTRATIVE MODERATOR VARIABLE TABLE FOR FEMALES: CORRELATIONS BETWEEN VARIABLE X AND VARIABLE Y FOR PERSONALITY SUBGROUPS

DEFENSIVENESS

		Low	High	Low + High
TEST ANXIETY	Low	r_{LL} $N = 28$	r_{LH} $N = 22$	r_{LL+LH} $\Sigma N = 50$
	High	r_{HL} $N = 24$	r_{HH} $N = 29$	r_{HL+HH} $\Sigma N = 53$
	Low + High	r_{LL+HL} $\Sigma N = 52$	r_{LH+HH} $\Sigma N = 51$	$\Sigma\Sigma N = 103$

$z =$

$z =$

cating the significance of the difference in correlations between high and low subgroups on each moderator. We shall not attempt to test for the significance of differences between correlation coefficients reported in the four cells of the table. Six comparisons are possible if each cell is compared with every other. This procedure would evidently be a highly cumbersome method of analysis. At the present stage of theoretical development in the problem area under investigation, where the appropriate emphasis is more one of exploration and discovery than of testing monolithic predictions, the authors will instead proceed by pointing up the pattern of correlational differences and showing how the consideration of both moderators simultaneously advances our knowledge a few steps beyond what we learn when treating test anxiety and defensiveness separately.

Descriptive data on the samples under study have been made available in the Appendix sections of the volume. Thus, Appendix A–1 lists means and sigmas for the major variables under examination in the male and female samples as a whole. Appendixes A–2 and A–3 provide means and sigmas for low and high test anxiety subgroups in males and females, respectively. Comparable data for low and high defensiveness subgroups are found in Appendixes A–4 and A–5. Descriptive data for the four-way moderator split are contained in Appendixes A–6 and A–7. Appendixes B–1 to B–9 provide the correlation matrices for the total samples and each of the moderator subgroups.

Reliabilities of the variables, computed for the male and female samples as a whole, are reported in Appendix C. Because the present study depends almost exclusively upon correlational analysis, the reliabilities of the variables assume considerable importance and hence warrant some discussion. Consider first the decision-making variables. The reliability of the choice dilemmas instrument conforms to values reported in the authors' previous work (Wallach & Kogan, 1961; Wallach et al., 1962) and can be considered satisfactory for a 12-item test. The various strategy measures in both the chance and the skill situations achieve quite high reliabilities. The fact that such clear individual consistencies exist in the usage of bet strategies is of considerable interest in its own right. The reliabilities for number judgments and clues, particularly the latter, are in the moderate range, but it should be emphasized that the average interitem r reported is a minimum estimate of reliability. The nature of the "final bet" variable precludes a reliability estimate. For the intellective and the cognitive-judgmental variables, reliabilities again reach quite satisfactory levels. Finally, we note that all of the personality inventory measures, with the possible exception of independence-yielding, achieve reliabilities in the moderate to high range. In sum, the substantial reliabilities of the study's measures are extremely encouraging. They indicate that we are dealing with variables tapping fairly stable phenomena. Further, these substantial reliabilities set quite high statistical ceilings for correlations between the major variables of the investigation. This fact implies also that any absence of relationships cannot be attributed to the measurement characteristics of the variables under scrutiny.

In closing this section, the authors would like to point to several factors that may militate against the emergence of statistically significant relationships and differences. With regard to the magnitude of relationships between the major variables of the study, it should be noted that none of the correlations to be reported in subsequent chapters has been corrected for attenuation (in other words, unreliability of measures). Although the reliabilities of measures are quite high, the fact remains that the actual relationships necessarily represent slight underestimates of the "true" values.

We turn now from the issue of magnitudes of correlations to the question of differences between correlations. Recall that moderator subgroups are composed by dividing the male and female samples at their respective medians on the dimensions of test anxiety and defensiveness. This technique clearly provides a conservative basis for constituting subgroups, for it includes all of the available cases rather than excluding those in the middle range of the dimensions in question. Because subjects on opposite sides of the median within this middle range must be more similar than different, the procedure necessarily has the effect of reducing correlational differences between subgroups. Again, this fact implies that the observed differences are conservative estimates of the "true" values.

A final consideration is the power of the statistical test that is used to determine the significance of the difference between correlations. Cohen (1962) has recently noted that the power of such a test is quite low for the sample sizes and the general range of correlational values with which we are here concerned. This finding implies that there is a special danger of committing Type II errors in the present circumstances — in other words, accepting the null hypothesis when it is false. Accordingly, it is worth keeping in mind that the .05 level of significance is an especially rigorous criterion for the statistical test at issue. Given the orientation of the present research toward discovery rather than strict hypothesis testing, the authors deemed it advisable to make occasional use of the .10 level of significance in interpreting findings.

3

Relationships within the Decision-Making Domain

Two questions will concern us in this chapter. First, we shall consider relationships between decision making in hypothetical and in payoff situations. Next, we shall turn to relationships among decision-making indexes in various payoff contexts.

DECISION MAKING IN HYPOTHETICAL VERSUS PAYOFF CONTEXTS

In the present section, evidence is described regarding consistencies in risk-taking behavior across hypothetical and monetary gain-loss situations. Decisions rendered in the choice dilemmas task are related to the strategy, information-seeking, and "final bet" procedures.

Choice dilemmas and chance strategies

Consider first the association between the "deterrence of failure" index derived from the choice dilemmas task and the five strategy indexes derived from the dice bets procedure. Listed here for males ($N = 114$) and females ($N = 103$), respectively, are the correlation coefficients.[1]

	Males	Females
Chance–max. of gain (CMG)	−.33**	−.22*
Chance–min. of loss (CML)	.21*	.22*
Chance–long shot (CLS)	−.31**	−.17
Chance–min. dev. from 1/2 (CMD)	.25**	.15
Chance–max. of variance (CMV)	−.32**	−.25**

[1] For all correlation coefficients reported in the text and in the tables, one and two asterisks indicate significance at the 5 and 1 percent levels, respectively.

The relationships are quite clear for both males and females, though of somewhat greater magnitude in the former case. As subjects' scores on deterrence of failure increase (greater conservatism), their strategies in a dice bets task also become more conservative — in other words, for both sexes, maximization of gain and of variance are avoided and a minimization of loss strategy is preferred. For males, furthermore, the other two strategies also achieve statistical significance: long shots are avoided and deviation from 1/2 is minimized.[2] It is evident, then, that what an individual does in a hypothetical decision context has some predictive value for a gambling type of task in which decisions represent a firm commitment in a subsequent playoff.

Table 1

CORRELATIONS FOR MALES BETWEEN CHOICE DILEMMAS AND CHANCE STRATEGIES FOR PERSONALITY SUBGROUPS

DEFENSIVENESS

			Low	High	Low + High	
TEST ANXIETY	Low	CMG	−.42*	−.32	−.38**	
		CML	.26	.33*	.33**	
		CLS	−.40*	−.21	−.30*	
		CMD	.34	.21	.26*	
		CMV	−.39*	−.33*	−.38**	
						z =
	High	CMG	.03	−.58**	−.32*	−.35
		CML	.06	.22	.10	1.25
		CLS	.05	−.62**	−.35**	.29
		CMD	−.04	.49*	.26	.00
		CMV	.01	−.53*	−.30*	−.47
					z =	
	Low + High	CMG	−.24	−.41**	.99	
		CML	.20	.23	−.16	
		CLS	−.22	−.38**	.91	
		CMD	.15	.32*	−.94	
		CMV	−.23	−.39**	.92	

Are these relationships subject to moderator influences? Tables 1 and 2 present the relevant findings. Consider first the results for males in Table 1.

---

[2]The authors emphasize again that the five strategy indexes are not independent. The five strategy scores are retained throughout because the differential magnitudes of relationships between the five strategy indexes and other variables are of considerable interest.

Table 2

CORRELATIONS FOR FEMALES BETWEEN CHOICE DILEMMAS AND CHANCE
STRATEGIES FOR PERSONALITY SUBGROUPS

			DEFENSIVENESS			
			Low	High	Low + High	
		CMG	−.42*	−.14	−.29*	
		CML	.30	.23	.25	
	Low	CLS	−.40*	−.10	−.28*	
		CMD	.28	.17	.23	
		CMV	−.45*	−.22	−.32*	
TEST						$z =$
ANXIETY		CMG	−.11	−.22	−.18	−.58
		CML	.24	.24	.27*	−.10
	High	CLS	−.06	−.15	−.10	−.93
		CMD	−.04	.16	.06	.86
		CMV	−.15	−.25	−.23	−.48
					$z =$	
		CMG	−.26	−.22	−.21	
	Low	CML	.19	.26	−.36	
	+	CLS	−.25	−.14	−.57	
	High	CMD	.15	.18	−.15	
		CMV	−.26	−.27	.05	

An examination of the marginal r's does not reveal any substantial differences when the moderators are treated separately. If we move into the cells of the table, however, it is quite apparent that the relationship in question breaks down for overtly test anxious males who are low in defensiveness. Note, on the other hand, the striking increase in the correlations when high test anxiety is accompanied by high defensiveness. It appears, then, that for test anxious males with highly vulnerable defenses (in other words, low defensiveness), the introduction of monetary payoffs radically changes the psychological character of the decision context. What these individuals do when nothing is at stake bears no relationship to what they do when monetary prizes are at issue and personal control over outcomes is lacking. Why high test anxiety in the presence of high defensiveness, on the other hand, should produce the highest correlations in the table is not immediately clear. Possibly, for such subjects, a consistent risky or conservative outlook serves defensively to allay anxiety across a variety of situational contexts. Lest we be accused of overinterpretation at this stage, however, let us postpone further discussion of this issue until we see whether these high correlations are maintained when deterrence of failure is related to other decision-making procedures involving payoffs.

Consider the results for females in Table 2. Here the pattern differs to some extent from that observed for the males in Table 1. Note that the significant correlations are all confined to the subgroup low in both test anxiety and defensiveness. When test anxiety and/or defensiveness is high, the corresponding r's show a slight drop in magnitude. So, unlike the males, the females show consistency between decisions of a hypothetical sort and strategies under chance conditions emerging most strongly when the level of motivational arousal or disturbance is low.

Of particular importance is the demonstration that r's for samples as a whole may conceal substantial variations across specific moderator subgroups. Indeed, even an analysis based on one or the other moderator taken separately tends to conceal effects that emerge with great clarity when test anxiety and defensiveness are considered simultaneously. Within the decision-making domain, these effects do not operate in identical ways for males and females. As the authors stated in the introduction, there is little reason to expect correspondences across sex groups, when the dimensions under study are particularly likely to have a differential psychological impact upon men and women.

Choice dilemmas and skill strategies

We turn next to relations between the choice dilemmas task and strategies employed in a context of skill. The latter context, like the chance context, also incorporates monetary payoffs. Results in the samples as a whole are as follows.

	Males	Females
Skill–max. of gain (SMG)	−.26**	−.14
Skill–min. of loss (SML)	.25**	.09
Skill–long shot (SLS)	−.21*	−.14
Skill–min. dev. from 1/2 (SMD)	.18	.24*
Skill–max. of variance (SMV)	−.26**	−.12

Again, the evidence points to an association between decisions in a hypothetical and a payoff context. For males, the correlations are smaller in magnitude in a skill task relative to a chance task, but the r's remain statistically significant. For females, on the other hand, it will be noted that only one of the skill strategies is significantly related to the deterrence-of-failure index. More conservative females on the latter show a preference for 50:50 probabilities of success in the shuffleboard bets procedure.

The moderator analysis for the variables in question is offered in Tables 3 and 4. Again, the marginal correlations fail to do justice to the nature and magnitude of the relationships that are present. The within-cell cor-

Table 3

CORRELATIONS FOR MALES BETWEEN CHOICE DILEMMAS AND SKILL STRATEGIES FOR PERSONALITY SUBGROUPS

DEFENSIVENESS

			Low	High	Low + High	
		SMG	−.24	−.22	−.27*	
		SML	.41*	.22	.30*	
	Low	SLS	−.17	−.17	−.20	
		SMD	.25	.09	.16	
		SMV	−.30	−.20	−.27*	
TEST ANXIETY						$z =$
		SMG	.05	−.55**	−.26	−.06
		SML	.29	.13	.18	.66
	High	SLS	.17	−.57**	−.23	.16
		SMD	−.07	.42*	.19	−.16
		SMV	−.04	−.46*	−.24	−.16
					$z =$	
		SMG	−.11	−.36**	1.39	
	Low	SML	.33*	.21	.67	
	+	SLS	.02	−.34**	1.94	
	High	SMD	.09	.24	−.81	
		SMV	−.17	−.32*	.83	

relations, on the other hand, once more are highly informative. For males, the resemblance to the results for chance strategies is quite strong, particularly with respect to the subgroup high on both moderators. Thus, we can add another piece of evidence to the observation that for males who are both highly test anxious and highly defensive, the risk-conservatism dimension is especially salient, with the consequence that strong consistencies hold across markedly dissimilar decision-making contexts. As suggested earlier, it is possible that the particular decision style such subjects adopt — risky or conservative — is enlisted in the service of defensively coping with test anxiety.

The results for females reported in Table 4 are highly consistent with those shown in Table 2. Again, it is in the "least disturbed" subgroup of females — those low on both moderators — that the relationships achieve statistically significant levels. Thus, under both chance and skill strategy conditions, women who are low both in test anxiety and in defensiveness exhibit generality of risk-taking behavior across hypothetical and payoff contexts. For males, on the other hand, such generality achieves its apex in the presence of both test anxiety and defensiveness. These divergent

Table 4

CORRELATIONS FOR FEMALES BETWEEN CHOICE DILEMMAS AND SKILL STRATEGIES FOR PERSONALITY SUBGROUPS

			DEFENSIVENESS			
			Low	High	Low + High	
TEST ANXIETY	Low	SMG	−.41*	.20	−.15	
		SML	.26	−.25	.07	
		SLS	−.41*	.13	−.18	
		SMD	.51**	.10	.34*	
		SMV	−.41*	.28	−.12	
						$z =$
	High	SMG	−.17	−.14	−.14	−.05
		SML	.28	.06	.17	−.50
		SLS	−.13	−.13	−.11	−.35
		SMD	.29	.12	.15	1.00
		SMV	−.22	−.14	−.17	.25
					$z =$	
	Low + High	SMG	−.31*	.01	−1.63	
		SML	.22	−.08	1.50	
		SLS	−.31*	−.02	−1.48	
		SMD	.44**	.11	1.78	
		SMV	−.32*	.05	−1.88	

findings for the two sexes raise the interesting possibility that generality for females is a matter of similarities between tasks in the decision-making domain, such similarities being most readily apprehended at low levels of motivational involvement — whereas generality for males may be based both on such task similarities (subjects low on both moderators) and on the extent to which the decision-making procedures engage relevant motivational processes (subjects high on both moderators).

Choice dilemmas and information seeking

Relations between choice dilemmas and information-seeking tasks — number judgments and clues — are considered next. For males, the correlations are negligible ($r = -.07$ and .04 for number judgments and clues, respectively). Further, these low coefficients are not concealing moderator effects. Coefficients range from .01 to −.23, for the four within-cell subgroups in the number judgments task, and from −.11 to .25 in the clues task. None of these r's approaches statistical significance.[3] For males, then,

---

[3] Where moderator effects are absent or negligible, the authors will not present the complete data in the text. The interested reader may obtain the exact values by consulting Appendix B.

the kinds of risks inherent in an information-seeking task with prizes and costs attached seem to bear little relationship to deterrence of failure in a hypothetical decision context. Possibly, the problem-solving character of the information-seeking procedures contributes to their remoteness from choice dilemmas in the male samples.

The female subjects, on the other hand, present a somewhat different picture. In the case of number judgments, the overall r with choice dilemmas is a mere .12. As Table 5 indicates, however, the subjects low on both

Table 5

CORRELATIONS FOR FEMALES BETWEEN CHOICE DILEMMAS AND NUMBER JUDGMENTS FOR PERSONALITY SUBGROUPS

DEFENSIVENESS

		Low	High	Low + High	
TEST ANXIETY	Low	**.38***	−.09	.19	$z = .45$
	High	**.16**	.06	.10	
	Low + High	.26	−.02	$z = 1.41$	

moderators yield a significant r of .38 between the two variables in question. As deterrence of failure increases on the choice dilemmas task, more information is requested before a decision is made on the number judgments task. None of the other coefficients approaches significance. Recall that the same female subgroup yielded the only significant correlations between choice dilemmas and the strategy indexes (Tables 2 and 4). Thus, in the case of the "least disturbed" female subjects, there is further evidence here for consistency of risk-conservatism across hypothetical and payoff contexts.

Turning to the relationship between choice dilemmas and performance on the clues task in female subjects, we observe that $r = .30$, $p < .01$. Again, a consistent effect is obtained, more conservative females in the choice dilemmas situation demanding more information before venturing a decision on the clues task. Unlike all of the preceding results reported for women, the results here show moderator effects to be absent, the four within-cells correlations falling within a fairly narrow band ranging from .23 to .38.

Choice dilemmas and final bet

We turn, finally, to the association between choice dilemmas and the final bet. As stated in the introductory chapter, the inclusion in the study of a procedure in which the subject gambled with his own newly acquired funds raised the problem of controlling for the magnitude of those funds. As the authors expected, significant correlations were obtained for both males ($r = .23$, $p < .05$) and females ($r = .31$, $p < .01$) between the final bet and the amount of money that had been accumulated prior to the final bet. The greater the sum earned, the more conservative is the final bet. The authors will later show that this relationship is in itself highly susceptible to moderator influences. For the present, however, we are interested in the relationship between decisions of a hypothetical kind and a final bet variable where the subject is making a decision based on his own newly acquired monetary resources. By using partial correlation analysis, we can control for the amount of those resources when relating final bet performance to the other variables under study.

The over-all partial r's (prior winnings held constant) between deterrence of failure in the choice dilemmas task and number of faces of the die chosen in the final bet are .05 for males and $-.05$ for females. Moderator effects are totally absent in the male sample. It is evident then, that a male subject's decision in the type of hypothetical context employed has no bearing on what he does when gambling with a newly acquired monetary prize. Because the hypothetical decisions do relate significantly to chance and skill strategies, one wonders why the relationship is not maintained when choice dilemmas and the final bet are correlated.

If the final bet is viewed as an "ultimate criterion" of risk taking and the strategy measures as "intermediate criteria," the results make eminently good sense. When we refer to the final bet as an "ultimate criterion," we highlight the greater salience of monetary risk where money is already in one's possession. In the strategy procedures, the subject is making decisions that will hopefully produce monetary gains, as opposed to gambling with funds already in hand. Thus, the greater indirectness of risks distinguishing the strategy measures suggests their "intermediate" criterion status. When viewed this way, it is not too surprising that the most indirect risk index — deterrence of failure — should relate to an "intermediate" rather than to an "ultimate criterion" measure. It must be emphasized that these distinctions between risk-taking measures on the basis of salience of outcomes are logically independent of the explicit-implicit distinction discussed earlier with reference to risk taking in decision-making and in cognitive-judgmental contexts. The latter distinction, it will be recalled, concerns the degree to which the task's ostensive purpose focuses on considerations of risk or on other matters.

Table 6

PARTIAL CORRELATIONS FOR FEMALES BETWEEN CHOICE DILEMMAS AND FINAL BET (PRIOR WINNINGS HELD CONSTANT) FOR PERSONALITY SUBGROUPS

DEFENSIVENESS

	Low	High	Low + High	
TEST ANXIETY Low	−.17	−.16	−.16	
TEST ANXIETY High	−.16	.46*	.14	$z = -1.49$
Low + High	−.19	.12		$z = -1.54$

How about moderator effects for women? The relevant information is provided by Table 6. Note that the significant association emerges in the subgroup high on both moderators. Greater deterrence of failure (conservatism) is associated with betting on more faces of the die (conservatism) for subjects who are high in both test anxiety and defensiveness. The correlations in the other three cells of the table are low and negative.

Of particular interest is the shift of the significant association from the subgroup *low* on both moderators (Tables 2, 4, and 5) to the subgroup *high* on both moderators. In this respect, the women in the latter subgroup bring to mind the correlational pattern for males between choice dilemmas, on the one hand, and chance and skill strategies on the other (Tables 1 and 3). It seems that the women begin to exhibit the male pattern when the stakes get to be quite high, as in the case of the final bet. The latter, by its very nature, is so remote from the choice dilemmas procedure that the task-similarity basis for an association seems to break down, only to be replaced by an association in the subgroup for whom the final bet is likely to articulate with motivational processes. Our results strongly suggest a differential threshold for males and females as to when this begins to happen.

Summary

The present section has offered evidence pertinent to the question raised in the introduction regarding the generality of risk-taking behavior across hypothetical and payoff contexts. The evidence for such generality, as we have seen, is strongly positive for females, moderately positive for males. For the latter, significant relationships with the hypothetical choice dilemmas situation are confined to chance and skill strategies. For the female sample, in contrast, significant relationships obtain between choice dilemmas and all of the other decision-making procedures employed in the study. Substantial moderator effects are found in both sexes, significant relationships emerging most strongly for non-test anxious, nondefensive subjects and/or for highly test anxious and highly defensive subjects.

These findings lead the authors to propose a dual process conceptualization. Specifically, for subjects low in motivational disturbance, linkages across hypothetical and payoff contexts in risk-taking behavior may conceivably arise through task-based similarities in the decision-making domain. When both test anxiety and defensiveness are high, however, the authors propose that a consistent mode of risk regulation becomes an integral, generalized part of the defensive apparatus employed to cope with the anxiety aroused in a success-failure context. Interestingly enough, least generality is found in the overtly test anxious-low defensive and the low test anxious-high defensive subgroups. In the case of the former, test anxiety in poorly defended individuals may contribute to sharp differentiation between decision-making contexts that do possess gain-loss or success-failure consequences and those that do not. Defensiveness in the absence of test anxiety, on the other hand, may enhance differentiation across varied decision-making contexts for reasons that have to do with distinctively different expectations of what is desirable or appropriate in a group-administered decision task of a hypothetical character as opposed to a face-to-face situation with an experimenter who is perceived as evaluating one's decisions.

DECISION MAKING IN DIFFERENT PAYOFF CONTEXTS

Chance and skill strategies

Recall that the paired comparisons procedure was virtually identical for dice and shuffleboard bets. Accordingly, we can examine the degree of consistency manifested across chance and skill conditions with the particular method of measurement held constant. Table 7 presents the relevant findings for the male and female samples as a whole. Consider first the cor-

Table 7
Correlations within and between Chance and Skill Strategies[a]

	CMG	CML	CLS	CMD	CMV	SMG	SML	SLS	SMD	SMV
Chance–max. of gain (CMG)	—	-.55	.95	-.82	.96	*.72*	-.40	.69	-.61	.69
Chance–min. of loss (CML)	-.54	—	-.32	.20	-.73	-.49	*.60*	-.37	.32	-.56
Chance–long shot (CLS)	.92	-.21	—	-.87	.86	.65	-.27	*.67*	-.59	.61
Chance–min. dev. from 1/2 (CMD)	-.72	.11	-.80	—	-.71	-.57	.22	-.58	*.60*	-.53
Chance–max. of variance (CMV)	.95	-.74	.78	-.59	—	.71	-.49	.66	-.58	*.71*
Skill–max. of gain (SMG)	*.60*	-.33	.54	-.37	.57	—	-.60	.96	-.80	.97
Skill–min. of loss (SML)	-.50	*.56*	-.30	.08	-.54	-.52	—	-.40	.29	-.75
Skill–long shot (SLS)	.51	-.20	*.51*	-.39	.47	.94	-.26	—	-.84	.89
Skill–min. dev. from 1/2 (SMD)	-.39	.07	-.43	*.41*	-.35	-.78	.10	-.87	—	-.74
Skill–max. of variance (SMV)	.63	-.41	.53	-.33	*.61*	.96	-.69	.85	-.67	—

[a]Correlations between matched chance and skill strategies are shown in italic. Results for males are above diagonal. With $N = 114$, r's of .19 and .24 are significant at the .05 and .01 levels, respectively. Results for females are below diagonal. With $N = 103$, r's of .19 and .25 are significant at the .05 and .01 levels, respectively.

relations among the strategy indexes *within* the chance and skill bet conditions. These r's are generally quite high, reflecting the experimental dependencies that are present. Note that "minimization of loss" is the most independent of the five strategy indexes used. Several correlations between that strategy and the others do not, in fact, achieve statistical significance. Note further the powerful consistencies that exist across chance and skill bets (r's in italic in Table 7). In the large majority of cases the largest r in any row or column of the chance-skill block belongs to the corresponding strategy for the two conditions. Finally, it can be seen that the magnitude of these correlations (in italic) is uniformly somewhat greater for males than females.

It is evident, then, that the risk-conservatism dimension generalizes across conditions in which subjects do and do not have control over the outcomes of their decisions. Is the foregoing relationship affected by moderator variables? For the males, no moderator effects whatever are observed. The largest difference in the magnitude of correlation coefficients across moderator subgroups is .16. With regard to absolute values, no r falls below .50.

Female subjects offer a somewhat different picture, and hence the findings are presented in detail in Table 8. Highly test anxious women who are low in defensiveness give some indication of differentiating the strategic requirements under chance and skill conditions. "Minimization of loss" appears consistent across chance and skill, but "maximization of gain" and "long shot" strategies, for example, are not employed in a consistent fashion in the two contexts. If highly test anxious women who are poorly defended are especially sensitized to failure-avoidance, it seems reasonable to expect that they will impose a different psychological meaning on a decision situation in which outcomes are under their personal control and a decision context where outcomes are determined by random processes.

Chance strategies and information seeking

In the matters of chance strategies and information seeking, we examine the relation of strategy preferences in the dice bets procedure to the amount of information requested in the number judgments and clues tasks. For male subjects, there appears to be no relationship whatever between decision making in the two contexts. Nonsignificant r's (ranging from $-.09$ to .12) obtain for the male sample as a whole, and the r's remain nonsignificant when moderator variables are introduced. Apparently, the mechanisms of risk regulation in chance bet preference and information-seeking situations are of a distinctly different order for males.

The results for females differ from those for males. Although the correlations between chance strategies and number judgments do not achieve statistical significance and moderator effects do not appear to operate in

Table 8

CORRELATIONS FOR FEMALES BETWEEN CHANCE STRATEGIES AND
SKILL STRATEGIES FOR PERSONALITY SUBGROUPS

			DEFENSIVENESS			
			Low	High	Low + High	
TEST ANXIETY	Low	MG	.68**	.78**	.71**	
		ML	.68**	.20	.48**	
		LS	.60**	.68**	.61**	
		MD	.42*	.53*	.46**	
		MV	.71**	.62**	.66**	
						z =
	High	MG	.23	.64**	.47**	1.86
		ML	.70**	.58**	.64**	−1.16
		LS	.07	.55**	.40**	1.40
		MD	.26	.42*	.36**	.59
		MV	.44*	.61**	.53**	1.00
					z =	
	Low + High	MG	.52**	.69**	−1.33	
		ML	.70**	.42**	2.06	
		LS	.42**	.58**	−1.06	
		MD	.36**	.46**	−.59	
		MV	.62**	.60**	.16	

their case, note in contrast the correlations of chance strategies with performance on the clues task.

Chance–max. of gain	−.23*
Chance–min. of loss	.25**
Chance–long shot	−.18
Chance–min. dev. from 1/2	.13
Chance–max. of variance	−.25**

For three of the five strategies, a significant relation is found. Subjects who request more clues before deciding on the identity of an object tend to prefer more conservative strategies in a dice bets procedure. Conversely, the less the information sought on the clues task, the greater the preference for risky strategies under chance conditions.

Are these relationships moderated by test anxiety and/or defensiveness? Table 9 reports the relevant data. Again, we note that consideration of moderators taken singly obscures the evident fact that the association between the variables in question reaches very strong proportions specifically in the case of those females who are high on both test anxiety and defensiveness. So, for the second time (see Table 6), we find this particular moderator subgroup accounting for whatever over-all relationship emerges in the sample as a whole. It should also be emphasized that for the first time we are relating decision making under payoff conditions in highly

Table 9

CORRELATIONS FOR FEMALES BETWEEN CHANCE STRATEGIES
AND CLUES FOR PERSONALITY SUBGROUPS

DEFENSIVENESS

			Low	High	Low + High	
		CMG	−.15	−.05	−.12	
		CML	.27	.03	.17	
	Low	CLS	−.09	−.10	−.09	
		CMD	.00	.28	.10	
		CMV	−.22	−.03	−.15	
TEST						$z =$
ANXIETY		CMG	−.03	−.60**	−.37**	1.32
		CML	.10	.49**	.34*	−.90
	High	CLS	−.03	−.43*	−.27*	.92
		CMD	−.05	.34	.16	−.30
		CMV	−.02	−.60**	−.36**	1.11
					$z =$	
		CMG	−.11	−.39**	1.49	
	Low	CML	.20	.31*	−.58	
	+	CLS	−.07	−.32*	1.29	
	High	CMD	−.02	.32*	−1.73	
		CMV	−.14	−.37**	1.22	

different procedural contexts — bet preference strategies on the one hand and information seeking on the other. In both of the tasks being correlated, in other words, the subject has the opportunity to increase her earnings, but the kinds of decisions required are markedly different in the two cases. Furthermore, the clues task is one in which outcomes depend upon the subject's problem-solving facility, whereas chance strategy outcomes are utterly beyond the subject's control. That such marked consistencies occur across these diverse situations suggests the extent to which a principle of risk regulation is operative in subjects who possess both strong failure-avoidance motivation and strong defenses for coping with motivational arousal in monetary gain-loss contexts. For the highly test anxious and defensive female, the clues task may be less a problem to be solved than a gamble to be taken.

Skill strategies and information seeking

Do the reported relationships also hold in the case of skill strategies? For males, moderator effects are negligible in the case of number judgments, but there is an indication of a moderator effect in the case of the clues task. Correlation coefficients between the clues task and the three skill strategies keyed in the risky direction — maximization of gain, long shot, and maximization of variance — are $-.35$, $-.35$, and $-.34$, respectively, in the subgroup high in both test anxiety and defensiveness. The p values associated with the r's cited are less than .10. Correlations for all of the other moderator subgroups are of negligible magnitude. Hence, here as well as in the other results for males discussed thus far (see Tables 1 and 3), consistencies within the decision-making domain emerge with greatest strength for individuals who are high in both test anxiety and defensiveness.

We turn next to the relationships observed in the female sample. Listed here are the correlations for the sample as a whole.

	Number judgments	Clues
Skill–max. of gain	$-.24*$	$-.21*$
Skill–min. of loss	$.25**$	$.29**$
Skill–long shot	$-.19*$	$-.17$
Skill–min. dev. from 1/2	$.11$	$.18$
Skill–max. of variance	$-.27**$	$-.26**$

It can be seen that statistically significant consistencies hold across the skill strategy and information-seeking domains. A preference for risky strategies on the shuffleboard bets procedure is associated with the requesting of fewer items of information in both the number judgments and clues tasks. In other words, the risk-taker in a motor skill context prefers the uncertainty of a larger prize to the certainty of a smaller one in an information-seeking context. Conversely, conservatism in a motor skill situation is associated, in the case of information seeking, with a preference for the smaller but more certain prize rather than the larger but more uncertain one.

Are these relationships influenced by moderator effects? Tables 10 and 11 present the relevant evidence. Although test anxiety and defensiveness do not exert a striking effect in the case of number judgments (Table 10), we may note that significant r's within the cells of the table occur only for the highly test anxious and defensive females. Hence, these results are quite consistent with the evidence reported earlier (see Table 9).

Turning to the clues task, Table 11 points up the substantial effects that ensue when test anxiety and defensiveness are considered simultaneously. Once again, substantial significant r's are found in females who

Table 10

CORRELATIONS FOR FEMALES BETWEEN SKILL STRATEGIES AND
NUMBER JUDGMENTS FOR PERSONALITY SUBGROUPS

DEFENSIVENESS

			Low	High	Low + High	
TEST ANXIETY	Low	SMG	−.27	−.23	−.26	
		SML	.21	.37	.27	
		SLS	−.21	−.18	−.20	
		SMD	.09	.05	.08	
		SMV	−.23	−.29	−.26	
						z =
	High	SMG	−.18	−.26	−.23	−.16
		SML	−.11	.41*	.21	.31
		SLS	−.24	−.13	−.17	−.15
		SMD	.36	.07	.17	−.45
		SMV	−.09	−.38*	−.27*	.05
					z =	
	Low + High	SMG	−.24	−.24	.00	
		SML	.14	.39**	−1.33	
		SLS	−.21	−.15	−.31	
		SMD	.15	.06	.45	
		SMV	−.20	−.34*	.74	

are both highly test anxious and defensive. In the present instance, however, we also find significant relations, although of somewhat lesser magnitude, in the subgroup low in both test anxiety and defensiveness. One may well wonder why the latter subgroup yields significant r's in the present case, when no such relationships appeared in that subgroup in Table 9 — clues versus chance strategies. Note, however, that the clues task and skill strategies have something in common that does not characterize the relationship between the clues task and chance strategies. The common element is the control that the subject possesses over decision outcomes. In the clues task and the shuffleboard bets procedure, the subject is aware that his payoffs depend upon his problem-solving and motor skill, respectively. No such personal control is involved when chance strategies are at issue.

The foregoing observations call for a further elaboration of the psychological processes tapped by the decision-making procedures employed in the study. The authors are suggesting that different decision contexts have distinctive features that contribute to associations or lack of associations between them. These associations can be expected to operate so as to

Table 11

CORRELATIONS FOR FEMALES BETWEEN SKILL STRATEGIES
AND CLUES FOR PERSONALITY SUBGROUPS

DEFENSIVENESS

			Low	High	Low + High	
TEST ANXIETY	Low	SMG	−.32	.02	−.18	
		SML	.37*	−.16	.18	
		SLS	−.32	−.08	−.23	
		SMD	.15	.32	.21	
		SMV	−.38*	.08	−.20	
						$z =$
	High	SMG	−.02	−.42*	−.25	.37
		SML	.21	.58**	.43**	−1.37
		SLS	.05	−.20	−.10	−.66
		SMD	.11	.18	.15	.31
		SMV	−.01	−.55**	−.34*	.74
					$z =$	
	Low + High	SMG	−.21	−.22	.05	
		SML	.31*	.28*	.16	
		SLS	−.19	−.15	−.20	
		SMD	.13	.23	−.51	
		SMV	−.25	−.27	.10	

enhance or depress relationships that are based on the more explicit risk-taking aspects of the phenomena. Of special importance, however, is the evidence that the task-centered and risk-regulatory components may have different weights in the various personality (moderator) subgroups. Consider Tables 9 and 11 once more. When the task properties are most dissimilar — Table 9 — no significant relationships emerge in the subgroup low on both moderators. Hence, the highly significant r's reported in Table 9 for highly test anxious and defensive females must be based on a risk-regulation mechanism, as we suggested earlier. The same mechanism can be invoked in Table 11 for the highly test anxious and defensive subjects. However, clues and skill strategies have, in addition, certain structural resemblances in the sense of requiring subjects to match the task requirements against their personal capacities and skills. Such structural resemblances might be expected to emerge most strongly in the subgroup ranking lowest in motivational disturbance — namely, the low test anxious and low defensive subjects. The authors are again affirming, in other words, that relations within the decision-making domain may be a joint product of structural task similarities and of underlying mechanisms of risk regulation. Further, the authors reiterate that these components appear to vary in strength in the personality subgroups under study here. While consistencies caused by similarities in task structure appear in the low test anxiety–low defensiveness subgroup, consistencies caused by the prominence of risk-regulation considerations are found in the subgroup high in both test anxiety and defensiveness.

Relationships within the information-seeking domain

To examine relationships within the information-seeking domain, we inquire into the relationship between the number judgments and clues procedures. For the male and female samples as a whole, the correlation

Table 12

CORRELATIONS FOR MALES BETWEEN NUMBER JUDGMENTS AND CLUES FOR PERSONALITY SUBGROUPS

DEFENSIVENESS

		Low	High	Low + High	
TEST ANXIETY	Low	.17	.31	.25	$z = -1.37$
	High	.41*	.56**	.48**	
	Low + High	.28*	.42**	$z = -.83$	

coefficients are .35 and .34, respectively. Both are significant well beyond the .01 level. The amount of information requested by a subject in attempting to identify an object is consistent with the amount of information he likes to have before deciding on the mean of a distribution of numbers. Again, we turn to the question of moderator influences. As Tables 12 and 13 show, the differential effects are not very strong. Yet the directions of moderator differences are sufficiently intriguing to merit brief comment. Note in each of the tables the cells containing the highest and lowest correlation coefficients. A striking sex difference is evident. Males *high* on

Table 13

CORRELATIONS FOR FEMALES BETWEEN NUMBER JUDGMENTS
AND CLUES FOR PERSONALITY SUBGROUPS

DEFENSIVENESS

		Low	High	Low + High
TEST ANXIETY	Low	.48**	.34	.43**
	High	.44*	.10	.25
	Low + High	.46**	.21	

$z = 1.00$

$z = 1.39$

both moderators exhibit the strongest consistency within the information-seeking domain; females *low* on both moderators manifest the greatest consistency. A comparable sex difference holds for the cells showing the weakest relationship between the clues and number judgments tasks.

The male results fit in nicely with findings reported earlier in the present chapter (see Tables 1 and 3). Highly test anxious and defensive males again show the greatest generality. Yet, this somehow comes as a bit of a surprise, because the two information-seeking tasks are structurally similar. One hence would have expected relationships based on structural considerations alone to have emerged most strongly in the subgroup low in test anxiety and defensiveness. Such, indeed, is the case in the female data (Table 13). But the corresponding coefficient in the male data, on the other hand, is the smallest in the table. We may speculate, then, that the "obvious" structural similarity across the two information-seeking tasks is somewhat illusory. Our "least disturbed" male does not perform the same way when behaving as a "statistician" (number judgments) and when responding as a "quiz contestant" (clues). Each task has its own specific properties, an observation that we can now begin to appreciate. Accordingly, it appears to be the comparability in payoff properties of the two tasks that engages the risk-sensitive motivational system of the highly test anxious and defensive males and brings about the highly significant consistency obtained for that subgroup.

In the present case, however, the males high in test anxiety and low in defensiveness also share in the relationship. This finding suggests that decision-making tasks with common procedural features can bring out risk-taking consistencies that do not otherwise emerge. Furthermore, the fact that both the number judgments and clues tasks are of a problem-solving type can be expected to enhance the influence of test anxiety, quite apart from the role played by defensiveness.

Returning to the female results (Table 13), we can merely speculate that females more than males ignore the subtle distinctions between the specific task requirements of number judgments and clues, and respond rather on the basis of their structural resemblances. Such tendencies should be strongest in the "least disturbed" females (those who are low on both moderators), and, as we have seen, the correlation is highly significant in that subgroup. As in the male sample, the subjects high in test anxiety and low in defensiveness also exhibit consistency within the information-seeking domain. The explanation previously advanced for the males can also be suggested here — namely, structural similarities (in this case, of a problem-solving sort) may push relationships into the range of statistical significance in subgroups of subjects for whom the risk-regulation aspects are not too salient. The major puzzle in the female data is the low, nonsignificant relationship for the subgroup high on both moderators. Recall (Tables 9, 10, and 11) that these females exhibit the strongest relationships between decision-making tasks that are markedly different in procedural format. Yet, when the format increases in similarity, the relationship declines sharply. We have no evident explanation for this surprising finding.

Chance strategies and final bet

In the instance of chance strategies and final bet, we are comparing bet preferences in which the subject, starting without funds, attempts to maximize future payoffs, and a final bet preference where the subject has the option of gambling at various levels of risk or not gambling at all with his accumulated winnings. It should be noted that the final bet procedure is a chance bet, and, accordingly, significant relationships with dice bet (chance) strategies can be anticipated. As in the case of choice dilemmas and the final bet (Table 6), the authors report partial r's in which the amount of the subject's winnings prior to the final bet was held constant. Listed here are the findings for the entire sample.

	Males	Females
Chance–max. of gain	−.26**	−.27**
Chance–min. of loss	.20*	.21*
Chance–long shot	−.20*	−.24*
Chance–min. dev. from 1/2	.18*	.17
Chance–max. of variance	−.24**	−.27**

These results conclusively demonstrate that subjects who pursue conservative strategies in their dice bet preferences are also conservative in their choice of probability on the final bet procedure. Correspondingly, risk taking on chance strategies is significantly associated with a penchant toward risk in the final bet. Note that the two sexes are highly comparable in the magnitude of the observed relationships.

Consider again the part played by moderator variables. For males, moderator effects are nonexistent. Thus, the over-all relationship reported is apparently not subject to personality influences. The same cannot be said for the female subjects, as Table 14 clearly indicates. Note the many

Table 14

Partial Correlations for Females between Chance Strategies and Final Bet (Prior Winnings Held Constant) for Personality Subgroups

DEFENSIVENESS

			Low	High	Low + High	
	Low	CMG	.18	−.39	−.01	
		CML	−.03	.44*	.15	
		CLS	.18	−.23	.06	
		CMD	−.15	.19	−.03	
		CMV	.17	−.44*	−.05	
TEST ANXIETY						z =
	High	CMG	−.30	−.65**	−.48**	2.52
		CML	.29	.27	.21	−.31
		CLS	−.26	−.58**	−.45**	2.68
		CMD	.13	.50**	.32*	−1.78
		CMV	−.39	−.57**	−.43**	2.02
					z =	
	Low + High	CMG	−.06	−.50**	2.41	
		CML	.14	.28*	−.72	
		CLS	−.03	−.44**	2.18	
		CMD	.00	.36**	−1.86	
		CMV	−.11	−.44**	1.78	

significant correlational differences obtained when test anxiety and defensiveness are treated one at a time. These differences indicate that high test anxiety and high defensiveness enhance relationships between the two variables under consideration.

Looking within the cells of the table, we observe that the subgroup low on both moderators does not participate in the general relationship. For these females, the kind of risk embodied in the dice bets task is quite independent of the risks inherent in a chance context where one's own newly acquired funds are at stake. Though outcomes are beyond one's control in both cases, the distinction between playing with the experimenter's resources and with one's own funds appears crucial. As has happened so often before, we find in turn that the highest r's are manifested by the highly test anxious and defensive subgroup. Here again, then, we find that where the appropriate motivational dynamics are present, risk-regulatory mechanisms are invoked that cause consistencies to appear across diverse decision-making contexts. These motivationally "disturbed" subjects appear to evaluate a wide variety of decision-making situations in terms of a single risk-conservatism dimension. At low levels of test anxiety and defensiveness, on the other hand, the decision-making domain may well become multidimensional.

Skill strategies and final bet

Because the final bet is conducted in a chance context, we can anticipate weaker relationships here than were obtained in the preceding case, where both indexes were derived from chance tasks. Again, partial r's were computed holding prior winnings constant. The over-all relationships are as follows.

	Males	Females
Skill–max. of gain	−.23*	−.16
Skill–min. of loss	.24**	.09
Skill–long shot	−.17	−.14
Skill–min. dev. from 1/2	.10	.07
Skill–max. of variance	−.24**	−.16

It can be seen that our expectation is borne out only in the case of the female subjects. For males, the correlations are virtually of the same magnitude as those obtained between the final bet and chance strategies. Subjects preferring more risky strategies in the shuffleboard task tend to select more risky (in other words, lower) probability-of-success values in their choice of a final bet.

Let us next check on moderator influences. Table 15 presents the results for males. It can be seen that the significant r's observed in the male sample as a whole can be attributed in large measure to the highly defensive subjects. Note further that, within the defensiveness subgroup, level of test anxiety does not have much of an effect. In short, across the highly dissimilar decision contexts of skill strategies and the final bet, we again find consistencies in risk taking emerging most clearly in the presence of a particular pattern of motivational disturbance. The reason that relation-

Table 15

PARTIAL CORRELATIONS FOR MALES BETWEEN SKILL STRATEGIES AND FINAL BET (PRIOR WINNINGS HELD CONSTANT) FOR PERSONALITY SUBGROUPS

DEFENSIVENESS

			Low	High	Low + High	
TEST ANXIETY	Low	SMG	−.01	−.34*	−.25*	
		SML	.26	.14	.25*	
		SLS	.09	−.31	−.17	
		SMD	−.20	.32	.11	
		SMV	−.09	−.28	−.26*	
						z =
	High	SMG	.02	−.38	−.20	−.27
		SML	.19	.26	.23	.11
		SLS	.10	−.38	−.16	−.06
		SMD	−.25	.25	.08	.15
		SMV	.01	−.39	−.22	−.22
					z =	
	Low + High	SMG	.00	−.35**	1.90	
		SML	.22	.19	.17	
		SLS	.09	−.34**	2.31	
		SMD	−.21	.28*	−2.61	
		SMV	−.04	−.32**	1.52	

ships hold in this case for both defensive subgroups, rather than solely for highly defensive *and* test anxious males, becomes clear when one takes account of the interpersonal contexts in which the skill strategies and final bet measures are obtained.

There can be little doubt that highly defensive males are going to be concerned with image maintenance. Such concern is especially likely when making decisions in a face-to-face interaction with an experimenter who is in the position of evaluating one's preferred risk or conservatism level and, subsequently, one's success or failure regarding decision outcomes. These conditions obtain for both skill strategies and the final bet. One may reasonably inquire why all defensive male subjects are not risk takers, on the grounds that this is a highly desirable masculine attribute. There is, in fact, a mean difference between high and low defensive males in that direction (see Appendix A–4, rows 7–11, 14) which turns out to be statistically significant for the final bet (row 14). However, there is also considerable variability. The basis for this variability can very probably be traced to the natural association between risky decision making and unfavorable outcomes. The latter can, of course, also be evaluated by the experimenter. Hence, the risk-taking propensities of defensive males depend on the differential relevance for image maintenance of boldness of decision making as opposed to successful implementation of decisions over and above their risky or conservative character.

The point to which this argument leads is a rather simple one. The highly defensive male adopts a consistently conservative or risky strategy across widely dissimilar tasks for the reason that such consistency follows from the image-maintenance requirements of his particular personality. The effects are especially pronounced when a respected other person (the experimenter) is present, for the defensive subject is quite concerned with the impression he conveys regarding his risk-taking prowess and judgment. Recall, in this connection, that chance strategies, a *group-administered* task, do not yield any moderator effects for males when related to the final bet measure.

Table 16

PARTIAL CORRELATIONS FOR FEMALES BETWEEN SKILL STRATEGIES AND FINAL BET (PRIOR WINNINGS HELD CONSTANT) FOR PERSONALITY SUBGROUPS

DEFENSIVENESS

			Low	High	Low + High	
TEST ANXIETY	Low	SMG	.37*	−.30	.08	
		SML	−.25	−.13	−.21	
		SLS	.32	−.40	.02	
		SMD	−.43*	.36	−.11	
		SMV	.32	−.17	.11	
						$z =$
	High	SMG	−.35	−.40*	−.38**	2.36
		SML	.15	.46*	.28*	−2.47
		SLS	−.35	−.21	−.27*	1.46
		SMD	.14	.20	.21	−1.59
		SMV	−.34	−.47**	−.40**	2.63
					$z =$	
	Low + High	SMG	.04	−.35*	2.00	
		SML	−.04	.25	−1.46	
		SLS	.02	−.28*	1.52	
		SMD	−.17	.26	−2.16	
		SMV	.03	−.33*	1.84	

Let us proceed to the female subjects. Table 16 presents the relevant moderator results. Recall that the partial correlations between skill strategies and the final bet are nonsignificant for the female sample in its entirety. As Table 16 indicates, however, these over-all nonsignificant r's are obscuring highly significant moderator differences. A comparison with Table 14 may prove instructive. There, it will be recalled, we found that the subgroup low in test anxiety and defensiveness was not participating in the general relationship between chance strategies and the final bet. Now, when skill strategies are at issue, we observe a significant reversal in the sign of the correlation for that subgroup — the subjects low in test anxiety and in defensiveness — relative to the three other moderator subgroups within the cells of Table 16. The low test anxious and low defensive females who prefer more risky strategies in the shuffleboard procedure turn out to be more conservative when selecting a probability level in the final bet situation. All of the other subgroups, and particularly the females high on both moderators, exhibit the very opposite, and more consistent, pattern. This latter pattern has been repeatedly described with reference to the salience of risk-regulatory mechanisms in subjects characterized by enduring states of motivational arousal. Once again, it is the high test anxious-high defensive individuals who exhibit the strongest risk-regulatory consistency. That low test anxious-low defensive females can exhibit such apparent inconsistency, in turn, suggests the extent to which these subjects can go in discriminating the contrasting features of the decision-making tasks confronting them. Thus, the shuffleboard task, to reiterate, places the responsibility for decision outcomes in the hands of the individual decision-maker, whereas the outcome of the final bet preference rests on the toss of a die. The decision context, in short, is quite different in the two cases, and the "least disturbed" or "least aroused" subjects appear to be most sensitive to this difference. The present findings suggest, in fact, that for low test anxious-low defensive people, confidence in one's capacity to implement one's decisions successfully is associated with a particularly pessimistic view about the laws of chance. Correspondingly, if this sort of person is quite conservative in decision making where outcomes depend on one's own performance, his decision-making behavior in a gambling context may reflect an optimistic outlook on the favorability of chance outcomes.

Information seeking and final bet

Is there any relationship between the amount of information demanded in a monetary payoff context and the level of risk preferred in a gambling context where one's own funds are at stake? For both males and females, the correlations in the samples as a whole are negligible for both information-seeking tasks — number judgments and clues. The partial r's of these tasks with the final bet (prior winnings held constant) range from .00 to .11.

Turning to the moderator analysis, we find no effects observed for the male samples. It is evident, then, that the decision-making domains under consideration here are quite independent of each other in male subjects. A comparable absence of any moderator influences has obtained for females in the number judgments procedure. Note, however, the results reported

Table 17

PARTIAL CORRELATIONS FOR FEMALES BETWEEN CLUES AND FINAL BET (PRIOR WINNINGS HELD CONSTANT) FOR PERSONALITY SUBGROUPS

DEFENSIVENESS

		Low	High	Low + High
TEST ANXIETY	Low	.02	.12	.04
	High	−.42*	.61**	.14
	Low + High	−.20	.42**	

$z = -.50$

$z = -3.21$

in Table 17. Again, we see that it is the clues task within the information-seeking domain that discriminates between the moderator subgroups. The significant difference in the marginal r's for defensiveness does not provide the sharpest delineation of the findings, as the r's within the cells of the table indicate. Once more, we observe that the highest r appears in the subgroup high on both test anxiety and defensiveness. For these subjects, a highly significant and consistent risk-regulatory relationship emerges — the requesting of more information on the clues task is associated with a preference for high probabilities of success in the final bet. Of further interest in Table 17 is the significant *negative* relationship manifested by the subjects high in test anxiety and low in defensiveness. These females, when conservative on the clues task, exhibit greater risk taking in a final bet context.

Recall that a similar inverse relationship was found in Table 16 — skill strategies versus final bet. In that case, however, the relationship in question emerged in the subgroup low on both moderators. How can we account for this apparent discrepancy? Both the skill strategies and clues measures involve reliance on personal resources — motor competence and verbal facility, respectively. In terms of the relevance of each to test anxiety, however, it seems quite reasonable to suppose that a task relying on verbal facility will rank above a procedure based on motor skill. The items in the test anxiety questionnaire are concerned, after all, with performance on achievement and intelligence tests. There can be no doubt that the clues task bears a much stronger relationship to classical intelligence measures than does a motor skill task. In short, the authors are suggesting that, of all the decision-making procedures employed, the clues task is the most likely to evoke the test anxious response in subjects high in overt test anxiety. For it is in the clues task that the subject's verbal skills are engaged, and, furthermore, monetary gain and loss depend on performance. Our results suggest that the subject who handles this anxiety by conservative decision making — requesting many clues — compensates in a gambling context by taking greater risks. Correspondingly, handling test anxiety by requesting few clues (one does not really fail if one has not truly tried) apparently produces a more conservative outlook when one's funds are at stake in a gambling situation.

Effect of prior winnings on final bet

Whenever the authors introduced the final bet variable in the preceding sections of the chapter, the authors resorted to partial correlation analysis. This step was necessary because significant relationships are found in both males and females between level of risk-taking manifested in the final bet and the amount of money won up to that point. Consistent with the authors' expectations, as subjects' winnings across bet strategy and information-seeking tasks increase, the subjects become more reluctant to take risks in a final gamble with the newly acquired winnings.

In Tables 18 and 19, this relationship is examined from a moderator standpoint. For both sexes, the effects are quite striking, though it can be seen that defensiveness is the critical moderator for males, whereas test anxiety fulfills that function for females. Considering first the results for males in Table 18, we note that the expected association between prior winnings and conservatism on the final bet holds only for subjects who are low in defensiveness. When defensiveness achieves high levels, the expected relationship vanishes, and we can consequently make no reliable prediction of what a subject will do in the final bet situation on the basis of his prior winnings.

Why does the amount of money earned cease to affect the final bet selection when defensiveness is high? Recall our earlier discussion of the implications of defensiveness for risk taking in males. There we emphasized the manner in which image-maintenance mechanisms operate to yield con-

Table 18

CORRELATIONS FOR MALES BETWEEN WINNINGS PRIOR TO FINAL BET AND FINAL BET FOR PERSONALITY SUBGROUPS

DEFENSIVENESS

		Low	High	Low + High	
TEST ANXIETY	Low	.39*	−.04	.20	$z = -.44$
	High	.45*	−.02	.28*	
	Low + High	.42	−.04	$z = 2.54$	

Table 19

CORRELATIONS FOR FEMALES BETWEEN WINNINGS PRIOR TO FINAL BET AND FINAL BET FOR PERSONALITY SUBGROUPS

DEFENSIVENESS

		Low	High	Low + High	
TEST ANXIETY	Low	.50**	.47*	.48**	$z = 1.63$
	High	.19	.14	.19	
	Low + High	.35**	.25	$z = .54$	

sistencies in risk-taking propensities across diverse decision-making contexts. Such mechanisms clearly exert their effects in the present case, for the need to maintain a self-image as a cautious or bold decision-maker (and/or to impress the experimenter as such) in the final bet situation will tend to dominate whatever influences derive from the magnitude of a subject's prior winnings. For these individuals, risk taking is an expression of inner motivational forces, rather than of such external (and rational) considerations as amount of monetary stake (within the range at issue in the present investigation). The subject low in defensiveness, on the other hand, being less driven by motivational factors to prove himself a particular sort of decision-maker, can adopt a more casual approach to the final bet situation. Such an approach encourages an evaluation of the external determinants at work. The most salient, of course, is the magnitude of the monetary winnings just acquired. The strategy adopted may be described as follows: Better that one leave the experimental situation with some winnings than none; and the more winnings one has acquired, the more satisfied one should be (and correspondingly, the more painful would be their loss). It is quite evident that the highly defensive males do not go through such a reasoning process.

Consider next the results for females reported in Table 19. Note that it is test anxiety, not defensiveness, that differentiates the females. This result is hardly surprising, for the risk-conservatism dimension is likely to be less critical for females than males when self-evaluation is at issue. Caution–boldness and success–failure in decision-making do not strike us as the kinds of dimensions that women need be maximally defensive about. Although considerations of risk may be an integral part of the masculine image, it is doubtful whether a female subject will perceive her femininity as being tied up to a comparable degree with the level of risk she displays in making decisions.

Test anxiety is another matter, however. College females are exposed to the stress of academic examinations. Success and failure in this context are a matter of some concern to college women, and of special concern to highly test anxious women. Again making the assumption that test anxiety represents a motive to avoid failure, we find that the results reported in Table 19 can be explained in terms of a preoccupation with the success and failure implications of the final bet. This motivational pattern again interferes with a proper evaluation of the monetary prize at stake. We are assuming now that test anxiety in females generalizes to a chance context. The Atkinson group (Atkinson *et al.*, 1960) has reported that some generalization is found in male samples across skill and chance tasks, but most investigators working in the McClelland-Atkinson tradition have scrupulously refrained from using female subjects. The high correlations found in the present sample of females between chance and skill strategy indexes certainly suggest that some generalization occurs.

If the Atkinson (1957) conceptualization of test anxiety is applicable in the present circumstances, highly test anxious women may seek to avoid failure either by responding conservatively to the final bet situation or by deciding impulsively — in other words, counterphobically. Again, these are inner motivational dynamics reflecting a condition in which rational consideration of the size of one's monetary stake is not likely to occur. The women who are low in test anxiety, on the other hand, take rational account of the size of their prior winnings, and bet conservatively if their prior winnings are large.

Summary

The present section has addressed itself to the generality of risk-taking behavior in a variety of payoff contexts. This generality is quite pronounced in both male and female subjects, particularly the latter. Again, division of the sample into test anxiety and defensiveness subgroups yields an array of moderator-differences. Does the dual process conceptualization, which has been employed to account for consistencies across hypothetical and payoff contexts, also prove to be valid *within* the latter domain? The answer to this question, on balance, seems to be "yes." Consider, in particular, relationships observed in the female sample between an information-seeking measure — clues — and chance and skill strategy indexes. When chance strategies are at issue, the relationship with the clues task emerges only in highly test anxious and defensive subjects. Skill strategies, on the other hand, correlate significantly with clues performance in *two* subgroups, those high *and* those low on both moderators. The authors have attempted to explain this difference in terms of the degree of similarity in the task requirements posed by the clues procedure, on the one hand, and the two strategy measures on the other. Clues and skill strategies are linked on the basis of the effect of personal competency upon outcomes, whereas clues and chance strategies do not possess this common element. In the latter instance, then, associations may obtain only when particular motivational processes relevant to risk regulation become engaged (in other words, especially in the case of high test anxious–high defensive persons). In the former case, on the other hand, correspondences may arise on the basis of similarities in task properties as well (similarities to which low test anxious–low defensive persons may be most sensitive). The findings are highly suggestive of this dual process conceptualization.

Sex differences intrude upon the picture outlined here. In the male sample, the link between information seeking (clues) and skill strategies apparently requires the presence of particular motivational predispositions — high test anxiety and defensiveness. No relationship emerges for the subgroup low on both moderators, suggesting that males make sharper differentiations than do females between the structural characteristics of information-seeking and skill strategy contexts. Despite the common element of dependence of outcomes on personal attributes — verbal capacity and motor skill — males low in motivational disturbance apparently do not find the task features comparable in the two cases.

Further evidence for the dual process conceptualization is contained in the relationships between the strategy indexes and the final bet variable. The presence of both high test anxiety and defensiveness in females appears to maximize relationships between the final bet and both chance and skill strategies. When test anxiety and defensiveness are low, on the other hand, a significant *inverse* relationship ensues between the final bet and skill strategy indexes. This latter finding suggests that, for subjects low in motivational disturbance or arousal, the perceived properties of different decision situations can overcome and actually reverse tendencies toward consistency in risk regulation.

The authors do not wish to imply that all of the findings in the present domain lend themselves to interpretation in terms of the proposed dual process conceptualization. In several cases, the authors have found it necessary to invoke other processes in order to give adequate psychological meaning to the results. Recall that the dual process interpretation has been based on results obtained in two of the four moderator subgroups — the subjects high on both moderators and those low on both moderators. Significant relationships are not confined, however, to those two subgroups in all cases, but also emerge in the remaining two cells of the table when various decision-making tasks involving payoffs are related to one another. When, for example, the procedural format of the decision-making tasks becomes highly comparable — chance versus skill strategies and number judgments versus clues — the magnitudes of relationships in the samples as a whole are quite high, and in addition, the low-high and/or high-low moderator subgroups sometimes begin to share in the general relationship. This sharing is more than a mere matter of identical procedural formats, however. Thus, where the decision tasks being related both involve face-to-face interaction with an experimenter, processes of image maintenance and the need for social approval begin to play an important role, with the consequence that defensiveness heightens relationships, and considerations of test anxiety become less relevant. Correspondingly, in those cases where the decision-making task is embedded in a format suggestive of an intelligence or aptitude assessment, the test anxiety moderator becomes more critical and defensiveness assumes more of a background role. One truly arrives at the impression that particular motivational predispositions are engaged in accordance with the total psychological "press" of the decision situation.

Finally, the authors have considered the influence of prior monetary winnings on the final bet selection. In general, the more money a subject has accumulated during the course of the experiment, the less risk he is willing to assume with it — an obviously rational response to the situation in which the subject finds himself. This association necessitates partial correlational analysis when relating the final bet index to all of the other decision-making measures. The authors found, however, that the prior winnings–final bet association is in itself strongly influenced by the moderator variables — defensiveness in the male subjects and test anxiety in the females. When defensiveness is high in the males and test anxiety is high in the females, the relationship between prior winnings and the final bet ceases to hold. The differential relevance of the two moderators for males and females makes good psychological sense in the domain of risk-taking behavior. The final bet, it will be recalled, is carried out in an interpersonal face-to-face encounter between experimenter and subject. This situation is precisely the kind in which the highly defensive male will feel that his masculine decision-making prowess is undergoing evaluation. Such concerns can hardly be expected to plague the female subject to the same degree. The highly test anxious female, on the other hand, motivated by a fear of failure, may well conceive of the loss of her winnings as a personal reflection on her critical judgment in choosing a probability level. There may well be an unwarranted generalization from an academic performance to a gambling context in such subjects. In both cases, motivational factors gain dominance over the rational consideration of amount of prior funds accumulated.

In closing this chapter, we may note that one point deserves particular underscoring. We have found that, of the four personality types under study, individuals high in both defensiveness and test anxiety are most likely to respond to a wide variety of decision-making situations in ways that indicate a primary sensitivity to the risk-taking implications of these situations — whether the direction of behavior of a particular person in that subgroup is more risky or more conservative. Correspondingly, it is evident that such persons are least sensitive to the particular task attributes that cause these decision-making situations to differ from one another. With a certain kind of motivational involvement on the part of the individual, therefore, considerations relating to risk regulation become of paramount importance. Their control over the person's behavior can interfere with his evaluation of specific situations in terms of whatever other characteristics they may possess.

4

Postdecisional Processes

Decisions generally have consequences. When these consequences are positive, the decision-maker's goals have been served; when the consequences are negative, the decision-maker's goals have been hindered or blocked. In the preceding chapter, we focused upon the decisions themselves. Here we shall examine postdecisional effects. Three specific questions will be probed. First, is there any relation between decision-making strategies and monetary outcomes? Here we inquire whether particular strategies are more optimal than others in the sense of their potentialities for monetary gain. Our second question concerns the degree of satisfaction the person expresses in his decisions as he becomes aware of the consequences that they bring. In particular, we are interested in the degree and form of the relationship between monetary winnings and postdecision satisfaction. One may expect, of course, that the bigger winner will indicate greater satisfaction with his previous decisions. Nevertheless, the matter must be put to a direct empirical test, for, as the preceding chapter has shown, relationships often are not as obvious as they seem, particularly when moderator influences are at work. Finally, we should like to know whether preferences for certain decision strategies are associated per se with postdecision satisfaction, over and beyond the effects of winnings on such satisfaction. Naturally, it is necessary to control for level of winnings when examining that question. In dealing with all of these questions, we shall pay close attention to moderator effects.

DECISION-MAKING STRATEGIES AND MONETARY OUTCOMES

Chance strategies

Listed here are the correlations for the male and female samples as a whole between the various chance strategies and two monetary outcome indexes. The "absolute" (Abs.) index refers to a subject's total winnings from the chance plays. The "relative" (Rel.) index takes account of the fact that maximum possible winnings vary as a function of the strategy selected — a person who chooses to maximize gain has the opportunity to win more money than does the individual who prefers to minimize loss. To correct for this factor, a "relative" index has been derived in which a subject's monetary gain is divided by the maximum he can win if each of his bets is successful.

	Males		Females	
	Abs.	Rel.	Abs.	Rel.
Chance–max. of gain	.24*	−.16	−.14	−.43**
Chance–min. of loss	−.11	.13	.05	.19*
Chance–long shot	.23*	−.16	−.15	−.43**
Chance–min. dev. from 1/2	−.20*	.13	.22*	.42**
Chance–max. of variance	.23*	−.17	−.13	−.40**

Despite the absence of control over outcomes in the chance plays, it can be seen that the pattern of correlations shows a substantial sex difference. With respect to absolute outcomes, the adoption of a more risky strategy by the males pays off in the form of bigger winnings. For the females, on the other hand, there is a tendency in the opposite direction; note the significant correlation with absolute winnings for the strategy that minimizes deviation from 1/2. The sex difference for relative winnings, in turn, is one of magnitude rather than sign. More risky strategies make for lesser winnings relative to a theoretical maximum, the effect being especially pronounced in the case of the females.[1]

How can we account for these obvious sex differences in a decision context that permits of no personal control over outcomes? We refuse to believe, of course, that males are simply luckier than females. The clue to the riddle lies in the mean differences in strategy preferences between the male and female samples (Appendix A–1, rows 2–6). Relative to the male sample, females appear to select more extreme strategies — risky or conservative — under chance conditions, and tend to avoid the intermediate strategy of minimizing deviation from 1/2. In short, males seem better able to judge threshold effects in risk taking under chance conditions. The females, by contrast, exceed the threshold, and as a consequence they experience less success in both absolute and particularly relative terms. It

---

[1] Although all bet pairs are of equal expected value, these results indicate that certain strategies are more optimal than others in the short run.

should be noted also that the males suffer somewhat in relative terms for greater risk taking. This statement may seem at first blush to be trivial, on the grounds that the individual at the conclusion of the chance plays is more interested in how much he did win than in any abstract ratio that takes account of the maximum he could have won. The issue must remain open, however, because the person who wins small sums consistently may derive as much satisfaction as the individual who wins large sums infrequently. The latter may wind up with greater absolute winnings than the former, with the reverse holding true for relative winnings, but we have no basis as yet for inferring levels of satisfaction from these differential outcome patterns.

Finally, mention should be made of the significant association for females between absolute winnings and the "minimization of deviation from 1/2" strategy. Against the background of excessive risk taking and overconservatism, the female who adopts a middle-of-the-road course is in monetary terms more successful. The identical strategy in the male sample is less successful for the reason that males seem more capable of finding the risk-taking threshold beyond which their luck cannot be expected to hold.

Let us inquire into the sums actually won by the males and females. Row 16 of Appendix A-1 reports this information. It can be seen that the males do win more on the average ($1.03) than the females ($.91). The difference is not statistically significant, however. Nor is the sex difference between relative winnings statistically significant.

The foregoing considerations seriously complicate the issue of moderator influences. If the correlation between chance strategies and associated monetary outcomes is dependent upon the level of risk-conservatism in strategy preferences, then any correlational differences among moderator subgroups may simply reflect mean differences in strategy preferences plus the operation of random processes. Appendix A-6 (rows 2 to 6) reports the chance strategy means for the four moderator subgroups of males. Note that the low test anxious–low defensive males are considerably more conservative than the other three subgroups. The associated F values are significant beyond the .05 level for both "minimization of loss" and "maximization of variance."

Row 16 of Appendix A-6 reports the chance winnings for the four subgroups. It can be seen that the high test anxious–low defensive subjects — those manifesting the highest risk levels — win the largest amount of money, though it will be noted that the F value does not achieve significance. Under decision conditions where outcomes depend upon random processes, high test anxious–low defensive males, then, show some tendency toward selecting optimal strategies. This outcome does not imply, of course, that these males are especially perspicacious with regard to assessing optimal strategies in a chance context. Rather, consistent with Atkinson (1957), the extreme risk-taking levels may well be a direct function of motivational dynamics, which coincidentally bring about quite favorable outcomes given the structure of the decision task. That structure, by the way, is one in which a successful high-risk bet (for example, 1/9 chance of winning $4.80, 8/9 chance of losing $.60) yields so very substantial a payoff that it more than compensates for the number of losses that can be experienced in a series of 22 bet plays. Of course, the high-risk bet may never pay off, in which case the subject's winnings will be negligible. Note, in this connection (Appendix A-6, row 16), that the chance winnings figure yields the highest variability for the high test anxious–low defensive subgroup.

How do the other three moderator subgroups fare in chance winnings? Especially interesting is the fact that the subjects low in both test anxiety and defensiveness — the most conservative group in strategy preferences — fare as well monetarily as the subgroups high in either test anxiety or defensiveness, though both of the latter are distinguished by higher risk levels. Furthermore, the low test anxious–low defensive subgroup obtains the highest value for relative winnings, suggesting that this subgroup prefers a strategy yielding consistent winnings of smaller magnitude to a strategy that looks for the "big killing." This may well be a chance phenomenon, of course, so we ought not to make too much of it. On the other hand, the observation is consistent with other evidence, to be considered in this chapter, of the strong adaptive quality shown in the decision-making behavior of the low test anxious–low defensive subjects.

Consider next the comparable findings for the female sample. With respect to the five chance strategies, the evidence (Appendix A-7, rows 2 to 6) is quite consistent with the male data. Again, it is the low test anxious–low defensive individuals who exhibit the greatest conservatism under chance conditions, although none of the F values achieves significance for females. In contrast with the result for males, however, the result for females is that the highly defensive (low test anxious) individuals, rather than the high test anxious–low defensives, appear to be the greatest risk-takers. Note, however, that such risk-taking levels in females bring about the lowest level of winnings, a reversal of the male findings. Hence, these females have exceeded the threshold to which the authors referred earlier. The more moderate level of risk taking that distinguishes the high test anxious–high defensive subgroup brings about the largest monetary payoff. Furthermore, this subgroup fares as well as the low test anxious–low defensive females in relative winnings. There is little evidence in the female sample, then, that low levels of motivational disturbance will produce optimal strategies in chance contexts. Again, this statement is not intended to imply that the greater winnings in the other moderator subgroups represent a higher level of acumen. An individual's strategy choice may be as much influenced by motivational dynamics as by cognitive apprehension of optimal decision making under conditions where personal control is lacking.

Skill strategies

We turn now to the relation between risk-taking indexes and monetary outcomes under conditions where the latter depend on the subject's own performance. Listed below for the male and female samples as a whole are the correlations between the five skill strategies, on the one hand, and absolute and relative skill winnings on the other.

	Males		Females	
	Abs.	Rel.	Abs.	Rel.
Skill–max. of gain	.15	−.33**	.23*	−.01
Skill–min. of loss	−.01	.31**	−.06	.02
Skill–long shot	.16	−.31**	.26**	.00
Skill–min. dev. from 1/2	−.20*	.23*	−.23*	−.01
Skill–max. of variance	.13	−.35**	.21*	−.02

A striking difference can be noted between these results and those obtained under chance conditions. With respect to the relationship between strategies and absolute winnings, males no longer show up to advantage when pursuing risky strategies. If anything, the female subjects (relative to their own group) profit more from an orientation of greater risk taking. In terms of absolute amounts, however, it can be seen (Appendix A-1, row 18) that the males fare somewhat better, winning $1.11 on the average in comparison with the $.92 earned by the females. But this difference is not statistically significant.

In the male sample, where it can be seen that the greater risk-taker wins proportionately less, relative to his maximum, relative winnings seem to be strongly affected by strategy selected. No such relation obtains in the female sample. The over-all magnitude of relative winnings (Appendix A-1, row 19) is significantly greater for the males ($t = 2.34$, $p < .05$), indicating that men approach their performance ceiling somewhat more closely than do women. This finding very likely reflects the males' superior motor skill.

Sex differences in skill strategies are negligible, with the exception of a significantly greater tendency on the part of the females to minimize deviation from 1/2. Hence, the correlational differences between the sexes do not seem to be associated with discrepancies in risk-taking levels. In this respect, the strategy-outcome relation is dissimilar for chance and skill conditions. Whereas the observed mean differences in risk taking under chance conditions preclude an examination of moderator effects, no such restrictions hold in the case of risk taking in a context of skill.

Table 20

CORRELATIONS FOR MALES BETWEEN SKILL STRATEGIES AND ABSOLUTE SKILL WINNINGS FOR PERSONALITY SUBGROUPS

DEFENSIVENESS

			Low	High	Low + High	
TEST ANXIETY	Low	SMG	.36*	.32	.30*	
		SML	−.05	−.20	−.12	
		SLS	.38*	.30	.31*	
		SMD	−.47**	−.23	−.33**	
		SMV	.37*	.32	.30*	
						$z =$
	High	SMG	−.04	.01	−.01	1.64
		SML	.24	−.08	.09	−1.08
		SLS	.05	−.07	−.01	1.70
		SMD	−.04	−.06	−.06	−1.45
		SMV	−.10	−.02	−.06	1.90
					$z =$	
	Low + High	SMG	.13	.18	−.26	
		SML	.12	−.14	1.36	
		SLS	.19	.13	.32	
		SMD	−.27*	−.15	−.65	
		SMV	.10	.17	−.37	

We turn, then, to moderator influences on relations between skill strategies and associated monetary outcomes. Table 20 shows the correlations for the male sample in the case of absolute winnings. The moderating influence of test anxiety is quite strong. When test anxiety is low, a preference for more risky strategies on the skill task is associated with larger winnings. The highly test anxious subjects, on the other hand, yield no relationship whatever between the two variables in question. Appendix A–2 (rows 7–11) further indicates no mean or variability differences between high and low test anxious subjects in skill strategy preferences. We conclude, then, that the presence of high levels of test anxiety disrupts skilled performance. If susceptible to anxiety under stress, a high risk taker in a context of skill is equally likely to succumb or succeed. By contrast, the high risk taker low in test anxiety generally does considerably better than his more conservative counterpart. Note that defensiveness does not play much of a moderator role in the present case, though it is of some interest that the only sig-

Table 21

CORRELATIONS FOR MALES BETWEEN SKILL STRATEGIES AND RELATIVE
SKILL WINNINGS FOR PERSONALITY SUBGROUPS

			DEFENSIVENESS			
			Low	High	Low + High	
		SMG	−.18	−.23	−.24	
		SML	.29	.20	.25*	
	Low	SLS	−.14	−.21	−.20	
		SMD	−.06	.24	.10	
		SMV	−.17	−.25	−.24	
TEST						$z =$
ANXIETY		SMG	−.41*	−.46*	−.43**	1.10
		SML	.44*	.26	.35*	−.57
	High	SLS	−.37	−.51*	−.44**	1.38
		SMD	.35	.40	.36**	−1.42
		SMV	−.47*	−.50*	−.47**	1.36
					$z =$	
		SMG	−.31*	−.35**	.23	
	Low	SML	.38**	.24	.81	
	+	SLS	−.26*	−.36**	.58	
	High	SMD	.13	.32*	−1.04	
		SMV	−.34**	−.38**	.24	

nificant r's within the body of the table are located in the cell containing the subjects low on both moderators. In sum, the less the motivational disturbance, the greater is the likelihood that the male subject will successfully implement a risky decision in a context of skilled performance.

In Table 21, we consider for the males the impact of skill strategy preferences on relative winnings. The results, although not as conclusive as those reported in Table 20, are nevertheless consistent with them. Higher levels of risk contribute to smaller monetary outcomes on a relative basis in all subgroups, but the effects are stronger in highly test anxious persons (though z's fall quite short of significance). Again, we are led to conclude that test anxiety interferes with the smooth efficiency of performance that characterizes the low test anxious individuals.

Consider next the results for female subjects. Table 22 presents the correlations between skill strategies and absolute skill winnings. Note that the significant association between those variables in the sample as a whole derives largely from two of the moderator subgroups. Again, we see that the marginal r's are not very informative, given the diagonal relation between the two subgroups in question — those low and high on both moder-

Table 22

CORRELATIONS FOR FEMALES BETWEEN SKILL STRATEGIES AND ABSOLUTE SKILL WINNINGS FOR PERSONALITY SUBGROUPS

DEFENSIVENESS

			Low	High	Low + High	
TEST ANXIETY	Low	SMG	.30	.14	.23	
		SML	−.04	−.21	−.10	
		SLS	.37*	.12	.27	
		SMD	−.32	.00	−.21	
		SMV	.24	.15	.20	
						$z =$
	High	SMG	.09	.36	.24	−.05
		SML	−.06	.01	−.04	−.30
		SLS	.12	.38*	.26	.05
		SMD	−.10	−.37*	−.25	.21
		SMV	.15	.29	.23	−.15
				$z =$		
Low + High		SMG	.21	.27*	−.31	
		SML	−.06	−.05	−.05	
		SLS	.26	.29*	−.16	
		SMD	−.21	−.27*	.31	
		SMV	.20	.23	−.15	

ators. Appendix A–7 (rows 7–11) indicates quite clearly that the moderator variations are not attributable to mean and variability differences in skill strategy preferences. Hence, we can conclude that skilled performance in females is least likely to be disrupted when motivational disturbance is at its lowest level or when a particular kind of motivational tension obtains, namely high test anxiety and high defensiveness. The former result is consistent with the male finding, and does not come as a great surprise. The significant correlations observed in the highly test anxious and defensive females, on the other hand, are not consistent with the male findings. There, we observed that test anxiety, regardless of defensiveness level, disrupted the successful implementation of decisions in a context of skill. For females, it appears that a set of strong, rigid defenses can overcome the debilitating effect of test anxiety. Recall that these are the women who show the highest degree of consistency in risk-conservatism level across a variety of decision-making tasks, from which we inferred that these subjects' decisions are more strongly determined by motivational dynamics than by situational influences. The present results indicate that the greater risk-takers within the test anxious–defensive subgroup manage to implement their decisions more successfully in a context of motor skill; but notice, on the other hand, that this is a within-group phenomenon. In terms of absolute skill winnings, it can be seen (Appendix A-7, row 18) that the test anxious–defensive subgroup yields the lowest mean value in the female sample. Their relative winnings are also lowest among the four moderator subgroups. Although these differences are not statistically significant, they suggest that the highly test anxious and defensive females perform more poorly generally. Within that subgroup, however, risk taking pays off when decisions under skill conditions are at issue. Correspondingly, the test anxious–defensive female who is also conservative in her strategy preferences apparently does most poorly of all in both absolute and relative terms.

Table 23 reports the correlations between skill strategies and relative skill winnings for females. The low test anxious–high defensive females manifest a trend toward greater winnings on a relative basis when adopting a more conservative strategy (minimizing deviation from 1/2). The authors find it difficult to interpret this finding, and suspect it may be due in part to the high variability of relative winnings in this subgroup (Appendix A-7, row 19).

Table 23

CORRELATIONS FOR FEMALES BETWEEN SKILL STRATEGIES AND RELATIVE SKILL WINNINGS FOR PERSONALITY SUBGROUPS

DEFENSIVENESS

			Low	High	Low + High	
		SMG	.24	−.37	−.09	
		SML	−.01	.19	.09	
	Low	SLS	.27	−.37	−.08	
		SMD	−.28	.43*	.09	
		SMV	.14	−.37	−.13	
TEST ANXIETY						z =
		SMG	−.08	.23	.07	−.79
		SML	−.02	−.01	−.05	.69
	High	SLS	−.09	.23	.07	−.74
		SMD	.05	−.24	−.09	.89
		SMV	.00	.19	.10	−1.14
					z =	
		SMG	.08	−.08	.79	
	Low	SML	−.04	.09	−.64	
	+	SLS	.08	−.06	.69	
	High	SMD	−.09	.05	−.69	
		SMV	.08	−.11	.94	

MONETARY OUTCOMES AND POSTDECISION SATISFACTION

It will be recalled that following the play of each chance or skill bet, subjects were requested to express their satisfaction with the subsequent bet in the series prior to its actual play. It was expected that as a consequence of positive or negative outcomes, some individuals might admit a willingness to shift to the previously unselected member of the bet pair, if given the opportunity to do so. Subjects remained committed, of course, to their decisions in accordance with the instructions for the decision-making tasks. Our concern, then, is with an individual's satisfaction with his decisions in the face of experienced monetary gain and loss.

In playing 22 bets, a subject has 21 opportunities to express dissatisfaction, because the first bet is necessarily excluded from consideration. Expressed dissatisfaction — a desire to change one's decision — is quite low for the samples as a whole. The mean numbers of desired shifts range from approximately 3.1 to 4.9 (Appendix A-1, rows 20–21). Women express a greater desire than men to shift in the chance condition ($t = 2.32$, $p < .05$). No significant sex difference obtains for skill bet dissatisfaction.

The relatively low level of decision dissatisfaction is quite congruent with the aspect of cognitive dissonance theory concerned with postdecision desirability of chosen and unchosen alternatives. An experiment by Brehm (1956) has clearly demonstrated individuals' increased preference for chosen relative to rejected alternatives following a decision. Thus, in our investigation, an expressed preference for the previously rejected member of the bet pair is an infrequent occurrence. Furthermore, there is a moderate degree of consistency in the extent of postdecision satisfaction expressed in chance and skill contexts ($r = .32$, $p < .01$ for males; and $r = .31$, $p < .01$ for females). Individual differences in this tendency toward dissonance reduction thus show a modicum of stability across these two situations.

Is this consistency in mode of handling dissonance moderated by test anxiety and defensiveness? Tables 24 and 25 contain the relevant information. It is evident from Table 24 that the consistency in question is found in the case of males among persons low in defensiveness but not among highly defensive subjects. For females, on the other hand, Table 25 indicates that it is the individuals low in test anxiety who exhibit consistent tolerance or intolerance for cognitive dissonance, those high in test anxiety showing no such consistency. As we have found before, defensiveness again turns out to be the more relevant moderator for males, test anxiety for females. In general, it is the individuals who are low in one or the other type of motivational disturbance who show the greater consistency in degree of satisfaction or dissatisfaction across chance and skill settings.

Table 24

CORRELATIONS FOR MALES BETWEEN CHANCE BET DISSATISFACTION AND
SKILL BET DISSATISFACTION FOR PERSONALITY SUBGROUPS

DEFENSIVENESS

		Low	High	Low + High	
TEST ANXIETY	Low	.47**	.15	.37**	$z = .52$
	High	.53**	−.15	.28*	
	Low + High	.45**	.06	$z = 2.21$	

Table 25

CORRELATIONS FOR FEMALES BETWEEN CHANCE BET DISSATISFACTION AND
SKILL BET DISSATISFACTION FOR PERSONALITY SUBGROUPS

DEFENSIVENESS

		Low	High	Low + High	
TEST ANXIETY	Low	.59**	.58**	.60**	$z = 3.21$
	High	−.20	.23	.04	
	Low + High	.29*	.35*	$z = -.33$	

Monetary Outcomes and Postdecision Satisfaction | 81

Recall that the payoff format of the chance and skill decision settings in fact is essentially identical; probabilities and monetary values are matched item by item in the two procedures. This matching implies that the average total winnings in chance and skill plays ought to be about the same, and indeed they are, both for males and females (Appendix A-1, rows 16 and 18). Individuals who are sensitive to actual environmental outcomes hence ought to feel about the same degree of characteristic satisfaction or dissatisfaction in the two settings, because the outcomes they in fact experience in the two settings are approximately equivalent. We find, then, that it is the persons low in one or the other type of motivational disturbance who exhibit this sensitivity to outcomes.

We turn now to the effect of winnings on postdecision satisfaction under chance and skill conditions.

Chance plays

Contrary to expectations, no relationship obtains in the male and female samples as a whole between absolute or relative winnings, on the one hand, and a desire to change one's decisions on the other. For males, the coefficients for absolute and relative winnings are .06 and .05, respectively. The corresponding r's for the females are $-.15$ and $-.14$, respectively.

Tables 26 and 27 present the relevant correlations for males with moder-

Table 26

Correlations for Males between Absolute Chance Winnings and Chance Bet Dissatisfaction for Personality Subgroups

DEFENSIVENESS

		Low	High	Low + High	
Test Anxiety	Low	.09	−.32	−.04	$z = -1.41$
	High	.20	.19	.23	
	Low + High	.10	−.17	$z = 1.41$	

ator effects taken into account. The two tables are quite similar, but the relationships are somewhat stronger for relative winnings (Table 27). It is only in the case of the defensive males low in test anxiety that a significant relationship emerges between winnings and a desire to change one's decision. The direction of this relation is consistent with expectations, greater winnings being associated with less dissatisfaction — in other words, with less desire to change one's decisions.

Table 27

CORRELATIONS FOR MALES BETWEEN RELATIVE CHANCE WINNINGS AND CHANCE BET DISSATISFACTION FOR PERSONALITY SUBGROUPS

DEFENSIVENESS

	Low	High	Low + High	
TEST ANXIETY — Low	.00	−.37*	.00	$z = -.88$
TEST ANXIETY — High	.11	.24	.17	
TEST ANXIETY — Low + High	.04	−.13	$z = .89$	

Consider the implications of this finding. First, it must be noted that defensiveness bears a low but significant over-all inverse relationship to chance bet dissatisfaction in the male sample as a whole ($r = -.23$, $p < .05$). The relationship is also significant, incidentally, in the case of skill bet dissatisfaction ($r = -.19, p < .05$). Defensive individuals, in other words, are less likely, in general, to admit having made a faulty decision, even in a context where luck is an important ingredient in the decision outcome.[2] Such persons, however, may well monitor the decision-making

---

[2]Deutsch, Krauss, and Rosenau (1962) have reported that defensiveness aroused through the mechanism of self-involving instructions produces greater postdecisional dissonance and consequent increased attractiveness of original decisions than occurs in the case where subjects are not involved in the decisions they make. These results are quite congruent with our finding that defensiveness as a personality characteristic contributes to an unwillingness to deviate from original decisions.

sequence quite carefully, so that when they do express a desire to shift, it comes only after a succession of negative outcomes. A set of this sort may well bring about the relationship observed in the high defensive–low test anxious subgroup.

Note that the defensive males who are also high on test anxiety do not share in the foregoing relationship. If anything, such males move in the opposite direction, showing more dissatisfaction with increasing winnings. For these subjects, as well as those in the low defensiveness subgroups, a desire to change one's decisions does not seem to be inexorably tied to monetary loss. Rather, one also finds a willingness to shift to riskier bets following a reasonable degree of success in decision outcomes. Ordinarily, the risky and conservative shifts balance each other out to yield the negligible relations observed in three out of the four moderator subgroups. The defensive males who are low in test anxiety, on the other hand, apparently find it essential to insist upon the wisdom and rectitude of their decisions (something that positive outcomes will reinforce), and therefore, they can modify their decisions only in the face of an incontrovertible lack of success.

Tables 28 and 29 offer comparable data for females. Once again, the pattern is quite different from that observed in the male sample. Further, defensiveness is unrelated to chance bet shifts in the female sample as a whole ($r = -.02$). Thus, in contrast with the circumstances prevailing in

Table 28

CORRELATIONS FOR FEMALES BETWEEN ABSOLUTE CHANCE WINNINGS AND CHANCE BET DISSATISFACTION FOR PERSONALITY SUBGROUPS

		DEFENSIVENESS			
		Low	High	Low + High	
TEST ANXIETY	Low	−.23	−.14	−.19	
	High	−.36	.13	−.13	$z = -.30$
	Low + High	−.29*	.05	$z = -1.72$	

the male sample, we observe that the defensive female does not resist the expression of dissatisfaction with decisions rendered in the dice bets procedure. It is evident that the female does not have the psychological stake in decision "correctness" that characterizes her defensive male counterpart. In agreement with our previous interpretation of sex differences in the prior winnings–final bet relationship, women, by virtue of their sex role, have less of a basis than males for being defensively involved in a decision task concerning chance bets.

Table 29

CORRELATIONS FOR FEMALES BETWEEN RELATIVE CHANCE WINNINGS AND CHANCE BET DISSATISFACTION FOR PERSONALITY SUBGROUPS

	DEFENSIVENESS			
	Low	High	Low + High	
Test Anxiety Low	−.23	−.14	−.18	
Test Anxiety High	−.38	.14	−.09	$z = -.45$
Low + High	−.27*	.08	$z = -1.76$	

Tables 28 and 29 indicate that it is the low defensive females who shift their decisions in the face of monetary loss. The effect is most pronounced for the low defensive women who are high in test anxiety. This finding suggests that for such persons the objective success-failure aspect of the decision task assumes importance. Not surprisingly, it is the test anxious females who are most sensitized to this feature, expressing a desire to change their decisions in proportion to the monetary losses experienced during the course of the chance plays.

In sum, close monitoring of monetary loss, as reflected in a desire to change one's prior decisions in a chance context, appears to have a different psychological basis for men and women. For females, such monitoring is attributable to failure-avoidance motivation. In the males, image-maintenance concerns seem to account for the phenomenon.

Skill plays

We turn next to the effect of monetary gain or loss derived from the subject's own performance on the expressed wish to change decisions. Consider first the relationships for the samples as a whole. The correlations between absolute skill winnings and desire to change prior decisions in the shuffleboard task are −.08 and −.01 for males and females, respectively. The corresponding r's for relative skill winnings are −.04 for males and −.09 for females. It is evident, then, that there is no relationship between skill winnings and dissatisfaction with skill bet decisions in the male and female samples as a whole.

Table 30

CORRELATIONS FOR MALES BETWEEN ABSOLUTE SKILL WINNINGS AND SKILL BET DISSATISFACTION FOR PERSONALITY SUBGROUPS

		DEFENSIVENESS			
		Low	High	Low + High	
TEST ANXIETY	Low	−.56**	.09	−.22	
	High	−.14	.41	.10	$z = -1.67$
	Low + High	−.38**	.23		$z = -3.29$

Consider now the moderator variable analysis. Tables 30 and 31 present the male results. Note first the significant and near-significant differences between the marginal r's. It is clear that test anxiety and defensiveness play an important role, but the full impact of the effect can be appreciated only when we consider both moderators simultaneously. For the male subjects low on both moderators, larger winnings (both absolute and relative) are associated with fewer desired shifts in decision making. These subjects, in other words, manifest greater contentment as their winnings increase. In the sense that such winnings may be expected to reinforce the subject's confidence in the wisdom of his original decisions, the observed relationship seems to reflect the kind of adaptively appropriate behavior that we have

Table 31

CORRELATIONS FOR MALES BETWEEN RELATIVE SKILL WINNINGS AND SKILL BET DISSATISFACTION FOR PERSONALITY SUBGROUPS

	DEFENSIVENESS		
	Low	High	Low + High
TEST ANXIETY Low	−.53**	−.03	−.25* $z = -2.20$
TEST ANXIETY High	−.06	.45*	.17
Low + High	−.31*	.23	$z = -2.88$

come to expect of this subgroup from the prior winnings–final bet relationship.

Turning to the subgroup high on both moderators, the magnitude and direction of the relationship appears to run counter to what would seem adaptively appropriate. For these subjects, greater winnings (again, both absolute and relative) are associated with *more* dissatisfaction — an increased willingness to alter previous decisions — and smaller winnings are associated with less dissatisfaction. How can we account for this paradoxical finding? In Chapter 3, we offered the interpretation that the highly test anxious and defensive subjects are most clearly characterized by a risk-conservatism syndrome. The risk-taking behavior of these individuals appears to be underinfluenced by situational aspects of the various decision-making tasks and overinfluenced by motivational requirements. The latter tendency obviously affects the postdecisional behavior of these subjects as well. If his risky or conservative outlook is motivationally based, we can expect the test anxious–defensive subject to do everything in his power to justify and maintain his original decisions. Postdecisional failures, then, are very likely to be interpreted in such a manner as to support a decision-making style. Thus, for the test anxious–defensive person of a risk-taking bent, to change decisions in the face of failure is to acknowledge that a risk-taking course was something less than wise. One must therefore pursue risk taking all the more irrevocably. Correspondingly, the more conservative members in the test anxious–defensive subgroup may use any semblance of failure as a basis for continuing all the more rigidly on a conservative path. Failure thus can push the test anxious–defensive individuals all the harder into their characteristic decision-making strategy, eventuating in the positive correlations between skill winnings and dissatisfaction that the tables report.

Although the behavior of the test anxious–defensive conservatives in the face of failure is not particularly unreasonable, that of the test anxious–defensive risk-takers clearly is maladaptive. Actually, there is a significant tendency (see Table 21) for the members of this test anxious–defensive subgroup to experience greater relative failure (in other words, smaller relative winnings) when pursuing a more risky strategy. Further, it is in the case of relative winnings (Table 31) that the positive correlation between failure and satisfaction that we have found for this subgroup reaches the conventional significance level. These considerations suggest that the correlations for the test anxious–defensive subgroup in Tables 30 and 31 are mostly or entirely a function of continued satisfaction with *risky* decisions after failure. And this, indeed, represents a maladaptive posture.

Also of interest is the absence of any relationship between winnings and satisfaction in the remaining two moderator subgroups. The subjects in these two subgroups seem to follow a more erratic course the outlines of which cannot be readily surmised.

A comparison of the present set of results with the analogous findings in the chance domain (Tables 26 and 27) may prove profitable. The dissimilarities are quite striking. The low test anxious–high defensive males, whose dissatisfaction level is inversely related to magnitude of winnings under chance conditions, manifest no relation between these variables in a context of skill. It should come as no surprise, of course, that postdecisional effects are not consistent across the chance and skill domains. In the latter case, the relevant components concern the level of risk inherent in the decision itself and the subject's skill in implementing his decision successfully. An unsuccessful trial can be attributed by the subject to a poor decision or to a faulty performance. Where decisions under chance conditions are at issue, however, the element of luck must be viewed by the subjects as playing the major role. Given the erratic nature of this element, it is perhaps not too surprising that most subjects' satisfactions with their decisions are not influenced in any systematic way by the outcomes of dice throws. That the low test anxious–high defensive subjects do manifest a significant relation here may well be a tribute to the "need for approval" characteristic of such subjects in an interpersonal context. Even though outcomes are beyond their control, these subjects apparently feel that success and failure in the chance task reflect upon their decision-making sagacity. Accordingly, a desire to change opinions is expressed when losses occur.

Why does the above relationship break down for low test anxious–high defensive subjects in a context of skill? Possibly, because there is more than one way of seeking approval and/or maintaining a favorable self-image in a decision situation where outcomes depend upon one's own performance. In other words, it can be viewed as socially acceptable either to express a desire to change a decision in the face of persistent loss, or alternatively, to persist in refusing to acknowledge that one's initial decisions were less than judicious. The former course may typify realism, the latter may suggest courage or perseverance. If some low test anxious–high defensive subjects adopt one course while the remainder adopt the other, a negligible correlation will necessarily ensue. In the chance condition, on the other hand, considerations of courage and perseverance seem less central.

Moderator effects for skill plays are considerably weaker in the female sample, though the correlational pattern, particularly for relative skill winnings, is quite similar to that obtained in the male subjects.

DECISION-MAKING STRATEGIES AND POSTDECISION SATISFACTION

In the present section, we inquire whether particular decision-making strategies differ in the extent to which they yield postdecision satisfaction. Is postdecision satisfaction entirely a function of monetary outcomes, or on the other hand, is it partly dependent upon a person's decision-making strategy regardless of the payoffs it may yield? In order to answer this question, it is necessary, of course, to control statistically the amount of money won by the subject in playing his bets. We shall use partial correlation analysis for this purpose.

Chance condition

Consider first the relationships in the male and female samples as a whole. Listed following are the partial correlations between degree of adherence to chance strategies and chance dissatisfaction, when absolute chance winnings are held constant.

	Males	Females
Chance–max. of gain	−.14	.07
Chance–min. of loss	.31**	−.13
Chance–long shot	−.07	.06
Chance–min. dev. from 1/2	−.05	−.13
Chance–max. of variance	−.17	.07

It is only the "minimization of loss" strategy in the male sample that is predictive of postdecision satisfaction under chance conditions. Those males who prefer to minimize potential losses when making dice-bet decisions express less satisfaction with their decisions regardless of the amount of money won. Thus, we can conclude that postdecision dissatisfaction reflects in part a particular decision-making strategy — minimization of loss. Those who adopt such a strategy express a desire to change their decisions without reference to the over-all successes or failures they may be experiencing.

Examination of moderator effects in the present case is not possible for either sex because of mean differences in chance strategies. Recall our earlier discussion of this problem.

Skill condition

Shown following are the partial correlations between skill strategies and skill shifts, with absolute skill winnings held constant.

	Males	Females
Skill–max. of gain	−.22*	−.12
Skill–min. of loss	.21*	.32**
Skill–long shot	−.19*	.00
Skill–min. dev. from 1/2	.16	−.11
Skill–max. of variance	−.24*	−.17

Under skill conditions, there is an evident tendency in males for stronger conservatism of strategy to be associated with greater postdecision dissatisfaction. This effect cannot be attributed to the degree of success experienced in implementing the decisions made in the shuffleboard procedure, because that factor is controlled. Indeed, as we have seen, more conservative strategies yield significantly higher relative winnings, a result that one might expect to produce greater postdecision satisfaction. Yet the findings are in the opposite direction.

The results for females are somewhat less impressive, though the significant r for "minimization of loss" is consistent with the male findings. Further, the female data for the skill condition strongly resemble the male results under chance conditions.

It is evident, then, that postdecision dissatisfaction is not a simple function of objective decision outcomes for the samples as a whole. Rather, it appears that the preference for conservative or risky strategies per se affects the degree of commitment that an individual feels toward his original decisions.

We turn next to moderator effects. It is possible to investigate these in the present case because the moderator subgroups are not distinguished by mean differences in risk-taking levels. Table 32 presents the relevant results for males. It is evident that the low and high test anxious subjects are characterized by a markedly different pattern of correlations. For the low test anxious males, decision-making strategies per se have little direct impact upon postdecision satisfaction. The satisfaction reported by the

Table 32

Partial Correlations for Males between Skill Strategies and Skill Bet Dissatisfaction (Absolute Skill Winnings Held Constant) for Personality Subgroups

			Defensiveness			
			Low	High	Low + High	
Test Anxiety	Low	SMG	−.13	.05	−.07	
		SML	.21	.03	.10	
		SLS	−.10	.10	−.05	
		SMD	−.05	−.07	.02	
		SMV	−.15	.05	−.09	
						$z =$
	High	SMG	−.38*	−.45*	−.39**	1.76
		SML	.44*	.27	.29*	−1.02
		SLS	−.29	−.41*	−.34*	1.56
		SMD	.06	.43*	.28*	−1.38
		SMV	−.42*	−.43*	−.40**	1.72
					$z =$	
	Low + High	SMG	−.26	−.19	−.38	
		SML	.35**	.15	1.12	
		SLS	−.20	−.14	−.32	
		SMD	.08	.17	−.48	
		SMV	−.33*	−.18	−.84	

high test anxious males, on the other hand, is clearly a function of strategy preference regardless of the monetary outcome level that the strategy produces. Greater risk taking in these subjects is associated with a firm commitment to original decisions. Correspondingly, greater conservatism contributes to greater dissatisfaction — in other words, to a ready willingness to shift from chosen to previously rejected alternatives. Because the level of winnings is statistically controlled, these results imply that, for test anxious males, we can make a reasonably good estimate of how satisfied they will be with their decisions, *before* these decisions are actually carried out. It is evident, then, that a decision-making preference in the subgroup of test anxious males carries with it a high degree of motivational investment. There appears to be no other way that we can adequately account for the insensitivity shown by test anxious males to the outcomes of their decisions than to view decision making in their case as a motivationally based internal disposition.

For the low test anxious male, in contrast, preference for a particular strategy bears little relation to the extent of satisfaction or dissatisfaction that the subject says he experiences with it. This finding implies a concern with intervening events — the outcomes of decisions — or the operation of personal dispositions, other than strategy preferences, that may conceivably influence the level of satisfaction or dissatisfaction reported. Certainly, as far as the low test anxious–low defensive males are concerned, the former interpretation applies, in view of the results reported in Tables 30 and 31. There, it will be recalled, we found that this subgroup expresses greater satisfaction if winnings are high, greater dissatisfaction if winnings are low. These subjects, in other words, are evidently monitoring in a careful way the influence of their performance upon monetary outcomes. On the other hand, the low test anxious–high defensive males do not yield a significant relationship between skill winnings and postdecision satisfaction — a result suggesting that satisfaction-dissatisfaction in their case may be determined by other personal or environmental characteristics about which we have little knowledge. In analogous fashion, it is possible that the high test anxious–low defensive and high test anxious–high defensive subgroups, although yielding a very similar pattern of relationships, may not do so for reasons of identical underlying processes.

Let us now turn to the female data (Table 33). The pattern of relationships bears little similarity to that described for the males. Rather, we find that it is the low defensive females for whom relationships between skill strategies and postdecision satisfaction assume statistical significance. There is a marked trend in that subgroup for greater conservatism of strategy to be associated with higher levels of postdecision dissatisfaction. On the other hand, evidence in favor of the converse — a preference for greater risk taking associated with lower levels of postdecision dissatisfaction — is quite equivocal.

When decisions and performance in the skill domain are at issue, conservative, low defensive females (whether low or high in test anxiety) seem to be characterized by a fundamental ambivalence. The general effect is a type of decision-making lability that is not too closely attuned to the payoff potential of one's own performance. Possibly, these subjects are premature in their expressed desire to shift to previously rejected decision alternatives. Their fundamental ambivalence respecting decisions in a context of skill may produce an overreactivity to isolated successes and failures as opposed to a more accurate appreciation of the effects of performance on over-all outcomes. It is possible, in other words, to err in the direction

Table 33

Partial Correlations for Females between Skill Strategies and Skill Bet Dissatisfaction (Absolute Skill Winnings Held Constant) for Personality Subgroups

			Defensiveness			
			Low	High	Low + High	
Test Anxiety	Low	SMG	−.20	−.15	−.19	
		SML	.52**	.22	.42**	
		SLS	.00	−.11	−.05	
		SMD	−.13	−.02	−.09	
		SMV	−.28	−.20	−.25	
						$z =$
	High	SMG	−.17	.01	−.02	−.85
		SML	.40*	.08	.23	1.05
		SLS	−.05	.08	.09	−.69
		SMD	.00	−.09	−.12	.15
		SMV	−.27	.02	.02	−1.36
					$z =$	
	Low + High	SMG	−.19	−.06	−.65	
		SML	.48**	.14	1.88	
		SLS	−.02	.01	−.15	
		SMD	−.09	−.10	.05	
		SMV	−.27*	−.07	−1.02	

of ignoring environmental feedback or to err in the direction of overreacting to it. Both processes can be expected to enhance relationships between predecisional and postdecisional phenomena.

SUMMARY

This chapter has been concerned with the consequences of decisions — with relationships between decision-making strategies and their outcomes, relationships between outcomes and expressed satisfaction-dissatisfaction, and relationships between decision-making strategies and expressed satisfaction-dissatisfaction. Consider each of these questions in turn.

Regarding decision-making strategies and monetary outcomes under skill conditions, for example, we find that those males who are lowest in motivational disturbance — in other words, the low defensive–low test anxiety subgroup — are most likely to fare successfully when deciding on risky courses of action. In contrast, presence of high test anxiety disrupts skilled performance, annulling the relationship between greater risk taking and greater success found when motivational disturbance is minimal. The results for females are in part consistent with the foregoing, and in part also suggest that the high defensive–high test anxiety subgroup experiences the lowest level of outcome success in a skill setting.

In a chance setting, females are found to select more extreme strategies than males in either the risky or conservative direction, and to experience less success through the pursuit of risky strategies than do males. It looks, therefore, as if males are more sensitive than females to the point beyond which risky strategies in a chance setting will not pay off.

Turning to monetary outcomes and postdecision satisfaction, low defensive–low test anxious males in a skill setting exhibit a degree of postdecision satisfaction that is proportional to their level of winnings. Interestingly enough, this adaptively appropriate behavior characterizes only this "least disturbed" of the four personality subgroups. In striking contrast, the male subgroup high on both test anxiety and defensiveness shows exactly the opposite behavior in a skill setting: the less these individuals win, the more satisfied they are with their bets. Failure seems to confirm them all the more in the rigid continuance of their decision-making strategy. Failure, furthermore, is more likely after risk taking than after conservatism. This finding suggests that the only effect negative environmental outcomes can have for the risk-takers in this subgroup is to push them all the harder into their characteristic high risk taking. Such evidence once again indicates with what single-mindedness the high defensive–high test anxious males are committed to a particular decision-making strategy. Failure makes the risk-takers among them adhere all the more firmly to their risky posture. In contrast, failure leads the subgroup lowest in motivational disturbance to express dissatisfaction with the decision strategy that they have been following — a more appropriate adaptation to environmental outcomes.

Consider, finally, the relationships that obtain between decision-making strategies and postdecision satisfaction. Regardless of winnings, there is a tendency on the whole toward dissatisfaction as a consequence of pursuing conservative strategies, satisfaction as a result of choosing risky strategies. This relationship is strongly subject to moderator effects, however. In particular, the low defensive–low test anxious males in a skill setting do not at all show this direct dependence of satisfaction-dissatisfaction on type of strategy pursued. Instead, as we have seen, decision *outcomes*, rather than decision strategies as such, determine the expressions of satisfaction or dissatisfaction of this subgroup. For test anxious males, in contrast, the individual's preferred decision strategy strongly influences his postdecision feelings and commitments, quite apart from outcomes. Once again, motivational disturbance is found to eventuate in a type of decisional commitment that is not appropriately responsive to feedback from the environment.

5

Decision-Making and Intellective Processes

As was stated in the introductory chapter, there have been few systematic efforts to spell out relationships between decision making and intellective abilities. The few empirical studies relevant to the issue have left a set of equivocal findings in their wake. Recall that intellective processes in the present exposition have been defined to include the conventional aptitude measures — verbal and mathematical — as well as the type of analytic functioning tapped by the embedded figures test. We begin with verbal aptitude.

VERBAL APTITUDE

Consider first the relationships observed in the male and female samples as a whole. It turns out that verbal aptitude is only minimally associated with the taking of risks in the various decision-making procedures employed. For males, the sole significant correlations are a tendency for the more verbally able to be less deterred by failure in the hypothetical choice dilemmas task ($r = -.21$, $p < .05$) and to avoid a "minimization of deviation from 1/2" strategy in the skill bets procedure ($r = -.20$, $p < .05$). In short, there is a very weak association in males between verbal ability and greater risk taking. For the female subjects, none of the correlations achieves significance.

There is also the possibility that the more verbally competent subjects may possess greater insight with regard to the payoff potential of decision alternatives. If this expectation were to be borne out, we would find a positive association between verbal aptitude and chance and/or skill winnings. The data clearly violate this expectation, however, for the only significant correlation obtained is an inverse relationship in females between verbal aptitude and absolute chance winnings ($r = -.20$, $p < .05$).

In sum, we must conclude that, for samples considered as a whole, verbal ability has little influence on risk levels in decision making and on postdecisional outcomes. Let us then proceed to an examination of moderator effects in the present domains.

No moderator influences hold, evidently, in the case of decisions rendered under hypothetical conditions — the choice dilemmas task. A very different set of results emerges, however, when verbal aptitude is related to the chance and skill strategy indexes. Table 34 presents the relevant findings for chance strategies in males. The marginals of the table indicate the moderating influence of test anxiety and defensiveness. An examination

Table 34

Correlations for Males between Chance Strategies and Verbal Aptitude for Personality Subgroups

DEFENSIVENESS

			Low	High	Low + High	
Test Anxiety	Low	CMG	.45*	.28	.33**	
		CML	−.31*	−.23	−.24*	
		CLS	.41*	.23	.29*	
		CMD	−.50**	−.05	−.24*	
		CMV	.46**	.33	.36**	
						$z =$
	High	CMG	−.39*	.33	.04	1.56
		CML	.24	−.11	.07	−1.62
		CLS	−.38*	.33	.05	1.28
		CMD	.36	−.26	−.01	−1.21
		CMV	−.37	.30	.03	1.78
						$z =$
	Low + High	CMG	.03	.29*		−1.40
		CML	.01	−.13		.73
		CLS	.01	.28*		−1.44
		CMD	−.06	−.14		.42
		CMV	.02	.29*		−1.45

of the within-cell correlations, however, again points to the importance of considering the interactive effect of the moderators. It can be seen that the high test anxious–low defensive males manifest a relationship that is quite the reverse of the other three subgroups. In the latter, higher verbal aptitude is associated with higher risk-taking levels, a relationship that achieves its greatest strength for those males who are low in both test anxiety and defensiveness. In sharp contrast, the high test anxious–low defensive males exhibit the very opposite pattern — greater verbal aptitude being associated with a preference for more conservative strategies.

Can these differences in correlational patterns be attributed to differential levels of ability obtaining in the four moderator subgroups? The statistically significant F value in row 22 of Appendix A–6 indicates that such differential levels do exist, the direction of the differences being quite consistent with the often-reported inverse relationship between test anxiety and intelligence measures. Note, however, that the mean verbal aptitude for males high in both test anxiety and defensiveness is the lowest of the four moderator subgroups, and yet the correlations shown in Table 34 for that subgroup are in the same direction as those emerging in the low test anxious–low defensive males, the subgroup manifesting the highest levels of verbal aptitude. Hence, the inverse relationship observed in highly test anxious–low defensive males between verbal intelligence and risk taking under chance conditions cannot be attributed to a ceiling on intelligence level in that subgroup.

Table 35

CORRELATIONS FOR MALES BETWEEN SKILL STRATEGIES AND VERBAL APTITUDE FOR PERSONALITY SUBGROUPS

			DEFENSIVENESS			
			Low	High	Low + High	
TEST ANXIETY	Low	SMG	.30	.30	.27*	
		SML	−.16	−.25	−.20	
		SLS	.30	.25	.25*	
		SMD	−.49**	−.07	−.23	
		SMV	.30	.31	.28*	
						$z =$
	High	SMG	−.37	.28	.00	1.42
		SML	.14	.21	.18	−1.97
		SLS	−.43*	.36	.02	1.21
		SMD	.39*	−.51*	−.15	−.43
		SMV	−.31	.18	−.05	1.74
					$z =$	
	Low + High	SMG	−.06	.30*	−1.92	
		SML	.01	−.09	.52	
		SLS	−.08	.31*	−2.08	
		SMD	−.11	−.27*	.87	
		SMV	−.04	.26*	−1.59	

Before attempting a theoretical explanation of the foregoing relationships, let us see whether they are maintained when decisions are made in a context of skill. As Table 35 demonstrates, the findings are reasonably consistent with those of Table 34. The effects are most pronounced in the case of the "minimization of deviation from 1/2" strategy. Males who are either low or high on both moderators manifest an inverse relationship between a preference for that strategy and verbal aptitude; higher verbal aptitude is associated with less conservatism. Highly test anxious–low defensive males, on the other hand, exhibit a direct relationship — in other words, the preference for a conservative "minimization of deviation from 1/2" strategy increases with higher levels of verbal aptitude. In agreement with this finding, the risky "long shot" strategy is inversely related to verbal aptitude in the test anxious–low defensive subgroup.

In sum, we have found that, irrespective of whether decisions are rendered under chance or skill conditions, test anxiety and defensiveness moderate relations for male subjects between the verbal aptitude and decision-making domains. Although intelligence as such has little predictive value for risk taking in a bet preference context, information regarding an individual's level of test anxiety and defensiveness makes for a drastic improvement in predictability. Subjects comparable in verbal intelligence but varying in test anxiety and defensiveness levels respond to a decision-making situation in distinctively different ways. If test anxiety is high and defensiveness is low, the more verbally able male adopts a more conservative course, whereas the less verbally competent pursues a more risky path. This particular result may be of considerable relevance to the Atkinson (1957) risk-taking theory of motivation. The theory maintains that test anxious subjects are motivated by failure avoidance and will therefore avoid intermediate risk levels in preference for the extremely risky or conservative alternatives.[1] There is no indication in the Atkinson theory of the basis for modal preferences for risk or conservatism within the test anxious subgroup, though that author does suggest the possibility of wild fluctuations from risk to conservatism on a within-person basis. The high reliability levels obtained for the chance and skill strategy procedures indicate that such fluctuations are quite rare in the present context. If, on the other hand, test anxious males can be subdivided into consistent risk-takers or conservatives, then a verbal intelligence measure provides a means of ascertaining which orientation will in all likelihood be adopted.

We still have not explained, of course, why the more verbally able

---

[1] Although "minimization of deviation from 1/2" may qualify as an intermediate risk strategy, it should be noted that, relative to the other probabilities employed — 1/8 (or 1/9), 1/4, and 3/4 — the particular strategy in question is on the conservative side of the probability distribution.

within the test anxious–low defensive subgroup select a more conservative strategy, whereas their less verbally intelligent counterparts are inclined toward risk taking. It is most unlikely that a sound explanation will be found so long as we insist on aptitude being a "determinant" of decision making. A more reasonable assumption is that the intelligence test score itself may be affected by risk-taking dispositions. The Scholastic Aptitude Test, by incorporating a penalty for guessing in the test's instructions to examinees, is subject to individual differences in risk-taking orientations.[2] This penalty-for-guessing characteristic, furthermore, is one that this test shares with many other intelligence tests. The reader will recall our discussion of the gambling response set in Chapter 1. In this view of the matter, the test anxious person who adopts a conservative stance may attempt fewer items of which he is not sure, hence receiving a smaller penalty for guessing and a consequent higher score. The test anxious individual predisposed toward risk taking, on the other hand, may well indulge a guessing penchant, thereby reducing his aptitude score. A further assumption that must be made — one for which a great deal of evidence exists — concerns the debilitating effect of test anxiety on problem-solving performance, especially where the latter takes place under ego-involving conditions (for example, Sarason, Mandler, & Craighill, 1952). It is hard to conceive of a more ego-involving setting, of course, than the conditions surrounding the administration of the SAT. Almost every examinee believes that admission to the college of his choice will depend to some extent upon his performance. Hence, the conditions are such that may make the highly test anxious subjects strongly prone to disruption in problem solving. Results reported by Sarason and Palola (1960) indicate that the disruption is greatest on difficult test items. Of course, these are the items that subjects are least confident of answering correctly and hence the items requiring a decision to guess or not to guess. Because the test anxious individual in an ego-involving test setting is at a severe motivational disadvantage, a conservative orientation with respect to guessing seems to be more optimal than a risk-taking orientation. It is the item about which the examinee is un-

---

[2]Exact instructions to examinees read as follows: "Many students wonder whether or not to guess the answers to questions about which they are not certain. In this test a percentage of the wrong answers will be subtracted from the number of right answers as a correction for haphazard guessing. It is improbable, therefore, that mere guessing will improve your score significantly; it may even lower your score, and it does take time. If, however, you are not sure of the correct answer but have some knowledge of the question and are able to eliminate one or more of the answer choices as wrong, your chance of getting the right answer is improved, and it will be to your advantage to answer such a question."

certain that is, after all, subject to motivational disruption, with a probable incorrect answer as a consequence.[3]

It should be emphasized that the foregoing interpretations apply only to test anxious males who are, at the same time, low in defensiveness. When test anxiety is present along with high defensiveness, the relationships in question actually undergo a reversal. For these latter males, greater risk taking is associated with higher verbal aptitude. This finding points up the role of defensiveness in counteracting the overt motivational disruption experienced by the test anxious person in an academic stress situation. This statement does not imply that defensiveness is an unalloyed asset in the test anxious individual, however, for these subjects yield the lowest mean SAT score (Appendix A-6, row 22). One can only wonder whether these subjects, apropos of the results reported in the previous chapter, do poorly in estimating probabilities of success on difficult items, thereby exceeding a threshold beyond which guessing (risk taking) on the test ceases to yield maximum payoff in the form of a high test score. Note that the low test anxious–low defensive subjects, although showing a similar correlational pattern, yield a mean SAT score that is approximately 45 points higher than the SAT mean for highly test anxious and defensive males (Appendix A-6, row 22). In view of the tendency in the latter subgroup toward a generalized risk-conservatism orientation, the possibility exists that these subjects' decisions about test items reflect risk-taking orientations as much as discrimination of specific item characteristics. Such a set will, of course, depress test scores, although it still favors the risk-taker in relative terms. We here assume that subjects have at least partial knowledge of most test items — absurd alternatives can be eliminated — with the consequence that guessing (risk taking) generally proves profitable. The large SAT score difference between the subgroups low and high on both moderators may well reflect a discriminating application of the foregoing rule in the former subgroup that takes account of item characteristics and subjective certainty levels, and an indiscriminate application in the latter subgroup in harmony with the generalized risky or conservative orientation that we have found the members of that group to exhibit.

The line of reasoning pursued here obviously does not consider intelligence as the causal agent and decision making as the effect. Rather, it appears more likely that general risk-taking tendencies influence behavior

---

[3]Ruebush (1960) has reported that sixth-grade boys who are high in test anxiety solve more embedded figures items when pursuing a "cautious" rather than a "noncautious" strategy. These results are congruent with those of the authors. However, Ruebush obtains a comparable effect for low test anxious subjects as well, a finding quite inconsistent with the results of the present study.

in both test-taking and decision-making contexts. Where a penalty for guessing is incorporated in aptitude test instructions, the element of risk that is introduced into the test can be expected to affect performance. The particular way in which risk-taking considerations impinge upon test performance further depends upon the subject's level of test anxiety and defensiveness.

We turn now to the moderator results for females. Although the direction of the correlations in the moderator subgroups between verbal aptitude, on the one hand, and chance and skill strategies, on the other, is quite similar in both sexes, the magnitudes of these r's are considerably smaller in the case of the females. This finding suggests that either the instructions to the SAT do not engage the risk-taking dispositions of women to the extent that is characteristic of men, or the verbal aptitude domain is more susceptible to such effects in males than females.

Are there particular conditions under which females' intellectual performances are susceptible to risk-taking influences? Recall that a brief vocabulary test is among the experimental procedures employed in the female sample. The instructions to this brief test specify that guessing will *always* improve the score. In contrast, the instructions to the SAT clearly state that guessing will prove profitable only if the examinee can positively eliminate incorrect alternatives. It is evident, of course, that a comparison focused specifically on the guessing issue is not possible in the present circumstances, given the difference in conditions of stress under which the SAT and the laboratory-administered test were taken. Further, a considerable period of time (varying with the subject's school class) separated the administration of the two tests. Nevertheless, it can be asserted with confidence that the context surrounding the respective tests varied along a dimension of permissiveness. Permissiveness was greater in the laboratory test, where guessing was encouraged and the consequences of error were less severe; permissiveness was reduced in the SAT, where guessing was discouraged and error possessed consequences of greater severity. It may prove instructive to compare the risk-taking implications of performance under these more and less permissive conditions. An over-all correlation coefficient of .37 ($p < .01$) between the SAT-Verbal and the brief vocabulary test is sufficiently high to suggest that similar aptitudes are tapped by the two tests, yet sufficiently low to point to the operation of unique factors in the respective test performances.

Table 36 lists the correlations for the moderator subgroups of females between the brief vocabulary test and the chance strategies. It can be seen that the reduction in stress and/or encouragement to guess bring out moderator effects that are not observed with the SAT as the measure of verbal aptitude. For the low test anxious females (especially the subgroup low in both test anxiety and defensiveness), a preference for more risky strategies

Table 36

CORRELATIONS FOR FEMALES BETWEEN CHANCE STRATEGIES AND VERBAL APTITUDE (BRIEF VOCABULARY TEST) FOR PERSONALITY SUBGROUPS

DEFENSIVENESS

			Low	High	Low + High	
TEST ANXIETY	Low	CMG	.39*	.17	.22	
		CML	−.09	−.01	.00	
		CLS	.41*	.35	.31*	
		CMD	−.36	−.47*	−.38**	
		CMV	.42*	.09	.19	
						$z =$
	High	CMG	−.05	−.08	−.07	1.45
		CML	.22	−.04	.14	−.69
		CLS	−.03	−.17	−.07	1.92
		CMD	−.14	.12	−.05	−1.72
		CMV	−.15	−.09	−.15	1.69
					$z =$	
	Low + High	CMG	.12	.01	.55	
		CML	.13	.01	.60	
		CLS	.17	.04	.65	
		CMD	−.25	−.15	−.52	
		CMV	.06	−.03	.44	

in the dice bets procedure is associated with higher verbal aptitude. Note that the relationships of opposite sign, so prominent in the case of high test anxious–low defensive males, do not emerge in the female sample. Conditions of lowered stress and encouragement to guess with impunity (conditions contrasting sharply with those of the SAT) can, of course, be expected to alter the form of moderator effects. Despite these changed conditions, however, we find that test anxiety continues to exert a moderating influence. Even under permissive conditions, a bent toward risk taking does not contribute to better performance in test anxious females, though such risk taking no longer is associated with poorer performance. The same risk-taking orientation in low test anxious females, on the other hand, is associated with higher verbal aptitude scores.

This latter finding is particularly intriguing, for it suggests that the kinds of risks implied by instruction and administration conditions for aptitude tests may have a differential impact upon performance as a function of the match between those conditions and one's natural disposition toward risk taking. For the basically conservative female who is low in test anxiety, a permissive context appears to bring about a performance decrement. Low test anxious females who prefer risky strategies in the dice bet procedure, on the other hand, seem to be favored by a permissive context.

Further evidence that instruction and administration conditions have consequences for test performance is available in the form of mean differences between low and high test anxious females on the two tests under consideration. For the SAT–Verbal, Appendix A–3 (row 22) indicates a near-significant score difference ($t = 1.91$, $p < .06$) favoring the low test anxious subjects. In the case of the brief vocabulary test, on the other hand, the difference in test performance between low and high test anxious females is negligible ($t = .43$). Hence, less stressful testing conditions and/or the elimination of penalty-for-guessing instructions appears to reduce substantially the decremental effects of test anxiety on intellective test performance.

Note, finally, that the relation between the brief verbal aptitude test and skill strategies in females does not show a pattern of moderator differences. This finding contrasts with the male results, where we observe fairly consistent effects when relating *both* chance and skill strategies to verbal aptitude.

Relations between information-seeking measures and verbal aptitude do not yield any moderator effects, except for a link between the brief vocabulary test and the clues task in female subjects. Table 37 presents the relevant findings. Because the clues task has many of the features of a verbal aptitude test, we can anticipate that the subjects with higher vocabulary scores will demand fewer clues before attempting an identification of the object. This is indeed what happens in the females who are low in test anxiety. Note, however, that the relationship disappears under conditions of high test anxiety. Hence, we have further evidence here of the manner in which test anxiety seems to interfere with the effective utilization of one's aptitude in a context where problem solving is suffused with monetary gain-loss considerations. Why a similar effect is not found in male subjects is not known. The negligible correlations between verbal aptitude and the clues procedure for all subgroups suggest that males, in general, do not approach the clues task as an exercise in verbal skill. For males, the costs and payoffs characteristic of our information-seeking procedures evidently engage psychological processes that have little to do with verbal aptitude as such or with that aspect of test-taking performance that is labelled the "gambling response set."

MATHEMATICAL APTITUDE

To the extent that tests of verbal and mathematical aptitude provide

Table 37

CORRELATIONS FOR FEMALES BETWEEN CLUES AND VERBAL APTITUDE
(BRIEF VOCABULARY TEST) FOR PERSONALITY SUBGROUPS

		DEFENSIVENESS		
		Low	High	Low + High
TEST ANXIETY	Low	−.43*	−.41	−.40**
	High	.21	−.14	.07
	Low + High	−.10	−.26	.82

z = −2.43

z = .82

instructions that allow the gambling response set to operate, the tests should yield a similar pattern of correlates with explicit risk-taking variables. There are, however, certain evident differences between the two forms of aptitude that may well produce discrepancies between the aptitudes in the general magnitude and direction of relationships with other variables. With regard to the gambling response set itself, we can conceive of its having greater relevance in the case of verbal than of mathematical aptitude measures. In the latter case, it seems more difficult to eliminate incorrect alternatives without going through the steps of actually solving the problem. This greater difficulty is certainly the case if none of the alternatives provided are patently absurd. In contrast, verbal aptitude items by their very nature lend themselves more readily to quick judgments about incorrect alternatives — on the basis of an "intuitive feel," if nothing else — and hence allow more play for the gambling response set to function.

Further, we must allow for the possibility that verbal and mathematical aptitude as such have different implications for personality and cognitive organization. In this connection, it may be noted that the correlation between the verbal and mathematical sections of the SAT in the present sample of male subjects is .26. Although this coefficient is significant at the .01 level, its relatively low magnitude quite clearly indicates that verbal and mathematical aptitude scores can hardly be considered different measures of the same underlying intellective ability. The corresponding correlation in the female sample is .05, which suggests that verbal and mathematical aptitude manifest even greater independence in females than in males.

We turn now to the relationship between the mathematical aptitude and decision-making domains. For the male sample as a whole, we find but a single statistically significant correlation. Males who prefer a strategy of "minimization of deviation from 1/2" on chance bets tend to have lower scores on the mathematical section of the SAT ($r = -.22$, $p < .05$). A more impressive array of over-all relationships is found in the female sample. Listed following are the correlations between mathematical aptitude, on the one hand, and chance and skill strategies on the other.

	Chance	Skill
Max. of gain	−.25*	−.09
Min. of loss	.09	.38**
Long shot	−.24*	.01
Min. dev. from 1/2	.06	−.03
Max. of variance	−.21*	−.18

In addition, the clues task is significantly related to mathematical aptitude in females ($r = .23$, $p < .05$). There is an evident tendency, then, for the more mathematically able women to be more conservative in decision-making contexts. We may seriously doubt that the penalty-for-guessing instruction distinguishing the SAT is the only element implicated in the foregoing results. Recall that a short mathematics test was included in the experimental procedures for the female sample. This test provided no instructions whatever concerning guessing. Rather, subjects were told that "you are to solve each problem and circle the answer you think is correct." Despite the difference between these instructions and those provided for the SAT, the two tests yield a correlation of .67 ($p < .001$). This correlation is a very substantial r indeed, considering that one to four years intervened between test administrations that also differed in stress-inducing properties.

Of further interest in the present context is the relationship between mathematical aptitude and embedded figures test performance in females ($r = .35$, $p < .01$ for the SAT; and $r = .33$, $p < .01$ for the brief mathematical aptitude test). This relationship suggests that mathematical aptitude in women may be related to the analytic functioning–field independence variable (to be discussed in the next section of the chapter). For males, mathematical aptitude and performance on the embedded figures test are quite independent ($r = .12$).

Consider next the outcomes of the moderator variable analysis. In Table 38, correlations for male subjects between chance strategies and mathematical aptitude are reported. The contrast with Table 34 — chance strategies versus verbal aptitude — is quite striking. It is in the high test anxious and defensive subgroup that the strongest relationships now

Table 38

CORRELATIONS FOR MALES BETWEEN CHANCE STRATEGIES AND MATHEMATICAL APTITUDE FOR PERSONALITY SUBGROUPS

DEFENSIVENESS

			Low	High	Low + High	
	Low	CMG	.19	.22	.14	
		CML	.05	.07	.12	
		CLS	.23	.24	.18	
		CMD	−.23	−.25	−.22	
		CMV	.11	.12	.05	
TEST ANXIETY						z =
	High	CMG	.03	.34	.20	−.32
		CML	−.03	.15	.07	.26
		CLS	.01	.39	.22	−.22
		CMD	.02	−.46*	−.24	.11
		CMV	.02	.26	.15	−.52
					z =	
	Low + High	CMG	.05	.27*	−1.18	
		CML	.06	.12	−.32	
		CLS	.06	.31*	−1.36	
		CMD	−.07	−.35**	1.54	
		CMV	−.01	.18	−.99	

emerge. For these males, a more conservative strategy on dice bets (particularly, minimization of deviation from 1/2) is associated with lower mathematical aptitude scores. Surprisingly, the relationship is not maintained when skill strategies are substituted for chance strategies. The surprise stems from finding that risk taking in a context in which there is no control over outcomes bears a stronger relationship to mathematical aptitude than does risk taking in a context of skill. These results suggest that the performance of the highly test anxious and defensive males on the mathematical aptitude test is indicative of a gambling response set. Although we have suggested that such a set is much less likely to manifest itself in the mathematical area, the salience of the risk-conservatism dimension may be so very high for the test anxious–defensive subgroup that considerations of risk are imposed even upon mathematical test performance. Thus, we may speak of such performance as having a considerably higher threshold than verbal aptitude for the gambling response set. Highly test anxious and defensive individuals can then be expected to exceed both thresholds.

In the sense that greater risk taking pays off — in other words, leads to a higher mathematical aptitude score — one may consider a gambling response set to be adaptive in the present case. Note, however, that although the mathematical aptitude score means across the four moderator subgroups do not yield a significant F value (Appendix A–6, row 23), the highly test anxious and defensive males manifest the lowest mean score (approximately 48 points lower than the mean for males low in test anxiety and defensiveness). Thus, although risk taking contributes to a higher mathematical aptitude score for a test anxious–defensive male *relative to his own subgroup*, he tends to do more poorly on an absolute basis — in other words, in comparison with the entire sample. Contrast this finding with the results reported in Table 34 for the low test anxious–low defensive males. There, it will be recalled, the gambling response set contributes to a higher verbal aptitude score on both a relative and an absolute basis. These findings tend to reinforce the speculation offered earlier that a mathematical aptitude test does not so readily lend itself to the operation of a gambling response set as does a test of verbal aptitude. The present results also contribute one more item of evidence regarding the tendency of highly test anxious and defensive subjects to bring a generalized, often inappropriate, risky or conservative orientation to a wide variety of decision-making situations.

We turn next to the results for the female subjects. In Tables 39–A and 39–B, correlations between chance strategies and two tests of mathematical aptitude are presented for moderator subgroups. Note the marked contrast between the results presented in these tables and those previously reported in Table 36. In the latter, higher verbal aptitude is associated with a choice of risky chance strategies in low test anxious females. A permissive test context, in other words, seems to profit the risk-taker, but only under conditions of low test anxiety. Tables 39–A and 39–B, in contrast, indicate that the female risk-taker does more poorly on a test of mathematical aptitude, but only under conditions of low defensiveness, and particularly, under conditions of low defensiveness and high test anxiety.

Note that both the magnitudes of r's and the discrepancies in r's between low and high test anxious females (low in defensiveness) are greater in Table 39–A than in Table 39–B. Test anxiety, in other words, makes more of a difference where the test context is less permissive (in other words, where stress is greater and there is a penalty for guessing). Under such conditions, the highly test anxious–low defensive female inclined toward risk taking is at a distinct disadvantage. Further evidence for the differential impact of test anxiety under conditions that vary in permissiveness is available in the form of a significant mean difference ($t = 1.98$, $p < .05$) on the SAT-Mathematical between high and low test anxious

Table 39-A

CORRELATIONS FOR FEMALES BETWEEN CHANCE STRATEGIES AND MATHEMATICAL APTITUDE (SAT) FOR PERSONALITY SUBGROUPS

DEFENSIVENESS

TEST ANXIETY			Low	High	Low + High	
	Low	CMG	−.34	.10	−.16	
		CML	.19	−.23	.00	
		CLS	−.33	.10	−.18	
		CMD	−.07	.00	−.05	
		CMV	−.35	.23	−.10	
						$z =$
	High	CMG	−.53**	−.22	−.33*	.90
		CML	.32	.13	.15	−.74
		CLS	−.53**	−.15	−.30*	.63
		CMD	.34	.03	.18	−1.14
		CMV	−.55**	−.19	−.30*	1.03
					$z =$	
	Low + High	CMG	−.42**	−.05	−1.96	
		CML	.24	−.05	1.45	
		CLS	−.40**	−.06	−1.79	
		CMD	.11	−.01	.59	
		CMV	−.42**	.03	−2.35	

females, in favor of the latter (Appendix A–3, row 23). The corresponding mean difference on the brief mathematical test administered as part of the experimental battery is nonsignificant ($t = 1.43$). Hence, for both verbal and mathematical aptitude in females, test anxiety is associated with performance decrements only in the case of the SAT — an examination that is taken under highly stressful circumstances and that contains a penalty for guessing. No such decrements are found for the verbal and mathematical tests that were administered under more permissive conditions.

Although the correlations for low test anxious–low defensive females in Tables 39–A and 39–B do not achieve statistical significance, the direction of relationships is quite the opposite of those observed in the case of verbal aptitude. Risk taking in a chance context, it will be recalled (Table 36), is associated with higher verbal aptitude, especially under more permissive conditions. Now we observe that the same subjects in a mathematical aptitude test do more poorly when disposed toward greater risk taking in the chance bets situation.

Earlier in the chapter, it was suggested that a mathematical aptitude

Table 39-B

CORRELATIONS FOR FEMALES BETWEEN CHANCE STRATEGIES AND MATHEMATICAL APTITUDE (BRIEF TEST) FOR PERSONALITY SUBGROUPS

DEFENSIVENESS

			Low	High	Low + High	
		CMG	−.28	.10	−.07	
		CML	.00	.15	.04	
	Low	CLS	−.36	.16	−.12	
		CMD	.00	−.22	−.11	
		CMV	−.25	.09	−.04	
Test Anxiety						$z =$
		CMG	−.37	.17	.00	−.34
		CML	.17	−.22	−.15	.94
	High	CLS	−.37	.14	−.03	−.45
		CMD	.32	−.13	.05	−.79
		CMV	−.33	.23	.07	−.54
					$z =$	
		CMG	−.30*	.18	−2.41	
	Low	CML	.04	−.12	.79	
	+	CLS	−.35**	.16	−2.59	
	High	CMD	.16	−.18	1.68	
		CMV	−.25	.22	−2.36	

test with multiple-choice alternatives does not as readily lend itself to the elimination of incorrect alternatives through "educated guessing" as does a verbal aptitude test. If risk-taking dispositions are associated with a gambling response set on aptitude tests, such a set seems to have greater payoff value in the verbal than in the mathematical domain. That the inverse correlations between mathematical performance and risk taking in chance strategies are somewhat higher in the case of the test anxious–low defensive females may well reflect the lessened capacity of such subjects to evaluate item alternatives in the face of anxiety symptoms evoked by the testing situation.

Consider, finally, the correlations between mathematical aptitude and skill strategies. Tables 40–A and 40–B offer the relevant findings. These are quite consistent with those reported in Tables 39–A and 39–B. Where the SAT score is used (Table 40–A), the effects are attenuated, relative to what is observed for chance strategies. There is, however, a trend toward a greater conservatism ("minimization of loss") associated with higher levels of mathematical aptitude in low defensive females. In Table 40–B,

Table 40-A

CORRELATIONS FOR FEMALES BETWEEN SKILL STRATEGIES AND MATHEMATICAL APTITUDE (SAT) FOR PERSONALITY SUBGROUPS

DEFENSIVENESS

			Low	High	Low + High	
TEST ANXIETY	Low	SMG	−.25	.22	−.05	
		SML	.47*	.10	.33*	
		SLS	−.15	.23	.01	
		SMD	−.08	−.16	−.11	
		SMV	−.32	.13	−.13	
						z =
	High	SMG	−.24	−.06	−.14	.45
		SML	.56**	.36	.40**	−.40
		SLS	−.10	.09	.00	.05
		SMD	.27	−.10	.05	−.79
		SMV	−.33	−.15	−.22	.46
					z =	
	Low + High	SMG	−.24	.06	−1.50	
		SML	.50**	.26	1.39	
		SLS	−.13	.13	−1.29	
		SMD	.05	−.11	.79	
		SMV	−.32*	−.03	−1.49	

we note that risk-taking dispositions are associated with poorer mathematics performance, in particular for females high in test anxiety and low in defensiveness. Conversely, a preference for conservative skill strategies in those subjects is related to better performance on the brief mathematical aptitude test. These findings parallel the results that have been presented for chance strategies.

It has been pointed out that mathematical performance is less susceptible to a gambling response set than is verbal performance. As long as penalty-for-guessing instructions are employed, however, the gambling response set may be expected to have some effect upon performance. The use of two separate mathematical tests, one with and one without penalty-for-guessing instructions, permits some assessment of the relative contribution of gambling response set to the relationships observed. Comparing Tables 39-A and 39-B, we noted that the test making use of penalty-for-guessing instructions (SAT) does yield a somewhat stronger set of relationships than is found for the mathematical test without the penalty-for-guessing provision. Nevertheless, the results in the latter case are substantial (for low defensive females), and hence we are forced to conclude

Table 40-B

Correlations for Females between Skill Strategies and Mathematical Aptitude (Brief Test) for Personality Subgroups

DEFENSIVENESS

			Low	High	Low + High	
TEST ANXIETY	Low	SMG	−.19	.15	.00	
		SML	.27	.08	.18	
		SLS	−.14	.18	.03	
		SMD	−.02	−.31	−.16	
		SMV	−.21	.08	−.05	
						z =
	High	SMG	−.34	.10	−.06	.30
		SML	.39	.11	.15	.15
		SLS	−.24	.17	.02	.05
		SMD	.45*	−.10	.09	−1.24
		SMV	−.40*	.08	−.08	.15
					z =	
	Low + High	SMG	−.25*	.12	−1.86	
		SML	.29*	.11	.93	
		SLS	−.18	.17	−1.74	
		SMD	.19	−.16	1.74	
		SMV	−.27*	.07	−1.71	

that the association between poorer mathematical aptitude and a preference for risky chance strategies is more than a matter of common gambling tendencies, although these play a role. Recall again that mathematical aptitude is positively related to performance on the embedded figures test — an index of analytic functioning. We may suspect, then, that mathematical aptitude in women may be part of a cognitive-personality syndrome, which as such has particular implications for decision-making behavior. More will be said on this topic in the subsequent section of the present chapter.

Turning next to skill strategies, we encounter more difficulty in accounting for the differences observed between Tables 40–A and 40–B. It should be noted that a resort to guessing on a mathematical aptitude test does partake of a real *gambling* flavor (in other words, the taking of a chance — a loss of control over outcomes), and for that reason, relations between mathematical aptitude and skill strategies are less likely to reflect gambling response set considerations than corresponding relations with chance strategies. Accordingly, no attempt will be made to account for the observed differences between Tables 40–A and 40–B. We strongly suspect that these differences involve considerations of cognitive control and personality, rather than the issue of the gambling response set elicited by test instructions, though the latter aspect may well be making some contribution to the differences in question. On the whole, however, the authors suspect that mathematical ability in females is part of a comprehensive cognitive structure in which the analytic functioning–field independence construct plays a major role. It is to this particular construct that we now turn.

ANALYTIC VERSUS GLOBAL FUNCTIONING

In attempting to account for relations between the traditional aptitude measures and risk-taking variables, we leaned quite heavily on the role of the gambling response set that is an intrinsic part of any aptitude measure with instructions informing the subject that indiscriminate guessing will be penalized. Aptitude tests using such instructions have, for all practical purposes, incorporated an explicit risk-taking component, and hence it follows that actual test performance will to some degree reflect individual risk-taking proclivities.

In the present section of the chapter, it seems relevant to consider the influence of another intellective ability variable — analytic versus global functioning. No explicit reference to guessing was made in the instructions accompanying the embedded figures measure of analytic functioning. Hence, any relations that emerge between this variable and risk-taking indexes cannot readily be attributed to the set with which the subject approaches the embedded figures task. Rather, we must conclude that analytic or global functioning as such bears upon the taking of risks in the decision-making procedures under study. If relationships are found, we will be in a position to link risk-taking behavior to the field-independence and field-dependence syndromes described by Witkin and his colleagues (Witkin *et al.*, 1954; Witkin *et al.*, 1962).

A first consideration is the extent to which analytic functioning is independent of verbal and mathematical aptitude. In the male sample, EFT performance correlates $-.17$ and $.12$ with SAT–Verbal and SAT–Mathematical performance, respectively. Neither correlation is statistically significant. For females, the corresponding r's with SAT performance are $-.14$ and $.35$ ($p < .01$). As noted in the previous section, this last coefficient points to an association between analytic functioning and mathematical aptitude in females.

We turn now to an examination of relations between embedded figures performance and risk-taking indexes. For the male sample as a whole, there is a barely significant correlation between the EFT and the choice dilemmas measure ($r = .19$, $p < .05$), analytic functioning being associated with greater conservatism in a hypothetical decision-making context. All other correlations of the EFT with decision-making measures are of negligible magnitude.

The female subjects yield a more impressive array of over-all relationships. Although an r of .04 is found between the EFT and choice dilemmas, note the r's listed between EFT performance, on the one hand, and chance and skill strategies on the other.

	Chance	Skill
Max. of gain	−.23*	−.17
Min. of loss	.14	.28**
Long shot	−.19*	−.11
Min. dev. from 1/2	.14	.08
Max. of variance	−.22*	−.20*

For both chance and skill strategies, there is a statistically significant trend toward greater risk taking on the part of females poor in analytic functioning. Further, a correlation coefficient of .26 ($p < .01$) is obtained between the EFT and number judgments — more information requested before decisional commitment is associated with better analytic functioning. In short, the evidence clearly points to conservatism as an integral part of the field-independence syndrome in women. Correspondingly, field-dependent women are characterized by higher risk-taking levels.

We must postpone a theoretical explanation of these general findings, for they may well be subject to moderator influences, to which we now turn. For both males and females, test anxiety and defensiveness have no effect whatever on associations between the EFT and the choice dilemmas task. Further, the negligible associations between EFT performance and chance and skill strategies in males remain that way in the various moderator subgroups. Such is not the case for the female samples, however, as Tables 41 and 42 point out. In a chance context (Table 41), significant relationships are confined to the high test anxiety–low defensiveness cell. By contrast, risk taking under skill conditions (Table 42) relates to analytic functioning when test anxiety is low, and especially so when defensiveness is low also. In both cases, field-independent, analytic functioning is associated with a preference for conservative strategies. Hence, the moderator analysis pinpoints the subgroups that are largely responsible for the over-all sample correlations reported earlier.

As far as the direction of the relationships is concerned, the reported findings support a psychodynamic rather than a surface-trait approach in accounting for the risk-taking implications of analytic versus global functioning. The impulse control that presumably distinguishes the field-in-

Table 41

CORRELATIONS FOR FEMALES BETWEEN CHANCE STRATEGIES AND ANALYTIC FUNCTIONING (EFT) FOR PERSONALITY SUBGROUPS

DEFENSIVENESS

			Low	High	Low + High	
TEST ANXIETY	Low	CMG	−.21	−.25	−.25	
		CML	.24	.13	.21	
		CLS	−.13	−.24	−.19	
		CMD	.02	.13	.08	
		CMV	−.24	−.16	−.24	
						$z =$
	High	CMG	−.38	−.03	−.19	−.32
		CML	.11	−.04	.04	.86
		CLS	−.40*	−.03	−.18	−.05
		CMD	.53**	−.11	.20	−.61
		CMV	−.35	−.01	−.18	−.32
					$z =$	
	Low + High	CMG	−.31*	−.13	−.94	
		CML	.24	.05	.96	
		CLS	−.26	−.11	−.77	
		CMD	.26	.00	1.31	
		CMV	−.33*	−.09	−1.25	

dependent person evidently contributes to a preference for conservative strategies. Note, however, that significant findings are confined to the female sample when risk taking is measured by strategy preferences. Further, as Tables 41 and 42 make clear, relationships are manifested within particular subgroups of females.

Because our findings thus far suggest that field independence and field dependence have evident motivational implications in the form of characteristic tendencies toward impulse control or lack of control, respectively, we may expect these implications to be most apparent in the absence of other motivational influences, such as test anxiety and general defensiveness. From this standpoint, that the strongest relationships in Table 42 emerge in the subgroup low on both moderators makes eminently good sense. Further, one may well expect field dependence–independence to be most relevant in a decision context where the subject exercises control over outcomes, because one of the criteria distinguishing field-independent, analytic functioning from field-dependent, global functioning is the capacity to differentiate oneself from the environment and achieve a certain measure of control over it. Skill strategies, from this point of view, are more

Table 42

CORRELATIONS FOR FEMALES BETWEEN SKILL STRATEGIES AND ANALYTIC FUNCTIONING (EFT) FOR PERSONALITY SUBGROUPS

DEFENSIVENESS

			Low	High	Low + High	
TEST ANXIETY	Low	SMG	−.36	−.26	−.31*	
		SML	.53**	.31	.40**	
		SLS	−.29	−.22	−.26	
		SMD	.26	.15	.20	
		SMV	−.39*	−.34	−.36**	
						$z =$
	High	SMG	−.17	.12	−.01	−1.53
		SML	.20	.08	.14	1.39
		SLS	−.13	.13	.03	−1.46
		SMD	.26	−.16	−.01	1.05
		SMV	−.16	.11	−.01	−1.81
					$z =$	
	Low + High	SMG	−.26	−.08	−.92	
		SML	.40**	.18	1.20	
		SLS	−.19	−.04	−.75	
		SMD	.21	−.03	1.20	
		SMV	−.28*	−.12	−.82	

relevant to EFT performance than chance strategies. In sum, Table 42 reinforces the impression that field-independent women manifesting the least amount of "motivational disturbance" structure a decision-making task in a way that ensures them "minimization of loss." These subjects apparently prefer to hang on to what they have rather than run the risk of losing it in an effort to earn bigger returns. Such conservatism is strongly suggestive of the tendency toward "overcontrol" so ably discussed by Witkin and his colleagues (1954; 1962) in their recent writings. At the other extreme of the present dimension — field-dependent, global functioning — the reckless impulsiveness allegedly characteristic of such persons seems to bring about a distinct preference for risky strategies.

Turning to Table 41 (EFT versus chance strategies), we note that the statistically significant relationships are confined to females high in test anxiety and low in defensiveness. The field-independence construct apparently has quite different implications for decision making in skill and chance contexts. Previously, we noted that the construct ought to be more relevant to skill than to chance situations, on the basis of the implied role of control over the environment. Yet, as Table 41 reveals quite clearly, a high level of test anxiety in conjunction with low defensiveness seems to bring about a link between field independence and conservatism under chance conditions. The test anxious, field-independent female attempts to impose control over an environment the outcomes of which are determined strictly on the basis of a random process. The need for control seems to become prominent for test anxious females who are field-independent specifically in a situation where direct control is removed because the outcomes have been made dependent on chance. The result is a conservative pulling back.

We turn now to relationships between embedded figures performance and information-seeking measures. Although the EFT and strategy indexes yield substantial moderator effects for females, such effects are minimal in the case of the association between the EFT and information-seeking indexes. The male subjects, on the other hand, manifest no relation whatever between the EFT and strategy indexes — but note the moderator effects evident in Tables 43 and 44, in which the EFT is related, respectively, to the number judgments and clues tasks.

Table 43

Correlations for Males between Number Judgments and Analytic Functioning (EFT) for Personality Subgroups

		Defensiveness			
		Low	High	Low + High	
Test Anxiety	Low	−.35	−.09	−.22	
	High	.29	−.42*	.01	$z = -1.20$
	Low + High	−.04	−.22	$z = .96$	

The direction of the significant r's is opposite to that observed in the female samples in the case of the chance and skill strategy measures. In the clues task (Table 44), and to a lesser extent in the number judgments procedure (Table 43), males high in both test anxiety and defensiveness turn out to be *less* conservative when field-independent and *more* con-

Table 44

CORRELATIONS FOR MALES BETWEEN CLUES AND ANALYTIC FUNCTIONING (EFT) FOR PERSONALITY SUBGROUPS

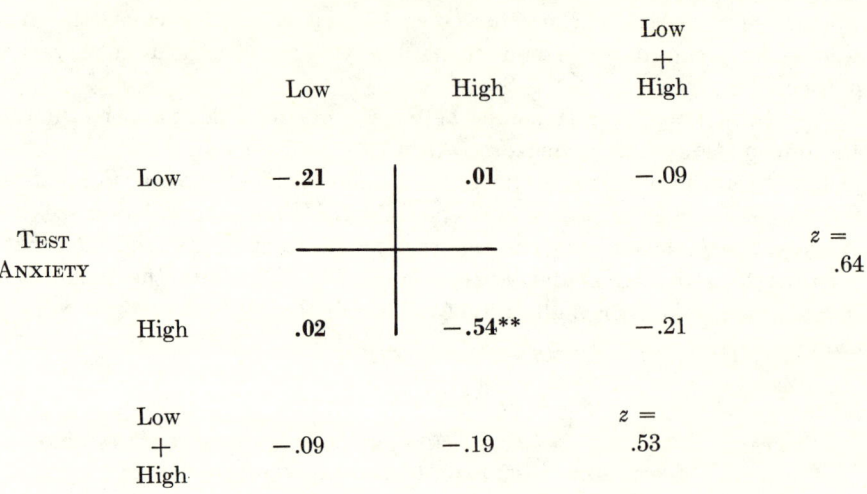

		Defensiveness			
		Low	High	Low + High	
Test Anxiety	Low	−.21	.01	−.09	z = .64
	High	.02	−.54**	−.21	
	Low + High	−.09	−.19		z = .53

servative when field-dependent. The affinity between field independence and conservatism, so characteristic of certain subgroups of females, is reversed for a particular class of males in the context of information seeking under payoff conditions.

In Chapters 3 and 4, evidence was presented indicating that test anxious and defensive males are the most likely of the four moderator subgroups to bring a consistently risky or conservative set to a variety of decision-making situations. We suggested that the decision-making behavior of those subjects is determined to a greater extent by internal dispositions brought to the situation than by the distinctive task requirements of the situation itself. A gap in the foregoing analysis was our inability to specify further, within the subgroup under consideration, the psychological characteristics of those subjects who gravitate toward risk taking as opposed to those inclined toward conservatism. Tables 43 and 44 offer data permitting a good start toward such further specification, at least with respect to risk taking in a context of information seeking.

As stated earlier, it appears that test anxiety and defensiveness provide a motivational foundation for a heightened salience of the risk-conservatism dimension. Field independence or field dependence, under these conditions of high motivational involvement, probably fills, in turn, the role of "cognitive control" mechanism, steering the organism along a risky or conservative path. Viewed in this particular manner, the present research becomes relevant to Klein's (1958) interpretation of the motivation-cognition relationship.

We may venture to suggest that a situation of choice produces high levels of arousal in the test anxious–defensive subject. Yet, arousal level as such cannot dictate the particular form a response to a complex situation will assume. It is here that intermediary cognitive processes take on importance. Recall that the number judgments and clues procedures require the subject to monitor information from the environment. Under conditions of low motivational involvement or arousal, one may expect the field-independent subject to postpone a response until certain of accuracy, in keeping with our expectations regarding such a person's strong control of impulses. However, under circumstances where the arousal level is exceedingly high, implying that a certain loss of control has already taken place, field-independence or field-dependence tendencies may no longer be able to influence impulse control but rather may simply affect the "style" of responding. Under these conditions, the activity-passivity aspect of field independence–field dependence may assume prominence. An active orientation implies risking a decision before all of the evidence is in; a passive orientation suggests waiting for the environment to inform one of the correct course. With the battle for impulse control already lost, in other words, the psychological significance of field dependence–independence may become more that of a cognitive steering mechanism than that of a motivational disposition. And as a cognitive factor "participant" behavior, in contrast with "spectator" behavior (Heidbreder, 1924), may function as the dominant attribute of a field-independent orientation.

Finally, we examine relationships between embedded figures performance and the final bet variable when the level of prior winnings is held constant. The two variables are totally unrelated for the male sample as a whole and for male moderator subgroups. Note, however, the pattern of results for females in Table 45. It can be seen that analytic functioning impinges upon the final bet selection in two of the four moderator subgroups and furthermore exerts diammetrically opposed effects in those two subgroups. Where subjects are low on both moderators, field-independent, analytic functioning is associated with greater risk taking in final bet selection, and field-dependent, global functioning is related to greater conservatism. For females high on both moderators, on the other hand, the relationship is reversed — analytic functioning being associated with greater conservatism and global functioning related to greater risk taking.

In some respects, the foregoing results point to the possibility that the field-independence construct may have distinctively different consequences in males and females. In an information-seeking context, it will be recalled, the test anxious and defensive males are more *conservative* when field dependent. Now, in the final bet context, we observe that the test anxious

Table 45

PARTIAL CORRELATIONS FOR FEMALES BETWEEN FINAL BET (PRIOR WINNINGS HELD CONSTANT) AND ANALYTIC FUNCTIONING (EFT) FOR PERSONALITY SUBGROUPS

DEFENSIVENESS

		Low	High	Low + High	
TEST ANXIETY	Low	−.45*	.09	−.16	$z = -2.01$
	High	.20	.38*	.25	
	Low + High	−.04	.21		$z = -1.26$

and defensive females show *greater risk taking* when field dependent. It may be that, on the whole, field dependence–independence is more likely to possess cognitive steering implications for males and therefore eventuate in a more risky posture for those who are field independent, whereas field dependence–independence is more likely to possess psychodynamic implications of impulse expression versus control for females and thus lead to a more conservative orientation for those who are field independent. Over and beyond this possible sex difference, however, there also is the fact of the very different task properties of the information-seeking and final bet procedures. We have here an indication of the complexity ensuing when various kinds of decision-making behavior are influenced by sex differences as well as by motivational, cognitive, and situational variables.

Some insight into the results reported in Table 45 may be gained by considering their relation to the findings shown in Table 19. Recall that the low test anxious females are influenced in their final bet selection by the amount of money they have accumulated in previous decision-making situations. The greater the level of prior winnings, the more conservative is the bet — a rational basis for decision. Holding such winnings constant, however, we note that field independence makes a separate contribution to the riskiness of final bet selection, but only in the case of low test anxious females who are also low in defensiveness. It almost appears as if, under conditions of low motivational disturbance, the field-independent female relaxes her controls at this point, possibly because she now understands that prior conservative decision-making behavior has minimized potential winnings (see Tables 42 and 22). Given the assurance that the regular salary will not be jeopardized by the final bet outcome, such subjects now opt for more risky alternatives. In a comparable vein, the low test anxious–low defensive female who is field-dependent apparently feels that she has done well enough in her previous decision-making encounters and prefers to protect her "nest egg" against possible loss. One gets the impression that, for a female sample, field independence or field dependence contributes to distinctive, but not inflexible, styles of decision making under conditions where motivational disturbance is low. For the low test anxious–low defensive subgroup of women, risk-taking behavior is quite sensitive to situational variations. This point has been stressed in earlier chapters; the embedded figures data support and extend it.

Let us turn now to the females who are high on test anxiety and defensiveness. For these subjects, a distinctly different set of circumstances prevail. Recall first (Table 19) that there is no association between level of prior winnings and risk taking in the final bet situation. As a beginning, then, we know that the risk-taking behavior of test anxious and defensive females is less subject to an apparent situational constraint — amount of money — than is the corresponding behavior of their low test anxious–low defensive counterparts. If the final bet selection is not based on considerations of monetary stake, on what basis does the test anxious–defensive female make her choice? Table 45 points to field-independent, analytic functioning as a major determinant. Where motivational involvement is high, in other words, field independence–field dependence in women determines which end of the bipolar risk-conservatism dimension will be favored. The field-independent subjects prefer the conservative way; the field dependent move in the risky direction.

A few words should be said about the two moderator subgroups for whom field independence exhibits no relation to the final bet selection. The low test anxious–defensive females are strongly influenced by prior winnings when making their choice in the final bet situation (Table 19). Field independence does not seem to be relevant for this subgroup. Turning to the high test anxious–low defensive women, Table 19 shows that these subjects do not pay much attention to prior winnings in selecting their final bet. Field independence, however, does not seem to be the key here either, so we remain quite in the dark regarding the basis on which high test anxious–low defensive females select a final bet.

In their recent volume, Witkin *et al.* (1962) concerned themselves with direct personality correlates of the dimension of field-independent, analytic functioning versus field-dependent, global functioning. On the basis of these investigations and the work of others, one may surmise that field-dependent subjects are both more anxious and more defensive than their field-independent counterparts. Our data lend no support whatever to those observations, however. As Appendixes A–6 and A–7 (row 24) demonstrate, mean EFT scores are highly similar across the various moderator subgroups employed in the study. F and t values do not even approach statistical significance. It is apparent, then, that analytic or global functioning is quite independent of test anxiety and general defensiveness.[4] These results clearly point to the existence of a limited number of field-independent and field-dependent types. We have shown that the pattern of decision-making behavior may vary as a function of the motivational context in which the field-independent or field-dependent mode of functioning is embedded. Witkin et al. (1962, pp. 229–269) in reporting case material have recognized the wide diversity of functioning within each of their bipolar types, but this diversity tends to be ignored in most empirical treatments of the problem. It may be suggested that the moderator breakdown employed in the present investigation provides a handle toward possible systematization of the within-type diversity so evident in case descriptions. Our results have shown that recognition of this diversity through the mechanism of moderator analysis does much to clarify the risk-taking consequences of analytic and global orientations. It is quite possible that such a moderator approach may also prove useful in exploring other correlates of field independence–dependence.

SUMMARY

The present chapter has explored the relationship between risk taking and three types of intellective skills — verbal aptitude, mathematical aptitude, and analytic functioning. We recognize, of course, that the last of these has ramifications beyond strictly intellective performance, but given its operational specification in the present context, we include it under that rubric.

The authors' initial orientation to the relationship between intellective abilities and decision making placed heavy emphasis upon the former as states or characteristics of the individual that might conceivably influence

---

[4] One might object, of course, that the multiple-choice EFT employed is faulty in some respect. Such an objection, however, receives no support in data reported by Jackson et al. (1964), indicating correlations between the present EFT and the original Witkin measures that approach the reliabilities of the respective tests. With regard to test anxiety and defensiveness, the Alpert-Haber and Marlowe-Crowne scales have demonstrated their validity in a variety of studies that have related scale scores to behavioral performance indexes.

decision-making behavior. This has been the conventional way of approaching the matter, prompted in large measure by the "common-sense" consideration that more intelligent subjects ought to tend toward optimal decision making. Our results in the case of verbal ability force a recasting of this traditional approach to the problem. In short, verbal aptitude itself (as measured by tests with instructional sets incorporating a penalty for guessing) may be partially determined by risk-taking dispositions. Under such conditions, each test item about which the examinee is uncertain becomes, for all practical purposes, a decision-making situation. Thus, the question that the examinee can (explicitly or implicitly) pose to himself may be of the following sort: "Having eliminated two or three patently incorrect alternatives, should I take a stab at choosing one of the remaining, even though I am quite uncertain which of these is correct?" Clearly, the resolution of such a decision-making situation must necessarily reflect individual propensities toward risk taking or conservatism.

The empirical evidence introduced, although indirect, is highly supportive of such an interpretation. For males, a sharp differentiation is observed between the high test anxious–low defensive subgroup, on the one hand, and the remaining three subgroups on the other. For the former, greater risk taking is associated with lower verbal ability as measured by the SAT, suggesting that males who experience severe anxiety in a stressful examination situation guess incorrectly when gambling on uncertain items. The test anxious–low defensive conservative, on the other hand, performs quite well on this verbal ability measure. Apparently, the disruptive influence of test anxiety is countered best by adopting a conservative course in dealing with the uncertainties of test items. Directly opposite effects are obtained in the other three subgroups — effects that emerge with greatest strength in low test anxious–low defensive males. Now it is the high risk-taker who obtains higher verbal aptitude scores and the conservative individual who secures lower scores. In the absence of anxiety symptoms and of defensiveness, risk taking clearly enhances test performance in the verbal aptitude domain.

Results for females, although in the same direction as the findings for males, are not nearly as clear-cut when verbal aptitude is measured by the SAT. Because the females also took a short vocabulary test with instructions encouraging guessing, however, we are permitted an examination of effects under relatively permissive testing conditions. Under these circumstances, only the low test anxious–low defensive females yield significant relationships, with risk taking again related to higher verbal aptitude scores. Associations of equal magnitude and opposite sign do not appear for high test anxious–low defensive females. In sum, encouragement to guess and/or less stressful testing conditions seem to alter the verbal aptitude–risk-taking relationship in an expected direction — in other words, test anxiety becomes less relevant as the testing context takes on a more permissive character.

Consider next the risk-taking implications of mathematical aptitude. We have speculated that the gambling response set may be less appropriate for mathematical than for verbal test items on the grounds that the former type of item does not lend itself to elimination of obviously incorrect alternatives unless the problem is actually worked through to solution. This speculation does not imply, of course, that a gambling response set will be totally absent in a mathematical problem-solving context. The multiple-choice framework of necessity involves decision-making considerations, even though the operation of a gambling response set ought to be markedly attenuated in the mathematical domain. Interestingly enough, the only evidence for the presence of the foregoing set emerges in the case of highly test anxious and defensive males. Recall that this is the subgroup that has been shown to exhibit a highly generalized risky or conservative orientation in a variety of decision-making contexts.

Turning to the females, we find significant positive correlations in the sample as a whole between mathematical aptitude test scores and a preference for conservative strategies in both chance and skill contexts. Subsequent moderator analysis indicates that these relationships are largely confined to subjects low in defensiveness. The general pattern of the results and the significant positive correlations between mathematical aptitude and analytic functioning (embedded figures test performance) strongly suggest that the gambling response set is of minor importance in the present context. Rather, mathematical aptitude in females seems to be part of a more comprehensive cognitive and personality organization, which, in turn, is quite relevant in its own right to matters of risk taking.

Consider, finally, the implications of field dependence–independence for risk taking. The general trend of results suggests that, for females, analytic versus global forms of intellective functioning possess their main significance for risk taking at the level of control versus release of impulses–analytic functioning contributing to greater conservatism through impulse inhibition, global functioning contributing to greater risk taking through impulse release. It may be that for males, in contrast, field dependence–independence has its main import for risk taking at the level of cognitive steering mechanism — analytic functioning contributing to greater risk taking through fostering an active, "participant" attitude, global functioning contributing to greater conservatism through supporting a passive, "spectator" attitude.

Apart from these possible sex differences, our findings also suggest the possibility that the impulse inhibition versus expression aspect of field independence–dependence is evidenced most clearly in the case of individuals lowest in motivational disturbance, as if these motivational implications can more readily come to the fore when other motivational influences such as test anxiety and defensiveness are absent. Females in this subgroup show more conservative betting behavior in a skill context if they are field-independent, more risky betting behavior in a skill context if field-dependent. This low defensive–low test anxious subgroup also seems to exhibit greater sensitivity to situational changes, however, in that circumstances do exist in which the field-independent individuals, rather than becoming more conservative, become greater risk-takers than their field-dependent counterparts. Once again, then, evidence is added testifying to the greater situational sensitivity of this least disturbed subgroup.

6

Decision-Making and Cognitive-Judgmental Processes

A major impetus for carrying out the research reported in the present volume derived from the generally inconclusive results obtained by the authors and by others in studies relating cognitive-judgmental indexes to explicit risk-taking measures. Despite the strategy implications attributed to categorization processes, for example, attempts to relate such processes to decision-making strategies have met with little success. In the introductory chapter, the authors suggested that past failures to obtain significant associations between cognitive-judgmental and risk-taking measures might be attributed to the use of exclusively hypothetical decision-making procedures and/or to the absence of consideration of relevant personality dispositions as moderator variables. The present investigation offers the opportunity to explore relations between the cognitive-judgmental domain, on the one hand, and decision making under various payoff conditions on the other, with moderator variables of test anxiety and defensiveness taken into account.

CONFIDENCE OF JUDGMENT

As an index of confidence, scores derived from the judgmental confidence-extremity procedure cited earlier were used. It has been observed that confidence estimates possess wide generality over a variety of judgment tasks (Johnson, 1957). In the present investigation, confidence of judgment is significantly correlated with the confidence index obtained from the number judgments procedure ($r = .38, p < .01$ for males; $r = .31, p < .01$ for females). The former was used in the present section because of the inherently greater reliability of an index based on 50 items than one based on 4 items.

It should be emphasized that confidence is evidently not a "strategy" variable in either an explicit or implicit sense. Rather, it is an index of a subject's introspective conviction regarding the correctness or appropriateness of his judgment or decision. Although we here put "confidence" into the cognitive-judgmental rubric, the variable has salient personality overtones.

We turn now to over-all sample correlations. Consistent with earlier findings (Wallach & Kogan, 1961), we find that risk taking under hypothetical conditions — the choice dilemmas procedure — does not relate significantly to confidence of judgment ($r = .06$ and $-.18$ for males and females, respectively). Further, negligible nonsignificant correlations obtain for males when confidence of judgment is related to decision making under payoff conditions. Note, however, the correlations reported for females between confidence of judgment, on the one hand, and chance and skill strategies on the other.

	Chance	Skill
Max. of gain	.17	.15
Min. of loss	−.31**	−.23*
Long shot	.07	.09
Min. dev. from 1/2	.01	−.02
Max. of variance	.24*	.19*

The most salient outcome is the inverse relationship between confidence and a preference for a minimization of loss strategy. Here, then, is the first evidence we have that a variable in the cognitive-judgmental domain bears some relation to decision making when the latter is measured in a context of monetary risks and payoffs. In the information-seeking area, number judgments performance does not relate significantly to judgmental confidence, but on the other hand, a significant inverse relationship is obtained with respect to the clues task ($r = -.24$, $p < .05$). The women who manifest greater confidence request fewer clues before irrevocably committing themselves to a decision. In sum, by employing tasks in which a subject's decisions have real outcomes, we have finally succeeded in bridging the gap, at least in women, between the cognitive-judgmental and decision-making domains.

Consider next the possibility of moderator influences. As noted previously, quite apart from the issue of decision making under hypothetical versus actual conditions, past failures to obtain significant relationships between cognitive-judgmental and decision-making variables may be attributable to the general neglect of possible moderator effects.

We consider first the association between confidence of judgment and the risk-conservatism index derived from the choice dilemmas procedure. The lack of over-all association in males does not appear to be affected by taking account of the moderators. Note, on the other hand, the findings for females in Table 46. The marginals indicate that the relationship is a statistically significant one for highly test anxious and for low defensive

Table 46

CORRELATIONS FOR FEMALES BETWEEN CHOICE DILEMMAS AND JUDGMENTAL CONFIDENCE FOR PERSONALITY SUBGROUPS

		DEFENSIVENESS			
		Low	High	Low + High	
TEST ANXIETY	Low	−.53**	.41	−.07	$z = 1.13$
	High	−.34	−.19	−.29*	
	Low + High	−.43**	.05	$z = -2.51$	

subjects. In both cases, selection of a higher probability level on choice dilemmas — greater deterrence of failure (conservatism) — is associated with lower confidence of judgment. Note, however, that only the difference between high and low defensive females yields a significant z value.

Moving into the cells of Table 46, we again observe in a striking way how much more can be learned by dividing the sample on both moderators simultaneously. It can readily be seen that within the low test anxious subgroup, level of defensiveness makes a great deal of difference. When defensiveness is low, the expected relation between confidence and risk taking achieves its highest value. By contrast, low test anxious females who are high in defensiveness exhibit the reverse relationship. For these subjects, high confidence of judgment is associated with *greater* conservatism in decision making under hypothetical conditions. The reported r of .41 is just short of the .42 value required for significance at the .05 level. Here, then, we find an apparent contradiction between explicit and implicit risk-taking indexes. Recall our earlier suggestion that certain cognitive-judgmental variables might be treated as implicit risk-taking indexes. It appears that, depending upon the moderator subgroup, these indexes may be directly or inversely related to one another.

Certain special conditions obtain in the case of the choice dilemmas task that very likely contribute to the correlational pattern noted in Table 46. The choice dilemmas instrument requires that the subject offer a protagonist advice with regard to the level of risk he ought to assume in pursuing a highly desirable goal. We have been proceeding on the assumption that the selection of a probability level on a "choice dilemmas" item is a reflection of one's own risk-taking propensities. The present data suggest that such an assumption may be entirely unwarranted for a particular subgroup. For low test anxious–highly defensive females, greater tolerance of risk when advising others in the choice dilemmas procedure is associated with lesser confidence in one's own judgments. Conversely, recommending a more conservative course to protagonists in choice dilemmas items is related to greater confidence of personal judgment. These subjects, in other words, are willing to advise a course of action to another that appears to be in contradiction with their own confidence level. Indeed, we may be dealing here with something akin to complementary projection; low personal confidence is compensated for by recommending that someone else adopt a risky course. Given such a tendency, it is hardly surprising that no significant associations appear for low test anxious–defensive females between the choice dilemmas scores and indexes derived from decision making in a payoff context (Tables 2, 4, 5, and 6).

We turn next to relationships between confidence of judgment and decision making under monetary payoff conditions. Tables 47 and 48 relate confidence of judgment to chance and skill strategies, respectively, in the male sample. In both cases, relationships appear to be confined to the low test anxious subjects. Note, however, that high or low defensiveness makes a considerable difference. Whether chance or skill strategies are at issue, the confident male who is low in test anxiety and high in defensiveness distinctly avoids the "minimization of loss" strategy. Correspondingly, his nonconfident counterpart prefers such a conservative strategy. When both test anxiety and defensiveness are low, on the other hand, the correlational pattern changes radically; especially in the case of skill strategies, high confidence is now associated with avoidance of risky strategies. In many respects, these data are in direct opposition to the female results reported in Table 46, which, it will be recalled, gives attention to decision making under hypothetical conditions.

How can we account for the pattern of results found in Tables 47 and 48? Let us briefly consider the nature of the probability estimation instrument (Appendix D) from which the confidence score is derived. The test

Table 47

CORRELATIONS FOR MALES BETWEEN CHANCE STRATEGIES AND JUDGMENTAL
CONFIDENCE FOR PERSONALITY SUBGROUPS

DEFENSIVENESS

			Low	High	Low + High	
TEST ANXIETY	Low	CMG	−.30	.10	−.06	
		CML	.21	−.39*	−.14	
		CLS	−.26	−.01	−.10	
		CMD	.29	.08	.17	
		CMV	−.32	.16	−.03	
						z =
	High	CMG	−.13	−.09	−.12	.31
		CML	−.14	.07	−.08	−.31
		CLS	−.26	−.06	−.20	.53
		CMD	.25	.07	.17	.00
		CMV	−.07	−.06	−.08	.26
					z =	
	Low + High	CMG	−.22	.03	−1.32	
		CML	.05	−.24	1.53	
		CLS	−.25	−.03	−1.17	
		CMD	.27*	.07	1.08	
		CMV	−.20	.08	−1.47	

items were deliberately selected to maximize the likelihood that the subject would not possess the detailed quantitative information required for "accurate" estimation. A high confidence score, then, for some people may be more an indication of a "desire for certainty" (Brim, 1955; Brim & Hoff, 1957) than of a realistic appraisal of the accuracy of one's estimations. Evidence for this formulation is available in terms of an r of $-.43$ ($p < .05$) between the confidence index and mathematical aptitude for the low test anxious–low defensive male subgroup. Further, it is only in the case of this subgroup that the foregoing relationship is statistically significant. For these subjects, in other words, greater confidence of judgment in making quantitative probability estimations is associated with *lower* levels of mathematical aptitude. The more mathematically sophisticated among them realistically adhere to lower confidence levels.

Given this indication that confidence may be reflecting a desire for certainty, the direction of the correlations for the low test anxious–low defensive males becomes meaningful. In a bet strategy context, certainty, in the sense of more frequent positive outcomes, will be advanced by adoption of a conservative course. In this context a desire for certainty can be

Table 48

CORRELATIONS FOR MALES BETWEEN SKILL STRATEGIES AND JUDGMENTAL CONFIDENCE FOR PERSONALITY SUBGROUPS

DEFENSIVENESS

			Low	High	Low + High	
TEST ANXIETY	Low	SMG	−.41*	.00	−.12	
		SML	.03	−.38*	−.26*	
		SLS	−.44*	−.11	−.21	
		SMD	.35	.06	.17	
		SMV	−.31	.09	−.03	
						$z =$
	High	SMG	−.11	−.07	−.08	−.21
		SML	.12	−.05	.04	−1.57
		SLS	−.16	−.08	−.12	−.48
		SMD	.08	.12	.07	.52
		SMV	−.12	−.03	−.07	.21
					$z =$	
	Low + High	SMG	−.26*	−.02	−1.28	
		SML	.08	−.27*	1.85	
		SLS	−.30*	−.10	−1.09	
		SMD	.24	.08	.86	
		SMV	−.21	.04	−1.32	

implemented, in other words, by placing conservative bets. The somewhat higher coefficients obtained under skill conditions (Table 48), where two of the five r's are significant, probably reflects the aspect of control over outcomes. The low test anxious–low defensive male in the probability estimation setting must feel, at a conscious level, that his judgments warrant the high confidence he places in them. The task, in other words, calls forth a controlled performance. In this respect, the stronger association of judgmental confidence with skill than with chance strategies becomes comprehensible.

For low test anxious–high defensive males, on the other hand, no discrimination between chance and skill seems to occur, and furthermore, the direction of the relationship is the converse of that reported for the males low on both moderators. In the low test anxious–high defensive subgroup, risk taking and judgmental confidence are positively related. We have repeatedly emphasized the importance of image-maintenance mechanisms in that subgroup. The results reported in Tables 47 and 48 suggest a need to maintain consistency as either a bold and risky or a cautious and conservative decision-maker across the exceedingly diverse situational contexts represented by a probability estimation questionnaire and the two bet strategy procedures. It is worthy of note that this relationship holds for confidence of judgment in particular. Recall our earlier discussion of this variable, where we stressed its introspective character. Given the disposition of low test anxious–high defensive subjects toward a preoccupation with self-evaluation, it is perhaps not too surprising that significant relationships emerge for that particular subgroup in the present case.

Do the foregoing relationships hold in the female sample? Tables 49 and 50 offer the relevant findings. Nowhere in the female data do we find the inverse relationships between confidence and risk taking so prominent in Table 48. On the other hand, the skill strategy results for low test anx-

Table 49

CORRELATIONS FOR FEMALES BETWEEN CHANCE STRATEGIES AND
JUDGMENTAL CONFIDENCE FOR PERSONALITY SUBGROUPS

DEFENSIVENESS

			Low	High	Low + High	
TEST ANXIETY	Low	CMG	.04	.35	.18	
		CML	−.15	−.27	−.22	
		CLS	.03	.31	.14	
		CMD	.11	−.25	−.06	
		CMV	.12	.32	.21	
						$z =$
	High	CMG	.00	.27	.16	.10
		CML	−.16	−.56**	−.43**	1.16
		CLS	−.05	.06	.00	.69
		CMD	.08	.09	.10	−.79
		CMV	.05	.41*	.28*	−.36
					$z =$	
	Low + High	CMG	.04	.32*	−1.44	
		CML	−.16	−.43**	1.47	
		CLS	.01	.16	−.74	
		CMD	.10	−.08	.89	
		CMV	.10	.38**	−1.48	

ious–high defensive subjects are quite consistent across sex, and indeed, the effect is somewhat more powerful in the female data (Table 50). Again, confidence and risk taking exhibit a direct relationship. Note, however, that the female results for chance strategies (Table 49) deviate somewhat from the corresponding male findings in Table 47. In the females, the highly test anxious and defensive subjects share in these direct relation-

Table 50

CORRELATIONS FOR FEMALES BETWEEN SKILL STRATEGIES AND
JUDGMENTAL CONFIDENCE FOR PERSONALITY SUBGROUPS

DEFENSIVENESS

			Low	High	Low + High	
TEST ANXIETY	Low	SMG	.20	.35	.28*	
		SML	−.17	−.45*	−.29*	
		SLS	.22	.28	.25	
		SMD	−.20	−.12	−.16	
		SMV	.25	.40	.33*	
						$z =$
	High	SMG	−.11	.09	−.01	1.47
		SML	−.09	−.20	−.19	−.53
		SLS	−.19	.00	−.09	1.70
		SMD	.00	.16	.13	−1.44
		SMV	−.18	.16	.01	1.64
					$z =$	
	Low + High	SMG	.08	.24	−.81	
		SML	−.15	−.30*	.78	
		SLS	.05	.14	−.45	
		SMD	−.11	.03	−.69	
		SMV	.09	.28*	−.97	

ships and, in fact, manifest the highest correlations between the confidence and strategy variables. Because confidence of judgment is measured in a context of knowledge, one may expect it to be more strongly related to skill than to chance strategies — in the former case, the subject is evaluating his own capacity. In other words, both the probability estimation and skill strategy tasks involve self-evaluative processes — retrospective in the case of a confidence judgment and prospective in the selection of a skill bet to be played at a subsequent time. Chance strategies, on the other hand, imply not a self-evaluation so much as an evaluation of environmental vagaries. Yet, as we have seen, the high test anxious–high defensive females exhibit a greater consistency between chance strategies and confidence than between skill strategies and confidence. The major point of note, however, is the extent to which defensiveness (whether or not test anxiety is also present) tends to promote a direct relationship in women between confidence of judgment and risk in decision making of the strategy type. When defensiveness is at a low level, on the other hand, the relationship in question is either absent (females) or reversed in direction (males). The latter is true, however, only where both defensiveness and test anxiety are low. In sum, a direct, reflective relationship — high confidence going with greater risk taking — apparently requires the presence of high levels of defensiveness in order to emerge with any strength. Under such conditions, a subject's self-appraisals of his judgmental confidence carry considerable weight in informing us of risks likely to be taken in payoff contexts.

Note, finally, that relationships between confidence of judgment, on the one hand, and information seeking and the final bet, on the other, are not subject to moderator influences.

EXTREMITY OF JUDGMENT

It will be recalled that separate extremity scores were obtained for judgments rendered with high and low degrees of confidence. The over-all correlations between these two kinds of extremity judgment are .16 and .11 in the male and female samples, respectively. Both r's are nonsignificant, thereby supporting the decision to separate the extremity score into these two distinct components.

Extremity under high confidence

Relations between extremity under high confidence and decision-making indexes are essentially absent in both the male and female samples considered as a whole. The only exception to this general trend is a partial r of $-.24$ ($p < .05$) in females between extremity under high confidence and the final bet variable when the amount of prior winnings is held constant. There is a tendency, then, for women who are extreme under high confidence to exhibit greater risk taking in the final bet situation. Given the fact that this statistically significant finding stands in relative isolation, we hesitate to make too much of it, and accordingly, we turn to an examination of moderator effects.

Tables 51 and 52 show the correlations of extremity under high confidence with chance and skill strategies, respectively, in the moderator subgroups of males. The effects are not overly strong in the case of chance strategies (Table 51). There is, however, some indication that low test anxious–high defensive males tend to minimize loss when extreme under high confidence. This finding may seem surprising in the light of the results reported in Table 47, where it can be seen that, for the same subgroup of males, confidence and "minimization of loss" on chance strategies are inversely related. The observation that over-all confidence and extremity under high confidence bear directly opposite relations to a particular strategy preference should be interpreted in the light of a correlation of $-.64$ ($p < .01$) in low test anxious–high defensive males between the two

Table 51

CORRELATIONS FOR MALES BETWEEN CHANCE STRATEGIES AND EXTREMITY
UNDER HIGH CONFIDENCE FOR PERSONALITY SUBGROUPS

DEFENSIVENESS

			Low	High	Low + High	
		CMG	.28	−.16	.05	
		CML	−.33	.36*	.02	
	Low	CLS	.19	−.09	.05	
		CMD	−.23	−.03	−.12	
		CMV	.34	−.18	.07	
TEST						$z =$
ANXIETY		CMG	−.25	−.09	−.17	1.14
		CML	.10	.05	.08	−.31
	High	CLS	−.21	−.07	−.14	.98
		CMD	.17	.07	.12	−1.24
		CMV	−.22	−.04	−.14	1.08
					$z =$	
		CMG	.04	−.13	.89	
	Low	CML	−.11	.27*	−2.01	
	+	CLS	.01	−.08	.47	
	High	CMD	−.02	.01	−.16	
		CMV	.08	−.14	1.15	

cognitive-judgmental measures under discussion. This correlation suggests that the male willing to go to extremes when quite sure of himself is, in general terms, fairly unsure of himself. In other words, the male lacking over-all confidence in his judgments seems to leap to extremes when he finally confronts an item the "correct" probability value of which seems quite apparent to him. It should be noted that this inverse relation between general confidence and extremity under high confidence is also obtained in low test anxious–low defensive males ($r = -.54$, $p < .01$) and high test anxious–low defensive males ($r = -.51$, $p < .01$). Only the males high on both moderators deviate from the general pattern ($r = -.15$).

In a previous paper (Wallach & Kogan, 1959), the authors explained sex differences in judgment on the present probability estimation instrument on the basis of a "counterphobic" mechanism in females, who turned out to be more extreme than males under high confidence, though less confident in general than males and less extreme than males under confidence conditions other than "very sure." Although the results of the present study do not replicate these earlier findings, the evidence outlined points to a more general effect — namely, an inverse relationship between over-all confidence and extremity under high confidence. Indeed, the fe-

Table 52

Correlations for Males between Skill Strategies and Extremity under High Confidence for Personality Subgroups

			DEFENSIVENESS			
			Low	High	Low + High	
	Low	SMG	.24	−.05	.07	
		SML	−.22	.32	.12	
		SLS	.20	.03	.11	
		SMD	−.30	−.04	−.16	
		SMV	.22	−.14	.01	
TEST ANXIETY						$z =$
	High	SMG	−.32	−.28	−.29*	1.90
		SML	−.02	.30	.08	.21
		SLS	−.37	−.22	−.30*	2.15
		SMD	.38*	.44*	.36**	−2.76
		SMV	−.26	−.32	−.26	1.42
					$z =$	
	Low + High	SMG	−.06	−.11	.26	
		SML	−.10	.30*	−2.13	
		SLS	−.09	−.04	−.26	
		SMD	.01	.12	−.58	
		SMV	−.04	−.18	.73	

males seem to share in this general effect, though to a considerably lesser degree ($r = -.21$, $p < .05$ for the female sample as a whole). Within both the male and female samples, then, we find evidence for an "overcompensation" or "counterphobic" mechanism in which the nonconfident individual "goes out on a limb" on those few occasions when his confidence level exceeds a certain threshold. Extremity under these conditions seems indeed to represent the desire-for-certainty or uncertainty-reduction tendency that has been described by Brim (1955) and Brim and Hoff (1957). If extremity of judgment represents an overcompensation for lowered confidence, one may expect such extremity to be inversely related to explicit risk-taking indicators. Returning to Table 51, we find that the results no longer appear inconsistent. The defensive male who goes to extremes in a judgmental context tends to be cautious and conservative in a decision-making situation in which control over outcomes is lacking.

The findings for skill strategies (Table 52) are consistent with those reported here, but are also revealing of additional effects. All of the results offer further support for the operation of a counterphobic risk mechanism. Note first that the significant difference between low and high defensive males is maintained with respect to the "minimization of loss" strategy. Again, those highly defensive males who are extreme under high confidence prefer to minimize loss when selecting a strategy. In the present instance, however, test anxiety also exerts a substantial moderator influence. When test anxiety is high, there is a significant relationship between greater extremity under high confidence and avoidance of risky strategies. Note further the significant z values between low and high test anxious subgroups.

In sum, we clearly observe how a shift from a chance to a skill context engages test anxiety as a moderator. Also of interest is the differential moderator effect of test anxiety and defensiveness with regard to specific strategy indexes. "Minimization of loss" is relevant to defensiveness; the other strategies are moderated by test anxiety. Depending upon the decision-making context, test anxiety and/or defensiveness enhances relations between cognitive-judgmental and explicit strategy variables. The direction of these associations links greater extremity under high confidence with a preference for conservative strategies. It is only the low test anxious–low defensive males who do not share in these relationships. Note in both Tables 51 and 52 that the correlations for these subjects, although uniformly nonsignificant, are in the direction opposite to that of the other three subgroups. It appears, then, that "counterphobic" extremity-confidence relations do not bear upon explicit risk taking in the low test anxious–low defensive males, implying a separation between cognitive-judgmental and explicit risk-taking effects in this "least disturbed" subgroup.

We have again found, then, that a cognitive-judgmental variable is of relevance to strategies in a decision-making situation involving monetary risks and payoffs. The association seems to be conditional upon the presence of test anxiety and/or defensiveness. Within those moderator subgroups, the direction of relationships among confidence, extremity under high confidence, and decision-making strategies suggests the operation of possible overcompensating or counterphobic mechanisms linking the cognitive-judgmental and risk-taking domains.

Consider next the female results in Tables 53 and 54. It is immediately evident that the findings for females do not parallel those obtained in the male samples. Rather, the few significant relationships observed suggest that greater extremity under high confidence is associated with a preference for risky strategies. These relationships occur in the case of subgroups high in either test anxiety or defensiveness. It appears, then, that extremity under high confidence has very different implications for males and females, particularly when the latter fall into one or the other of the two subgroups cited. It may be noted in this connection that the correlations between over-all confidence and extremity under high confidence are .15 in the low test anxious–highly defensive females and $-.17$ in the high test anxious–low defensive women. Neither approaches statistical significance. Hence,

Table 53

CORRELATIONS FOR FEMALES BETWEEN CHANCE STRATEGIES AND EXTREMITY UNDER HIGH CONFIDENCE FOR PERSONALITY SUBGROUPS

DEFENSIVENESS

			Low	High	Low + High	
TEST ANXIETY	Low	CMG	−.16	.22	−.08	
		CML	.11	−.19	.03	
		CLS	−.14	.18	−.08	
		CMD	.02	−.42*	−.14	
		CMV	−.23	.24	−.10	
						$z =$
	High	CMG	.33	−.05	.09	−.84
		CML	.06	−.12	.00	.15
		CLS	.33	−.08	.08	−.79
		CMD	−.32	−.02	−.16	.10
		CMV	.29	−.05	.06	−.79
					$z =$	
	Low + High	CMG	.00	.01	−.05	
		CML	.13	−.10	1.14	
		CLS	.02	.00	.10	
		CMD	−.14	−.15	.05	
		CMV	−.07	.02	−.44	

the pattern typical of the males — a substantial inverse relation between over-all confidence and extremity under high confidence — is virtually absent in the two female subgroups under consideration. This finding suggests that the overcompensatory, counterphobic aspects of an extremity judgment under high confidence are much less salient in these women than in the corresponding subgroups of men. Rather, going to extremes in a probability estimation task seems to have a direct, reflective relation to risk taking in women who are high in either test anxiety or defensiveness.

If extremity under high confidence does not partake of counterphobic qualities in test anxious or defensive women, what are the critical features of such judgments that bring about their association with risk taking? Obviously, more than simple knowledge must be involved when making such high-confidence judgments, or the observed relationships with risk taking could not have occurred. Knowledge can never be complete, of course, in the judgmental situation we have chosen to employ, involving as it does ambiguity as a criterion of item selection. Hence, other factors must necessarily contribute to the probability estimations of the subjects.

It may be that where test anxious or defensive women are concerned,

Table 54

CORRELATIONS FOR FEMALES BETWEEN SKILL STRATEGIES AND EXTREMITY
UNDER HIGH CONFIDENCE FOR PERSONALITY SUBGROUPS

			DEFENSIVENESS			
			Low	High	Low + High	
TEST ANXIETY	Low	SMG	−.04	.27	.08	
		SML	.14	−.11	.03	
		SLS	.00	.31	.12	
		SMD	.09	−.46*	−.14	
		SMV	−.04	.24	.07	
						$z =$
	High	SMG	.44*	−.17	.09	−.05
		SML	−.29	−.34	−.28*	1.57
		SLS	.38	−.35	−.05	.84
		SMD	−.25	.31	.08	−1.09
		SMV	.43*	−.06	.13	−.30
					$z =$	
	Low + High	SMG	.14	.04	.50	
		SML	.01	−.24	1.26	
		SLS	.15	−.04	.94	
		SMD	−.06	−.01	−.25	
		SMV	.12	.09	.15	

greater subjective safety lies in probability estimates that are biased in the direction of the midpoint of the probability scale, as opposed to biases in the direction of the 0 in 100 and 100 in 100 extremes. In short, biases in the direction of an "all-or-none" principle when dealing with human events are likely to be perceived by these women as entailing a greater risk of error. Such a principle may account for the direct relationship between extremity under high confidence and risk taking in the present circumstances. Why low test anxious–low defensive females are not susceptible to such an "all-or-none" bias is not immediately evident. Possibly, these subjects are the most likely to operate strictly on the basis of personal knowledge, thereby making them less prone to the judgmental distortions that the "all-or-none" principle implies. Note, however, that it is only in the low test anxious–low defensive females that extremity under high confidence and over-all confidence are negatively correlated ($r = -.51, p < .01$). This correlation means that a very different kind of bias presumably operates in these women, one similar to that previously observed for males — namely, a desire for certainty (greater extremity) under high confidence conditions that compensates for an over-all feeling of low confidence. It must be stressed, however, that these cognitive-judgmental effects in the subgroup of females low in test anxiety and defensiveness yield no relationships whatever to decision-making indexes. This pattern corresponds exactly to that of the low test anxious–low defensive males, thus providing evidence that extremity under high confidence and explicit risk taking remain independent for this subgroup.

Note, finally, that test anxiety plays a stronger role in skill (Table 54) than in chance (Table 53) strategies. Defensiveness, on the other hand, is engaged to about the same extent regardless of the chance or skill nature of the decision context. A comparable effect is observed in the male sample (Tables 51 and 52).

Few moderator effects are observed when extremity of judgment under high confidence is related to the information-seeking and final bet variables. The sole exception to this trend is represented by Table 55, where it will be noted that a highly significant inverse r is found in the low test anxious–

Table 55

CORRELATIONS FOR FEMALES BETWEEN CLUES AND EXTREMITY UNDER HIGH CONFIDENCE FOR PERSONALITY SUBGROUPS

DEFENSIVENESS

		Low	High	Low + High	
TEST ANXIETY	Low	−.05	−.57**	−.25	$z = -1.11$
	High	.06	−.10	−.03	
	Low + High	−.01	−.29*	$z = 1.42$	

defensive females between extremity under high confidence and the clues total. Greater extremity is associated with fewer clues demanded (greater risk taking). The direction of the relationship is quite consistent with that observed in Tables 53 and 54, thus supporting the general view that when extremity under high confidence is related to risk-taking indexes in females, it is in the reflective direction — greater extremity being linked with greater risk taking.

Earlier, we suggested that the male and female results are not wholly congruent. This is certainly true insofar as a counterphobic link with risk taking seems to distinguish the males, whereas the females are characterized by a reflective function. A different form of consistency does prevail across the sexes, however, in the sense that some motivational disturbance must be present if any sort of relationship between the cognitive-judgmental and decision-making domains is to emerge. The data from both sexes suggest, then, that conditions of motivational disturbance are required in order for the cognitive-judgmental domain to be infused with risk-relevant properties. This statement is, of course, intended to apply only to the variable of extremity under high confidence. Let us note next what happens when the other form of extremity is examined.

Extremity under low confidence

In the matter of extremity under low confidence, consider first the correlations between this second form of judgmental extremity and the various decision-making indexes for the samples as a whole. The result is quite straightforward; not a single correlation achieves statistical significance. Once again, then, we obtain a general pattern of relationships for total samples suggestive of independence between the cognitive-judgmental and decision-making domains. Let us examine whether this independence is maintained when a moderator analysis is applied.

Tables 56 and 57 provide the correlations in the male subgroups between extremity under low confidence and chance and skill strategies, respectively. It is instructive to compare these tables with those for extremity under high confidence (Tables 51 and 52). Before proceeding to such a comparison, however, we must give some consideration to the psychological distinction between the two forms of extremity. We have already noted that extremity under high confidence in males is negatively related to over-all confidence, a relation that suggests a possible counterphobic effect whereby the nonconfident individual leaps to extremes on those few occasions when his confidence achieves high levels. The relation between extremity under low confidence and over-all confidence, on the other hand, is much lower, and indeed achieves significance ($r = -.34$, $p < .05$) only in the case of the low test anxious–high defensive males. Because this subgroup also yields a very substantial relation between extremity under high confidence and over-all confidence ($r = -.64$, $p < .01$), there seems to be a general tendency in low test anxious-defensive males toward a compensatory confidence-extremity relationship. If one goes up, the other declines. Note in Table 57 that it is only in the subgroup we have been discussing that extremity

Table 56

CORRELATIONS FOR MALES BETWEEN CHANCE STRATEGIES AND EXTREMITY UNDER LOW CONFIDENCE FOR PERSONALITY SUBGROUPS

DEFENSIVENESS

			Low	High	Low + High	
		CMG	.05	−.01	−.01	
		CML	−.01	.29	.17	
	Low	CLS	.06	.10	.05	
		CMD	.09	−.16	−.04	
		CMV	.04	−.06	−.04	
TEST ANXIETY						$z =$
		CMG	.03	.36	.22	−1.20
		CML	−.23	−.03	−.13	1.56
	High	CLS	−.06	.41	.20	−.79
		CMD	.14	−.49*	−.22	.95
		CMV	.06	.32	.20	−1.25
					$z =$	
		CMG	.00	.14	−.73	
	Low	CML	−.04	.17	−1.10	
	+	CLS	−.03	.22	−1.32	
	High	CMD	.12	−.30*	2.23	
		CMV	−.01	.09	−.52	

manifests any relation with skill strategies. Greater extremity under low confidence is associated with the conservative "minimization of loss" strategy. Because we now know that extremity tends to increase as confidence declines in low test anxious–high defensive males, the association between extremity and strategy conservatism makes a great deal of sense. In sum, regardless of confidence level, greater extremity in the low test anxious–high defensive male is related to greater conservatism in decision making.

We have repeatedly stressed the image-maintenance and social approval aspects of defensiveness. With regard to the former, it is quite conceivable that uncertainty is so very difficult to tolerate for these subjects that its admission requires that particular compensatory mechanisms be set in motion. Such a conceptualization is consistent with the view that confidence and extremity reflect a desire for certainty (Brim, 1955; Brim & Hoff, 1957). However, Brim and Brim and Hoff maintained that confidence and extremity work in a supplementary fashion, and, accordingly, they multiplied the two components to obtain a total desire-for-certainty score. Our data, on the other hand, indicate that such an operation is unjustified in that it conceals the basic processes involved. The association

Table 57

CORRELATIONS FOR MALES BETWEEN SKILL STRATEGIES AND EXTREMITY UNDER LOW CONFIDENCE FOR PERSONALITY SUBGROUPS

			DEFENSIVENESS			
			Low	High	Low + High	
TEST ANXIETY	Low	SMG	.11	−.08	−.03	
		SML	.17	.35*	.30*	
		SLS	.18	.04	.07	
		SMD	−.32	−.01	−.13	
		SMV	.04	−.18	−.11	
						z =
	High	SMG	−.06	.13	.05	−.41
		SML	−.21	.10	−.05	1.84
		SLS	−.14	.16	.03	.21
		SMD	.33	−.05	.09	−1.14
		SMV	−.03	.10	.04	−.77
					z =	
	Low + High	SMG	.01	.01	.00	
		SML	−.02	.26*	−1.49	
		SLS	.02	.09	−.36	
		SMD	−.08	−.03	−.26	
		SMV	−.01	−.07	.31	

between extremity and confidence is dependent upon the confidence level at which extremity judgments are rendered and upon the motivational state of the subjects in question.

Notice further in Table 57 how the relationships for high test anxious subjects have declined relative to the data reported in Table 52. It is apparent that extremity under low confidence does not have the implication for skill strategy preferences that characterizes judgmental extremity under high confidence. In the sense that high confidence in one's judgments implies a measure of control, the discrepancies between the two forms of extremity may be of a systematic kind.

We turn next to a comparison of the results provided in Table 56 with the previously reported findings in Table 51. Note particularly how the highly test anxious and defensive males show up in Table 56. For these subjects, extremity under low confidence is associated with risk taking in a chance bet context, though only the "minimization of deviation from 1/2" strategy achieves significance. No such relationships emerge in Table 51, where extremity under high confidence is at issue. Indeed, the finding in Table 56 represents the first instance in which greater extremity is significantly related to greater risk taking in males. For highly test anxious and defensive subjects, then, estimating probabilities when quite uncertain of the "correct" answer apparently becomes imbued with a risk-taking flavor. The fact of a considerably higher correlation with chance than with skill strategies (Table 56 versus Table 57) is congruent in certain respects with the lack of effective control that low confidence implies. For the high-high male subgroup, greater deviation from a 50 in 100 probability judgment seems to have aspects in common with greater risk taking in a dice bet situation. Recall, furthermore, that this is the only male subgroup failing to manifest an inverse relationship between extremity under high confidence and over-all confidence. This fact may help to explain why the linkage with risk just described takes a reflective rather than counterphobic form.

Associations between extremity under low confidence and the two kinds of strategy indexes are reported for females in Tables 58 and 59. Again, the

Table 58

CORRELATIONS FOR FEMALES BETWEEN CHANCE STRATEGIES AND EXTREMITY UNDER LOW CONFIDENCE FOR PERSONALITY SUBGROUPS

			DEFENSIVENESS			
			Low	High	Low + High	
TEST ANXIETY	Low	CMG	−.44*	.07	−.27	
		CML	.37*	.03	.24	
		CLS	−.34	.21	−.18	
		CMD	.16	−.23	.01	
		CMV	−.49**	.12	−.26	
						$z =$
	High	CMG	−.13	.04	−.05	−1.12
		CML	.07	−.09	.01	1.16
		CLS	−.03	.06	.02	−.99
		CMD	.09	.08	.08	−.34
		CMV	−.06	.10	−.01	−1.26
					$z =$	
	Low + High	CMG	−.29*	.05	−1.72	
		CML	.24	−.03	1.35	
		CLS	−.19	.11	−1.49	
		CMD	.11	−.05	.79	
		CMV	−.29*	.10	−1.96	

discrepancy with the analogous male results is quite evident. For the female subjects, the significant r's occur in the low test anxious–low defensive subgroup. In contrast, male subjects in the corresponding moderator sub-

Table 59

CORRELATIONS FOR FEMALES BETWEEN SKILL STRATEGIES AND EXTREMITY
UNDER LOW CONFIDENCE FOR PERSONALITY SUBGROUPS

			DEFENSIVENESS			
			Low	High	Low + High	
TEST ANXIETY	Low	SMG	−.29	.13	−.12	
		SML	.45*	.28	.39**	
		SLS	−.18	.25	.00	
		SMD	.15	−.40	−.06	
		SMV	−.29	.01	−.17	
						$z =$
	High	SMG	.02	−.10	−.03	−.45
		SML	.00	−.03	.00	2.03
		SLS	.05	−.12	−.02	.10
		SMD	.10	.19	.12	−.89
		SMV	.03	−.10	−.02	−.75
					$z =$	
	Low + High	SMG	−.14	.01	−.74	
		SML	.24	.11	.66	
		SLS	−.06	.05	−.54	
		SMD	.11	−.05	.79	
		SMV	−.14	−.04	−.50	

group manifest a sharp differentiation between the cognitive-judgmental and decision-making domains.

Within the low test anxious–low defensive subgroup of females, extremity under low confidence is associated with a preference for conservative strategies in both a chance and skill context, but particularly in the former. A comparison of Tables 58 and 59 with their matched equivalents for extremity under high confidence — Tables 53 and 54 — indicates quite clearly that the two forms of extremity have distinctly different implications for risk taking in women. Under conditions of high confidence, extremity is associated with risk taking, though only in the presence of test anxiety or defensiveness. When confidence is low, on the other hand, extremity is linked with conservatism, but only in the absence of test anxiety and defensiveness.

Recall that low test anxious–low defensive women do not exhibit any association between extremity under high confidence and risk-taking indexes. This is the case despite the indication that these women make some use of a counterphobic or desire-for-certainty mechanism (going to extremes when highly confident, though generally lacking confidence). It therefore is evident that, for this "least disturbed" subgroup of females, the effect of a counterphobic mechanism on explicit risk-taking processes is attenuated when judgments are made with high confidence.

Turning to the case of judgment under low confidence, a very different set of conditions can be expected to prevail. The very fact of low confidence implies that the subject makes a judgment in the total or substantial absence of available knowledge. Under such conditions, extremity judgments, as we have seen in Tables 58 and 59, turn out to have distinct risk-taking implications. Why, however, do they assume the direction they do (an association between extremity and conservatism), and why particularly for women low in test anxiety and defensiveness? A most important piece of information in this regard is the correlation between high-confidence and low-confidence extremity judgments in the various female subgroups. It is only for the women low in test anxiety and defensiveness that this correlation is significant ($r = .45$, $p < .05$). The r's in the other three subgroups range from .07 to $-.16$. On the basis of these findings we must infer that, in the low test anxious–low defensive females, greater extremity of judgment per se, regardless of confidence level, is a reflection of uncertainty reduction (in other words, of a desire for certainty). Lesser extremity of judgment is correspondingly indicative of a greater tolerance for uncertainty. Consistent with expectations, we note that such tolerance is associated with a preference for risky strategies (Tables 58 and 59).

Why do not similar relationships occur in the other three subgroups of Tables 58 and 59? Is it not reasonable to suppose that all individuals are subject to a stronger or weaker desire for uncertainty reduction under low confidence conditions? The authors believe that the answers to these questions lie in the interaction of desire-for-certainty and "all-or-none" mechanisms. The relevance of the latter has already been considered in the case of extremity judgments rendered under high confidence. There is no a priori reason why this mechanism should cease to function when confidence declines. Because, however, the "all-or-none" principle operates in a direction opposite to that of uncertainty reduction, any relationships between judgment under low confidence and risk-taking indexes are bound to be attenuated. Accordingly, significant associations emerge only in the case of the low test anxious–low defensive females, because only one of the processes — uncertainty reduction — seems to be relevant for this subgroup.

No moderator effects are observed in the correlations between extremity under low confidence and the information-seeking measures. Similarly, the correlation of extremity with the final bet index is not affected by moderators in the female sample. Note, however, the correlational pattern in the male sample (Table 60). For high test anxious–low defensive males, there is a very substantial relationship between extremity under low confidence

Table 60

PARTIAL CORRELATIONS FOR MALES BETWEEN FINAL BET (PRIOR WINNINGS HELD CONSTANT) AND EXTREMITY UNDER LOW CONFIDENCE FOR PERSONALITY SUBGROUPS

	DEFENSIVENESS			
	Low	High	Low + High	
TEST ANXIETY — Low	.22	−.21	.04	
TEST ANXIETY — High	−.61**	−.28	−.38**	$z = 2.22$
Low + High	−.12	−.24	$z = .68$	

and the final bet variable, greater extremity being associated with a riskier final bet selection. The direction of the relationship is consistent with that between extremity under low confidence and chance strategies reported in Table 56. We find, however, that the relationships emerge in different moderator subgroups.

The pattern of results presented in Table 60 is especially impressive in the light of the findings reported in Table 18. The latter shows a significant r of .45 between winnings prior to final bet and conservatism of the final bet itself in males high in test anxiety and low in defensiveness. Now, we see that, holding the foregoing relationship constant, we can substantially improve our prediction of the final bet selection by taking account of judgmental extremity in a context of low confidence. For high test anxious–low defensive males, then, performance on a neutral probability estimation task has considerable predictive value for a highly involving decision-making situation in which monetary winnings are at stake. This finding reinforces the view that cognitive-judgmental behavior has genuine risk-taking implications for male subjects with distinctive patterns of motivational disturbance.

CATEGORY BREADTH

In the present section, we focus on relationships between scores derived from the Pettigrew (1958) category width test and the various decision-making indexes. Although two scores were derived from the Pettigrew instrument corresponding to that author's Factor 1 and 2 components, we shall in the present exposition concern ourselves exclusively with Factor 1. The authors found that Factor 2 is significantly correlated with mathematical aptitude, and ignored it for that reason.[1]

Consider first the correlations between category breadth and decision-making variables in the samples taken as a whole. For males, all correlations hover around 0. In contrast, females yield a significant set of relationships involving decision-making indexes derived from payoff contexts. Listed following are the correlations between category breadth and chance and skill strategies.

	Chance	Skill
Max. of gain	−.21*	−.25**
Min. of loss	.17	.23*
Long shot	−.19*	−.17
Min. dev. from 1/2	.16	.09
Max. of variance	−.18	−.25**

Further, a correlation coefficient of .26 ($p < .01$) is obtained between category breadth and number judgments, and of .24 ($p < .05$) between category breadth and clues.

The results reported here come as a bit of a surprise in the light of the conceptual assumptions and indirect empirical evidence tending to support the view that broader categorization has strategic implications indicative of a willingness to take greater risks. Our data run directly counter to this prevalent conception. Greater breadth of categorization in females is significantly associated with conservatism in most of the decision-making tasks employed in the study. Apparently, as far as female subjects are concerned, a preference for committing errors of exclusion reflects a form of conceptual risk taking that generalizes to more explicit risk-taking behavior.

Broad as opposed to narrow categorization, then, may really imply a

---

[1]Pettigrew (1958) reported that his Factor 1 score was significantly correlated with mathematical aptitude. The authors are quite puzzled by this discrepancy. Additional support for the authors' finding that it is Factor 2, not Factor 1, that is correlated with mathematical aptitude is available in an unpublished investigation by Messick and Kogan.

conservative approach. In the absence of information regarding the categories in the Pettigrew task, the conservative subject may decide to "blanket the field," for there is always the nagging possibility that at least one highly deviant case exists for almost all natural and man-made events. Such an interpretation receives considerable support from the inverse relationship existing between category breadth and confidence of judgment in females ($r = -.25$, $p < .01$). The broad categorizer tends to be less confident in judgments. In the presence of ambiguity and uncertainty, narrow categorization seems to entail greater risks from a strategic standpoint. A narrow categorizer may assume that the physical and organic environment is free of highly deviant occurrences, a risky assumption under conditions where but a single instance is required to violate it.

Although the female results run counter to prevalent conceptions regarding the strategic implications of breadth of categorization, indirect suggestive evidence has been available (Wallach, 1959) from which one might have inferred the direction of the relationships actually obtained in the present investigation. Recall the earlier discussion respecting the greater psychological value that subjects apparently attribute to inclusion as opposed to exclusion classes. Our female data tend to reinforce these earlier observations. Those subjects who find broad inclusion categories more comfortable are basically conservative in their decision-making orientations; they are maximizing the class of greater value, an approach that constitutes the lesser risk. A preference for large exclusion categories (and hence narrow inclusion categories), on the other hand, is associated with greater risk taking; here the class of greater value is minimized, an act that represents the higher risk.

We turn next to a consideration of moderator effects. None is observed in the male sample. For females, Tables 61 and 62 relate category width to chance and skill strategies, respectively. The effects reported above for the female sample as a whole seem to be concentrated in the low test anxious subgroups. Where chance strategies are concerned, the associations are of approximately equal strength in the low test anxious–low defensive and the low test anxious–high defensive subgroups, although slightly stronger in the latter (Table 61). The magnitudes of the relationships show a sharp divergence, however, when skill strategies are at issue (Table 62). In this case, relationships become nonsignificant in the subgroup low on both moderators, but increase markedly in the low test anxious–high defensive subgroup.

In order to explain the exceptionally high correlations in the low test anxiety–high defensiveness cell of Table 62, we find it necessary to introduce the confidence variable. The particular subgroup of females in question exhibits the highest and indeed the only significant relation between category width and judgmental confidence among the four female subgroups

Table 61

CORRELATIONS FOR FEMALES BETWEEN CHANCE STRATEGIES AND
CATEGORY WIDTH FOR PERSONALITY SUBGROUPS

DEFENSIVENESS

			Low	High	Low + High	
TEST ANXIETY	Low	CMG	−.35	−.43*	−.32*	
		CML	−.01	.26	.12	
		CLS	−.40*	−.42*	−.33*	
		CMD	.33	.27	.27	
		CMV	−.28	−.32	−.25	
						$z =$
	High	CMG	.06	−.17	−.08	−1.24
		CML	.02	.33	.22	−.51
		CLS	.06	−.10	−.04	−1.49
		CMD	−.09	.20	.06	1.07
		CMV	.06	−.20	−.10	−.77
					$z =$	
	Low + High	CMG	−.15	−.28*	.67	
		CML	.00	.28*	−1.42	
		CLS	−.18	−.22	.21	
		CMD	.11	.23	−.61	
		CMV	−.11	−.25	.72	

($r = -.44$, $p < .05$). The highly confident among this subgroup, then, keep their categories narrow, whereas their less confident counterparts are distinguished by a preference for broader categories. A directional implication is not intended, of course, for it is possible that preferred styles of categorization influence confidence levels. In general, these confidence data indicate that the mechanism engaged by the category width test may again be one of uncertainty reduction. This point suggests that the processes underlying performance for females on the Pettigrew instrument and on the probability estimation task under low general confidence may be quite similar.

This may be an appropriate juncture at which to consider further the conceptual status of category breadth as a cognitive construct. Our data suggest that the level of confidence with which a judgment is rendered may well influence the set of determinants of which that judgment is a function. On the whole, it probably is the case that category judgments on the Pettigrew instrument are made with relatively low levels of confidence by females. The issues with which the items deal, involving as they do estimations of quantities, magnitudes, and rates, are ones that possess less

Table 62

CORRELATIONS FOR FEMALES BETWEEN SKILL STRATEGIES AND
CATEGORY WIDTH FOR PERSONALITY SUBGROUPS

			DEFENSIVENESS			
			Low	High	Low + High	
TEST ANXIETY	Low	SMG	−.29	−.61**	−.45**	
		SML	.09	.51*	.31*	
		SLS	−.29	−.56**	−.42**	
		SMD	.20	.44*	.32*	
		SMV	−.24	−.62**	−.44**	
						$z =$
	High	SMG	−.17	.12	.01	−2.44
		SML	.12	.15	.14	.89
		SLS	−.12	.24	.11	−2.75
		SMD	.28	−.36	−.14	2.33
		SMV	−.14	.10	.00	−2.32
					$z =$	
	Low + High	SMG	−.23	−.28*	.27	
		SML	.10	.33*	−1.20	
		SLS	−.20	−.17	−.15	
		SMD	.23	.00	1.15	
		SMV	−.19	−.30*	.58	

familiarity for women than for men. With low confidence as a general baseline for the females' category width judgments, then, we find that broader categorizing is carried out by the less confident, narrower categorizing by the more confident females. This inverse direction of the category width–confidence relationship suggests that broader categorizing may be reflecting a desire for reduction of uncertainty. Individuals of lower confidence opt for errors of inclusion on the Pettigrew test, and also bias their probability judgments toward greater extremity on the extremity-confidence instrument. In the former case, we find that a desire for certainty favors an inclusion rather than an exclusion bias. On intuitive grounds, we may reason that an ideal way of reducing uncertainty is to make sure that every conceivable member of the category has been included. Possibly, the assignment to limbo implied by the failure to include a potential category instance is incompatible with the total accounting of category membership toward which a desire for certainty may be directed. As mentioned, the present direction of category width findings also is consistent with the implications of Wallach's (1959) work on classes defined by inclusion and exclusion.

When confidence on a particular task is high for females, another set of considerations may well prevail. Our expectation is that judgments made with high confidence by females will be less susceptible to uncertainty-reduction effects, and that other tendencies will then begin to exert their influence. Evidence supportive of this view has already been introduced, when we observed that females making more extreme judgments under high confidence conditions are more inclined toward risk taking (rather than toward conservatism) in bet strategy contexts.

While we may thus surmise that confidence level provides some leverage on predicting the operation of uncertainty-reduction tendencies in females, further and perhaps more general leverage (which also accounts for the male extremity data) is provided by reference to the presence or absence of an inverse relationship between judgmental extremity or category breadth, on the one hand, and general level of confidence on the other. When an inverse relationship obtains, the operation of an uncertainty-reduction mechanism is suggested, and we tend to find greater extremity of judgment and broader categorizing on the part of conservative individuals.

In the light of the results reported in this section, we are forced to reconsider the implications of the often-replicated finding that males exceed females in breadth of categorization on the Pettigrew test. Recall that no associations whatever are obtained in males between category width and explicit risk-taking indexes. On the other hand, female subjects generally (and certain subgroups in particular) manifest significant relationships between the two domains in question. We may conclude, therefore, that the Pettigrew test taps somewhat different dimensions in the two sexes — more strictly cognitive in males, more motivational in females. If this is indeed the case, sex differences on the test have little psychological meaning and most certainly do not reflect differential risk-taking proclivities in males and females.

Let us return briefly to Tables 61 and 62. Why do relationships emerge with such overwhelming clarity in low test anxious–high defensive females in the case of skill strategies in particular (Table 62)? We have already noted the significant negative association between confidence and category width in that subgroup, the only subgroup where such an association is significant. Hence, the characteristic strategy adopted in this subgroup with regard to errors of inclusion or exclusion is likely to reflect the extent of uncertainty tolerated: the more uncertainty tolerated, the greater is the willingness to commit errors of exclusion. The subject decides what the appropriate level ought to be, thereby exerting complete control over the level of risk assumed. The mechanisms of personal control are much stronger for skill than for chance strategies, hence linking the former somewhat more closely to the controls exerted in the category width context. Where chance strategies are at issue, on the other hand, control over outcomes declines, with the consequence of a drop in the magnitude of correlations in low test anxious–high defensive females and an increase in correlations in the subgroup low in test anxiety and defensiveness. Possibly, the latter regard their judgments on the category width test as something of a gamble, which may well be a realistic appraisal given the informational lack that the subjects must experience in coping with the test's items.

Moderator effects for the number judgments and clues tasks in relation to category width in women are less pronounced than those observed for strategy indexes. Yet, in both of the information-seeking procedures, the highest correlation coefficients are located in the cell containing the low test anxious–high defensive females ($r = .41$, $p < .06$ for number judgments; $r = .42$, $p < .05$ for clues). The r's in the remaining three cells range from .11 to .36 for number judgments and from .10 to .23 for clues. Note that category breadth is associated with the demand for more information before decisional commitment. The broader categorizer, in other words, prefers the greater certainty of a small prize to the uncertainty of a larger one. Although the moderator differences may not be substantial, the results are quite consistent with those reported in Tables 61 and 62, and thereby offer still further support for an uncertainty-reduction interpretation of the phenomenon that has been called breadth of categorization.

EXTREMITY OF SELF-RATING

Evidence has been available (Peabody, 1962) that the extremity of response on attitude inventories employing the Likert-type format is quite independent of the item content of such inventories. Further support for this generalization is given in the data of the present investigation. For the male sample, none of the correlations between extremity of self-rating and the various personality scales achieves statistical significance. In the sample of females, but two of the eleven scales correlate significantly with extremity of self-rating — the Edwards Social Desirability Scale ($r = -.21$, $p < .05$) and the Self-sufficiency Scale from the Personality Research Inventory ($r = .20$, $p < .05$). Women who rate themselves more extremely, then, tend to respond in the undesirable and self-sufficient direction on the respective scales. These relationships suggest that extremity of self-rating may not be entirely independent of item content in the personality realm for females. It should be noted that Peabody's work was based largely on attitude and value items worded in the third person. When first-person personality items are used, it appears that significant low-level content-style interactions may occur, at least in the case of females. This finding does not constitute a serious problem from our standpoint, and indeed, these effects may help clarify the psychological meaning of extremity of self-rating as a judgmental response style. The fact remains, however, that extremity of self-rating stands relatively independent of item content in our research.

A further consideration with regard to extremity of self-rating concerns the extent to which it is independent of over-all confidence. Is it conceivable that the use of extreme categories on a personality inventory reflects a form of conviction or confidence respecting the self-descriptive appropriateness of the various items, and that, in turn, this form of self-referent confidence is part of a more inclusive confidence syndrome? Our data lend no support whatever to this conceptualization. Correlations between extremity of self-rating and both forms of confidence (indexes derived from the confidence-extremity questionnaire and from the number judgments procedure) are uniformly nonsignificant. Furthermore, there is no evidence of a moderator effect in the present case. If extremity of self-rating is reflecting a form of self-confidence, then, such confidence is of a different order from that derived by means of judgments about external events.

Let us now proceed to the examination of relationships between extremity of self-rating and decision making. For the male sample, all correlations are nonsignificant. In contrast, the females yield the following relationships for chance and skill strategies.

	Chance	Skill
Max. of gain	.18	.20*
Min. of loss	−.01	−.05
Long shot	.21*	.21*
Min. dev. from 1/2	−.24*	−.27**
Max. of variance	.14	.17

Those women who use more extreme alternatives in rating themselves show a clear trend toward greater risk taking in both chance and skill contexts. Endorsing less extreme alternatives on the personality inventory employed is associated with greater conservatism. It is evident, then, that extremity of self-rating in women constitutes a judgmental response style with clear implications for risk taking. Recall that extremity of self-rating is associated negatively with social desirability and positively with self-sufficiency. If the endorsement of socially undesirable statements is viewed as relevant to unconventionality, it is possible that the latter, in association with self-sufficiency (the antithesis of a "sweet femininity" syndrome), is at the basis of or at least a contributor to the extremity–risk-taking relationship.

Note, finally, that extremity of self-rating is not related to the choice dilemmas, information-seeking, and final bet variables in females.

Turning to moderator influences, we can report that few effects are observed in the male sample. The only significant correlations emerge in the high test anxious–low defensive subgroup, where extremity of self-rating is positively related to the "minimization of deviation from 1/2" strategy under both chance ($r = .38$, $p < .05$) and skill ($r = .41$, $p < .05$) conditions. The r's for that strategy in the remaining three male subgroups range from $-.08$ to $.19$ for the chance condition and from $-.19$ to $.16$ for the skill condition. Highly test anxious males who are low in defensiveness, then, seem inclined toward a conservative or middle-of-the-road strategy, if they rate themselves extremely. Such extremity of rating in test anxious males with poor defensive structures may well represent an attempt to shore up and repair a less than satisfactory self-image. Once again, then, an interpretation in terms of counterphobic mechanisms seems called for.

We turn next to the female subjects. Table 63 reports the moderator relationship between extremity of self-rating and the choice dilemmas questionnaire. Although both marginal z's are significant, it is in large part the correlation for low test anxious–low defensive women that is responsible

Table 63

CORRELATIONS FOR FEMALES BETWEEN CHOICE DILEMMAS AND EXTREMITY OF SELF-RATING FOR PERSONALITY SUBGROUPS

		DEFENSIVENESS			
		Low	High	Low + High	
TEST ANXIETY	Low	$-.48**$	$.12$	$-.23$	$z = -1.94$
	High	$.03$	$.22$	$.16$	
	Low + High	$-.29*$	$.15$	$z = -2.22$	

for these effects. Greater extremity of self-rating in this subgroup of females is associated with the recommendation of a more risky course of action in the choice dilemmas procedure. The correlations in the other three subgroups are of negligible magnitude. Test anxiety and/or defensiveness quite clearly represents motivational conditions that serve to block the manifestation of a relationship between the particular variables under consideration. Where an association does emerge between a judgmental and an explicit risk-taking measure in the present instance, it assumes the reflective rather than the counterphobic form and emerges in the subgroup distinguished by the lowest level of motivational disturbance.

Turning to decision making under payoff conditions, we find that moderator effects prove to be quite weak in the case of chance strategies. The one finding worthy of note concerns the correlation between extremity of self-rating and minimization of loss for low ($r = -.24$) and high ($r = .20$) test anxious females. Although neither r achieves significance in its own right, the difference between them yields a z of 2.21 ($p < .05$). Extremity of self-rating appears to have antithetical effects on preference for a "minimization of loss" strategy in women, depending upon level of test anxiety. Again, the relationship appears to be reflective under low test anxiety, counterphobic under high test anxiety.

For skill strategies, the effects are more pronounced, as Table 64 demonstrates. A direct relationship between extremity of self-rating and choice of risky skill strategies distinguishes the women low in test anxiety. Their

Table 64

CORRELATIONS FOR FEMALES BETWEEN SKILL STRATEGIES AND EXTREMITY OF SELF-RATING FOR PERSONALITY SUBGROUPS

DEFENSIVENESS

			Low	High	Low + High	
TEST ANXIETY	Low	SMG	.36	.31	.32*	
		SML	−.17	−.23	−.20	
		SLS	.38*	.36	.36**	
		SMD	−.38*	−.26	−.32*	
		SMV	.32	.27	.29*	
						$z =$
	High	SMG	−.12	.20	.05	1.39
		SML	.22	−.17	.05	−1.24
		SLS	−.10	.14	.06	1.56
		SMD	−.09	−.26	−.21	−.58
		SMV	−.15	.20	.04	1.27
					$z =$	
	Low + High	SMG	.14	.26	−.62	
		SML	.06	−.19	1.24	
		SLS	.18	.24	−.31	
		SMD	−.28*	−.25	−.16	
		SMV	.10	.24	−.71	

high test anxious counterparts, on the other hand, yield no relationships whatever between the domains in question.

In the case of both chance and skill strategies, then, there is suggestive evidence that the emergence of a direct, reflective relationship between extremity of self-rating and risk taking requires that test anxiety be at a low level. Note in Table 64 that the presence of high defensiveness (when test anxiety is low) does not especially inhibit the reflective function of extremity of self-rating with respect to strategy preference. That such a function is not found in the hypothetical decision-making case (Table 63) is not overly surprising, given the earlier evidence pointing to the special forces that seem to be at work in low test anxious–high defensive subjects when decisions are couched in the form of advice to a protagonist. No such considerations enter into the dice and skill bet procedures, of course. Note, finally, that the information-seeking and final bet variables are not susceptible to moderator effects in the present case.

SUMMARY

The present chapter has endeavored to shed detailed empirical light on the general hypothesis that certain cognitive-judgmental processes (for example, categorization behavior) involve considerations of strategy and risk taking. Our findings indicate that there is a very substantial basis to the hypothesis, though the empirical relationships are of a complex order and often contrary to various speculative assertions that have gained currency in the psychological literature. The complexity stems largely from the evidence that the various cognitive-judgmental indexes — confidence, extremity, category width — do not behave in identical ways when impinging upon the area of decision making. To complicate the issue further, sex differences are almost always present, though it is rare that inconsistencies are found when all relevant empirical information is taken into account.

Two fundamental questions concerned us in the present chapter. First, would the introduction of monetary risks and payoffs into the decision-making realm bring about empirical relationships with cognitive-judgmental measures, where almost no such relationships had been found before? Second, was it possible that the pattern of prior negative results could be attributed to the general neglect of key moderator variables? On the basis of the evidence offered in the present chapter, both questions can be given an affirmative answer. The employment of decision-making procedures having real outcomes does make a difference; associations between cognitive-judgmental and decision-making variables are moderated by test anxiety and defensiveness.

With respect to relationships in the samples as a whole between cognitive-judgmental indexes and decision making under payoff conditions, a strong sex difference is obtained. Without exception, significant relationships are confined to the female sample. Associated with risk taking in a strategy context are confidence of judgment, extremity under high confidence (associated with final bet only), narrow category width, and extremity of self-rating. Somewhat surprising is the direction of the relationship between risk taking and category width, given prevalent conceptions in the literature regarding the latter.

The uniformly nonsignificant pattern of results in the male sample changes radically when moderator effects are taken into account. Such effects are also quite substantial in the female sample. The direction of moderator influences, however, is dissimilar for males and females, thereby complicating the problem of interpretation. It is quite evident that the psychological meaning of various cognitive-judgmental processes is sex-linked.

Considering first confidence of judgment, there is an inverse relationship between confidence and risk taking in low test anxious–low defensive males, a direct relationship in low test anxious–highly defensive males. The former can in part be ascribed to a desire-for-certainty mechanism with its evident implications for conservatism. The latter is attributed to the fact that confidence in a context of image-maintenance needs has phenomenological risk-taking properties. An examination of moderator relationships for females provides results that are only partially congruent with the male data. Again, a direct relationship is manifested between confidence and risk taking in low test anxious–high defensive subjects, though the high test anxious and defensive females now share in the relationship. The inverse relationship characteristic of males low on both moderators is not found in the females. Quite clear and consistent for both sexes, however, is the extent to which defensiveness enhances a direct association between confidence and risk taking. The direction of this moderator effect is attributed to the introspective character of the confidence variable. For subjects who are preoccupied with matters of self-evaluation (high defensives), confidence can be expected to have certain distinctive connotations that bear upon the risk-conservatism dimension.

Two kinds of judgmental extremity are derived — extremity under conditions of high confidence and low confidence. In the chapter, we considered first the variable of extremity under high confidence. For males, this form of extremity is inversely related to risk taking in the presence of defensiveness or test anxiety. This unexpected result can be explained on the basis of substantial negative relationships between extremity under high confidence and over-all confidence. In brief, extremity under high confidence seems to involve counterphobic mechanisms in test anxious and/or defensive males. Evidence of such counterphobic mechanisms is notably absent in low test anxious–low defensive males, a finding congruent with theoretical expectations to the effect that these mechanisms come into play under conditions of motivational disturbance.

A different set of results prevails for females. Test anxiety and defensiveness contribute to a direct, reflective relation between extremity under high confidence and risk taking. The inverse relation between extremity under high confidence and over-all confidence, so indicative of overcompensatory or counterphobic mechanisms in males, does not appear in the motivationally disturbed groups of females. We may account for the female data in terms of an "all-or-none" principle in probability estimations. Greater subjective safety may lie in judgments that do not approach the 0 in 100 or 100 in 100 extremes too closely, because complete certainty of occurrence or nonoccurrence is quite uncharacteristic of most human events.

Although relationships between extremity under high confidence and risk taking are of the counterphobic type in males and of the reflective sort in females, the presence of test anxiety and/or defensiveness is essential for the emergence of significant associations of either form in the present context.

Judgmental extremity under low confidence concerned us next. The over-compensatory inverse relationship between over-all confidence and extremity so characteristic of high-confidence extremity in males, now appears only in the low test anxious–high defensive subgroup. Consistent with this observation, low-confidence extremity is again inversely associated with risk taking in that particular subgroup. For low test anxious–high defensive males, then, counterphobic mechanisms seem to be operative regardless of confidence level. A further finding of interest in the present context is the direct, reflective relation between extremity under low confidence and risk taking (chance strategies) in highly test anxious and defensive males. For these subjects, the link between extremity and risk taking is not a matter of overcompensation, but rather derives from other psychological processes.

Again, the female subjects yield a pattern of results that bears little similarity to the corresponding data for males. Significant associations appear only in the least disturbed females, extremity under low confidence now being related to greater strategy conservatism. We can account for these results in terms of uncertainty-reduction mechanisms unique to the low test anxious–low defensive subgroup.

In general, our findings tend to indicate that an inverse relationship between judgmental extremity and risk taking obtains when extremity is linked with low over-all confidence, suggesting that extremity under these conditions expresses an attempt to reduce uncertainty in a basically uncertain individual (operation of the "desire-for-certainty" principle). On the other hand, a direct relationship between judgmental extremity and risk taking tends to be found when extremity has no connection with over-all confidence level, suggesting that sensitivity to the greater error potential of extreme judgments (operation of the "all-or-none" principle) comes to the fore only if extremity does not possess an uncertainty-reduction significance.

Moderator effects for category breadth are confined to female subjects.

Relationships are most pronounced in low test anxious–defensive females, broader category width being associated with greater conservatism. The observation that confidence and category width are inversely related in that subgroup leads us to the conclusion that the psychological process underlying category breadth is uncertainty reduction. This finding is consistent with earlier evidence to the effect that inclusion classes possess greater psychological value than exclusion classes. A preference for errors of inclusion (in other words, broader categories) rather than errors of exclusion (in other words, narrower categories) hence constitutes the conservative course. Inclusion implies greater certainty of class membership than does exclusion.

Finally, there is a strong indication that the extremity with which an individual describes himself bears some relation to the kind of decision-maker he is in hypothetical and payoff contexts. For female subjects, a disposition toward extremity of self-rating (which is associated in their case with unconventionality and self-sufficiency) contributes to a preference for risk taking in low test anxious individuals. When the level of test anxiety is increased, however, the relationship is markedly attenuated. For the males, significant associations assume the form of an inverse relation between extremity of self-rating and risk taking in high test anxious–low defensive subjects. Thus, in the case of extremity of self-rating, a reflective relation with risk taking emerges under conditions of low disturbance, whereas a counterphobic relation with risk taking is found in a context of high disturbance.

7

Personality Correlates of Decision Making

RELATIONSHIPS FOR SAMPLES AS A WHOLE

In the first chapter, a number of hypotheses were advanced concerning over-all associations between personality dispositions and decision making. The authors predicted that risk taking would be positively related to impulsiveness, negatively related to manifest anxiety and rigidity, and curvilinearly associated with self-sufficiency and independence. In this last instance, the authors expected that self-sufficient and independent persons would prefer intermediate risk levels.

The fit between hypotheses and empirical findings can be estimated from the correlations reported for males and females in Tables 65 and 66, respectively. Consider first the evidence with regard to the predicted positive association between risk taking and impulsiveness. As the first column in both tables shows, the hypothesis clearly is not confirmed; none of the correlations achieves statistical significance.

Turning to self-sufficiency and independence, we find that there is no evidence in support of the curvilinear hypothesis. Confirmation of the hypothesis would have required that a strategy of "minimization of deviation from 1/2" yield significant positive associations with the two personality variables in question. Recall, however, that the 50 : 50 probability is biased in the conservative direction (see Footnote 1, Chapter 5). This bias may conceivably contribute to the nonconfirmation of the hypothesis. Somewhat contrary to expectations, there are indications in the data of linear relationships between self-sufficiency and independence, on the one hand, and the various decision-making measures on the other. Thus, in the case of self-sufficiency, there is a trend for males in which self-sufficiency is *inversely* associated with a preference for more risky skill strategies.

Table 65
INTERCORRELATIONS BETWEEN PERSONALITY AND DECISION-MAKING VARIABLES FOR MALES

	Content Scales			Manifest		Style Scales	
	Impulsiveness	Self-sufficiency	Independence	Anxiety	Rigidity	Social Desirability	Acquiescence
Choice dilemmas	−.05	−.16	−.12	−.05	.26**	.08	−.15
Chance–max. of gain	.13	−.05	.08	−.19*	−.13	.12	−.06
Chance–min. of loss	−.15	−.01	−.02	.14	.11	−.13	.06
Chance–long shot	.12	−.08	.10	−.15	−.12	.07	−.05
Chance–min. dev. from 1/2	−.06	.02	−.16	.13	.10	−.05	.10
Chance–max. of variance	.16	−.04	.06	−.19*	−.13	.13	−.07
Skill–max. of gain	.02	−.18	−.06	−.18	.02	.17	−.07
Skill–min. of loss	−.09	.05	.02	.18	.05	−.12	.04
Skill–long shot	−.01	−.21*	−.08	−.13	.03	.12	−.07
Skill–min. dev. from 1/2	.02	.16	.01	.13	−.07	−.09	.03
Skill–max. of variance	.05	−.18	−.05	−.19*	.00	.16	−.09
Number judgments	.05	−.02	.20*	−.16	−.13	.20*	−.07
Clues	.02	.01	−.06	−.06	.06	.06	−.12
Final bet	−.08	−.04	−.15	.11	−.05	−.09	.09

Relationships for Samples as a Whole | **161**

Table 66

INTERCORRELATIONS BETWEEN PERSONALITY AND DECISION-MAKING VARIABLES FOR FEMALES

	Content Scales			Manifest		Style Scales	
	Impulsiveness	Self-sufficiency	Independence	Anxiety	Rigidity	Social Desirability	Acquiescence
Choice dilemmas	−.11	−.27**	−.42**	−.09	.26**	.07	−.16
Chance–max. of gain	.07	.05	.22*	−.07	−.20*	.04	.15
Chance–min. of loss	.06	−.04	.04	.13	.02	−.05	−.02
Chance–long shot	.13	.05	.28**	−.02	−.19*	.03	.17
Chance–min. dev. from 1/2	−.04	−.14	−.19*	.11	.11	−.04	−.09
Chance–max. of variance	.03	.02	.16	−.08	−.15	.03	.14
Skill–max. of gain	.01	.01	.11	−.04	−.07	.03	.16
Skill–min. of loss	−.11	.03	−.07	.03	.12	.02	−.19*
Skill–long shot	−.01	.03	.11	−.02	−.07	.03	.13
Skill–min. dev. from 1/2	.06	−.06	−.17	−.02	.15	−.04	−.10
Skill–max. of variance	.04	.01	.12	−.07	−.08	.05	.16
Number judgments	−.12	−.02	−.05	−.01	.10	.02	−.11
Clues	−.13	.00	−.03	−.01	.20*	−.07	−.12
Final bet	.07	−.06	−.03	.18	.04	−.12	.03

For females, on the other hand, self-sufficiency is directly related to greater risk taking on choice dilemmas. Turning to independence, we note that this personality variable is related to greater conservatism in the number judgments task for males and to greater risk taking in choice dilemmas and chance strategies for females.

It is quite evident that, with the exception of relationships with choice dilemmas in females, the self-sufficiency and independence scales do not bear upon the decision-making domain in the same manner. Further, the scales have different consequences for risk taking in males and females. Note in this connection that the r between the scales is $-.01$ for males and $.35$ ($p < .01$) for females. The self-sufficiency measure employed was derived on the basis of a priori content, whereas the independence items were selected for their capacity to discriminate between independents and yielders in an Asch-type (1952) conformity situation. The latter items possess a strong component of conventionality-unconventionality. It may well be this component that is responsible for the absence of any association between independence and self-sufficiency in males. Unconventionality and self-sufficiency apparently have a greater bearing upon one another in female subjects, and both in turn seem to contribute to greater risk taking. In contrast, the associations emerging in the male sample, although quite weak, suggest that self-sufficiency and independence may enhance conservatism in decision making.

We turn next to manifest anxiety and rigidity, both of which were expected to relate to conservatism. It is in this instance that the hypotheses regarding direct personality correlates of decision making receive their most positive support, though the absolute magnitude of the correlations is quite low and differential effects obtain across sex. Thus, manifest anxiety is related to conservatism of strategy preferences in males only, whereas rigidity yields a much more pervasive pattern of relationships with conservatism in females than in males. It is only the choice dilemmas task that is associated with rigidity in the male sample as a whole. Note further that this particular significant relationship represents the only such consistency across sex in Tables 65 and 66.

Consider finally the two scales of response style — social desirability and acquiescence. It can be noted that there are but two correlations achieving significance, both at the .05 level. This finding serves to strengthen the content basis of the few significant relationships observed in Tables 65 and 66. Given the extremely high negative r between manifest anxiety and social desirability ($r = -.81$, $p < .001$ for males), it is particularly noteworthy that the associations with risk taking in Table 65 appear to be somewhat stronger for manifest anxiety than for social desirability. Where acquiescence is concerned, we observe an inverse relation with a preference for a "minimization of loss" strategy in females' skill bets, though the r is of borderline significance. The Couch-Keniston acquiescence items have a distinct "impulsiveness" flavor (as contrasted with a tendency toward impulse control), and hence, this connotation may be contributing to the relationship in question. Recall that the authors predicted a direct association between risk taking and impulsiveness, though the authors failed to achieve empirical confirmation when using the Barratt impulsiveness scale. Possibly, for the particular sample of females employed in the present investigation, the Couch-Keniston scale is superior to the Barratt scale in tapping that aspect of impulsiveness bearing upon risk-taking behavior.

In sum, consistent with results presented in previous chapters, correlations observed in the male and female samples as a whole tend to be of low magnitude, though occasionally reaching statistical significance. But if past experience is an effective guide in these matters, there is every reason to doubt that the correlations reported in Tables 65 and 66 are revealing of the entire story with regard to personality correlates of decision-making behavior. In the light of the impressive evidence concerning moderator effects when we examine relationships in the decision-making and post-decisional domains and when we relate decision-making to intellective ability and cognitive-judgmental variables, we find that it is clearly incumbent upon us to explore the possibility that the impact of personality upon decision making may also be subject to moderator influences. Recall in this connection the statement in Chapter 1, where we warned that the personality variables under investigation might be strongly associated with the moderators themselves. Because the latter — test anxiety and defensiveness — are measured by the same type of personality inventory that is used for the other personality dispositions under investigation, the likelihood arises that the moderators and these other personality variables are empirically associated, if only as a consequence of shared method or instrument variance. This association would, of course, introduce a problem of restriction of range, thereby reducing the probability of obtaining moderator effects of any consequence. Accordingly, the authors will eliminate from consideration in further moderator analyses those personality variables that are significantly correlated (5 percent level or better) with one or both of the moderators. Using this criterion, the authors exclude manifest anxiety, social desirability, and acquiescence. In addition, rigidity is excluded from the male sample on the grounds of a significant association with defensiveness. No such dependency occurs in the female sample.

It should be noted that the personality scales included in the moderator analysis are not entirely independent of one another in either the male or female samples. In the males, impulsiveness and independence are related ($r = .27$, $p < .01$). The females yield an even larger number of significant linkages. Earlier, we observed an r of .35 ($p < .01$) between self-sufficiency and independence. In addition, independence is related to impulsiveness ($r = .28$, $p < .01$) and to rigidity ($r = -.41$, $p < .01$). The former correlation is consistent with the male data. Finally, rigidity and impulsiveness are inversely associated ($r = -.36$, $p < .01$). Although these correlations point to the presence of experimental dependencies, their magnitude is sufficiently low to suggest that a considerable portion of each scale's variance remains unshared with that of the others. We turn now to the results of major interest — moderator effects in relations between impulsiveness, self-sufficiency, independence, and rigidity (females), on the one hand, and the various risk-taking indexes on the other.

EXAMINATION OF MODERATOR EFFECTS

Impulsiveness

Recall that in Tables 65 and 66 impulsiveness is not related to any of the decision-making variables. What happens when a moderator analysis is applied? Consider first the results for males. Although choice dilemmas — the hypothetical decision task — remains immune to moderator effects, such is not the case in monetary payoff contexts. As Tables 67 and 68 indicate, moderator effects emerge for males under these conditions. For both chance and skill strategies, impulsiveness is associated with greater risk taking only in the case of the subgroup low in both test anxiety and defensiveness.

These findings point to the possibility that some personality characteristics, impulsiveness among them, may influence risk taking only under those conditions where sources of motivational disturbance are at a minimum. The distinctive psychodynamics of test anxiety and defensiveness exert fairly powerful effects upon decision-making behavior, as we have seen, and these in turn may well obscure influences stemming from certain other personality sources.

Beginning with Chapter 3 and at various points thereafter, we have emphasized the situationally determined character shown by the decision-making behavior of the subgroup lowest in motivational disturbance. How do we reconcile this observation with the data of Tables 67 and 68? First, it must be noted that individual differences in the subgroup in question, as reflected in distribution variances, are approximately of the same magnitude as those observed in other subgroups. Hence, low test anxious–low defensive individuals may be quite similar, in other words, homogeneous, in the sense that their decision-making behavior reflects situational variation — and nevertheless be quite heterogeneous in terms of the direction their decision-making behavior takes in different task contexts. Thus, subject A may be more conservative on choice dilemmas than he is on number

Table 67

CORRELATIONS FOR MALES BETWEEN CHANCE STRATEGIES AND
IMPULSIVENESS FOR PERSONALITY SUBGROUPS

DEFENSIVENESS

			Low	High	Low + High	
		CMG	.43*	−.07	.16	
		CML	−.36*	.08	−.12	
	Low	CLS	.36*	−.03	.16	
		CMD	−.21	.09	−.06	
		CMV	.45*	−.08	.17	
TEST ANXIETY						$z =$
		CMG	−.02	.27	.13	.15
		CML	−.31	−.21	−.25	.67
	High	CLS	−.07	.25	.10	.31
		CMD	.02	−.16	−.07	.05
		CMV	.15	.28	.21	−.21
					$z =$	
		CMG	.20	.08	.62	
	Low + High	CML	−.29*	−.02	−1.40	
		CLS	.14	.11	.16	
		CMD	−.08	−.03	−.26	
		CMV	.26*	.07	.99	

judgments. For subject B, the relation may be in the reverse direction. Subject C may show a high degree of consistency on both. If all these various types are represented in the low test anxious–low defensive subgroup in reasonably equal numbers, the net effect, of course, is a negligible correlation coefficient. Yet this kind of situational specificity does not rule out the possibility that each specific situation may have its particular correlates — ability, cognitive-judgmental, and personality.

In the present instance, it is the strategy preference indexes that relate to impulsiveness. Both chance and skill strategies are engaged, reflecting the procedural similarities between them. Note that impulsiveness yields no moderated relationships in the "least disturbed" male subgroup with choice dilemmas, information-seeking, or the final bet index. As we shall later note, these other decision-making indexes have their own distinctive correlates. We are then led to the conclusion that various decision-making tasks, depending on their nature, may engage certain distinctive personality characteristics when powerful motivational forces are not present to disrupt such effects.

Sex differences distinguish relationships, consistent with results pre-

Table 68

CORRELATIONS FOR MALES BETWEEN SKILL STRATEGIES AND
IMPULSIVENESS FOR PERSONALITY SUBGROUPS

DEFENSIVENESS

			Low	High	Low + High	
TEST ANXIETY	Low	SMG	.38*	−.18	.05	
		SML	−.29	.09	−.04	
		SLS	.32	−.20	.03	
		SMD	−.28	.23	−.01	
		SMV	.38*	−.16	.05	
						$z =$
	High	SMG	.01	−.01	.00	.26
		SML	−.13	−.16	−.13	.46
		SLS	−.01	−.06	−.03	.31
		SMD	−.06	.18	.08	−.46
		SMV	.04	.07	.05	.00
				$z =$		
Low + High		SMG	.17	−.09	1.35	
		SML	−.19	−.03	−.83	
		SLS	.13	−.12	1.30	
		SMD	−.19	.20	−2.03	
		SMV	.19	−.05	1.25	

sented in earlier chapters, between personality and decision making. Note in Table 69 that, unlike the findings for males, these findings indicate that the association between impulsiveness and the choice dilemmas procedure does show a marked moderator effect. High test anxious–low defensive females, in particular, exhibit a direct relation between impulsiveness and risk taking under hypothetical conditions. A trend in the same direction is found among female subjects who are high in defensiveness but low in test anxiety. It thus is apparent that impulsiveness has quite different implications for decision making in males and females. Whereas the characteristic in males becomes linked with decision making under conditions of minimal motivational disturbance, impulsiveness in females — as we have noted thus far — becomes engaged with decision making under particular circumstances of motivational disturbance. In the latter case, impulsiveness can no longer be expected to possess the same psychological qualities that it has when it characterizes members of the "least disturbed" subgroup. That is, we can expect impulsiveness to relate differently to risk taking when impulsiveness is added to an already "disturbed" motivational context than when impulsiveness operates in the absence of such

Table 69

CORRELATIONS FOR FEMALES BETWEEN CHOICE DILEMMAS AND
IMPULSIVENESS FOR PERSONALITY SUBGROUPS

DEFENSIVENESS

		Low	High	Low + High	
TEST ANXIETY	Low	−.02	−.35	−.14	$z = -.25$
	High	−.45*	.19	−.09	
	Low + High	−.23	.04	−1.33	$z = $

disturbance. When added to another source of motivational disturbance, impulsiveness may, for example, indicate "acting out" or counterphobic qualities that can lead to extreme behavior in *either* a risky *or* a conservative direction.

Such an interpretation receives some support in Table 70, where impulsiveness is related to skill strategies. No moderator effects are observed in the case of chance strategies. Note in Table 70 how the relationship between risk taking and impulsiveness ceases to hold for the female subgroup high in test anxiety and low in defensiveness. Further, consider the inverse relationship between risk taking and impulsiveness that now emerges in the high defensive–low test anxious subjects. Where real payoffs are at issue in a context of personal control over outcomes, impulsive females who are highly defensive and low in test anxiety reverse their decision-making pattern (in other words, become conservative) relative to choices rendered in a hypothetical decision context.

Although the correlations do not quite achieve statistical significance, the pattern of a link between impulsiveness and conservatism is maintained in the final bet situation (Table 71), with the additional feature that the high test anxious–low defensive females also exhibit the effect. Note that these females, when impulsive, tend to be more conservative in the final bet task, but are greater risk-takers — as you recall — in the hypothetical decision situation. Thus, impulsiveness in the presence of test anxiety *or*

Table 70

CORRELATIONS FOR FEMALES BETWEEN SKILL STRATEGIES AND IMPULSIVENESS FOR PERSONALITY SUBGROUPS

DEFENSIVENESS

			Low	High	Low + High	
TEST ANXIETY	Low	SMG	.21	−.37	−.02	
		SML	−.34	.08	−.20	
		SLS	.13	−.40	−.07	
		SMD	.12	.46*	.24	
		SMV	.30	−.35	.05	
						$z =$
	High	SMG	.15	−.04	.04	−.30
		SML	−.09	.00	−.02	−.89
		SLS	.14	−.03	.05	−.59
		SMD	−.31	.06	−.09	1.62
		SMV	.16	−.07	.02	.15
					$z =$	
	Low + High	SMG	.18	−.18	1.77	
		SML	−.20	.02	−1.08	
		SLS	.14	−.16	1.48	
		SMD	−.07	.19	−1.28	
		SMV	.23	−.18	2.02	

defensiveness appears to polarize decisions, orienting them toward either risk taking or conservatism as the decision context is altered in its payoff characteristics (in other words, when payoffs change from hypothetical to real). In many respects, the process is suggestive of the identity of opposites that characterizes reaction formation in the psychoanalytic framework. Risk and conservatism can stand side by side in the same personality, representing an exaggerated bipolarity in responding to shifting situational contexts. These violent swings from conservatism to risk taking as a function of impulsiveness in test anxious *or* defensive females may account for the low level of generality across decision-making contexts displayed by these subjects. The latter stand in sharp contrast to highly test anxious *and* defensive subjects, who, it will be recalled, are especially prone to consistency of risk-conservatism in diverse decision situations. The exaggerated bipolarity described can also be contrasted with the greater situational specificity that distinguishes the low test anxious–low defensive females, who show intermediate degrees of generality based on structural similarities between decision tasks.

Further evidence in favor of the interpretation offered here is available

Table 71

PARTIAL CORRELATIONS FOR FEMALES BETWEEN FINAL BET (PRIOR WINNINGS HELD CONSTANT) AND IMPULSIVENESS FOR PERSONALITY SUBGROUPS

		DEFENSIVENESS			
		Low	High	Low + High	
TEST ANXIETY	Low	−.40*	.37	−.14	$z = -1.53$
	High	.35	.06	.17	
	Low + High	.00	.10	−.49	$z = -.49$

in the final bet procedure for the "least disturbed" female subgroup. It can be seen in Table 71 that the low test anxious–low defensive females yield a direct association between impulsiveness and risk taking in the final bet situation. Hence, the kind of relationship that emerges in males in strategy contexts (Tables 67 and 68) becomes manifest in females only in the case of the final bet decision. Again, we note the element of specificity — the association is confined to a single decision index. When the relationship does emerge in the "least disturbed" female subgroup, its direction parallels that found in the "least disturbed" male subgroup. In short, the function that impulsiveness serves with regard to risk taking depends upon the personality or motivational structure in which it is embedded.

A final point must be made regarding this significant association between impulsiveness and riskiness of final bet in the low test anxious–low defensive subgroup (Table 71). Recall that these women, as well as their low test anxious–high defensive counterparts, choose a final bet that is in part based upon prior winnings accumulated. The results reported in Table 71 indicate that the variable of impulsiveness also contributes substantially to the final bet decision. Yet the contribution is in opposite directions for the low and high defensive subjects within the subgroup low in test anxiety. The direction of the relationship in the low defensives is a reflective one. In the high defensives, on the other hand, the direction of the relationship (relative to that in Table 69, showing hypothetical payoffs) seems to indicate that impulsiveness is in the service of reaction formation or some related defensive process.

Self-sufficiency

Recall that the authors' initial hypothesis with regard to the influence of self-sufficiency on risk taking was a curvilinear one. No evidence in support of this hypothesis is found in either the male or female sample as a whole. If anything, a tendency toward an inverse association between self-sufficiency and a preference for more risky strategies in a skill context is noted in males (Table 65). We shall now examine whether a moderator analysis of the present domain clarifies the relationships observed in the total samples.

Table 72 considers the association between choice dilemmas and self-sufficiency for the moderator subgroups of males. It is apparent that the low test anxious–high defensive males stand apart from the remaining subgroups, in that there is a highly significant association between self-sufficiency and lesser deterrence of failure (greater risk taking) in the choice dilemmas task. In order to clarify this finding, the authors need to say a

Table 72

CORRELATIONS FOR MALES BETWEEN CHOICE DILEMMAS AND SELF-SUFFICIENCY FOR PERSONALITY SUBGROUPS

DEFENSIVENESS

		Low	High	Low + High	
TEST ANXIETY	Low	.08	−.47**	−.25*	$z = -1.13$
	High	−.13	.23	−.03	
	Low + High	−.03	−.26*	$z = 1.20$	

few words about the self-sufficiency scale. It contains items that concern a general willingness to arrive at decisions and take action alone, as opposed to a need to seek the advice and assistance of others before making decisions. Our index of defensiveness — the Marlowe-Crowne scale — has been conceptualized by its authors as measuring a need for social approval. Accordingly, defensive males who score low in self-sufficiency — in other words, show greater dependency upon others — are distinguished by a form of "social conservatism." On the other hand, if males are high in need for social approval — in other words, are defensive — but if, in addition, they are high in self-sufficiency, the latter characteristic evidently represents a conscious attempt at counteracting the former. For the defensive individual to follow such a course, he must be willing to accept evident risks. The significant correlation reported in Table 72 supports this view. It must be emphasized, however, that the present results concern decision making in a context that is both hypothetical and projective, because there are no real outcomes and the subject advises a course of action for another.

In sum, we note here how the personality variable of self-sufficiency becomes relevant to risk taking for persons in whom the variable in question has a special kind of role. By implication, self-sufficiency in a different personality type may change in character and hence have other kinds of consequences for decision-making behavior. Note, in particular, the results reported in Table 73. In low test anxious–low defensive subjects, self-sufficiency is inversely related to risk taking in a context of skill. These

Table 73

CORRELATIONS FOR MALES BETWEEN SKILL STRATEGIES AND SELF-SUFFICIENCY FOR PERSONALITY SUBGROUPS

DEFENSIVENESS

			Low	High	Low + High	
TEST ANXIETY	Low	SMG	−.37*	.02	−.14	
		SML	.19	−.07	.03	
		SLS	−.39*	−.03	−.19	
		SMD	.29	−.01	.13	
		SMV	−.41*	.00	−.17	
						z =
	High	SMG	−.15	−.34	−.24	.51
		SML	.01	.17	.10	−.36
		SLS	−.20	−.34	−.25	.31
		SMD	.12	.24	.20	−.36
		SMV	−.08	−.33	−.20	.15
					z =	
	Low + High	SMG	−.25	−.10	−.78	
		SML	.09	−.01	.52	
		SLS	−.29*	−.13	−.83	
		SMD	.22	.08	.73	
		SMV	−.24	−.11	−.68	

results stand in sharp contrast with those reported in Table 72, though it must be noted that we are presently concerned with decision making in a motor skill situation. Where there is personal control over outcomes, self-sufficiency in our "least disturbed" males is associated with avoidance of risky strategies. The original prediction was that self-sufficient subjects would prefer strategies entailing intermediate degrees of risk taking. There is some evidence of this result in the low test anxious–low defensive subgroup, though the correlation for the strategy of minimizing deviation from 1/2 falls considerably short of statistical significance. Still, the r for "minimization of loss" is quite low indeed, suggesting that the self-sufficient subjects show little disposition toward extreme conservatism. Where the level of motivational disturbance is low, then, there is evidence of a sort for the original curvilinear hypothesis. It must be granted, however, that the authors rendered the hypothesis quite difficult to test. Although a 50 : 50 probability of success is the objective midpoint of the probability distribution, the authors did not employ a symmetrical set of probability alternatives on either side of the midpoint. As noted previously, therefore, a strategy minimizing deviation from 1/2 may be biased in the conservative direction.

No moderator effects are observed in the case of chance strategies. We turn, then, to the information-seeking procedures. Table 74 reports the correlations between self-sufficiency and number judgments. Again, the

Table 74

CORRELATIONS FOR MALES BETWEEN NUMBER JUDGMENTS AND SELF-SUFFICIENCY FOR PERSONALITY SUBGROUPS

DEFENSIVENESS

		Low	High	Low + High	
TEST ANXIETY	Low	−.44*	.16	−.13	$z = -1.39$
	High	.01	.31	.14	
	Low + High	−.24	.20	$z = -2.29$	

relationship is significant for the low test anxious–low defensive subjects, though opposite in direction to results previously reported for skill strategies. Within the subgroup in question, more self-sufficient males request less information before committing themselves to a decision in the number judgments procedure.

Here is further evidence of the situational specificity that characterizes male subjects low in test anxiety and defensiveness. One may in fact wonder whether the results reported in Tables 73 and 74 reflect the same type of exaggerated intra-individual bipolarity described earlier in the case of impulsiveness in test anxious or defensive females. The authors think not, for two reasons: first, self-sufficiency and impulsiveness are of a quite different character; and second, and more important, the task variation in the present case remains *within* a payoff context, in contrast with the hypothetical versus payoff distinction observed earlier. Hence, the switch from relative conservatism to risk taking in the low-low subgroup as a function of self-sufficiency may simply reflect a differential perception of the optimal strategy in the two payoff contexts. The more self-sufficient member of this subgroup may realistically perceive that conservatism brings higher returns in the skill strategy context but lower returns in an information-seeking situation. In the latter case, he naturally adopts a more risky strategy.

Note, in contrast, the consistent trends displayed by the high-high subgroup in Tables 73 and 74. Although the correlations fall quite short of significance, it is of some interest that they are in the same direction for both decision contexts: self-sufficiency is linked with conservatism. Again, consistency has been demonstrated to hold in that subgroup, despite the considerable discrepancy in the kinds of decision contexts involved.

We turn, finally, to Table 75, in which self-sufficiency is related to the final bet in males. The resemblance to Table 72 is quite striking. Once again, it is the low test anxious–high defensive males who manifest a significant relation. For these subjects, greater self-sufficiency is associated with a more risky final bet selection (again, prior winnings are held constant in a partial correlation analysis). Hence, the interpretation advanced to account for the significant relation in Table 72 is also applicable here, thereby increasing somewhat the finding's generality. The argument, it will be recalled, stressed that high self-sufficiency in low test anxious–high defensive males represents an attempt to counteract the strong need for social approval that characterizes such persons. It is as if these subjects insist that solitary effort may pay off in the form of social approval. Such a course, however, represents a greater risk than is true for the person who checks his social-approval standing with relevant others every step of the way. In short, the authors are suggesting that risk and conservatism in the social realm may have implications for the type of risk taking under investigation in the present volume. This is hardly a new issue, for there

Table 75

Partial Correlations for Males between Final Bet (Prior Winnings Held Constant) and Self-sufficiency for Personality Subgroups

		DEFENSIVENESS			
		Low	High	Low + High	
TEST ANXIETY	Low	−.04	−.35*	−.22	z = −2.00
	High	−.08	.23	.17	
	Low + High	−.04	−.09	.26	z =

were many references in Chapter 3 to the special relevance of interpersonal contexts to defensive subjects.

Consider next the results obtained for females. We find that the choice dilemmas procedure does not yield any moderator effects. A very different situation obtains, however, with the decision-making procedures that involve monetary payoffs. We discuss first the relation between chance strategies and self-sufficiency reported in Table 76. Again, a striking sex difference is evident. Only in the case of females high on both test anxiety and defensiveness are there significant relationships to be found. Within this subgroup, greater self-sufficiency is linked to a preference for risky strategies.

Table 77 presents the correlations between self-sufficiency and skill strategies in the moderator subgroups of females. The findings are highly consistent with those reported in the preceding table. Regardless of whether chance or skill strategies are at issue, then, the significant relationships emerge in the subgroup high on both moderators, and the direction of linkage is between risk taking and self-sufficiency.

No moderator influences are evident in the case of the information-seeking procedures. The final bet variable, on the other hand, yields the pattern shown in Table 78. Its resemblance to the preceding two tables is quite striking. Once again, it is in the case of the subgroup high on both

Table 76
CORRELATIONS FOR FEMALES BETWEEN CHANCE STRATEGIES AND SELF-SUFFICIENCY FOR PERSONALITY SUBGROUPS

DEFENSIVENESS

			Low	High	Low + High	
TEST ANXIETY	Low	CMG	.06	−.02	−.02	
		CML	−.25	.18	−.03	
		CLS	−.03	.01	−.06	
		CMD	−.19	−.03	−.11	
		CMV	.09	−.12	−.05	
						z =
	High	CMG	−.25	.43*	.13	−.74
		CML	.09	−.11	−.08	.25
		CLS	−.18	.43*	.16	−1.08
		CMD	.25	−.57**	−.15	.20
		CMV	−.19	.31	.12	−.84
					z =	
	Low + High	CMG	−.08	.26	−1.67	
		CML	−.08	.00	−.39	
		CLS	−.09	.28*	−1.82	
		CMD	.01	−.35*	1.77	
		CMV	−.05	.14	−.94	

moderators, and only in the case of this subgroup, that a significant relationship emerges between risk taking and self-sufficiency.

Thus, on three separate decision-making tasks — chance strategies, skill strategies, and the final bet — self-sufficiency contributes to greater risk taking specifically in the case of test anxious and defensive females. Hence, knowledge of the self-sufficiency score in this particular subgroup of females allows us to make a reasonably good estimate of whether the highly generalized decision-making behavior so characteristic of this subgroup will take a risky or conservative form.

It is evident, on the basis of these findings, that self-sufficiency has quite different implications for decision-making in men and women. As Appendix A–1 (row 30) indicates, males' self-sufficiency scores are significantly higher than those of females. The latter are presumed to have stronger affiliative orientations, which may militate against self-sufficiency. In short, self-sufficiency entails risks of disaffiliation for women that are of lesser consequence for males. If such social risks have anything at all to do with the kinds of risk taking with which this volume is concerned, we can expect the link between risk taking in the social and nonsocial spheres to

Table 77

CORRELATIONS FOR FEMALES BETWEEN SKILL STRATEGIES AND SELF-SUFFICIENCY FOR PERSONALITY SUBGROUPS

DEFENSIVENESS

			Low	High	Low + High	
	Low	SMG	−.01	−.07	−.05	
		SML	.07	−.07	.01	
		SLS	.05	−.11	−.03	
		SMD	−.06	.18	.04	
		SMV	−.03	−.06	−.05	
TEST ANXIETY						$z =$
	High	SMG	−.24	.37*	.09	−.69
		SML	.27	−.10	.02	−.05
		SLS	−.13	.31	.10	−.64
		SMD	.08	−.35	−.14	.89
		SMV	−.25	.37*	.10	−.74
					$z =$	
	Low + High	SMG	−.10	.16	−1.28	
		SML	.16	−.08	1.18	
		SLS	−.02	.13	−.74	
		SMD	−.02	−.15	.64	
		SMV	−.11	.16	−1.33	

Table 78

PARTIAL CORRELATIONS FOR FEMALES BETWEEN FINAL BET (PRIOR WINNINGS HELD CONSTANT) AND SELF-SUFFICIENCY FOR PERSONALITY SUBGROUPS

DEFENSIVENESS

		Low	High	Low + High	
	Low	−.19	.14	−.05	
TEST ANXIETY					$z =$ 1.18
	High	−.17	−.51**	−.29*	
				$z =$	
	Low + High	−.15	−.21	.30	

be forged in test anxious defensives, because these are the subjects for whom considerations of risk and conservatism are most pervasive. For males, on the other hand, the alternatives of being self-sufficient or not are more equally balanced in desirability, and as a result, we cannot expect a commitment to one or the other to have the powerful consequences for risk taking that we find in the females. Rather, self-sufficiency appears to have more varied meanings for males, dependent upon motivational dynamics and task specifications.

Independence

Relationships between the personality dimension of independence and decision making are negligible in the male sample as a whole. Turning to moderator effects, we consider first the choice dilemmas procedure (Table

Table 79

CORRELATIONS FOR MALES BETWEEN CHOICE DILEMMAS AND INDEPENDENCE FOR PERSONALITY SUBGROUPS

		DEFENSIVENESS			
		Low	High	Low + High	
TEST ANXIETY	Low	−.15	.12	.02	
	High	−.06	−.43*	−.30*	$z = 1.64$
	Low + High	−.11	−.12		$z = .05$

79). It can be seen that independence relates to lesser deterrence of failure (greater risk taking) only in the case of males who are high in both test anxiety and defensiveness.

Comparable results are obtained when independence is related to chance strategies (Table 80). Again the same subgroup is involved, and again the more independent males in this subgroup show greater risk-taking preferences. The relation disappears, however, in the case of skill strategies. With respect to Table 80, it can be seen that the largest r in the high–high

Table 80

CORRELATIONS FOR MALES BETWEEN CHANCE STRATEGIES AND
INDEPENDENCE FOR PERSONALITY SUBGROUPS

DEFENSIVENESS

			Low	High	Low + High	
TEST ANXIETY	Low	CMG	.11	−.12	−.01	
		CML	−.12	.15	.02	
		CLS	.10	−.07	.02	
		CMD	−.23	.05	−.08	
		CMV	.12	−.17	−.03	
						z =
	High	CMG	.11	.43*	.29*	−1.54
		CML	−.35	.00	−.16	.92
		CLS	−.01	.49*	.27	−1.28
		CMD	−.04	−.57**	−.31*	1.18
		CMV	.21	.37	.29*	−1.64
					z =	
	Low + High	CMG	.11	.07	.21	
		CML	−.20	.13	−1.71	
		CLS	.06	.14	−.42	
		CMD	−.15	−.18	.16	
		CMV	.14	.01	.68	

cell belongs to the "minimization of deviation from 1/2" strategy. The sign of the correlation is negative, indicating an inverse relationship between independence and a preference for intermediate risk levels. Recall that the authors initially hypothesized a direct relationship.

For test anxious and defensive males, the subgroup most disposed toward a highly generalized risky or conservative orientation, the Barron-Asch-Crutchfield Independence-Yielding Scale is able to inform us in which particular direction — toward risk or conservatism — the male subject's decisions will gravitate. Note, however, that the relation holds only in a decision context in which personal control over outcomes is lacking. The authors suspect that the associations observed in Tables 79 and 80 represent the engagement of the conventionality-unconventionality aspect of the independence scale as discussed earlier in the chapter. In a context where personal control over outcomes is lacking, the subject for whom the risk-conservatism dimension is salient may adopt a "devil-may-care" attitude if independent, an attitude of refusal to "relax one's guard" if yielding. In short, the authors are suggesting that the social risks tapped by such measures as the independence scale are especially likely to become assimilated to the forms of risk here under investigation in subjects for whom issues of risk and conservatism are central.

In Table 81, we examine the relation in males between independence and the final bet, with level of prior winnings held constant. The direction of the relation is maintained — independence associated with greater risk taking — but the significant r is now located in the male subgroup low in both test anxiety and defensiveness.

Table 81

PARTIAL CORRELATIONS FOR MALES BETWEEN FINAL BET (PRIOR WINNINGS HELD CONSTANT) AND INDEPENDENCE FOR PERSONALITY SUBGROUPS

	DEFENSIVENESS			
	Low	High	Low + High	
TEST ANXIETY — Low	−.52**	.14	−.13	$z =$ −.36
TEST ANXIETY — High	−.09	−.16	−.06	
Low + High	−.34*	.05		$z =$ −2.03

The shift in the critical moderator subgroup in Table 81 constitutes something of a puzzle. The explanation of the shift may possibly lie in the fact that the reliability of the independence scale is quite low (Appendix C), suggesting that the scale is multidimensional. Hence, the independence scale may be tapping different dimensions in the low-low and high-high subgroups. For the latter, the authors have proposed that the conventionality-unconventionality aspect of the scale may be crucial. Where both test anxiety and defensiveness are low, on the other hand, the scale may yield scores that are reflective of the construct that the original authors of the scale intended it to measure. The highly autonomous behavior of the independent in the Asch-type conformity situation is in many respects incompatible with high levels of test anxiety and defensiveness. Hence, a scale that attempts to discriminate between those who behave in an independent and yielding manner may prove most effective where related sources of motivational disturbance are low. In sum, the present authors are suggesting that the independence scale is most adequately measuring what it purports to measure in the case of the low test anxious–low defensive subgroup.

Returning to Table 81, we note that the independent male makes a more risky choice of a final bet. A great deal is at stake in the final bet task, and it is possible that the independent male is better able to quell the fear of monetary loss that assails his yielding counterpart when contemplating a more risky decision. To lose all one's gradually accumulated winnings on the toss of a die is, after all, an outcome that can brand one as stupid in the eyes of the experimenter, and hence can be tolerated better if one is less in need of social support. Of course, this is a speculative assertion, and must be put to systematic empirical test.

Next, we inquire into the results for females. Recall, from Table 66, that these subjects yield significant associations between independence and greater risk taking in the choice dilemmas and chance bets tasks. To what extent do moderator influences bear upon the female data? With regard to choice dilemmas, such influences are negligible. Hence, the willingness of independent female subjects to take greater risks in a hypothetical decision-making context is relatively unaffected by test anxiety and defensiveness.

Chance strategies present a distinctly different picture. As Table 82 shows, the strongest relationships are obtained in the low test anxious–low defensive subgroup, though the high-high subgroup yields a comparable pattern of results. Moderator effects, not evident in the case of skill strategies, are very substantial in the final bet situation (Table 83). It is now the highly test anxious and defensive females for whom independence and the final bet are related. Again, independence contributes to greater risk taking.

A comparison of Tables 82 and 83 with 80 and 81, respectively, reveals a marked sex difference. The difference is especially pronounced in the case of the final bet situation, where it can be seen that the significant association shifts from the low-low to the high-high cell as a function of sex of subject.

Let us attempt to account for the observed differences between males and females in the present context. The place to start, perhaps, is with the matter of sex differences in the Asch-type group pressure situation. Krech, Crutchfield, and Ballachey (1962, pp. 524–525) have recently reviewed the empirical evidence on this issue, noting a consistent tendency for females to earn higher conformity scores than do males and for females who resist group pressure to experience greater conflict with regard to the conventional feminine role. These observations make it clear that conformity and independence may have distinctly different meanings for men and women — and hence, that scores on an independence scale intended to discriminate independents and yielders may not have the same significance

Table 82

CORRELATIONS FOR FEMALES BETWEEN CHANCE STRATEGIES AND INDEPENDENCE FOR PERSONALITY SUBGROUPS

			DEFENSIVENESS			
			Low	High	Low + High	
TEST ANXIETY	Low	CMG	.47*	−.04	.19	
		CML	−.05	.16	.10	
		CLS	.51**	−.03	.25	
		CMD	−.45*	.11	−.21	
		CMV	.43*	−.15	.10	
						z =
	High	CMG	.24	.31	.25	−.30
		CML	−.32	.15	−.01	.54
		CLS	.23	.40*	.31*	−.30
		CMD	−.07	−.31	−.18	−.15
		CMV	.31	.23	.22	−.59
					z =	
	Low + High	CMG	.30*	.12	.89	
		CML	−.09	.19	−1.38	
		CLS	.34*	.23	.54	
		CMD	−.25	−.11	−.69	
		CMV	.28*	.02	1.28	

Table 83

PARTIAL CORRELATIONS FOR FEMALES BETWEEN FINAL BET (PRIOR WINNINGS HELD CONSTANT) AND INDEPENDENCE FOR PERSONALITY SUBGROUPS

		DEFENSIVENESS			
		Low	High	Low + High	
TEST ANXIETY	Low	.11	.07	.09	
					z = 1.77
	High	.04	−.58**	−.27	
	Low + High	.08	−.42**	z = 2.46	

for males and females. Indeed, it is quite conceivable that high levels of independence in females, by running counter to prevalent sex norms, constitute a type of social risk taking, which in turn may be expected to prove highly relevant for those women who, in other contexts, are particularly oriented to matters of risk and conservatism in decision making. In short, we are led to the conclusion that the kinds of risk taking we have been exploring in a laboratory context may have broad implications for social behaviors that have not usually been conceptualized in risk-taking terms. More will be said on this point in the subsequent chapter.

We are now in a considerably better position to interpret the data of Tables 82 and 83. In the case of the latter we are dealing with a situation where the risks are at their most severe and salient. It is apparently under such conditions that a neat match is achieved between the highly generalized orientation of risk taking or conservatism implied by the simultaneous presence of test anxiety and defensiveness, on the one hand — and on the other, the social risk taking or social conservatism (conventionality) inherent for women who are independents or yielders, respectively.

The results we have been discussing take us a step beyond the observation of highly generalized tendencies toward risk taking or conservatism in test anxious and defensive subjects. With certain key personality variables of the sort measured by the Barron-Asch-Crutchfield scale, we can begin to make reasonably accurate predictions regarding the specific direction that the choice behavior will assume in various decision-making contexts.

Finally, one may well ask why it is the low test anxious–low defensive females who yield the strongest associations between independence and chance strategies (Table 82). We can merely surmise that independence also has risk-taking implications for those subjects in certain decision situations.

Somewhat surprising is the absence in both males and females of any relation between independence, on the one hand, and skill strategies and information-seeking measures on the other. An "independent" orientation does connote a sense of personal control over environmental events, and yet all of the significant relationships observed involve decision-making procedures in which outcomes are beyond the subject's control. This is one of those intriguing findings that resists interpretation and literally cries out for further investigation.

Rigidity

The final personality variable to fall within our purview is rigidity. We shall concern ourselves only with the female data here, in view of the significant relationship between rigidity and defensiveness in males. Recall from Table 66 that rigidity is associated with greater conservatism in several decision-making tasks. We turn now to the matter of moderator influences. None are obtained in the case of the choice dilemmas task. With chance strategies, on the other hand, the moderator pattern assumes the form shown in Table 84. It is apparent that significant relations are

Table 84

CORRELATIONS FOR FEMALES BETWEEN CHANCE STRATEGIES AND RIGIDITY FOR PERSONALITY SUBGROUPS

			DEFENSIVENESS			
			Low	High	Low + High	
TEST ANXIETY	Low	CMG	−.20	−.18	−.19	
		CML	.15	−.01	.08	
		CLS	−.12	−.15	−.13	
		CMD	.05	.10	.07	
		CMV	−.25	−.10	−.19	
						$z =$
	High	CMG	−.13	−.36	−.21	.10
		CML	.18	−.20	−.03	.54
		CLS	−.10	−.44*	−.25	.59
		CMD	−.07	.43*	.13	−.30
		CMV	−.13	−.20	−.13	−.30
					$z =$	
	Low + High	CMG	−.14	−.28*	.69	
		CML	.11	−.11	1.08	
		CLS	−.10	−.32*	1.08	
		CMD	.00	.28*	−1.38	
		CMV	−.15	−.16	.05	

confined to high test anxious–high defensive subjects. The more rigid members of that subgroup tend to avoid the more risky strategies and exhibit a preference for a strategy that minimizes deviation from a probability of 1/2.

The foregoing relationships are maintained and in fact exhibit even greater strength when rigidity is correlated with skill strategies (Table 85). Once more, significant relationships are found only in the high test anxious–high defensive subgroup, greater rigidity being clearly associated with greater conservatism on four of the five strategy indexes. Finally, Table 86 presents the partial correlations between rigidity and the final bet index, with the amount of prior winnings held constant. Again, it is

Table 85

CORRELATIONS FOR FEMALES BETWEEN SKILL STRATEGIES AND RIGIDITY FOR PERSONALITY SUBGROUPS

DEFENSIVENESS

			Low	High	Low + High	
TEST ANXIETY	Low	SMG	.08	−.08	.02	
		SML	.24	−.11	.12	
		SLS	.17	−.18	.03	
		SMD	−.20	.25	−.03	
		SMV	.03	−.05	−.01	
						$z =$
	High	SMG	.06	−.44*	−.16	.89
		SML	.24	.10	.15	−.15
		SLS	.12	−.46*	−.16	.94
		SMD	.03	.58**	.29*	−1.58
		SMV	−.02	−.38*	−.18	.84
					$z =$	
	Low + High	SMG	.07	−.26	1.62	
		SML	.21	.00	1.03	
		SLS	.14	−.33*	2.31	
		SMD	−.07	.44**	−2.51	
		SMV	.01	−.22	1.13	

the females high on both test anxiety and defensiveness who yield the significant association between rigidity and greater conservatism.

In sum, all the decision-making procedures involving bet selections under payoff conditions yield significant associations with the Gough-Sanford Rigidity Scale, but only in the case where female subjects are high in both test anxiety and defensiveness. Apparently, rigidity impinges upon decision-making behavior, channeling it in a conservative direction, but only for those subjects in whom the risk-conservatism dimension constitutes a major focus. Although we might have expected the more rigid females generally to be quite inhibited and hence conservative in decision-making contexts, it is quite clear that rigidity has no influence along these lines until it comes into contact with a particular pattern of motivational dynamics. Much the same is true for the other personality variables that we have considered. Hence, the relative lack of success that psychologists have experienced in finding direct personality correlates of risk-taking behavior may well be a consequence of the neglect of relevant moderators.

It is perhaps of particular interest to note that the results of this chapter have permitted us to make significant progress in specifying *which direction*

Table 86

PARTIAL CORRELATIONS FOR FEMALES BETWEEN FINAL BET (PRIOR WINNINGS HELD CONSTANT) AND RIGIDITY FOR PERSONALITY SUBGROUPS

		DEFENSIVENESS			
		Low	High	Low + High	
TEST ANXIETY	Low	.10	.27	.17	$z = .30$
	High	−.17	.48**	.11	
	Low + High	−.07	.34*		$z = -2.02$

— toward risk or toward conservatism — the highly generalized decision-making behavior of the high test anxious–high defensive subjects will take. Among the females in this high-high subgroup, decisions will gravitate in the risky direction in the case of individuals high in self-sufficiency, high in independence, and low in rigidity; decisions will gravitate toward conservatism, on the other hand, in the case of persons low in self-sufficiency, high in yielding tendencies, and high in rigidity. Among the males in this high-high subgroup, decisions will tend toward risk taking for persons high in independence, toward conservatism for persons high in the tendency to yield.

SUMMARY

Hypotheses respecting direct personality correlates of decision-making behavior have received only partial confirmation in the present chapter. Thus, for male and female samples as a whole, no evidence has been obtained to support the hypothesis of a direct association between impulsiveness and risk taking. The hypothesis that self-sufficiency and independence would be related to a preference for chance and skill strategies entailing intermediate risk levels (in other words, minimization of deviation from 1/2) also has failed to be confirmed. Rather, the evidence suggests that self-sufficiency may be related to conservatism in males, and independence to risk taking in females. Hypotheses regarding the relation of manifest anxiety and rigidity to conservatism in decision-making receive some support, the former yielding low-level significant associations for males, the latter for females. Finally, relationships between response-style measures — social desirability and acquiescence — and decision-making indexes are negligible.

Turning to the examination of moderator effects, we retained for analysis those inventory scales that are not significantly related to either moderator. The scales meeting this criterion are impulsiveness, self-sufficiency, and independence for both sexes, and rigidity for females.

Very substantial moderator effects are obtained between the personality and decision-making domains. These effects are quite dissimilar across sex, however, indicating that the implications of personality for risk-taking behavior are strongly sex-linked. Thus, the expected relationship between impulsiveness and risk taking, which is absent in the male sample taken as a whole, emerges in striking fashion for strategy measures in males low in test anxiety and defensiveness. On the basis of this finding, we can suggest that there may be personality determinants of risk-taking behavior that become manifest only in the absence of motivational disturbance. Impulsiveness in females, on the other hand, has a significant impact on decision making when test anxiety or defensiveness is present. Test anxious or defensive females yield relationships between impulsiveness and risk-taking measures that are of opposite sign in hypothetical and payoff contexts, suggesting a type of exaggerated bipolarity in decision making. We can conclude, therefore, that impulsiveness may well serve in an "acting out" capacity for females.

Moderator relations between self-sufficiency and decision-making are quite complex in the case of the male sample. Where decision outcomes are not under personal control (choice dilemmas and the final bet), self-sufficiency is associated with greater risk taking in low test anxious–high defensive subjects. Because our defensiveness measure implies a high need for social approval, such individuals when high in self-sufficiency are apparently attempting to counteract that need — a course that involves evident risks. The consequence, indeed, is a higher level of risk taking than ensues when low levels of self-sufficiency are found in a context of defensiveness.

Where decision outcomes are under personal control, self-sufficiency exerts its influence in low test anxious–low defensive males. For skill strategies, self-sufficiency contributes to conservatism; for number judgments, it enhances risk taking. This kind of situational specificity may reflect the differential perception of optimal requirements in the two tasks and is consistent in this respect with other evidence regarding the sensitivity to task or situational contexts that characterizes subjects low in test anxiety and defensiveness.

The self-sufficiency results for females exhibit a much higher degree of internal consistency. For the chance and skill strategy indexes and the final bet, self-sufficiency is associated with greater risk taking in highly test anxious and defensive females. Interpretation of the striking differences between males and females in the present context stresses the more salient risk-taking aspects attached to self-sufficiency for females in our culture. Accordingly, that particular personality dimension proves especially relevant for test anxious defensives, because considerations of risk and conservatism are of central concern in their case.

Independence and risk taking are positively related in both sexes. The complex pattern of relationships found in the case of males suggests that this personality dimension may not have the same psychological meaning for subjects with varying degrees and kinds of motivational disturbance. In particular, the evidence suggests that conventionality-unconventionality is implicated for the high-high subgroup, whereas genuine independence or autonomy may be involved for the low-low subgroup. Certain sex differences are observed, and we may attempt to account for these in terms of the differential meaning of conformity and independence in males and females. Independence in females may constitute a type of social risk taking that bears directly upon the kinds of risk under study in the present investigation.

Turning to rigidity in the female sample, we find that relationships are confined to the subgroup high in both test anxiety and defensiveness. Consistent results are obtained across chance and skill strategies and the final bet, more rigid females being more conservative.

It is of particular interest that the findings of the present chapter contributed significantly to specifying the *direction* that will be taken — toward risk or conservatism — in the highly generalized decision-making behavior of the high test anxious–high defensive subgroup.

It is evident that the use of appropriate moderator variables facilitates the search for personality correlates of decision-making behavior. Such a procedure does lead to the inescapable conclusion, however, that the phenomena are more complex than had been imagined by those seeking direct linear relationships in unselected samples.

8

Conclusions and Implications

In the course of presenting our findings in Chapters 3 through 7, specific implications have been drawn and interpretations provided. It is our purpose in the present chapter to consider some of the broader consequences — methodological, theoretical, and practical — that our results seem to possess.

IMPLICATIONS FOR METHOD

It is evident that the consideration of personality dispositions of test anxiety and defensiveness as moderator variables has rendered clear a psychological picture that otherwise would have been totally ambiguous. Overall sample correlations that were nonsignificant or, although statistically significant, so low as to be of doubtful psychological value have been found to be substantial in one moderator subgroup, negligible in another. In some cases, these over-all correlations have been found to be significant in a positive direction in one moderator subgroup, significant in a negative direction in another. Such findings require the conclusion that consideration of potential moderator variables is nothing less than essential in psychological research involving the study of correlations. In most of the authors' present work, the assumption of linearity that has typically been made in previous studies of the over-all relationship between two psychological variables simply does not hold. The present authors found that correlation coefficients depicting over-all relationships often conceal more psychological truth than they reveal. Time and again, consideration of one or the other of our two moderator variables has considerably clarified the correlational picture in comparison with what the state of affairs seemed to be when neither moderator was considered. And consideration of the joint effect of both moderator variables operating simultaneously has provided a sizeable further clarification of the correlational picture in comparison with the results obtained by considering the effect of either moderator alone.

These findings possess serious import for the extensive published literature based on correlational approaches to the study of personality and personality-related psychological processes. This literature includes, of course, studies involving the factor analysis of a matrix of correlation coefficients. In the vast majority of these researches, the correlations have been computed for the sample as a whole, without regard for the effects of possible moderator variables. At best, the results of such studies are not as clear-cut as they might be. At worst, the results of such studies may be positively misleading. It is no exaggeration to presume that a large proportion of this literature has led to what will turn out to be serious errors of interpretation. The correlation coefficients in question, when statistically significant, usually are not large, so that the degree of over-all association between variables often is not very great. Yet interpretations of such results have typically proceeded on the assumption that the relatively weak association obtained was actually symptomatic of a much stronger "real" correlation that failed to reveal itself only because of the combined effect of a host of error tendencies. The results reported in this volume cast serious doubt on the tenability of such an assumption. Negligible associations observed for a sample as a whole may conceivably manifest dramatically different magnitudes and directions in subgroups defined in terms of relevant moderators.

How can the investigator decide on the particular variables to be cast in the role of moderators? The authors make no claim to the universal efficacy of test anxiety and defensiveness in moderator capacities. For the specific domain in which the authors chose to work — risk taking broadly defined — test anxiety and defensiveness appeared *on theoretical grounds* to be good bets as moderators. In other substantive areas, those two variables may prove relatively useless in that role. When choosing moderator variables, in other words, "There is nothing so practical as a good theory," to quote Kurt Lewin's well-known dictum. It may be technically feasible with high-speed computers to treat each variable as a moderator in turn, examining its effects upon associations between all possible pairs of other variables. The authors doubt, however, that this will prove to be the most fruitful way to proceed. Quite apart from deluging the investigator with masses of data, such a procedure cannot inform him which among dozens of variables ought to be included in the study in the first place. Here the role of theory is indispensable.

IMPLICATIONS FOR RISK-TAKING AND POST-DECISIONAL PROCESSES

One thread runs rather prominently through the discussion of our findings concerning generality within the decision-making domain. It is the suggestion that two psychological sources for such generality can be identified, one more motivational and the other more cognitive.

The motivational source, in the authors' view, is responsible for producing consistencies of risk or conservatism across highly divergent domains of psychological functioning. It consists of risk-regulatory tendencies, taking their origin in the motivational predispositions of the individual, that arise from the fact that he selectively scans the environment in terms of its success and failure potentials rather than in terms of its other multifarious attributes, and from the fact that he is particularly sensitized to the image that his behavior creates in the eyes of others as well as in the "inner eye" of his own self-evaluation system. We infer the presence of the first of these contributors to risk regulation from high levels of test anxiety, the second from high levels of defensiveness. When both of these sources of motivational disturbance reach high levels, the generality of risk taking or conservatism appears to be maximized. Under certain conditions, this generality of risk taking or conservatism is also found when either test anxiety or defensiveness is high, assuming a form that is consistent with the particular motivational disposition in question.

The cognitive source of generality, in turn, accounts for consistencies of risk or conservatism across narrow bands of situations that share common structural properties. The consistencies in question possess a task-centered rather than a motivation-centered quality because they arise from discriminable similarities between procedures. Risk-conservatism consistencies that take their origin in such structural similarities are most strongly in evidence within the "least disturbed" subgroup of each sex — those persons who are low both in test anxiety and in defensiveness tendencies.

The juxtaposition of these two psychological sources of consistent risk or conservatism tendencies across situational differences requires the conclusion that what may look like the same type of outcome — consistency within the risk-taking domain — actually may be the product of very different psychological processes. When consistency is born of motivational sources, it is overgeneralized; it ignores patent differences in task properties. Such consistency emerges on the basis of the fact that various procedures can be viewed within an image-maintenance or success-failure (payoff) context. When, on the other hand, consistency takes its origin from cognitive sources, it tends to respect discriminable task differences and confine itself to those procedures that are similar in one or more aspects of their intrinsic structure, rather than similar in terms of their extrinsic motivational consequences.

These findings underscore the fact that the behavior of the "least disturbed" subgroup is quite sensitive to the nature of each task at hand. Members of this subgroup tend to treat different tasks differently; but when task similarities are pervasive, they again respond appropriately. Although these tendencies are evident in both sexes, they are somewhat more prominent in the case of the "least disturbed" males than in the corresponding subgroup of females. For the high test anxious–high defensive subgroups, on the other hand, the sex difference is in the opposite direction, the highly generalized risk taking or conservatism being somewhat more pronounced in the females than in the males.

In sum, the general psychological portraits generated by the low test anxious–low defensive and by the high test anxious–high defensive subgroups are quite different from each other. When these two types of individuals do look similar, the evident similarity turns out to be a concealment of striking functional differences in the psychological meaning of the behavior in question. The majority of the evidence in Chapter 3 thus leads us to conceptualize these subgroups in terms of the predominance of cognitive versus motivational determinants, respectively. To talk about the dominance of cognitive factors in the behavior of the "least disturbed" individuals is to emphasize that they tend to respond in a situationally specific manner. The universe of procedures with which they are confronted has a more multidimensional impact on them than it does on their high test anxious–high defensive counterparts. Consistencies in the treatment of different situations along risky or conservative lines are less frequent in the case of the former individuals and, when found, are premised upon structural commonalities.

The evidence in Chapter 3 concerning the relationship between amount of prior winnings and the final bet, and some of the evidence in Chapter 4 concerning postdecisional phenomena permit us to proceed even further in characterizing the behavior of this "least disturbed" subgroup. Besides exhibiting greater situational discrimination and sensitivity, some of the decisional behavior of this subgroup appears to be more "adaptive," in terms of its antecedents and its effects, than that of the motivationally disturbed subgroups. Consider some of the evidence on this point.

In making a risky or conservative final bet, the "least disturbed" subgroup for both sexes is significantly influenced by amount of prior winnings; the larger these winnings, the more conservative the final bet. No such relationship is obtained for the high test anxious–high defensive individuals, whose risk or conservatism on the final bet depends on whether risk or conservatism is their preferred strategy in other decision-making contexts.

Turning now to what happens after decision making has occurred, we note that only the "least disturbed" subgroup of males exhibits greater dissatisfaction with their skill bets as an inverse function of the amount of money their skill bets have earned them. The less they have earned, the more dissatisfied they are with their bets; the more they have earned, the less dissatisfied. Degree of dissatisfaction with their skill bet decisions hence is adaptively tuned to the monetary outcomes of these decisions only in the case of this subgroup. Recall that the paradoxical converse of such adaptiveness is observed in the high test anxious–high defensive males. The risk-takers among them are driven by low earnings into all the more inflexible insistence upon the rectitude of their prior decisions.

Viewing these findings on satisfaction-dissatisfaction in terms of dissonance reduction, we find that the two subgroups in question pursue distinctively different routes toward eliminating dissonance when faced with an inconsistency between the decision alternatives they have chosen and the desirability of the outcomes to which these alternatives lead. When committed to risky decision alternatives yielding undesirable outcomes, members of the high test anxious–high defensive subgroup insist all the more strongly that they are satisfied with the strategy that they have followed. They distort their evaluation of their decision making in an adaptively inappropriate direction. In contrast, when members of the "least disturbed" subgroup find that risky decision alternatives to which they committed themselves are yielding undesirable outcomes, they relinquish their commitment and express a preference for the formerly unchosen alternatives. They are more sensitive to the negative effects of the decision strategy that they followed, and hence they undo it. Both of these courses of action obviously serve to reduce dissonance — one by emphasizing the desirability of chosen alternatives, the other by undoing the commitment to those choices. But the former course involves a lack of appreciation of the consequences of one's own behavior, whereas the latter does not. Withdrawal of commitment is easier for the "least disturbed" subgroup than for the high test anxious–high defensive subgroup.

The present findings hence specify certain personality conditions under which distinctively different routes toward dissonance reduction will be followed. Brehm and Cohen (1962) have noted that little attention has thus far been given to this issue of individual differences in preferred mode of dissonance reduction. Viewed in the light of dissonance theory, the findings we have described provide a contribution to that problem.

Further evidence of adaptiveness in the "least disturbed" subgroup comes from the findings concerning skill bet strategies and absolute winnings for males. Within this subgroup, and within none of the others, the pursuit of risky skill strategies is productive of significantly greater winnings than the pursuit of conservative strategies. Thus, only members of the "least disturbed" subgroup of males can successfully implement the decision to take greater risks in a motor skill task. For the other subgroups, and especially for those involving the presence of high test anxiety, skilled performance undergoes motivational disruption.

Finally, consider the fact that, for males in the skill bet context, the subgroups high in test anxiety exhibit a direct dependence of postdecision satisfaction-dissatisfaction on risk-conservatism of decisional strategy quite apart from the level of winnings. Regardless of whether their monetary outcomes are favorable or unfavorable — in other words, with monetary outcomes held constant — these individuals express greater satisfaction if they have been more risky in their betting, greater dissatisfaction if they have been more conservative. This behavior is especially perverse in view of the fact that their relative winnings are larger when the subjects are more conservative, smaller when they are more risky. In contrast, the "least disturbed" subgroup shows no such direct dependence of postdecision satisfaction-dissatisfaction on the nature of the strategy pursued. Rather, as we have seen, satisfaction in their case arises quite reasonably from high winnings, dissatisfaction in their case arises quite reasonably from low winnings. They exhibit no relationship between decision-making strategies as such and postdecision satisfaction-dissatisfaction. For satisfaction-dissatisfaction to show a direct dependence on decisional strategies quite apart from outcomes betokens in yet another way the kind of insensitivity to relevant environmental factors that we have found to characterize individuals subject to motivational disturbance.

Thus, we have seen that certain contrasting findings for the "least disturbed" individuals, on the one hand, and those high in test anxiety and/or defensiveness, on the other, support the view that cognitive considerations more prominently determine the behavior of the former, whereas motivational considerations contribute more heavily to the behavior of the latter. In addition, further contrasts between these personality types support the view that some of the behavior of the former subgroup is more "adaptive" or "reasonable" than the corresponding behavior of the latter.

IMPLICATIONS FOR COGNITIVE-JUDGMENTAL PROCESSES

We have found that explicit dispositions toward risk and conservatism are associated with various cognitive-judgmental behaviors. The demonstration of such relationships and the delineation of their structure requires, however, that risk taking be considered under payoff rather than hypothetical conditions, and that the moderator variables of test anxiety and defensiveness be taken into account.

Considering sample-wide relationships, it is of considerable interest that these are found for females but not for males. Although associations obtain for both sexes when moderator variables are considered, the fact that associations obtain only for females when moderator effects are ignored suggests that, other things being equal, risk-taking considerations permeate the cognitive-judgmental realm more strongly for females than males. The cognitive-judgmental behaviors under study — confidence, category width, extremity — do not, of course, possess explicit risk-taking connotations. The manifestation of consistencies between the cognitive-judgmental and decision-making domains, then, suggests the extent to which the former may be invested with reward-punishment or gain-loss properties. It betokens what Lewin (for example, 1936) would conceptualize as weaker, more permeable boundaries between lifespace regions concerning habitual modes of dealing with the cognitive-judgmental tasks at hand, and lifespace regions concerning characteristic ways of handling payoff contingencies in decision-making situations.

Turning to the effects when personality moderators are taken into account, consider first general confidence of judgment. Consistent for both sexes is the finding that, for individuals high in defensiveness, judgmental confidence exhibits a direct, reflective association with risk-taking proclivities under payoff conditions. Among persons who have a strong inclination to be defensive in self-evaluation, those who take greater risks in chance and skill bet strategy contexts possess greater introspective conviction about the correctness of judgments rendered in a probability estimation task; those who are more conservative in the former contexts are less sure of their judgmental correctness in the cognitive task. With no criteria for success or failure ever provided in the judgment task, risk taking is evidently not inherent in one's self-appraisals of confidence or nonconfidence. Such confidence appraisals, rather, may be expected to exhibit a high degree of task relevance, reflecting almost exclusively a subjective conviction of greater or lesser knowledge concerning each item at hand. For defensive individuals, however, high and low judgmental confidence seem to involve implicit risk taking and conservatism, respectively. Depending, then, on whether they behave as risk-takers or conservatives in their bet strategies under payoff conditions, these individuals manifest high or low judgmental confidence.

Such a finding is quite supportive of the view that defensiveness implies a strong concern with image maintenance. Either risk taking or conservatism may be a component of the self-image held by a defensive person. Whichever is preferred, the person's introspections concerning judgmental confidence seem to follow suit in a reflective fashion. Confidence of judgment in a context where information is incomplete may well possess phenomenological risk-taking properties for such an individual; hence, consistency between the realms of decision making and judgmental confidence may derive from a common base of image-maintenance motivation.

Next consider breadth of categorizing — how far out an individual wishes to go from the typical instance of a class in determining where the boundaries of that class should be placed. Among defensive women who also are low in test anxiety (persons whom, in the introductory chapter, we characterized as "successful defenders"), risk taking and category breadth prove to be inversely correlated. This is the case for risk taking in chance and skill bet contexts and in number judgments and clues information-seeking contexts, but the relationships reach their strongest levels in the case of skill bets.

That risk taking under payoff conditions is related to narrow categorization behavior, whereas conservatism is related to broad categorizing, constitutes a provocative finding that helps clarify the implications of risk-taking and conservatism penchants for categorizing breadth. When direct relationships with risk-taking behaviors are investigated, we find that errors of inclusion (constructing broad categories) imply a conservative course, whereas errors of exclusion (constructing narrow categories) are indicative of a risky course. It is especially important to consider the fact that these are the results that obtain when no explicit rewards or punishments are attached to either of these two mutually exclusive types of error. It is obvious that, were one of the types of error to be made more costly than the other, conservatism would become linked with the less costly error tendency, risk taking with the more costly error tendency. Our intent, of course, lay in quite a different direction. We wished to leave this categorization task as "strictly cognitive" as possible — in other words, we wished to provide the two error tendencies with no explicit costs whatsoever. The intriguing outcome, then, is that under these "cost-free" conditions, a certain class of individuals — high defensive-low test anxious women — assign differential implicit costs of a particular kind: inclusion errors are treated as less costly, exclusion errors are treated as more costly. We infer these differential cost assignments from the fact that, within the subgroup of persons in question, those who are conservatives in decision-making situations involving payoffs prefer to make errors of inclusion in their categorizing behavior, whereas those who are risk-takers in decision-making situations involving payoffs prefer to make errors of exclusion in their categorizing behavior.

Why are errors of exclusion treated as more costly, errors of inclusion as less costly, when no explicit costs have been introduced? Earlier research on classification tendencies (Wallach, 1959) has indicated that greater psychological value is possessed by classes defined in terms of the factors determining inclusion than by classes defined in terms of the factors determining exclusion. This implies, therefore, that to call an event a member of class X when it is not, constitutes an error tendency that maximizes the class of greater value (namely, class X); whereas to call an event not a member of class X when it is, constitutes an error tendency that maximizes the class of lesser value (namely, the class of not-X). Given a value bias in favor of inclusion-defined classes, then, it follows that errors of exclusion are more costly and hence constitute greater risks than do errors of inclusion.

Inclusion-defined classes seem to be of greater psychological value than exclusion-defined classes because definition by inclusion provides greater certainty of class membership than does definition by exclusion. As was pointed out in the research cited in the preceding paragraph, to know what something *is* provides information of a more direct, applicable kind than to know what something is *not*. Inclusion classes thus represent knowns, whereas exclusion classes represent unknowns. Individuals who strive after certainty — who seek to reduce uncertainty in their cognitive activities — hence can be expected to maximize inclusion-defined categories. The fact that, among high defensive-low test anxious females, broad categorizers possess generally lower judgmental confidence supports the view that wider inclusion classes within this subgroup reflect an attempt to reduce uncertainty. Widening an inclusion class seems to constitute a maneuver adopted by a basically uncertain individual in order to keep uncertainty to a minimum. It comes as no surprise, therefore, that these are the same individuals who ask for a great deal of information before commiting themselves to a decision in the information-seeking tasks. As we have noted, such individuals prefer to be more certain of a smaller prize than to be less certain of a larger prize.

It is evident from our data that category breadth has no implications whatsoever for risk taking in the case of males. Females, on the other hand, exhibit significant sample-wide relationships between the two domains in question. The often-reported finding that males are broader categorizers than females, which has been used as a basis for postulating an association between broader categorizing and greater risk-taking tendencies, hence turns out not to possess any implications for risk taking at all. Knowing, as we now do, that no direct relationships exist for males between category breadth and risk-conservatism, we can assert with a substantial degree of confidence that different psychological processes underlie breadth versus narrowness of categorization in the case of the two sexes. Only in the case of females do these processes concern risk-conservatism tendencies.

That relationships between risk-conservatism and narrow versus broad categorizing turn out to be heavily localized within the high defensive-low test anxious subgroup of females provides further support for an image-maintenance conception of defensiveness. Individuals who are heavily committed to maintaining a favorable self-image may view either boldness or caution as a component of that image. Whichever they favor, a penchant for consistency in image maintenance may well be expected to lead them to assume congruent postures in their categorizing behavior. Even in "cost-free" categorizing situations, these individuals are sensitive to whatever bases for differential cost assignments can be found, no matter how implicit, and they guide their breadth of categorizing in a manner consistent with their preferences for accepting or avoiding the more costly risks.

We turn now to a different aspect of cognitive functioning: the degree of extremity a person exhibits in rendering probability judgments about ambiguous external events. Although judgmental extremity is obviously different from breadth of categorizing, our evidence suggests that, under some conditions, extremity of probability judgments is subject to influence by the same mechanism of tolerance for versus reduction of uncertainty that we invoked in interpreting the category width findings. In the area of judging probabilities, the person who seeks to reduce uncertainty is led to estimate that an event is either very likely or very unlikely — in other words, his judgments are extreme. In contrast, the person who tolerates uncertainty is more willing to estimate that events possess likelihoods in the middle range. Evidence for the operation of such an uncertainty-reduction or desire-for-certainty mechanism is found mainly in particular subgroups characterized by an inverse relationship between judgmental extremity and general level of confidence. That is, in most of the subgroups where extremity of judgments is related to low general confidence and in almost none of the subgroups where this relationship fails to obtain, the making of extreme probability estimates turns out to be associated with conservatism in payoff situations, whereas the making of more moderate probability estimates is associated with risk taking in payoff situations. When judgmental extremity seems to represent what may be characterized as a "counterphobic" going to extremes in compensation for a feeling of low general confidence, then such extremity is found in the case of individuals whose decision making under payoff conditions is conservative. Extremity under these circumstances seems indeed to represent an attempt to reduce or minimize uncertainty in a basically uncertain person.

In contrast, when judgmental extremity is independent of general confidence, a mechanism other than uncertainty reduction seems to operate. For most of the subgroups where such independence prevails, extremity in probability estimation tends to be directly, rather than inversely, correlated with dispositions toward risk taking. Such a direct relationship between risk taking in payoff contexts and judgmental extremity suggests the operation of what can be called an "all-or-none" mechanism — a perception of extreme (in other words, "all-or-none") judgments as more likely to be in error than judgments that keep to the middle of the road. If it is to reveal itself, such a sensitivity to the greater error potential of extreme judgments seems to require the absence of an inverse relationship between judgmental extremity and general confidence. When, in other words, extremity serves as an expression of tendencies toward reducing general uncertainty, then the individual is not sensitive, by and large, to the greater potential for error that lurks in extreme judgments. If extremity does not have an uncertainty-reduction function, on the other hand, then a person is more likely to respond as if aware of the greater chance for error that extremity entails. Under such conditions, greater judgmental extremity characterizes persons who take greater risks rather than persons who are more conservative in payoff situations.

Recourse to these two concepts — the "desire-for-certainty" and the "all-or-none" principles — provides us with a sufficient basis for interpreting our findings concerning the relationships between extremity of judgment and risk taking. It is clear that once we have described evidence for the operation of these principles, the critical next question becomes one of specifying the conditions under which one or the other of these principles gains sway. The authors feel that a significant advance in this direction is provided by consideration of the relationship between judgmental extremity and general confidence level. On the whole, the authors' findings are rather well summarized in the generalization that the "desire-for-certainty" principle, and hence an inverse linkage between extremity and risk taking, operates when extremity bears an inverse correlation with general level of confidence; whereas the "all-or-none" principle, and hence a direct linkage between extremity and risk taking, operates when extremity is unrelated to general level of confidence. Although the authors believe that this generalization represents an important and useful signpost, it is evident nonetheless that there is still much to be learned concerning the conditions that lead one or the other of these two principles to gain control over the extremity–risk-taking relationship.[1]

Decision making under payoff conditions and judgmental extremity in rendering probability estimations about external events hence do possess demonstrable interconnections. These interconnections are no less complicated, however, than they are intriguing.

Finally, recall our findings concerning extremity in self-referent judgments — extremity in affirming or denying self-descriptive statements. On the whole, it is under conditions of motivational disturbance that extremity in self-description is related to conservatism in decision making; it is under conditions of low disturbance, on the other hand, that such extremity is related to risk taking. Once again, then, we find two directions of relationships between an aspect of judgmental extremity — this time, extremity in judgments about self-descriptive statements — and risk-conservatism of decision making. Not only extremity in judging external events but also extremity in self-referent judgments hence serve under some conditions as a counterphobic or compensatory attempt at uncertainty reduction on the part of a basically conservative individual, and serve under other conditions as a willingness to tolerate the risk of error on the part of a high risk taker.

---

[1] See Kogan and Wallach (1964) for further work on this issue.

In sum, we have been able to demonstrate that various cognitive-judgmental behaviors — namely, general confidence of judgment, breadth of categorizing, extremity concerning judgments about external events, and extremity concerning self-referent judgments — do possess particular kinds of risk-conservatism implications for particular subgroups of individuals.

IMPLICATIONS FOR INTELLECTIVE ABILITIES

A frequent approach to the study of intellective abilities has been to cast them in the role of antecedents and to assume that if such abilities should turn out to be associated with other realms of psychological functioning, then the intellective abilities have been responsible for the associations in question. The evidence the authors have obtained on the relationship between verbal ability and decision making, however, forces the authors to propose a reversal of this causal sequence for the particular case in question. The authors' results suggest that the classic indexes of such ability, incorporating penalty-for-guessing instructions as they do, are partially reflecting individual differences in tendencies toward risk taking or conservatism. Rather than supposing verbal ability to serve as a cause of risk-taking dispositions, in other words, the authors find it more reasonable to assert that risk-taking dispositions influence verbal ability measures. The evidence indicates that when a subject faces a verbal aptitude test item that he cannot answer with certainty and when guessing carries a penalty in the cases where guessing leads to error, individual differences in risk-taking dispositions apparently become a significant determinant of what the subject does. Uncertainty is often the case during test taking, of course, and a penalty for guessing forms part of the instructions in many classic assessment techniques for measuring verbal aptitude (such as the College Entrance Examination Board's Scholastic Aptitude Test). Some share of measured verbal ability under these conditions, therefore, seems to be bound up with individual dispositions toward risk or conservatism.

The direction of the effect of risk-taking dispositions upon verbal performance as measured by the SAT depends, in turn, upon personality considerations. If a male subject is a member of the "least disturbed" subgroup, then a penchant for taking greater risks in chance and skill bet contexts pays off in the form of higher verbal ability scores. Just the opposite situation prevails, on the other hand, if a male subject is characterized by a particular pattern of motivational disturbance — high test anxiety and low defensiveness. For such persons, greater risk taking in chance and skill bet settings results in lower verbal ability scores. The implications of such findings are not far to seek. A gambling orientation on this verbal aptitude test lowers the scores of those individuals who react to such a stress situation with anxiety and who are devoid of any tendencies toward defensive control. In contrast, a gambling orientation does not have a harmful effect on verbal aptitude scores in the other subgroups, and most clearly exercises a beneficial effect upon verbal aptitude scores in the case of the "least disturbed" subgroup. The authors propose that test anxiety renders risk taking an inappropriate strategy by disrupting performance on difficult items — items in which the element of uncertainty is present. In contrast, minimal motivational disturbance seems to make risk taking an appropriate posture by leaving the individual in adequate command of his faculties when facing difficult items. Such a person, in other words, can indulge in "educated guessing," and this redounds to his advantage.

We feel that the present findings permit us some insight into the ever-elusive problem of explicating the psychological nature of verbal ability. Our results suggest that decision-making dispositions may be intimately woven into the fabric of the verbal ability concept. Part of the concept inevitably must concern the manner in which individuals can function with knowledge that is partial rather than complete, because the former situation is much more representative of everyday life than the latter. A modicum of uncertainty, in other words, is likely to accompany us in most of our verbal dominated intellectual pursuits. Part of the concept also must inevitably bear upon the case where blind guessing about answers does us more harm than good, because again, this situation is likely in the majority of our general experiences. It is no accident, in other words, that such a widely accepted assessor of verbal ability as the SAT has incorporated a penalty for guessing in its instructions. A verbal ability construct ought to reflect the capacity to judge when one has enough information to undertake the solution of a problem as well as the skill in problem-solving itself.

Under these conditions, then, risk-taking dispositions in interaction with personality considerations play a distinct role in verbal ability performances. The authors' suggestion is that this risk-conservatism element constitutes part of the psychological definition of such ability. Interestingly enough, furthermore, the contribution of that element to the verbal ability concept cannot be specified in isolation, but rather requires reference to the contextual personality conditions that obtain for the given individual. Recall that, whereas a risk-taking penchant in the context of minimal motivational disturbance leads to higher verbal aptitude scores, a risk-taking penchant in the context of a particular pattern of motivational disturbance — high test anxiety when defensiveness is low — leads to lower verbal aptitude scores. The authors submit, therefore, that risk-conservatism dispositions operating in a matrix of personality functioning constitute psychological processes of some importance for our understanding of what is involved in verbal ability.

There are, in turn, other cases of relationships between an ability measure, on the one hand, and decision-making on the other where the causal sequence seems to run in the more expected direction — from ability index to decision-making dispositions. Recall, for instance, our examination of the implications for risk taking of field dependence–independence, a mode of intellective functioning originally defined by Witkin and his colleagues in perceptual situations. The field dependence–independence concept refers to an individual's ability to extract an item perceptually from its context, as inferred from his proficiency at perceptually dealing with the item separately despite misleading contextual or "field" influences. A typical measure of this concept, and the one that we employed in the present research, requires the subject to locate a particular simple figure which is "hidden" as part of a larger, complex, and perceptually misleading figure. The field-independent person is one who performs well at this task, the field-dependent person one who performs poorly.

Recall that we found the *direction* of relationship between field dependence–independence, on the one hand, and risk-conservatism, on the other, itself to depend upon certain factors. For example, the evidence suggests that, on the whole, risk taking in men tends to be associated with a field-independent perceptual orientation, conservatism with field dependence — whereas risk taking in women tends to be linked with a field-dependent perceptual orientation, conservatism with field independence. These results suggest that field dependence–independence may well possess different psychological meanings for the two sexes.

The recent clinical formulation by Witkin and his colleagues (1962) proposed that field independence might possess psychodynamic implications of overcontrol and inhibition of impulses, whereas field dependence might imply impulsiveness and undercontrol. In relation to risk-conservatism, then, one would predict field-independent functioning to be linked with conservatism, field dependence with risk taking. As we have noted, such does tend to be the case with females. One can alternatively propose, however, that field independence–dependence may possess the function of a cognitive steering mechanism, the field-independent individual being characterized by a pattern of active, "participant" behavior, the field-dependent person by a pattern of passive, "spectator" behavior. This formulation implies what in fact has turned out to be the predominant finding for males: an association between field independence and risk taking on the one hand, a link between field dependence and conservatism on the other. On the whole, then, the differing directions of association with risk taking in the two sexes suggest that field-dependent versus field-independent modes of perceptual functioning may possess implications of a more psychodynamic, motivational nature for women, implications of a more cognitive nature for men.

The particular findings just discussed were obtained in the course of a moderator variable analysis. This analysis not only pinpoints the foregoing sex differences within particular subgroups, but also suggests that the members of the "least disturbed" subgroup of females react in a maximally flexible manner in regard to the impact of field dependence–independence upon risk taking and conservatism. Once again, sensitivity to situational factors seems to be particularly characteristic of this minimally disturbed subgroup.

In general, however, it is clear that our work on the risk-taking implications of perceptual field dependence–independence but scratches the surface of what needs to be done. What seems heartening to the authors is the progress we have been able to make in revealing and systematizing the diversity of psychological functioning subsumed under each pole of the field dependence–independence concept.

IMPLICATIONS FOR PERSONALITY CORRELATES

The authors' purpose in including inventory measures of personality in the present investigation was twofold. First and foremost, the authors wished to determine whether certain of the better-known personality scales impinge upon the decision-making domain. With this objective in mind, the authors selected personality dimensions likely to possess risk-taking implications. Second, it seemed possible that the emergence of significant relationships between personality inventory scales and risk-taking indexes would clarify the psychological meaning of the former as well as the latter.

It is the authors' considered view that these interdependent purposes were well served by the empirical outcomes. The data are quite revealing of some of the personality dimensions that have an impact upon risk taking. As a valuable by-product, we have acquired a deeper knowledge of the kinds of psychological processes tapped by some of the better-known scales. Both of these outcomes were rendered feasible through the application of a moderator analysis. Correlations obtained for the male and female samples as a whole are not especially revealing of personality-risk-taking relationships. When, however, test anxiety and defensiveness (personality variables in their own right) are cast in a moderator role, a reasonably meaningful pattern of relationships emerges. The implications of this finding for personality research are quite far-reaching, for it indicates that a particular personality dimension may have quite different meaning for individuals varying in other psychological characteristics. Impulsiveness in males, for example, has distinctively different consequences for risk taking when test anxiety and defensiveness are present and when they are absent. The evidence suggests that impulsiveness in males has an impact upon risk taking only in a context of low motivational disturbance. Had we remained at the level of working with entire samples (whether confined to correlational analysis or proceeding to a factor analysis), we would have been forced to conclude that impulsiveness and risk taking have little bearing upon one another in male subjects. Now, however, it appears that certain traits may require a context of low motivational disturbance in order for their effects to be felt in the area of decision-making behavior. Other traits, as we have seen, seem to require various types of motivational arousal if they are to have any influence on risk taking.

Psychologists in search of the basis for individual differences in behaviors of interest to them have often turned to relevant personality scales as the solution to their problem; reports of this type have been legion in psychological literature. Yet, the general outcome of such studies has been reflected in the often-repeated statement that the number of significant correlations obtained did not exceed some chance baseline. The present authors do not wish to maintain that a moderator analysis will improve the situation in all such cases. It is the authors' suspicion, however, that a moderator approach will provide significant clarification in many of these circumstances. The authors can only hope that the outcomes of the present investigation will encourage an increased alertness to the possibility that important relationships may be obscured as a consequence of neglecting potentially critical moderator effects. In the personality realm, the results reported in Chapter 7 strongly suggest that various personality characteristics that do not themselves possess direct relevance to psychological disturbance nevertheless have different consequences for behavior in individuals varying in degree and type of motivational disturbance. It does not seem to be the identical form of independence or self-sufficiency, for example, that is represented in subjects who are low in test anxiety and defensiveness, on the one hand, and who are high in one or both moderators on the other. In short, it may be necessary, when dealing with a particular personality variable, to give some consideration to the magnitude of other key personality variables that function as a motivational context. The major problem, of course, is one of delineating these key variables. Within the risk-taking domain, test anxiety and defensiveness play a critical moderator role. Whether these dimensions influence associations among other kinds of psychological variables is a moot question, though the authors are inclined toward a positive view of the matter, at least for related domains, given the central motivational significance of the two moderators under discussion.

Sex differences, so prevalent throughout the study, are especially prominent in the case of the personality–risk-taking relationships. Although such differences are always of interest in their own right, they are of particular significance in the present context, for in the course of observing how various personality dimensions relate to risk taking in different moderator subgroups for males and females, it becomes clear that the decision-making tasks used in the laboratory may bear directly upon risk and conservatism in everyday social contexts. For example, females expressing sentiments indicative of self-sufficiency and independence may be indulging in a type of "social risk taking" relative to certain normative expectations for women in our culture. Correspondingly, rigidity in females may reflect a way of ordering life so as to preclude the risk of having to cope with the unexpected. Interpretations of this kind receive some support on the basis of low-level significant relationships in the female sample as a whole. Especially noteworthy, however, is the evidence obtained from the moderator analysis, where it can be observed that females high in both test anxiety and defensiveness are largely responsible for the significant associations uncovered in the entire sample. This particular subgroup, in other words, exhibits a highly overgeneralized risk-conservatism orientation that may well encompass interpersonal behaviors bearing little formal resemblance to the type of risk-taking behaviors under study in the present investigation.

Recall, for example, that the independence scale is comprised of items that empirically distinguish between resistors and yielders in the Asch group-pressure situation. The relations observed between that scale and the decision-making indexes of the present study suggest the extent to which a risk-taking model may be applied to a broad net of "social decision-making" phenomena. The kinds of risks taken in a context of monetary gain or loss may be related to the forms of risk assumed when one deviates from the majority opinion of a group of which one is a member.[2] The relationships in question never appear to be direct, however. Rather, they vary with sex and with the pattern of motivational dynamics reflected by membership in one or another moderator subgroup. Such variations, it should be noted, may be put to systematic use in studies attempting to predict social behavior from personality inventory measures.

In conclusion, the personality evidence has served to fill in the psychological portrait of individuals located in the four moderator subgroups delineated in the study. With regard to the subjects high in test anxiety and defensiveness, those who (figuratively speaking) view their world through risky or conservative spectacles, we can now specify some of the forces that determine the direction of their highly generalized decision making toward risk or conservatism. Similarly, for those subjects who exhibit lesser degrees of generality in the risk-taking domain, we are now able to pinpoint some of the personality determinants contributing to risk taking or conservatism in particular situational contexts. On the whole, the relationships between

---

[2]Homans (1961) and Thibaut and Kelley (1959) have recently described the risks and payoffs inherent in conformity and innovation for group members at different status levels.

personality and risk taking neatly complement the other portions of the study. What may be equally important in the long run, however, are the intriguing possibilities for future research suggested by the presence of those relationships. There are indications in the present work that the risk-conservatism dimension may have implications for a wide variety of behavioral and social phenomena.

IMPLICATIONS FOR THE STUDY OF THINKING

Much attention has been devoted to the issue of whether thinking represents a unitary process or a set of relatively independent, diverse processes. Possibly the strongest exponent of the latter point of view has been Guilford (1960), who has cautioned against assuming that one name means one process. More recently, Taylor (1963) has maintained that the question of the degree to which various forms of thinking (for example, creativity, problem solving, decision making) represent similar or different processes is a matter for empirical investigation, rather than of definition. Taylor's preferences were more clearly revealed, however, when he proposed that an optimal research strategy in the present area will concentrate on limited theories of particular kinds of thinking rather than on a general, all-encompassing theory.

An alternative approach to the study of thinking has been reflected in attempts to divide the thinking process into phases. Brim *et al.* (1962, p. 9) distinguished six such phases: "(1) Identification of the problem; (2) obtaining necessary information; (3) production of possible solutions; (4) evaluation of such solutions; (5) selection of a strategy for performance; and (6) actual performance of an action or actions, and subsequent learning and revision." A somewhat similar phase conception has been proposed by Gagné (1959). In both cases, the intention has been one of linking problem solving and decision making as parts of a single continuous sequence. When one realizes, however, that different parts of the thinking sequence are omitted or engaged for particular kinds of "problems" or "decisions," the disparity between a unitary and multiprocess view loses much of its force.

How do the results of the present study bear upon the issues outlined here? The upshot of our research points neither toward a unitary nor multiple conception, but rather suggests that there are wide individual differences in the degree to which thinking may reflect a single as opposed to a variety of processes. As we have seen, it is the particular motivational matrix within which thinking activities occur that determines its dimensionality. Where test anxiety and defensiveness are high, risk-conservatism considerations seem to be highly salient, with the consequence that most of the thinking tasks used are approached from that perspective. Similarly, individuals who are high in test anxiety but low in defensiveness are most likely to demonstrate generalities when tasks have manifest problem-solving characteristics. Persons low in test anxiety and high in defensiveness, on the other hand, seem to exhibit the greatest generality under conditions where one's decisions (or problem solutions) are rendered in an interpersonal context and hence are presumed to have image-maintenance implications. Finally, it is the low test anxious–low defensive subjects who seem to respond to diverse thinking tasks on the basis of structural similarities and differences (for example, lack of control as opposed to direct personal control in decision implementation).

These findings make it quite clear that motivational influences may intrude upon thinking in various ways and to differing degrees. It is at this point that our results bear upon the long-standing problem of the relative dominance of external and internal determinants in thinking processes. In recent decades, we have witnessed the embodiment of the first set of determinants in the writings of Gestalt psychologists such as Wertheimer (for example, 1959), Köhler (for example, 1929), Duncker (for example, 1945), and Asch (for example, 1952). The emphasis has been upon viewing man's thinking as an enterprise primarily responsive to data offered by the environment and generally responsive in adaptively appropriate ways. Various experimental demonstrations have been adduced in support of viewing man as more of a task-centered than a self-centered being — in other words, as discriminating and responding to vectors or demands arising from the environment rather than seeing in it only a mirror of his own needs and other internal dispositions. Piaget (for example, 1951), indeed, has contrasted these two tendencies developmentally, finding "accommodation" to the environment's nature and "assimilation" of the environment to one's own nature as more and less mature modes of cognitive functioning, respectively.

The second set of determinants, in turn, has been embodied in the writings of S. Freud (for example, 1925) and in related orthodox psychoanalytic doctrine (for example, Fenichel, 1945). According to this viewpoint, thinking activities emerge from a motivational source. Man comes to take account of the environment's features only grudgingly as an indirect route toward achieving motivational gratifications ("reality principle") when completely solipsistic, projective behavior such as the hallucination of desired goal-objects ("pleasure principle") fails to gratify. Reality gains acknowledgement only as an instrument toward furthering gratificational ends; thinking constantly slips back toward nonveridicality because it remains the servant of affective processes. These cause projection and other forms of distortion to replace accurate evaluation of the environment wherever possible.

It will be granted that the two approaches outlined represent the extreme positions regarding the issue of motivational influences upon thinking. A major contemporary view, as reflected in the writings of the "ego-psychologists" (for example, Hartmann, 1951; Rapaport, 1957; Klein, 1958), has placed a heavy emphasis upon the controlling psychic structures that intervene between motivational states and environmental stimulation. Klein (1958), for example, has distinguished between control structures having an accommodative function in behavior and drive structures involving goal sets and requirements for particular forms of stimulation. The adaptive or nonadaptive quality of behavior, in this theory, depends on the relative dominance of the two types of structures. It should be noted that maladaptive behaviors, in this view, may derive from maximal drive "recruitment" and minimal accommodation (akin to what Freud has called primary-process thought), or from *capricious* steering of behavior by environmental stimulation. Although these propositions appear eminently reasonable, investigators working within the framework of ego psychology have devoted little empirical effort to specifying the relationships between motivational and cognitive variables.[3] Rather, there has been a concerted effort to explore the interrelationships among the cognitive controls themselves (for example, Gardner et al., 1959). By choosing to move in this direction, experimenters have sidestepped the issue of the relative dominance of motivational and environmental factors, and individual variations in cognitive controls have been considered to reflect diverse ways of adapting successfully to reality (Klein, 1958). This latter interpretation appears somewhat paradoxical, however, in the light of later evidence that has demonstrated that the cognitive control of leveling is related to repression tendencies (Holzman & Gardner, 1960).

It should be noted that most of the studies stemming from the Menninger Foundation have concentrated largely on perception, short-term memory, and sensorimotor interference. All of these functions are subject to powerful reality constraints. The subject's goal is generally one of achieving a workable approximation to veridicality, and gross deviations from reality, suggestive of psychopathology, must appear before one can apply the "maladaptive" label. In contrast, the domain of human thinking, particularly the form of thinking that encompasses decision-making processes, is less constrained by situational forces, with the consequence that motivational influences are allowed more freedom to operate. In the present study, we have tried to explore the relative contributions of motivational and situational variables to thinking processes. A consistently risky or conservative orientation across the various tasks included in the decision-making domain seems to imply the dominance of motivational influences.

---

[3]One of the few relevant studies (Klein, 1954) has concerned the manner in which relationships between thirst and perception are mediated by cognitive structures.

Correspondingly, a differential sensitivity to the stimulus character of the various decision-making procedures employed suggests that situational and task variables receive major emphasis.

Is it feasible to make the transition from motivational versus task dominance to irrationality versus rationality of thought processes? At first blush, such a transition appears quite reasonable, but the issue upon further reflection is an exceedingly complicated one. Rationality in the realm of decision making implies that the individual follows a set of rules in an effort to optimize outcomes. Within a decision framework, this principle has usually implied maximizing subjectively expected utility (W. Edwards, 1954). This model has recently been challenged by March and Simon (1958), who have argued that most decision making involves "satisficing" rather than "maximizing." It is only in exceptional cases, according to those authors, that the individual seeks the optimal alternative.

The authors make no claim to an independent criterion for "maximizing" or "satisficing." Indeed, where possible, the authors deliberately arranged decision alternatives so that they were equal in objectively expected value. In other words, the authors wanted to find out whether, under such conditions, individuals would show consistent preferences for gain maximization, loss minimization, and so forth. Strategies of these kinds are reflective of risk-taking or conservative orientations, not of rationality or irrationality as such.

Nevertheless, it must be granted that information on level of winnings was available, and could have served as a criterion for rationality. By this product-centered view, one can maintain that the persons winning the most money have made the most rational decisions. Despite the theoretically equal expected values in the strategy procedures, for example, subjects are making a finite series of decisions, and, hence, certain decision patterns may prove more rational (optimal) than others in the short run. In each of our decision-making procedures, however, there are factors that can impinge upon the process to upset the expected relation between rational decisions and favorable consequences. Thus, where chance strategies are concerned, random processes can be expected to produce runs of good and bad luck, thereby yielding outcomes that have little to do with prior decisions. In the case of skill strategies, a slight increase in muscle tension can readily reduce payoffs to a less than optimal level relative to potential payoffs based on level of performance during the practice trials. Finally, for the number judgments and clues tasks, optimal decision-making implies requesting the minimum amount of information necessary to identify correctly the sign of a distribution (number judgments) or the identity of an object (clues). An incorrect identification is by definition nonoptimal, but in the case of an accurate decision there is no way of knowing how soon in the series an accurate hypothesis was formed but withheld pending the receipt of further confirmatory information.[4]

Given the circumstances described here, the authors feel that a product-centered approach to the question of rationality of decision making is inappropriate in the present context. This is not to imply that there is no relation between process and product. If one could sample a wide variety of decision-making behavior over an extended period of time, one would expect less favorable outcomes to eventuate for those individuals who are committed to a consistently risky or conservative orientation. Correspondingly, we should expect more favorable consequences to flow from decisions that are in large part influenced by external situational requirements. A modicum of evidence to support this expectation is available in the form of performance in a natural life situation — the Scholastic Aptitude Test — where the examinee's academic career is influenced by his performance. In this context, there is a clear trend in which least disturbed males achieve the highest SAT-Verbal scores, whereas the test anxious defensives — those most strongly committed to a consistently risky or conservative outlook — obtain the lowest scores. As we have seen, the evidence strongly suggests that objective test performance (and, hence, an individual's "aptitude") is, in part, determined by risk-taking dispositions.

Although these data do strengthen the authors' case for a conceptualization in terms of rationality and irrationality, there are other pieces of evidence that better lend themselves to consideration from that point of view. For example, recall the results on postdecisional processes reported in Chapter 4. There are persons who, when faced with the failure of a risky decision-making strategy, react by insistently affirming their satisfaction with that strategy. These are the males who are high both in test anxiety and defensiveness. In contrast, others display the more reasonable approach of reacting to the failure of a risky strategy by expressing dissatisfaction and a desire to switch to more conservative alternatives. This behavior is characteristic of the males who are low in both test anxiety and defensiveness.

Further confirmatory evidence for rationality and irrationality in the low-low and high-high subgroups, respectively, is provided by the observed relation between decision strategies and postdecision dissatisfaction. For the high test anxious–high defensive males, these domains are significantly linked — the risk-takers remain more committed to their original decisions than do the conservatives, quite apart from level of monetary winnings. The low test anxious–low defensive males, on the other hand, manifest no

---

[4]Note that had the authors tried to obtain information on this point, a radical change in the nature of the procedure would have resulted.

association between strategies and postdecision dissatisfaction when monetary winnings are held constant. There is, then, a clear distinction between the subgroups in the degree to which postdecision dissatisfaction is predetermined by initial strategy selection. The greater the predetermination, the more irrational the behavior appears to be, for the subject's postdecisional satisfaction under these conditions reflects a personal decision-making style rather than an objective evaluation of decision outcomes. As we have seen, it is the more motivationally disturbed males who are susceptible to these effects. Correspondingly, the lack of an association between decision-making strategies and postdecisional dissatisfaction implies the close monitoring of outcomes so strongly suggestive of a rational approach. Recall that the least disturbed males exhibit this pattern.

Also relevant to the rationality-irrationality issue are the observed relationships between the final bet index and the level of prior winnings. There are persons who, when making a final dice bet the stake of which consists of their own newly acquired funds, disregard the amount of their money that is at stake and bet largely according to a generalized disposition for risk or conservatism. Again, this general disregard of monetary amount when betting on a single toss of a die has clear overtones of irrationality. It is the motivationally disturbed subgroups who manifest this irrational pattern. Other individuals, in contrast, follow the more rational strategem of betting in a conservative manner if they have a lot that can be lost and betting in a risky manner if they do not have much to lose. Included here are the "least disturbed" subgroups in the study.

The picture in its full detail is more complicated, of course, than the over-all generalizations that we have presented. There are circumstances, for example, under which the locus of responsibility for a particular form of irrationality resides more strongly in one or the other of these two aspects of motivational disturbance — defensiveness or test anxiety. There also are certain sex differences. In general, however, irrationality and rationality assume their pristine form in the high test anxious–high defensive and low test anxious–low defensive subjects, respectively.

Interestingly enough, the two subgroups that we have been discussing are distinguished most clearly in terms of the relative dominance of motivational and situational forces in their decision-making behavior. Recall that the high-high subjects manifest a highly generalized risky or conservative outlook in their decision-making behavior, whereas the low-lows respond to decision-making situations on the basis of structural similarities and differences. Although these findings may not constitute evidence for rationality-irrationality in their own right, they do tend to buttress the evidence outlined earlier in the section. The general neglect of environmental outcomes in postdecisional responses, so suggestive of irrationality, seems to have its counterpart in the decision-making process itself, in the sense that motivational dispositions achieve dominance over the inherent structural aspects of the decision tasks. Correspondingly, the apparent rationality displayed by the "least disturbed" subjects in postdecisional contexts is consonant with the sensitivity to task structure reflected in the more differentiated decision-making behavior of those subjects. Although we do not choose to render equivalent the rational-irrational and structural-motivational dichotomies, there is an empirical warrant in the present context for assuming some degree of overlap.

IMPLICATIONS FOR DECISION MAKING ON NATIONAL AND MILITARY ISSUES

It is apparent that none of the research reported in this volume has been explicitly concerned with decision making of a kind that has import for questions of human survival. The authors believe, however, that their work may possess some implications for such matters. In view of the findings, there may be much to be gained by considering what they suggest concerning decision making on national and military issues. The topic in question is obviously of extreme importance to mankind. Under such circumstances, we cannot afford to ignore the relevance that the present findings may have for this area, even though the discussion here must consist of extrapolations rather than direct evidence.

In general, it has become all too clear in the nuclear age that we cannot assign a positive or negative value judgment to one or the other end of the risk-conservatism continuum. Risk taking or conservatism may be equally disastrous, depending upon the particular circumstances and situation in question. We can, however, begin to make value judgments about behavior that is *consistently* risky or *consistently* conservative — in other words, behavior that relegates situational inducements and constraints to a secondary role. Such behavior in policy-making contexts may well constitute a prime threat in decision making about national and military affairs. The authors have described an all-pervasive orientation toward risk or conservatism as possibly having implications for irrationality in decision making, and the authors believe that this outlook on the matter of irrationality may provide a highly relevant way of specifying the meaning of that term as it applies to international affairs. Osgood (1962) has written as follows on the dangers of irrationality in the conduct of relations between nations: "In a situation where the consequences of wrong decisions are so awesome, where a single bit of irrationality can set a whole chain of traumatic events in motion, I do not think that we can be satisfied with the assurance that 'most people behave rationally most of the time' " (p. 120). Osgood then went on to ask about the conditions that contribute to irrationality in decision making. To quote him again, "Increases in tension, beyond some optimal level, serve to magnify the ratio of nonrational to rational alternatives. Under stress men are more likely to act irrationally, to strike out blindly, or even to freeze into stupid immobility. In other words, both flexibility and rationality 'ride on the back' of tension level" (p. 121).

Osgood's points obviously are very well taken. The present work suggests, however, that the argument has to be extended further. Tension and stress can lead to greater irrationality in decision making by men in general; but the present findings strongly suggest that *particular kinds of individuals* — namely, persons who are high in defensiveness and in the tendency to react to stress with anxiety — may be especially susceptible to such irrationality. The present work also has specified and provided evidence for an operational meaning of irrationality that appears to be especially relevant to the kinds of decision making under examination in this section. Further, the presence of relatively strong tendencies toward rationality in such decision making may characterize but a minority of men — namely, ones who are low both in defensiveness and in stress-induced anxiety. In short, the present results bear upon the question of the forms that irrationality and rationality may take in decision making concerning national and military policy, and upon the question of the kinds of persons most likely to display more rational and more nonrational behavior in such situations.

The need to cast psychological light on these very questions is quite evident from recent writings on national policy. Thus, for example, Brodie (1962) has remarked that political leaders "are *bound* to act at times irrationally, even in important matters, simply because all men do so. Neurotics tend to do so more than others, but there is not the slightest evidence that the Soviet Union has a lower incidence of neurosis than other countries or that neurotics are less likely there to climb into high political positions" (p. 744). Lest the United States be considered an exception to this issue, he went on to point out, "In periods of intense crisis, we are probably as capable as the Russians of acting out what may seem to be the imperatives of the moment. Our conceptions of what we are compelled to do will be molded, like theirs, by a range of rational, semirational, and nonrational judgments or impressions, all coming out of human beings charged with emotion, including emotions of which the possessors are not even conscious" (p. 745). So also, Deutsch (1961) has remarked, "Nervousness, the need to respond quickly because of the fear that one will lose either the desire or ability to respond, enhances the likelihood that a response will be triggered off by an insufficient stimulus and thus, makes for instability" (p. 62). The kind of predispositional "trigger" to which the present research has called attention consists of a heightened salience of the risk-conservatism dimension; and the kind of people whom we find to be most highly sensitized to this dimension are those who are both defensive and anxious in response to stress.

Finally, we must note Kahn's (1960) ordering of the ways in which a nuclear war can arise. Although acknowledging that accidents are improbable, he nevertheless has felt compelled by his analysis of the various contingencies to assign accidental war the top ranking. Among the types of accidents at issue are ones that arise from the very kinds of human irrationality that we have been considering. Other writers, too, have stressed the dangers of war by accident. Deutsch (1961) has called attention to the "possibility that the decision to use the bomb would be made by an irresponsible local unit — by a 'mischievous' missile squad, a 'grandiose' bomber crew, a 'paranoid' submarine crew — which could carry out its own decision" (p. 62). Frank (1960) has pointed out that responsibility for nuclear weapons has been filtering progressively down the chain of command as a joint result of the increased number of such weapons and the decreased warning time available for retaliation. It is especially in the examination of possible sources of accidental war that attention must be focused upon personality predispositions toward rational and irrational behavior, and upon the psychological forms that these classes of behavior can take. The very definition of *accidental* implies a situation where essentially "irrelevant" factors have the potential for becoming dominant and determining. It is obviously of the utmost importance to know just what these irrelevant factors may be, and what kinds of effects they may have.

Let us step back now to consider somewhat less ultimate but still very critical decisions of policy. We turn to the customary state of affairs in international relations, where nations are acting out long-range policies toward each other in which particular maneuvers lead to a particular failure or success of limited consequence and are followed by other particular maneuvers. This is the situation, of course, in diplomacy and in "limited" war. Recall, in this connection, our examination of reactions to the *failure* of a risky strategy. We found that, among the individuals high in both test anxiety and defensiveness, the failure of a risky strategy leads to a heightened affirmation of that strategy. In contrast, for the low test anxious–low defensive persons, just the reverse pattern obtains — failure of a risky strategy leads to an increase in desired shifts toward conservatism. The kind of behavior exhibited by the high test anxious–high defensive risktakers has evident maladaptive aspects. The type of behavior shown by the persons low in test anxiety and defensiveness, on the other hand, is more clearly adaptive. These contrasting types of reactions to a risky strategy's failure may well possess some striking implications for questions of national and military policy. The failure of a risky policy pursued by political and military decision-makers of a particular personality make-up may well exacerbate their inclination toward risk taking.

The published literature on national and military affairs has emphasized the presence of irrational elements in decision making and the possible impact of such elements on international conflict. Nowhere in this literature has any specific attempt been found, however, to isolate and describe in detail the forms of irrationality that possess particular implications for the decision making involved in matters of human survival. Nor is there evidence of attempts to delineate and document systematically the varying personality dispositions that can exacerbate or dampen tendencies toward irrationality in times of international tension and stress. The authors would like to think that the research reported in this volume represents a start in the direction of dealing with these issues. The authors must confess, in fact, to being burdened at times by a nagging curiosity as to how the various individuals who control our destiny would distribute themselves across the personality subgroups that have been investigated in the present volume.

References

ALPERT, R., & HABER, R. N. Anxiety in academic achievement situations. *J. abnorm. soc. Psychol.*, 1960, *61*, 207–215.
ASCH, S. E. *Social psychology.* Englewood Cliffs, N. J.: Prentice-Hall, 1952.
ATKINSON, J. W. Motivational determinants of risk-taking behavior. *Psychol. Rev.*, 1957, *64*, 359–372.
ATKINSON, J. W., BASTIAN, J. R., EARL, R. W., & LITWIN, G. H. The achievement motive, goal setting, and probability preferences. *J. abnorm. soc. Psychol.*, 1960, *60*, 27–36.
ATKINSON, J. W., & LITWIN, G. H. Achievement motive and test anxiety conceived as motive to approach success and motive to avoid failure. *J. abnorm. soc. Psychol.*, 1960, *60*, 52–63.
BARRATT, E. S. Anxiety and impulsiveness related to psychomotor efficiency. *Percept. mot. Skills*, 1959, *9*, 191–198.
BARRON, F. Some personality correlates of independence of judgment. *J. Pers.*, 1953, *21*, 287–297.
BENDIG, A. W. The development of a short form of the Manifest Anxiety Scale. *J. consult. Psychol.*, 1956, *20*, 384.
BREHM, J. W. Postdecision changes in the desirability of alternatives. *J. abnorm. soc. Psychol.*, 1956, *52*, 384–389.
BREHM, J. W., & COHEN, A. R. *Explorations in cognitive dissonance.* New York: Wiley, 1962.
BRIM, O. G., JR. Attitude content-intensity and probability expectations. *Amer. sociol. Rev.*, 1955, *20*, 68–76.
BRIM, O. G., JR., GLASS, D. C., LAVIN, D. E., & GOODMAN, N. *Personality and decision processes.* Stanford, Cal.: Stanford Univer. Press, 1962.
BRIM, O. G., JR., & HOFF, D. B. Individual and situational differences in desire for certainty. *J. abnorm. soc. Psychol.*, 1957, *54*, 225–229.
BRODIE, B. Defense policy and the possibility of total war. *Daedalus*, 1962, *91*, 733–748.

BRUNER, J. S., GOODNOW, JACQUELINE J., & AUSTIN, G. A. A study of thinking. New York: Wiley, 1956.

BRUNER, J. S., & TAJFEL, H. Cognitive risk and environmental change. J. abnorm. soc. Psychol., 1961, 62, 231–241.

COHEN, J. Chance, skill, and luck. Baltimore, Md.: Penguin, 1960.

COHEN, J. The statistical power of abnormal-social psychological research: A review. J. abnorm. soc. Psychol., 1962, 65, 145–153.

COLLEGE ENTRANCE EXAMINATION BOARD. College Board score reports: A guide for counselors. Princeton, N. J.: Author, 1962.

COOMBS, C. H., MILHOLLAND, J. E., & WOMER, F. B. The assessment of partial knowledge. Educ. psychol. Measmt, 1956, 16, 13–37.

COOMBS, C. H., & PRUITT, D. G. Components of risk in decision-making: Probability and variance preferences. J. exp. Psychol., 1960, 60, 265–277.

COUCH, A., & KENISTON, K. Yea-sayers and nay-sayers: Agreeing response set as a personality variable. J. abnorm. soc. Psychol., 1960, 60, 151–174.

CRONBACH, L. J. Response sets and test validity. Educ. psychol. Measmt, 1946, 6, 475–494.

CRONBACH, L. J. Coefficient alpha and the internal structure of tests. Psychometrika, 1951, 16, 297–334.

CRONBACH, L. J., & MEEHL, P. E. Construct validity in psychological tests. Psychol. Bull., 1955, 52, 281–302.

CROWNE, D. P., & MARLOWE, D. A new scale of social desirability independent of psychopathology. J. consult. Psychol., 1960, 24, 349–354.

CRUTCHFIELD, R. S. Conformity and character. Amer. Psychologist, 1955, 10, 191–198.

CRUTCHFIELD, R. S., & STARKWEATHER, J. A. Differences among officer personnel in perception of the vertical under distorting influence of a tilted frame. Berkeley, Cal.: IPAR, Univer. of California, 1953.

DEUTSCH, M. Some considerations relevant to national policy. J. soc. Issues, 1961, 17, 57–68.

DEUTSCH, M., KRAUSS, R. M., & ROSENAU, NORAH. Dissonance or defensiveness? J. Pers., 1962, 30, 16–28.

DUNCKER, K. On problem solving. Psychol. Monogr., 1945, 58, No. 5 (Whole No. 270).

EDWARDS, A. L. The social desirability variable in personality assessment and research. New York: Holt, 1957.

EDWARDS, W. The theory of decision-making. Psychol. Bull., 1954, 51, 380–417.

EDWARDS, W. Behavioral decision theory. Annu. Rev. Psychol., 1961, 12, 473–498.

ELLIOTT, R. Interrelationships among measures of field dependence, ability, and personality traits. J. abnorm. soc. Psychol., 1961, 63, 27–36.

FENICHEL, O. The psychoanalytic theory of neurosis. New York: Norton, 1945.

FESTINGER, L. A theory of cognitive dissonance. Stanford, Cal.: Stanford Univer. Press, 1957.

FILLENBAUM, S. Some stylistic aspects of categorizing behavior. J. Pers., 1959, 27, 187–195.

FOREHAND, G. A. Relationships among response sets and cognitive behaviors. Educ. psychol. Measmt, 1962, 22, 287–302.

FRANK, J. D. Breaking the thought barrier: Psychological challenges of the nuclear age. *Psychiatry*, 1960, *23*, 245–266.
FRENCH, J. W. *Manual for kit of selected tests for reference aptitude and achievement factors.* Princeton, N. J.: Educational Testing Service, 1954.
FREUD, ANNA. *The ego and the mechanisms of defense.* New York: International Univer. Press., 1946.
FREUD, S. *Collected papers.* Vol. IV. London: Hogarth, 1925.
FREUD, S. *The problem of anxiety.* New York: Norton, 1936.
GAGNÉ, R. M. Problem solving and thinking. *Annu. Rev. Psychol.*, 1959, *10*, 147–173.
GARDNER, R. W., HOLZMAN, P. S., KLEIN, G. S., LINTON, HARRIET, & SPENCE, D. P. Cognitive control: A study of individual consistencies in cognitive behavior. *Psychol. Issues*, 1959, *1*, No. 4 (Monogr. 4).
GARDNER, R. W., JACKSON, D. N., & MESSICK, S. Personality organization in cognitive controls and intellectual abilities. *Psychol. Issues*, 1960, *2*, No. 4 (Monogr. 8).
GARDNER, R. W., & SCHOEN, R. A. Differentiation and abstraction in concept formation. *Psychol. Monogr.*, 1962, *76*, No. 41 (Whole No. 560).
GHISELLI, E. E. Differentiation of individuals in terms of their predictability. *J. appl. Psychol.*, 1956, *40*, 374–377.
GHISELLI, E. E. Differentiation of tests in terms of the accuracy with which they predict for a given individual. *Educ. psychol. Measmt*, 1960, *20*, 675–684. (a)
GHISELLI, E. E. The prediction of predictability. *Educ. psychol. Measmt*, 1960, *20*, 3–8. (b)
GHISELLI, E. E. Moderating effects and differential reliability and validity. *J. appl. Psychol.*, 1963, *47*, 81–86.
GUILFORD, J. P. Basic conceptual problems in the psychology of thinking. *Ann. N. Y. Acad. Sci.*, 1960, *91*, 6–21.
HAMILTON, V. Perceptual and personality dynamics in reactions to ambiguity. *Brit. J. Psychol.*, 1957, *48*, 200–215.
HARTMANN, H. Ego psychology and the problem of adaptation. In D. Rapaport (Ed.), *Organization and pathology of thought.* New York: Columbia Univer. Press, 1951. Pp. 362–398.
HEIDBREDER, EDNA. An experimental study of thinking. *Arch. Psychol.*, 1924, *11*, No. 73.
HEIDER, F. *The psychology of interpersonal relations.* New York: Wiley, 1958.
HOLZMAN, P. S., & GARDNER. R. W. Leveling-sharpening and memory organization. *J. abnorm. soc. Psychol.*, 1960, *61*, 176–180.
HOMANS, G. C. *Social behavior: Its elementary forms.* New York: Harcourt, Brace, 1961.
IRWIN, F. W., & SMITH, W. A. S. Further tests of theories of decision in an "expanded judgment" situation. *J. exp. Psychol.*, 1956, *52*, 345–348.
IRWIN, F. W., & SMITH, W. A. S. Value, cost, and information as determiners of decision. *J. exp. Psychol.*, 1957, *54*, 229–232.
JACKSON, D. N., & MESSICK, S. Content and style in personality assessment. *Psychol. Bull.*, 1958, *55*, 243–252.

JACKSON, D. N., MESSICK, S., & MYERS, C. T. The role of memory and color in group and individual embedded-figures measures of field independence. *Educ. psychol. Measmt*, 1964, in press.

JOHNSON, L. C. Generality of speed and confidence of judgment. *J. abnorm. soc. Psychol.*, 1957, *54*, 264–265.

KAHN, H. The arms race and some of its hazards. *Daedalus*, 1960, *89*, 744–780.

KLEIN, G. S. Need and regulation. In M. R. Jones (Ed.), *Nebraska symposium on motivation*. Lincoln, Neb.: Univer. of Nebraska Press, 1954. Pp. 224–274.

KLEIN, G. S. Cognitive control and motivation. In G. Lindzey (Ed.), *Assessment of human motives*. New York: Rinehart, 1958. Pp. 87–115.

KOGAN, N., & WALLACH, M. A. Certainty of judgment and the evaluation of risk. *Psychol. Rep.*, 1960, *6*, 207–213.

KOGAN, N., & WALLACH, M. A. The effect of anxiety on relations between subjective age and caution in an older sample. In P. H. Hoch & J. Zubin (Eds.), *Psychopathology of aging*. New York: Grune and Stratton, 1961. Pp. 123–135.

KOGAN, N., & WALLACH, M. A. Personality and situational determinants of judgmental confidence and extremity. *Brit. J. soc. clin. Psychol.*, 1964, in press.

KÖHLER, W. *Gestalt psychology*. New York: Liveright, 1929.

KRECH, D., CRUTCHFIELD, R. S., & BALLACHEY, E. L. *Individual in society: A textbook of social psychology*. New York: McGraw-Hill, 1962.

LEWIN, K. *Principles of topological psychology*. New York: McGraw-Hill, 1936.

LITTIG, L. W. Effects of skill and chance orientations on probability preferences. *Psychol. Rep.*, 1962, *10*, 67–70.

LIVERANT, S., & SCODEL, A. Internal and external control as determinants of decision-making under conditions of risk. *Psychol. Rep.*, 1960, *7*, 59–67.

MARCH, J. C., & SIMON, H. A. *Organizations*. New York: Wiley, 1958.

MCGEE, R. K. Response style as a personality variable: By what criterion? *Psychol. Bull.*, 1962, *59*, 284–295.

MESSICK, S. Response style and content measures from personality inventories. *Educ. psychol. Measmt*, 1962, *22*, 41–56.

MESSICK, S., & HILLS, J. Objective measurement of personality: Cautiousness and intolerance of ambiguity. *Educ. psychol. Measmt*, 1960, *20*, 685–698.

MESSICK, S., & KOGAN, N. Differentiation and compartmentalization in object-sorting measures of categorizing style. *Percept. mot. Skills*, 1963, *16*, 47–51.

OSGOOD, C. E. Toward international behavior appropriate to a nuclear age. In G. S. Nielsen (Ed.), *Psychology and international affairs*. Copenhagen: Munksgaard, 1962. Pp. 109–132.

PEABODY, D. Two components in bipolar scales: Direction and extremeness. *Psychol. Rev.*, 1962, *69*, 65–73.

PETTIGREW, T. F. The measurement and correlates of category width as a cognitive variable. *J. Pers.*, 1958, *26*, 532–544.

PIAGET, J. *Play, dreams, and imitation in childhood*. New York: Norton, 1951.

QUERESHI, M. Y. Mental test performance as a function of payoff conditions, item difficulty, and degree of speeding. *J. appl. Psychol.*, 1960, *44*, 65–77.

RAPAPORT, D. Cognitive structures. In *Contemporary approaches to cognition*. Cambridge, Mass.: Harvard Univer. Press, 1957. Pp. 157–200.

ROBERTS, J. S., JR. Information-seeking in sequential decision-making as dependent upon test anxiety and upon prior success or failure in problem solving. In D. W. Taylor (Ed.), *Experiments on decision-making and other studies.* Arlington, Va.: ASTIA, 1960. (Technical Report No. 6, AD 253952.) Pp. 26–37.

ROGERS, C. R. A theory of therapy, personality, and interpersonal relationships, as developed in the client-centered framework. In S. Koch (Ed.), *Psychology: A study of a science.* Vol. 3. *Formulations of the person and the social context.* New York: McGraw-Hill, 1959. Pp. 184–256.

ROKEACH, M. *The open and closed mind.* New York: Basic Books, 1960.

ROSEN, S. Post-decision affinity for incompatible information. *J. abnorm. soc. Psychol.,* 1961, *63,* 188–190.

RUEBUSH, B. K. Interfering and facilitating effects of test anxiety. *J. abnorm. soc. Psychol.,* 1960, *60,* 205–212.

SARASON, I. G. Interrelationships among individual difference variables, behavior in psychotherapy, and verbal conditioning. *J. abnorm. soc. Psychol.,* 1958, *56,* 339–344.

SARASON, I. G., & PALOLA, E. G. The relationship of test and general anxiety, difficulty of task, and experimental instructions to performance. *J. exp. Psychol.,* 1960, *59,* 185–191.

SARASON, S. B., MANDLER, G., & CRAIGHILL, P. G. The effect of differential instructions on anxiety and learning. *J. abnorm. soc. Psychol.,* 1952, *47,* 561–565.

SAUNDERS, D. R. Some preliminary interpretive material for the PRI. Research Memorandum 55-15. Princeton, N. J.: Educational Testing Service, 1955.

SAUNDERS, D. R. Moderator variables in prediction. *Educ. psychol. Measmt,* 1956, *16,* 209–222.

SCODEL, A., RATOOSH, P., & MINAS, J. S. Some personality correlates of decision making under conditions of risk. *Behav. Sci.,* 1959, *4,* 19–28.

SHERIFFS, A. C., & BOOMER, D. S. Who is penalized by the penalty for guessing? *J. educ. Psychol.,* 1954, *45,* 81–90.

SLOVIC, P. Convergent validation of risk taking measures. *J. abnorm. soc. Psychol.,* 1962, *65,* 68–70.

STRICKLAND, BONNIE R., & CROWNE, D. P. Need for approval and the premature termination of psychotherapy. *J. consult. Psychol.,* 1963, *27,* 95–101.

TAYLOR, D. W. Thinking. In M. H. Marx (Ed.), *Psychological theory: Contemporary readings.* New York: Macmillan, 1963.

THIBAUT, J. W., & KELLEY, H. H. *The social psychology of groups.* New York: Wiley, 1959.

WALLACH, M. A. The influence of classification requirements on gradients of response. *Psychol. Monogr.,* 1959, *73,* No. 8 (Whole No. 478).

WALLACH, M. A. Commentary: Active-analytical vs. passive-global cognitive functioning. In S. Messick & J. Ross (Eds.), *Measurement in personality and cognition.* New York: Wiley, 1962. Pp. 199–215.

WALLACH, M. A., & CARON, A. J. Attribute criteriality and sex-linked conservatism as determinants of psychological similarity. *J. abnorm. soc. Psychol.,* 1959, *59,* 43–50.

WALLACH, M. A., & GAHM, RUTHELLEN C. Personality functions of graphic constriction and expansiveness. *J. Pers.*, 1960, *28*, 73–88.

WALLACH, M. A., GREEN, L. R., LIPSITT, P. D., & MINEHART, JEAN B. Contradiction between overt and projective personality indicators as a function of defensiveness. *Psychol. Monogr.*, 1962, *76*, No. 1 (Whole No. 520).

WALLACH, M. A., & GREENBERG, CAROL. Personality functions of symbolic sexual arousal to music. *Psychol. Monogr.*, 1960, *74*, No. 7 (Whole No. 494).

WALLACH, M. A., & KOGAN, N. Sex differences and judgment processes. *J. Pers.*, 1959, *27*, 555–564.

WALLACH, M. A., & KOGAN, N. Aspects of judgment and decision-making: Interrelationships and changes with age. *Behav. Sci.*, 1961, *6*, 23–36.

WALLACH, M. A., KOGAN, N., & BEM, D. J. Group influence on individual risk taking. *J. abnorm. soc. Psychol.*, 1962, *65*, 75–86.

WERTHEIMER, M. *Productive thinking.* New York: Harper, 1959.

WHITE, R. W. *The abnormal personality.* New York: Ronald, 1956.

WITKIN, H. A., DYK, R. B., FATERSON, H. F., GOODENOUGH, D. R., & KARP, S. A. *Psychological differentiation.* New York: Wiley, 1962.

WITKIN, H. A., LEWIS, HELEN B., HERTZMAN, M., MACHOVER, KAREN, MEISSNER, PEARL B., & WAPNER, S. *Personality through perception.* New York: Harper, 1954.

WORLEY, D. R. Amount and generality of information-seeking behavior in sequential decision-making as dependent on level of incentive. In D. W. Taylor (Ed.), *Experiments on decision-making and other studies.* Arlington, Va.: ASTIA, 1960. (Technical Report No. 6, AD 253952.) Pp. 1–11.

ZILLER, R. C. A measure of the gambling response set in objective tests. *Psychometrika*, 1957, *22*, 289–292.

Appendixes

Appendix A-1

Means and Sigmas of Major Variables for Total Male and Female Samples

	Variable	Males (N = 114) Mean	SD	Females (N = 103) Mean	SD	t[a]
1.	Choice dilemmas	66.84	11.61	67.08	12.99	-.14
2.	Chance-max. of gain	37.14	14.77	38.99	12.02	-1.01
3.	Chance-min. of loss	21.79	7.62	23.63	8.05	-1.72
4.	Chance-long shot	29.80	13.01	32.45	10.52	-1.65
5.	Chance-min. dev. from 1/2	24.41	8.73	22.68	7.52	1.56
6.	Chance-max. of variance	37.09	12.70	37.75	10.82	-.41
7.	Skill-max. of gain	35.32	14.64	35.68	11.83	-.20
8.	Skill-min. of loss	21.68	6.96	20.61	6.68	1.14
9.	Skill-long shot	27.64	12.64	26.61	10.54	.65
10.	Skill-min. dev. from 1/2	26.18	8.90	28.83	8.35	-2.25
11.	Skill-max. of variance	35.45	12.53	36.13	10.59	-.43
12.	Number judgments	56.64	23.78	45.23	21.91	3.66
13.	Clues	60.61	11.56	53.16	13.56	4.31
14.	Final bet	4.11	1.51	4.03	1.55	.41
15.	Total winnings	3.63	1.56	3.38	1.51	1.19
16.	Chance-abs. winnings	1.03	1.21	.91	1.06	.76
17.	Chance-rel. winnings	.13	.14	.12	.16	.31
18.	Skill-abs. winnings	1.11	1.17	.92	1.03	1.27
19.	Skill-rel. winnings	.18	.18	.13	.14	2.34
20.	Chance bet dissatisfaction	3.89	3.01	4.90	3.43	-2.32
21.	Skill bet dissatisfaction	3.11	2.55	3.26	2.10	-.49
22.	Verbal aptitude (SAT)	654.14	61.36	659.86	46.96	-.77
23.	Math. aptitude (SAT)	691.42	73.16	626.12	64.04	6.98
24.	Analytic functioning (EFT)	18.68	6.91	19.15	5.99	-.53
25.	Judgmental confidence	2.84	.55	2.77	.50	1.01
26.	Extremity-high confidence	31.01	6.91	31.23	8.19	-.21
27.	Extremity-low confidence	18.32	5.07	17.08	5.52	1.71
28.	Category width	16.57	3.46	15.79	3.14	1.72
29.	Extremity of self-rating	111.40	18.37	110.96	14.67	.20
30.	Self-sufficiency	4.96	2.46	4.23	2.31	2.25
31.	Independence	8.46	2.10	8.19	1.72	1.03
32.	Impulsiveness	11.91	3.45	11.93	2.98	-.05
33.	Rigidity	12.82	3.66	13.54	3.40	-1.49

[a] For 215 df, t's of 1.97 and 2.60 are significant at the .05 and .01 levels, respectively.

Appendix A-2

Means and Sigmas of Major Variables for Low and High Test Anxious Males

	Variable	Low (N = 65)		High (N = 49)		t^a
		Mean	SD	Mean	SD	
1.	Choice dilemmas	65.88	11.10	68.12	12.14	-1.00
2.	Chance-max. of gain	35.35	15.12	39.51	13.94	-1.51
3.	Chance-min. of loss	23.18	7.74	19.94	7.06	2.31
4.	Chance-long shot	28.43	13.02	31.61	12.76	-1.29
5.	Chance-min. dev. from 1/2	24.92	7.93	23.73	9.64	.70
6.	Chance-max. of variance	34.98	12.75	39.88	12.08	-2.07
7.	Skill-max. of gain	35.03	14.19	35.71	15.20	-.24
8.	Skill-min. of loss	21.31	6.60	22.16	7.37	-.64
9.	Skill-long shot	27.15	12.36	28.29	12.98	-.47
10.	Skill-min. dev. from 1/2	25.88	8.68	26.57	9.17	-.41
11.	Skill-max. of variance	35.25	12.20	35.71	12.94	-.19
12.	Number judgments	56.25	22.92	57.16	24.87	-.20
13.	Clues	60.82	11.48	60.35	11.66	.21
14.	Final bet	4.12	1.43	4.10	1.61	.07
15.	Total winnings	3.49	1.64	3.81	1.42	-1.10
16.	Chance-abs. winnings	.85	1.02	1.26	1.38	-1.71
17.	Chance-rel. winnings	.12	.14	.14	.13	-.70
18.	Skill-abs. winnings	1.11	1.12	1.10	1.24	.07
19.	Skill-rel. winnings	.17	.16	.19	.20	-.78
20.	Chance bet dissatisfaction	4.05	3.44	3.67	2.28	.69
21.	Skill bet dissatisfaction	2.74	2.59	3.59	2.42	-1.79
22.	Verbal aptitude (SAT)	666.74	57.72	637.43	62.04	2.59
23.	Math. aptitude (SAT)	699.85	66.75	680.24	79.52	1.38
24.	Analytic functioning (EFT)	18.80	6.93	18.51	6.87	.22
25.	Judgmental confidence	2.84	.57	2.83	.53	.10
26.	Extremity-high confidence	31.19	7.10	30.76	6.64	.31
27.	Extremity-low confidence	18.59	5.40	17.96	4.57	.66
28.	Category width	16.86	3.17	16.18	3.77	1.00
29.	Extremity of self-rating	109.54	16.96	113.88	19.81	-1.23
30.	Self-sufficiency	5.12	2.52	4.73	2.36	.84
31.	Independence	8.66	2.27	8.18	1.83	1.2
32.	Impulsiveness	12.26	3.30	11.45	3.58	1.2
33.	Rigidity	12.63	3.29	13.06	4.09	-.6

[a] For 112 df, t's of 1.98 and 2.63 are significant at the .05 and .01 levels, respectively.

Appendix A-3

MEANS AND SIGMAS OF MAJOR VARIABLES FOR LOW AND HIGH TEST ANXIOUS FEMALES

	Variable	Low (N = 50) Mean	SD	High (N = 53) Mean	SD	t[a]
1.	Choice dilemmas	63.86	12.65	70.11	12.58	-2.49
2.	Chance-max. of gain	38.54	12.78	39.42	11.23	-.36
3.	Chance-min. of loss	24.44	8.26	22.87	7.77	.98
4.	Chance-long shot	32.06	10.62	32.81	10.41	-.36
5.	Chance-min. dev. from 1/2	22.06	7.28	23.26	7.68	-.81
6.	Chance-max. of variance	36.98	11.50	38.47	10.08	-.69
7.	Skill-max. of gain	35.64	13.01	35.72	10.61	-.03
8.	Skill-min. of loss	21.46	6.90	19.81	6.35	1.25
9.	Skill-long shot	26.76	10.97	26.47	10.12	.14
10.	Skill-min. dev. from 1/2	28.34	8.00	29.28	8.64	-.57
11.	Skill-max. of variance	35.68	11.76	36.55	9.34	-.41
12.	Number judgments	47.70	24.55	42.91	18.78	1.10
13.	Clues	53.12	14.01	53.21	13.11	-.03
14.	Final bet	4.28	1.40	3.79	1.65	1.60
15.	Total winnings	3.23	1.66	3.52	1.34	-.96
16.	Chance-abs. winnings	.80	1.08	1.01	1.04	-1.00
17.	Chance-rel. winnings	.12	.18	.12	.13	-.05
18.	Skill-abs. winnings	.90	.88	.94	1.15	-.19
19.	Skill-rel. winnings	.13	.13	.13	.14	.13
20.	Chance bet dissatisfaction	4.60	3.35	5.19	3.47	-.87
21.	Skill bet dissatisfaction	3.16	2.16	3.36	2.04	-.47
22.	Verbal aptitude (SAT)	668.96	52.88	651.28	38.69	1.91
23.	Math. aptitude (SAT)	638.86	61.14	614.09	64.39	1.98
24.	Analytic functioning (EFT)	19.78	5.90	18.55	6.02	1.04
25.	Judgmental confidence	2.81	.54	2.73	.47	.73
26.	Extremity-high confidence	30.40	8.80	32.02	7.49	-.99
27.	Extremity-low confidence	17.27	5.19	16.90	5.80	.34
28.	Category width	15.80	3.31	15.78	2.97	.03
29.	Extremity of self-rating	114.18	14.84	107.92	13.84	2.19
30.	Self-sufficiency	4.52	2.33	3.96	2.25	1.23
31.	Independence	8.14	1.56	8.25	1.85	-.32
32.	Impulsiveness	11.96	2.92	11.91	3.04	.08
33.	Rigidity	13.28	3.29	13.79	3.47	-.76

[a] For 101 df, t's of 1.98 and 2.63 are significant at the .05 and .01 levels, respectively.

Appendix A-4

MEANS AND SIGMAS OF MAJOR VARIABLES FOR LOW AND HIGH DEFENSIVE MALES

	Variable	Low (N = 57) Mean	SD	High (N = 57) Mean	SD	t[a]
1.	Choice dilemmas	66.81	9.68	66.88	13.27	-.0
2.	Chance-max. of gain	36.02	14.55	38.26	14.89	-.8
3.	Chance-min. of loss	23.12	7.73	20.46	7.27	1.8
4.	Chance-long shot	29.42	13.29	30.18	12.70	-.3
5.	Chance-min. dev. from 1/2	24.46	8.29	24.37	9.14	.0
6.	Chance-max. of variance	35.74	12.72	38.44	12.53	-1.1
7.	Skill-max. of gain	33.05	13.18	37.60	15.63	-1.6
8.	Skill-min. of loss	22.70	6.02	20.65	7.64	1.5
9.	Skill-long shot	26.18	11.85	29.11	13.22	-1.2
10.	Skill-min. dev. from 1/2	27.19	7.90	25.16	9.70	1.2
11.	Skill-max. of variance	33.37	11.28	37.53	13.34	-1.7
12.	Number judgments	57.44	23.84	55.84	23.70	.3
13.	Clues	61.28	10.62	59.95	12.39	.6
14.	Final bet	4.44	1.44	3.79	1.51	2.3
15.	Total winnings	3.82	1.74	3.44	1.32	1.3
16.	Chance-abs. winnings	1.22	1.37	.83	.99	1.6
17.	Chance-rel. winnings	.16	.16	.10	.11	2.3
18.	Skill-abs. winnings	1.10	1.24	1.11	1.10	-.0
19.	Skill-rel. winnings	.19	.19	.17	.17	.4
20.	Chance bet dissatisfaction	4.77	3.39	3.00	2.24	3.2
21.	Skill bet dissatisfaction	3.65	2.44	2.56	2.54	2.3
22.	Verbal aptitude (SAT)	659.53	54.06	648.75	67.44	.9
23.	Math. aptitude (SAT)	703.91	70.76	678.93	73.39	1.8
24.	Analytic functioning (EFT)	18.51	7.59	18.84	6.14	-.2
25.	Judgmental confidence	2.73	.58	2.95	.50	-2.2
26.	Extremity-high confidence	30.98	7.52	31.04	6.24	-.0
27.	Extremity-low confidence	18.60	4.82	18.04	5.30	.5
28.	Category width	17.02	3.04	16.12	3.78	1.3
29.	Extremity of self-rating	111.74	19.25	111.07	17.44	.2
30.	Self-sufficiency	5.21	2.48	4.70	2.42	1.
31.	Independence	8.63	2.01	8.28	2.18	.8
32.	Impulsiveness	12.19	3.60	11.63	3.26	.8
33.	Rigidity	12.14	3.31	13.49	3.87	-1.

[a] For 112 df, t's of 1.98 and 2.63 are significant at the .05 and .01 levels, respectively.

Appendix A-5

Means and Sigmas of Major Variables for Low and High Defensive Females

	Variable	Low (N = 52) Mean	SD	High (N = 51) Mean	SD	t[a]
1.	Choice dilemmas	65.19	12.88	69.00	12.83	-1.49
2.	Chance-max. of gain	37.71	12.56	40.29	11.29	-1.09
3.	Chance-min. of loss	23.56	7.78	23.71	8.31	-.09
4.	Chance-long shot	31.02	10.81	33.90	10.00	-1.39
5.	Chance-min. dev. from 1/2	23.04	7.94	22.31	7.04	.49
6.	Chance-max. of variance	37.02	11.13	38.49	10.44	-.69
7.	Skill-max. of gain	34.79	11.61	36.59	11.99	-.77
8.	Skill-min. of loss	20.10	6.75	21.14	6.56	-.79
9.	Skill-long shot	25.60	9.84	27.65	11.11	-.98
10.	Skill-min. dev. from 1/2	29.62	7.68	28.02	8.91	.96
11.	Skill-max. of variance	35.63	10.28	36.63	10.88	-.47
12.	Number judgments	46.52	22.74	43.92	20.94	.60
13.	Clues	53.15	14.07	53.18	13.01	-.01
14.	Final bet	4.23	1.55	3.82	1.53	1.33
15.	Total winnings	3.49	1.57	3.28	1.43	.70
16.	Chance-abs. winnings	.87	1.12	.95	1.00	-.37
17.	Chance-rel. winnings	.12	.17	.12	.14	.04
18.	Skill-abs. winnings	1.02	1.05	.83	.99	.94
19.	Skill-rel. winnings	.13	.13	.12	.14	.47
20.	Chance bet dissatisfaction	5.19	3.79	4.61	2.98	.86
21.	Skill bet dissatisfaction	3.21	2.18	3.31	2.01	-.24
22.	Verbal aptitude (SAT)	662.02	47.91	657.67	45.87	.47
23.	Math. aptitude (SAT)	628.79	63.69	623.39	64.28	.42
24.	Analytic functioning (EFT)	19.50	5.74	18.78	6.22	.60
25.	Judgmental confidence	2.81	.47	2.73	.53	.83
26.	Extremity-high confidence	31.58	7.68	30.88	8.67	.43
27.	Extremity-low confidence	17.00	6.36	17.16	4.49	-.15
28.	Category width	15.59	2.58	16.00	3.60	-.64
29.	Extremity of self-rating	110.60	15.75	111.33	13.47	-.25
30.	Self-sufficiency	4.71	2.34	3.75	2.17	2.14
31.	Independence	8.25	1.86	8.14	1.56	.32
32.	Impulsiveness	12.10	3.22	11.76	2.70	.58
33.	Rigidity	13.69	3.93	13.39	2.73	.45

[a] For 101 df, t's of 1.98 and 2.63 are significant at the .05 and .01 levels, respectively.

Appendix A-6

MEANS AND SIGMAS OF MAJOR VARIABLES FOR THE FOUR MODERATOR SUBGROUPS OF MALES

	Variable	Low test anxiety Low defensiveness (N = 30)		Low test anxiety High defensiveness (N = 35)		High test anxiety Low defensiveness (N = 27)		High test anxiety High defensiveness (N = 22)		F^a
		Mean	SD	Mean	SD	Mean	SD	Mean	SD	
1.	Choice dilemmas	68.30	8.54	63.80	12.54	65.15	10.56	71.77	12.92	2.68
2.	Chance-max. of gain	31.90	15.27	38.31	14.33	40.59	12.18	38.18	15.74	1.80
3.	Chance-min. of loss	25.40	7.66	21.29	7.28	20.59	7.00	19.14	7.05	3.64
4.	Chance-long shot	25.77	13.84	30.71	11.81	33.48	11.34	29.32	13.97	1.71
5.	Chance-min. dev. from 1/2	25.33	8.06	24.57	7.79	23.48	8.43	24.05	10.95	.22
6.	Chance-max. of variance	31.30	12.71	38.14	11.91	40.67	10.77	38.91	13.45	3.04
7.	Skill-max. of gain	30.93	12.28	38.54	14.77	35.41	13.74	36.09	16.81	1.31
8.	Skill-min. of loss	22.83	4.83	20.00	7.56	22.56	7.11	21.68	7.65	.93
9.	Skill-long shot	24.10	11.55	29.77	12.44	28.48	11.76	28.05	14.32	1.03
10.	Skill-min. dev. from 1/2	27.00	8.48	24.91	8.74	27.41	7.20	25.55	11.04	.47
11.	Skill-max. of variance	31.73	10.30	38.26	12.89	35.19	12.02	36.36	13.96	1.33
12.	Number judgments	57.37	23.57	55.29	22.30	57.52	24.13	56.73	25.74	.05
13.	Clues	62.63	10.56	59.26	12.01	59.78	10.49	61.05	12.91	.46
14.	Final bet	4.37	1.45	3.91	1.38	4.52	1.42	3.59	1.67	2.23
15.	Total winnings	3.68	1.86	3.33	1.41	3.98	1.59	3.60	1.13	.80
16.	Chance-abs. winnings	.98	1.02	.74	1.01	1.47	1.63	.99	.94	1.83
17.	Chance-rel. winnings	.16	.17	.08	.09	.15	.14	.13	.13	1.71
18.	Skill-abs. winnings	1.20	1.18	1.04	1.06	1.00	1.30	1.22	1.16	.23
19.	Skill-rel. winnings	.19	.17	.14	.14	.18	.20	.22	.20	.76
20.	Chance bet dissatisfaction	5.27	3.96	3.00	2.50	4.22	2.50	3.00	1.76	3.94
21.	Skill bet dissatisfaction	3.30	2.64	2.26	2.44	4.04	2.13	3.05	2.62	2.38
22.	Verbal aptitude (SAT)	670.30	53.20	663.69	61.17	647.56	52.48	625.00	70.09	3.11
23.	Math. aptitude (SAT)	716.27	62.80	685.77	66.82	690.19	76.35	668.05	81.60	2.09
24.	Analytic functioning (EFT)	18.93	7.53	18.69	6.37	18.04	7.62	19.09	5.75	.12
25.	Judgmental confidence	2.73	.58	2.94	.54	2.73	.57	2.97	.43	1.55
26.	Extremity-high confidence	31.00	7.07	31.36	7.12	30.95	7.98	30.54	4.47	.06
27.	Extremity-low confidence	19.24	5.36	18.03	5.38	17.88	4.00	18.06	5.18	.42
28.	Category width	17.29	2.98	16.49	3.28	16.72	3.07	15.53	4.40	1.24
29.	Extremity of self-rating	110.60	16.02	108.63	17.68	113.00	22.22	114.95	16.32	.61
30.	Self-sufficiency	5.13	2.59	5.11	2.46	5.30	2.34	4.05	2.20	1.50
31.	Independence	8.63	2.21	8.69	2.31	8.63	1.75	7.64	1.77	1.61
32.	Impulsiveness	12.53	3.53	12.03	3.07	11.81	3.63	11.00	3.46	.94
33.	Rigidity	12.43	3.23	12.80	3.34	11.81	3.37	14.59	4.38	3.03

^{a}For 3 and 110 df, F's of 2.70 and 3.97 are significant at the .05 and .01 levels, respectively.

Appendix A-7

MEANS AND SIGMAS OF MAJOR VARIABLES FOR THE FOUR MODERATOR SUBGROUPS OF FEMALES

Variable	Low test anxiety Low defensiveness (N = 28)		Low test anxiety High defensiveness (N = 22)		High test anxiety Low defensiveness (N = 24)		High test anxiety High defensiveness (N = 29)		F [a]
	Mean	SD	Mean	SD	Mean	SD	Mean	SD	
Choice dilemmas	63.07	13.14	64.86	11.93	67.67	12.12	72.14	12.59	2.44
Chance-max. of gain	35.61	13.72	42.27	10.34	40.17	10.53	38.79	11.75	1.38
Chance-min. of loss	26.04	8.11	22.41	8.00	20.67	6.25	24.69	8.41	2.29
Chance-long shot	30.18	12.13	34.45	7.67	32.00	8.94	33.48	11.44	.79
Chance-min. dev. from 1/2	22.46	7.81	21.55	6.51	23.71	8.04	22.90	7.35	.35
Chance-max. of variance	34.11	11.68	40.64	10.16	40.42	9.36	36.86	10.36	2.17
Skill-max. of gain	34.57	12.87	37.00	13.05	35.04	9.93	36.28	11.10	.22
Skill-min. of loss	21.43	7.29	21.50	6.37	18.54	5.67	20.86	6.69	1.09
Skill-long shot	25.96	10.89	27.77	10.99	25.17	8.44	27.55	11.20	.35
Skill-min. dev. from 1/2	28.61	8.26	28.00	7.64	30.79	6.75	28.03	9.77	.62
Skill-max. of variance	35.00	11.70	36.55	11.78	36.38	8.26	36.69	10.14	.13
Number judgments	49.93	25.53	44.86	22.94	42.54	18.19	43.21	19.26	.58
Clues	53.32	15.05	52.86	12.55	52.96	12.82	53.41	13.35	.01
Final bet	4.25	1.45	4.32	1.33	4.21	1.66	3.45	1.57	1.78
Total winnings	3.26	1.75	3.20	1.54	3.75	1.29	3.33	1.34	.68
Chance-abs. winnings	.82	1.09	.78	1.06	.93	1.15	1.07	.93	.39
Chance-rel. winnings	.14	.20	.09	.13	.10	.12	.14	.14	.73
Skill-abs. winnings	.94	1.00	.86	.70	1.11	1.09	.80	1.17	.42
Skill-rel. winnings	.12	.10	.15	.16	.16	.15	.10	.13	.86
Chance bet dissatisfaction	5.07	3.93	4.00	2.30	5.33	3.62	5.07	3.33	.74
Skill bet dissatisfaction	3.39	2.44	2.86	1.69	3.00	1.80	3.66	2.17	.75
Verbal aptitude (SAT)	678.18	50.10	657.23	53.99	643.17	37.23	658.00	38.58	2.48
Math. aptitude (SAT)	632.61	65.42	646.82	54.18	624.33	61.31	605.62	65.63	1.86
Analytic functioning (EFT)	20.82	4.77	18.45	6.86	17.96	6.37	19.03	5.67	1.10
Judgmental confidence	2.78	.47	2.84	.61	2.84	.47	2.64	.45	.89
Extremity-high confidence	32.49	8.06	27.74	8.98	30.51	7.05	33.27	7.61	2.37
Extremity-low confidence	17.48	5.45	17.01	4.84	16.45	7.25	17.27	4.21	.16
Category width	15.56	2.25	16.11	4.27	15.63	2.92	15.91	3.00	.16
Extremity of self-rating	115.57	14.48	112.41	15.10	104.79	15.17	110.52	12.03	2.51
Self-sufficiency	4.89	2.37	4.05	2.20	4.50	2.29	3.52	2.11	1.70
Independence	8.57	1.55	7.59	1.40	7.88	2.11	8.55	1.54	2.13
Impulsiveness	12.50	3.25	11.27	2.26	11.62	3.13	12.14	2.93	.83
Rigidity	13.29	3.54	13.27	2.94	14.17	4.30	13.48	2.55	.38

[a] For 3 and 99 df, F's of 2.70 and 3.98 are significant at the .05 and .01 levels, respectively.

Appendix B-1

Intercorrelations of Major Variables for Total Male ($N = 114$) and Female ($N = 103$) Samples

	Variable	1	2	3	4	5	6	7	8	9	10	11	12	13	14
1.	Choice dilemmas		-33	21	-31	25	-32	-26	25	-21	18	-26	-07	04	03
2.	Chance-max. of gain	-22		-55	95	-82	96	72	-40	69	-61	69	11	-05	-16
3.	Chance-min. of loss	22	-54		-32	20	-73	-49	60	-37	32	-56	-04	03	17
4.	Chance-long shot	-17	92	-21		-87	86	65	-27	67	-59	61	12	-06	-12
5.	Chance-min. dev. from 1/2	15	-72	11	-80		-71	-57	22	-58	60	-53	-09	07	11
6.	Chance-max. of variance	-25	95	-74	78	-59		72	-49	66	-58	71	10	-04	-16
7.	Skill-max. of gain	-14	60	-33	54	-37	57		-60	96	-80	97	-01	-12	-18
8.	Skill-min. of loss	09	-50	56	-30	08	-54	-52		-40	29	-75	07	05	22
9.	Skill-long shot	-14	51	-20	51	-39	47	94	-26		-84	89	01	-12	-12
10.	Skill-min. dev. from 1/2	24	-39	07	-43	41	-35	-78	10	-87		-74	-03	11	05
11.	Skill-max. of variance	-12	63	-41	53	-33	61	96	-69	85	-67		-01	-11	-19
12.	Number judgments	12	-17	07	-14	-02	-14	-24	25	-19	11	-27		35	-02
13.	Clues	30	-23	25	-18	13	-24	-21	29	-17	18	-26	34		10
14.	Final bet	-11	-23	19	-21	17	-23	-11	06	-09	03	-12	01	11	
15.	Total winnings	-22	07	-03	05	03	07	13	-09	13	-11	11	-15	06	31
16.	Chance-abs. winnings	-20	-14	05	-15	22	-13	-08	-02	-08	03	-08	-17	04	26
17.	Chance-rel. winnings	-13	-43	19	-43	42	-40	-26	12	-25	14	-27	-05	21	30
18.	Skill-abs. winnings	-13	21	-08	21	-19	20	23	-06	26	-23	21	12	01	13
19.	Skill-rel. winnings	-11	09	03	10	-08	07	-01	02	00	-01	-02	11	09	21
20.	Chance bet dissatisfaction	02	09	-14	08	-16	09	-07	-08	-11	03	-03	-04	-10	-11
21.	Skill bet dissatisfaction	-01	-11	00	-09	-12	-09	-12	32	00	-10	-17	08	-11	-14
22.	Verbal aptitude (SAT)	-11	05	-09	01	-12	06	11	-04	09	-05	09	12	-06	09
23.	Math. aptitude (SAT)	16	-25	09	-24	06	-21	-09	38	01	-03	-18	12	23	15
24.	Analytic functioning (EFT)	04	-23	14	-19	14	-22	-17	28	-11	08	-20	26	14	07
25.	Judgmental confidence	-19	17	-31	07	01	24	15	-23	09	-02	19	-01	-24	02
26.	Extremity-high confidence	22	00	01	00	-14	-02	08	-12	04	-03	10	02	-15	-29
27.	Extremity-low confidence	12	-16	12	-07	05	-13	-08	19	-01	04	-10	12	-06	-16
28.	Category width	-01	-21	17	-19	16	-18	-25	23	-17	09	-25	26	24	07
29.	Extremity of self-rating	-09	18	-01	21	-24	14	20	-05	21	-27	17	-11	-09	-02
30.	Self-sufficiency	-27	05	-04	05	-14	02	01	03	03	-06	01	-02	00	-06
31.	Independence	-42	22	04	28	-19	16	11	-07	11	-17	12	-05	-03	-03
32.	Impulsiveness	-11	07	06	13	-04	03	01	-11	-01	06	04	-12	-13	07
33.	Rigidity	26	-20	02	-19	11	-15	-07	12	-07	15	-08	10	20	04

Note: On this and all other tables in Appendix B, correlations for males are above the diagonal and those for females are below. All decimal points are omitted.

Appendix B-1 (Continued)

5	16	17	18	19	20	21	22	23	24	25	26	27	28	29	30	31	32	33
8	-04	15	-09	10	04	04	-21	-09	19	-06	01	-13	-08	-06	-16	-12	-05	26
3	24	-16	21	-21	-12	-12	17	15	06	-08	-04	07	09	-06	-05	08	13	-13
1	-11	13	-07	14	30	13	-05	12	10	-11	05	07	-06	-04	-01	-02	-15	11
0	23	-16	19	-22	-05	-09	15	18	09	-14	-03	10	11	-12	-08	10	12	-12
7	-20	13	-18	21	-06	13	-10	-22	-16	17	-01	-11	-14	13	02	-16	-06	10
9	23	-17	17	-22	-15	-13	16	07	02	-05	-02	04	09	-05	-04	06	16	-13
9	09	-23	15	-33	-05	-23	13	12	03	-10	-08	00	03	-11	-18	-06	02	02
6	-09	12	-01	31	10	21	-03	03	00	-13	10	15	-04	01	05	02	-09	05
9	07	-24	16	-31	-02	-20	13	14	04	-17	-06	05	05	-13	-21	-08	00	03
1	-07	15	-20	23	08	17	-20	-18	-01	13	06	-05	-05	10	16	01	02	-07
9	12	-19	13	-35	-07	-25	12	09	00	-05	-11	-05	04	-08	-18	-05	05	-01
1	-07	-17	12	07	-02	09	14	06	-12	-12	-12	04	07	13	-02	20	05	-12
3	-02	-02	02	08	10	16	01	11	-14	10	-10	05	-03	09	01	-06	02	06
3	23	21	00	07	09	12	-06	06	-05	-04	-09	-14	-03	-03	-04	-15	-08	-05
	65	51	61	42	-06	-03	13	02	10	08	-16	-02	-11	19	-02	-25	-12	01
6		78	-14	-17	06	05	03	-16	06	12	-07	-09	-09	15	-03	-21	04	-02
3	85		-10	03	05	09	-02	-15	08	14	-04	-01	-09	15	02	-19	-04	01
6	-05	-10		76	-15	-08	10	19	08	04	-19	10	02	11	02	-06	-18	-03
4	07	06	84		-12	-04	-02	08	-01	15	-09	07	-04	15	05	-09	-24	11
1	-15	-14	-13	-05		32	-01	13	12	03	-12	-03	03	-02	07	-01	07	-02
0	-09	-02	-01	-09	31		-01	00	03	02	-12	-05	01	06	15	-01	16	-17
3	-20	-17	15	05	01	08		26	-17	-12	10	13	00	10	15	13	09	-05
9	-13	03	-11	-11	04	15	05		12	-23	08	20	03	-10	-08	10	-14	-10
1	03	08	01	08	-08	08	-14	35		-03	10	06	07	-02	-09	-02	-03	13
0	-03	-03	06	-08	-15	-05	-07	-02	-04		-51	-24	-09	16	12	-09	02	05
3	-15	-13	-16	-26	32	01	02	-01	-06	-21		16	-03	-12	-17	21	16	-08
9	-04	-05	-05	-08	05	12	-11	11	15	-20	11		14	06	-04	-12	-07	-13
4	11	16	01	15	08	06	-05	01	19	-25	-18	09		-06	-03	02	10	-18
6	-01	-05	11	-01	-05	14	06	-01	02	14	-11	-07	-02		13	-08	11	-14
5	09	09	30	27	08	06	23	07	04	02	-04	01	10	20		-01	-10	-03
2	14	08	31	29	10	-05	22	-21	-06	-17	-03	-06	08	03	35		27	-31
9	00	-08	12	09	11	-14	-01	-30	-14	-10	21	-01	08	12	07	28		-51
7	-12	-04	-16	-14	05	17	-19	26	16	10	-05	07	-04	07	-11	-41	-36	

Appendix B-2

Intercorrelations of Major Variables for Low Test Anxious Males ($N = 65$) and Females ($N = 50$)

Variable	1	2	3	4	5	6	7	8	9	10	11	12	13
1. Choice dilemmas		-38	33	-30	26	-38	-27	30	-20	16	-27	-04	03
2. Chance-max. of gain	-29		-55	95	-80	96	75	-47	71	-67	74	03	-11
3. Chance-min. of loss	25	-58		-31	18	-73	-48	67	-34	30	-57	-05	04
4. Chance-long shot	-28	93	-29		-85	86	68	-33	68	-66	65	04	-13
5. Chance-min. dev. from 1/2	23	-70	26	-73		-68	-54	20	-56	65	-51	-02	09
6. Chance-max. of variance	-32	96	-75	82	-64		74	-56	67	-62	76	03	-08
7. Skill-max. of gain	-15	71	-48	65	-44	68		-57	96	-79	96	06	-09
8. Skill-min. of loss	07	-59	48	-46	20	-56	-65		-37	22	-73	-01	-03
9. Skill-long shot	-18	64	-44	61	-47	63	96	-45		-85	89	07	-11
10. Skill-min. dev. from 1/2	34	-48	26	-50	46	-49	-78	21	-87		-71	-04	14
11. Skill-max. of variance	-12	69	-48	62	-37	66	97	-78	89	-68		06	-09
12. Number judgments	19	-27	06	-26	03	-19	-26	27	-20	08	-26		25
13. Clues	25	-12	17	-09	10	-15	-18	18	-23	21	-20	43	
14. Final bet	-31	00	18	05	03	-06	09	-20	05	-12	11	-01	07
15. Total winnings	-37	01	11	00	11	-04	04	-04	07	-05	02	-33	08
16. Chance-abs. winnings	-33	-15	15	-15	24	-17	-19	10	-17	10	-21	-22	12
17. Chance-rel. winnings	-21	-45	28	-45	47	-44	-34	18	-34	17	-34	-07	23
18. Skill-abs. winnings	-25	07	03	07	-06	04	23	-10	27	-21	20	-13	-02
19. Skill-rel. winnings	-21	-07	21	-05	13	-12	-09	09	-08	09	-13	-16	14
20. Chance bet dissatisfaction	03	-02	-06	01	-14	-03	02	04	06	-12	02	05	-09
21. Skill bet dissatisfaction	01	-29	08	-26	-08	-23	-22	43	-09	-05	-27	22	-04
22. Verbal aptitude (SAT)	-16	15	-23	11	-18	20	11	-18	08	-04	11	10	-07
23. Math. aptitude (SAT)	11	-16	00	-18	-05	-10	-05	33	01	-11	-13	25	24
24. Analytic functioning (EFT)	04	-25	21	-19	08	-24	-31	40	-26	20	-36	33	25
25. Judgmental confidence	-07	18	-22	14	-06	21	28	-29	25	-16	33	-02	-16
26. Extremity-high confidence	29	-08	03	-08	-14	-10	08	03	12	-14	07	04	-25
27. Extremity-low confidence	15	-27	24	-18	02	-26	-12	39	00	-06	-17	13	-07
28. Category width	-02	-32	12	-33	27	-25	-45	31	-42	32	-44	29	31
29. Extremity of self-rating	-23	25	-24	23	-24	27	32	-20	36	-32	29	-13	-13
30. Self-sufficiency	-22	-02	-03	-06	-11	-04	-05	01	-03	04	-05	-10	-03
31. Independence	-46	19	10	25	-21	10	06	-05	04	-11	07	-16	06
32. Impulsiveness	-14	07	-02	11	03	02	-02	-20	-07	24	05	-17	-26
33. Rigidity	31	-19	08	-13	07	-19	02	12	03	-03	-01	27	27

Appendix B-2 (Continued)

16	17	18	19	20	21	22	23	24	25	26	27	28	29	30	31	32	33
19	28	-10	18	06	01	-24	-15	13	00	-08	-16	-13	-02	-25	02	-05	31
22	-21	32	-20	-18	-07	33	14	02	-06	05	-01	05	00	-06	-01	16	-19
-14	15	-10	20	40	14	-24	12	19	-14	02	17	-12	00	-04	02	-12	09
19	-22	27	-21	-11	-06	29	18	06	-10	05	05	02	-04	-10	02	16	-19
-11	25	-33	08	00	07	-24	-22	-12	17	-12	-04	-11	-03	-03	-08	-06	09
21	-23	27	-21	-25	-10	36	05	-07	-03	07	-04	07	-02	-04	-03	17	-15
07	-26	30	-24	-12	-13	27	10	-04	-12	07	-03	-02	-17	-14	-14	05	-03
-12	15	-12	25	16	12	-20	-06	01	-26	12	30	02	12	03	02	-04	02
05	-26	31	-20	-08	-11	25	11	-04	-21	11	07	-01	-18	-19	-18	03	-02
-12	15	-33	10	16	09	-23	-12	05	17	-16	-13	-13	08	13	13	-01	05
11	-23	30	-24	-14	-15	28	11	-06	-03	01	-11	00	-16	-17	-12	05	-05
-08	-19	-08	-14	00	03	15	13	-22	-24	-11	06	16	10	-13	19	03	-24
02	06	-20	-05	19	15	02	10	-09	-01	-07	09	-10	13	-02	-04	04	16
17	21	12	20	07	14	-11	08	-02	-15	-10	04	-08	00	-24	-18	-08	-14
67	52	76	52	-09	-10	21	12	31	05	-05	03	-05	21	-15	-28	-12	-03
	74	08	00	-04	10	04	03	25	16	-08	-10	-11	23	-12	-26	06	-11
87		13	28	00	08	-10	04	22	22	-14	02	-10	22	-02	-19	-12	-03
21	10		73	-13	-22	27	17	19	-02	-05	14	08	10	-07	-15	-22	00
45	37	71		-09	-25	11	03	10	03	02	13	05	10	-08	-12	-26	18
-19	-18	-26	-22		37	05	13	-04	-06	-14	01	05	10	18	-05	-02	03
-18	-10	-16	-24	60		02	10	02	08	-22	08	02	21	08	-04	11	-14
-04	-11	19	-03	03	-01		26	-13	-17	04	26	17	18	04	01	11	-04
-02	12	04	-04	09	22	-08		07	-35	14	16	11	03	-19	02	-11	-12
-05	02	-12	07	05	16	-23	33		04	15	01	05	-01	07	03	-11	19
-07	-04	07	-21	-25	-21	-18	01	-17		-58	-26	00	19	28	-10	00	00
-34	-26	-21	-41	34	16	-02	17	15	-17		10	-07	-21	-23	27	13	10
-20	-11	11	-03	19	47	01	31	25	-26	25		16	02	03	-23	-16	04
30	34	-13	18	27	26	-03	04	25	-31	-16	18		-01	12	-02	10	-24
03	-03	29	02	-01	16	10	-04	-01	26	-11	13	-11		28	-10	22	-32
30	22	25	17	02	06	31	03	-07	06	-01	14	09	40		-14	-17	05
41	27	21	22	03	-02	45	-12	-08	-19	-14	-12	01	16	47		31	-19
-01	-08	11	06	09	-03	00	-30	-04	-12	19	11	00	10	11	21		-49
-27	-14	-14	-07	31	28	-29	26	25	07	09	13	00	01	04	-40	-26	

Appendix B-3

INTERCORRELATIONS OF MAJOR VARIABLES FOR HIGH TEST ANXIOUS MALES ($N = 49$) AND FEMALES ($N = 53$)

	Variable	1	2	3	4	5	6	7	8	9	10	11	12	13
1.	Choice dilemmas		-32	10	-35	26	-30	-26	18	-23	19	-24	-12	05
2.	Chance-max. of gain	-18		-52	95	-85	96	69	-33	67	-56	63	22	05
3.	Chance-min. of loss	27	-49		-29	21	-70	-53	59	-41	39	-56	-03	00
4.	Chance-long shot	-10	91	-13		-91	86	63	-22	65	-52	56	22	04
5.	Chance-min. dev. from 1/2	06	-75	-01	-87		-76	-59	24	-61	57	-55	-15	05
6.	Chance-max. of variance	-23	94	-72	75	-57		71	-44	66	-56	67	19	04
7.	Skill-max. of gain	-14	47	-16	40	-30	43		-63	97	-82	97	-08	-15
8.	Skill-min. of loss	17	-40	64	-12	00	-51	-37		-44	36	-77	16	15
9.	Skill-long shot	-11	36	05	40	-31	29	93	-04		-84	90	-06	-14
10.	Skill-min. dev. from 1/2	15	-31	-11	-37	36	-22	-79	01	-88		-77	-03	09
11.	Skill-max. of variance	-17	54	-31	42	-30	53	95	-59	80	-69		-09	-14
12.	Number judgments	10	-03	06	01	-05	-05	-23	21	-17	17	-27		48
13.	Clues	36	-37	34	-27	16	-36	-25	43	-10	15	-34	25	
14.	Final bet	11	-44	17	-42	30	-38	-32	25	-22	17	-34	00	14
15.	Total winnings	-13	15	-17	10	-08	20	24	-13	22	-19	24	14	04
16.	Chance-abs. winnings	-13	-14	-03	-16	18	-09	06	-11	02	-03	06	-09	-03
17.	Chance-rel. winnings	-03	-41	08	-42	37	-35	-13	04	-14	11	-15	-02	19
18.	Skill-abs. winnings	-05	33	-16	31	-29	33	24	-04	26	-25	23	37	03
19.	Skill-rel. winnings	-02	26	-14	24	-26	27	07	-05	07	-09	10	43	05
20.	Chance bet dissatisfaction	-03	21	-20	13	-19	21	-17	-18	-27	15	-11	-14	-11
21.	Skill bet dissatisfaction	-05	10	-07	08	-16	06	00	22	11	-14	-04	-09	-19
22.	Verbal aptitude (SAT)	06	-06	05	-09	-03	-11	12	10	10	-04	09	09	-05
23.	Math. aptitude (SAT)	31	-33	15	-30	18	-30	-14	40	00	05	-22	-07	23
24.	Analytic functioning (EFT)	10	-19	04	-18	20	-18	-01	14	03	-01	-01	16	04
25.	Judgmental confidence	-29	16	-43	00	10	28	-01	-19	-09	13	01	-02	-34
26.	Extremity-high confidence	12	09	00	08	-16	06	09	-28	-05	08	13	02	-03
27.	Extremity-low confidence	12	-05	01	02	08	-01	-03	00	-02	12	-02	10	-05
28.	Category width	00	-08	22	-04	06	-10	01	14	11	-14	00	22	16
29.	Extremity of self-rating	16	13	20	21	-22	02	05	05	06	-21	04	-15	-04
30.	Self-sufficiency	-28	13	-08	16	-15	12	08	02	10	-14	10	06	03
31.	Independence	-42	25	-01	31	-18	22	17	-08	18	-22	17	06	-10
32.	Impulsiveness	-09	06	13	14	-11	03	04	-02	05	-09	02	-06	-01
33.	Rigidity	20	-21	-03	-25	13	-13	-16	15	-16	29	-18	-07	13

Appendix B-3 (Continued)

16	17	18	19	20	21	22	23	24	25	26	27	28	29	30	31	32	33
-28	-02	-09	01	04	05	-16	00	27	-14	12	-06	00	-12	-03	-30	-03	20
23	-12	08	-26	04	-28	04	20	12	-12	-17	22	18	-16	01	29	13	-09
00	14	-03	11	07	21	07	07	-04	-08	08	-13	-04	-03	-01	-16	-25	17
25	-11	10	-26	09	-20	05	22	14	-20	-14	20	24	-25	-03	27	10	-07
-25	01	-05	34	-16	24	-01	-24	-22	17	12	-22	-19	29	08	-31	-07	11
20	-14	06	-27	06	-26	03	15	15	-08	-14	20	16	-13	01	29	21	-14
10	-21	-01	-43	08	-39	00	16	12	-08	-29	05	09	-05	-24	08	00	07
-10	08	09	35	00	30	18	14	-01	04	08	-05	-08	-11	10	04	-13	08
07	-22	-01	-44	09	-34	02	20	14	-12	-30	03	12	-10	-25	10	-03	09
-04	14	-06	36	-04	27	-15	-23	-08	07	36	09	04	11	20	-16	08	-20
14	-15	-06	-47	06	-40	-04	08	08	-07	-26	04	09	-01	-20	04	05	04
-07	-15	35	28	-05	16	15	-01	01	03	-13	02	-01	17	14	24	08	-02
-06	-12	29	21	-08	19	-01	12	-21	25	-15	-01	03	05	04	-10	-02	-05
29	21	-12	-05	11	09	-02	03	-08	10	-09	-39	02	-06	22	-10	-09	04
65	49	41	30	03	03	08	-08	-22	15	-34	-11	-17	14	21	-17	-11	05
	86	-34	-33	23	-05	11	-28	-12	10	-06	-06	-05	06	09	-14	07	04
86		-38	-26	17	07	13	-36	-13	02	11	-03	-07	06	09	-19	08	04
-25	-30		79	-18	10	-08	21	-08	11	-37	03	-04	11	15	07	-16	-07
-27	-31	94		-18	17	-10	15	-13	29	-20	02	-10	17	21	-04	-21	05
-13	-09	-04	10		28	-17	13	42	21	-09	-12	-03	-19	-17	08	23	-09
00	07	10	05	04		05	-06	07	-07	03	-24	04	-17	30	08	28	-23
-38	-28	14	15	04	22		22	-25	-07	16	-10	-22	08	27	25	02	-03
-20	-07	-21	-18	03	11	12		18	-10	-01	24	-06	-20	02	18	-22	-07
12	15	11	09	-18	00	-09	34		-13	04	13	10	-03	-33	-11	05	08
04	-02	05	04	-03	15	05	-09	08		-41	-22	-20	13	-13	-07	05	10
04	05	-12	-10	30	-17	13	-16	-27	-25		27	01	00	-08	10	19	-29
12	02	-15	-12	-07	-19	-26	-07	06	-15	-02		11	13	-16	07	04	-35
-10	-10	13	13	-11	-15	-10	-02	13	-17	-22	01		-09	-22	04	08	-13
-01	-09	-02	-04	-05	16	-09	-06	01	-02	-08	-27	08		-02	-02	03	00
-10	-08	36	36	16	07	09	06	12	-04	-04	-12	11	-05		19	-04	-11
-07	-11	38	35	14	-07	-01	-28	-04	-14	07	-02	14	-07	27		19	-48
01	-09	13	12	13	-25	-02	-31	-24	-09	25	-11	16	15	02	34		-52
00	08	-17	-20	-18	07	-05	31	09	14	-21	02	-08	16	-23	-43	-45	

Appendix B-4

INTERCORRELATIONS OF MAJOR VARIABLES FOR LOW DEFENSIVE MALES ($N = 57$) AND FEMALES ($N = 52$)

	Variable	1	2	3	4	5	6	7	8	9	10	11	12	13
1.	Choice dilemmas		-24	20	-22	15	-23	-11	33	-02	09	-17	-01	25
2.	Chance-max. of gain	-26		-53	95	-82	96	73	-46	71	-58	73	13	-05
3.	Chance-min. of loss	19	-56		-30	20	-73	-52	55	-41	31	-54	-03	14
4.	Chance-long shot	-25	93	-27		-88	85	68	-37	69	-58	67	15	-04
5.	Chance-min. dev. from 1/2	15	-70	11	-75		-71	-55	30	-57	58	-55	-17	-01
6.	Chance-max. of variance	-26	96	-73	83	-58		75	-54	69	-55	75	14	-08
7.	Skill-max. of gain	-31	52	-34	48	-32	54		-59	97	-73	97	03	-07
8.	Skill-min. of loss	22	-58	70	-39	07	-67	-57		-39	20	-72	09	03
9.	Skill-long shot	-31	41	-22	42	-36	43	95	-35		-80	90	09	-05
10.	Skill-min. dev. from 1/2	44	-27	05	-33	36	-26	-77	18	-84		-66	-07	03
11.	Skill-max. of variance	-32	58	-45	51	-29	62	96	-72	87	-66		04	-09
12.	Number judgments	26	-16	-04	-22	08	-12	-24	14	-21	15	-20		28
13.	Clues	29	-11	20	-07	-02	-14	-21	31	-19	13	-25	46	
14.	Final bet	-30	-01	10	01	-01	-05	13	-08	12	-25	10	-13	-18
15.	Total winnings	-40	12	-08	11	-03	15	27	-12	30	-28	22	-32	03
16.	Chance-abs. winnings	-37	-04	-08	-08	15	01	10	-07	11	-17	05	-30	-02
17.	Chance-rel. winnings	-30	-39	12	-41	41	-34	-13	11	-13	-06	-18	-11	15
18.	Skill-abs. winnings	-22	13	-03	15	-16	14	21	-06	26	-21	20	01	05
19.	Skill-rel. winnings	-15	10	00	14	-14	10	08	-04	08	-09	08	-02	16
20.	Chance bet dissatisfaction	-02	16	-05	20	-28	09	-06	-04	-06	-08	-03	06	-11
21.	Skill bet dissatisfaction	20	-34	29	-29	-08	-38	-21	48	-05	-06	-29	15	-08
22.	Verbal aptitude (SAT)	-05	07	05	04	-15	01	06	-08	02	-02	06	13	03
23.	Math. aptitude (SAT)	14	-42	24	-40	11	-42	-24	50	-13	05	-32	16	21
24.	Analytic functioning (EFT)	00	-31	24	-26	26	-33	-26	40	-19	21	-28	15	11
25.	Judgmental confidence	-43	04	-16	01	10	10	08	-15	05	-11	09	-09	-28
26.	Extremity-high confidence	33	00	13	02	-14	-07	14	01	15	-06	12	13	-01
27.	Extremity-low confidence	23	-29	24	-19	11	-29	-14	24	-06	11	-14	15	-14
28.	Category width	03	-15	00	-18	11	-11	-22	10	-20	23	-19	26	22
29.	Extremity of self-rating	-29	12	07	17	-27	06	14	06	18	-28	10	-24	-17
30.	Self-sufficiency	-34	-08	-08	-09	01	-05	-10	16	-02	-02	-11	-12	01
31.	Independence	-57	30	-09	34	-25	28	18	-10	17	-25	19	-09	01
32.	Impulsiveness	-22	17	-06	21	-11	14	18	-20	14	-07	23	-23	-29
33.	Rigidity	32	-14	11	-10	00	-15	07	21	14	-07	01	04	16

Appendix B-4 (Continued)

16	17	18	19	20	21	22	23	24	25	26	27	28	29	30	31	32	33
-29	-06	-01	10	19	11	-07	01	16	03	-07	-01	08	-10	-03	-11	-04	22
31	-16	15	-24	-13	-17	03	05	10	-22	04	00	08	-11	-11	11	20	-19
-03	24	05	20	29	20	01	06	10	05	-11	-04	03	-03	04	-20	-29	27
32	-13	17	-23	-07	-12	01	06	14	-25	01	-03	12	-19	-15	06	14	-13
-27	13	-21	20	-05	10	-06	-07	-19	27	-02	12	-17	17	-02	-15	-08	06
27	-20	07	-28	-17	-17	02	-01	06	-20	08	-01	06	-09	-10	14	26	-23
12	-28	13	-31	-03	-29	-06	22	11	-26	-06	01	02	-16	-25	-02	17	-15
-09	18	12	38	01	28	01	-03	01	08	-10	-02	07	08	09	-16	-19	18
09	-28	19	-26	-03	-25	-08	22	15	-30	-09	02	04	-19	-29	-06	13	-14
-06	16	-27	13	10	17	-11	-23	-11	24	01	-08	-07	19	22	-01	-19	12
15	-25	10	-34	-03	-34	-04	18	08	-21	-04	-01	00	-16	-24	04	19	-20
00	-16	00	-01	10	-13	11	-04	-04	-11	-02	-11	19	09	-24	14	04	-07
-02	01	01	02	19	07	-02	08	-09	24	-21	12	-10	10	-03	-07	-16	20
38	32	12	05	03	05	-03	15	03	01	-25	-07	-16	04	-04	-43	-21	01
69	52	61	41	-11	-16	15	11	08	05	-18	08	-11	22	-01	-33	-10	01
	72	-11	-16	10	14	10	-10	02	08	-11	-06	-23	08	-07	-26	05	04
82		-02	10	04	15	05	-10	03	19	-09	05	-17	12	00	-21	-05	05
-03	-05		77	-25	-38	12	23	06	03	-18	18	20	20	07	-11	-20	-07
-06	00	88		-21	-31	18	17	-09	25	-14	17	17	28	14	-13	-31	14
-29	-27	-01	08		45	-09	18	31	11	-19	-14	-09	-02	04	13	10	07
-12	-05	-13	-22	29		-10	-06	18	08	-11	-17	-21	-10	15	01	16	02
-23	-17	25	18	-15	-10		20	-21	-14	30	11	09	17	05	05	14	00
-10	12	-06	-03	-05	33	08		09	-21	14	18	02	-17	-17	-12	-28	06
-03	02	-25	-20	-07	15	-18	30		-08	08	-04	17	07	-07	-12	13	17
19	19	01	-05	-10	-09	-17	-08	-04		-53	-15	-22	18	17	07	-02	09
-24	-22	-05	-12	25	01	-07	01	-05	-37		14	13	-05	-20	16	30	-19
-01	-02	00	-03	13	29	-17	15	14	-20	26		-02	10	-21	-35	-09	-06
-11	08	05	09	31	25	-17	13	26	-04	02	06		-02	-13	11	-03	18
06	06	09	-04	03	28	19	-01	-03	19	-21	-20	-08		08	06	20	-12
10	10	43	34	04	05	26	24	08	03	-10	13	21	24		12	-11	-01
11	05	38	29	07	-28	33	-08	-03	-07	-12	-05	06	05	41		35	-28
-16	-20	19	06	19	-14	08	-31	-09	04	35	-06	02	14	16	38		-44
-10	-05	-21	-19	11	33	-27	35	09	-10	04	12	10	14	-14	-42	-45	

Appendix B-5

Intercorrelations of Major Variables for High Defensive Males ($N = 57$) and Females ($N = 51$)

	Variable	1	2	3	4	5	6	7	8	9	10	11	12	13
1.	Choice dilemmas		-41	23	-38	32	-39	-36	21	-34	24	-32	-12	-09
2.	Chance-max. of gain	-22		-56	96	-81	96	70	-34	67	-63	66	10	-03
3.	Chance-min. of loss	26	-52		-34	21	-73	-45	64	-32	31	-55	-08	-09
4.	Chance-long shot	-14	90	-16		-87	87	64	-18	65	-62	57	09	-08
5.	Chance-min. dev. from 1/2	18	-75	12	-86		-72	-59	16	-60	63	-52	-01	13
6.	Chance-max. of variance	-27	93	-75	73	-60		69	-44	63	-60	68	07	01
7.	Skill-max. of gain	01	69	-33	59	-42	61		-59	96	-85	96	-02	-14
8.	Skill-min. of loss	-08	-43	42	-22	11	-41	-50		-39	33	-76	05	05
9.	Skill-long shot	-02	60	-19	58	-42	52	93	-19		-86	88	-05	-18
10.	Skill-min. dev. from 1/2	11	-50	08	-52	46	-42	-78	05	-89		-78	-01	16
11.	Skill-max. of variance	05	68	-37	55	-37	60	96	-68	83	-67		-03	-11
12.	Number judgments	-02	-18	18	-03	-14	-15	-24	39	-15	06	-34		42
13.	Clues	31	-39	31	-32	32	-37	-22	28	-15	23	-27	21	
14.	Final bet	11	-47	28	-43	37	-43	-34	23	-27	26	-32	16	43
15.	Total winnings	-02	04	03	00	09	-01	-02	-05	-01	04	01	05	10
16.	Chance-abs. winnings	-01	-28	19	-26	30	-30	-28	04	-28	24	-23	00	12
17.	Chance-rel. winnings	08	-49	28	-47	43	-49	-42	14	-39	35	-37	03	28
18.	Skill-abs. winnings	00	34	-13	31	-24	28	27	-05	29	-27	23	24	-04
19.	Skill-rel. winnings	-06	10	05	08	-03	05	-08	09	-06	05	-11	23	03
20.	Chance bet dissatisfaction	10	02	-25	-07	00	11	-07	-12	-15	13	-03	-20	-08
21.	Skill bet dissatisfaction	-24	17	-30	13	-17	25	-02	13	05	-13	-04	00	-16
22.	Verbal aptitude (SAT)	-16	05	-23	00	-09	12	17	01	16	-08	13	10	-16
23.	Math. aptitude (SAT)	20	-05	-05	-06	-01	03	06	26	13	-11	-03	07	24
24.	Analytic functioning (EFT)	10	-13	05	-11	00	-09	-08	18	-04	-03	-12	37	17
25.	Judgmental confidence	05	32	-43	16	-08	38	24	-30	14	03	28	05	-20
26.	Extremity-high confidence	15	01	-10	00	-15	02	04	-24	-04	-01	09	-09	-29
27.	Extremity-low confidence	-03	05	-03	11	-05	10	01	11	05	-05	-04	07	08
28.	Category width	-06	-28	28	-22	23	-25	-28	33	-17	00	-30	28	26
29.	Extremity of self-rating	15	25	-10	25	-19	23	26	-19	24	-25	24	06	02
30.	Self-sufficiency	-14	26	00	28	-35	14	16	-08	13	-15	16	07	-01
31.	Independence	-23	12	19	23	-11	02	05	-02	07	-11	04	-01	-06
32.	Impulsiveness	04	-06	19	04	04	-11	-18	02	-16	19	-18	02	06
33.	Rigidity	21	-28	-11	-32	28	-16	-26	00	-33	44	-22	20	27

Appendix B-5 (Continued)

	16	17	18	19	20	21	22	23	24	25	26	27	28	29	30	31	32	33
	20	41	-18	09	-10	00	-30	-16	23	-14	07	-21	-17	-02	-26	-12	-07	29
	19	-15	27	-18	-05	-05	29	27	01	03	-13	14	12	00	03	07	08	-11
	-30	-13	-21	05	23	-01	-13	12	12	-24	27	17	-19	-05	-11	13	-02	03
	13	-22	21	-21	-01	-06	28	31	03	-03	-08	22	11	-04	00	14	11	-12
	-14	16	-16	22	-07	17	-14	-35	-14	07	01	-30	-12	08	06	-18	-03	13
	23	-10	29	-14	-07	-05	29	18	-04	08	-14	09	14	01	05	01	07	-09
	11	-13	18	-35	02	-14	30	10	-06	-02	-11	01	08	-06	-10	-07	-09	10
	-16	00	-14	24	12	11	-09	03	00	-27	30	26	-14	-05	-01	13	-03	02
	08	-15	13	-36	06	-11	31	12	-08	-10	-04	09	08	-08	-13	-07	-12	13
	-13	10	-15	32	00	13	-27	-18	09	08	12	-03	-06	01	08	01	20	-18
	16	-08	17	-38	-01	-13	26	08	-09	04	-18	-07	11	-01	-11	-11	-05	08
	-18	-23	26	17	-22	30	17	14	-22	-13	-24	17	-03	18	20	26	05	-16
	-05	-08	03	13	-04	23	02	12	-19	-01	01	00	00	08	03	-07	18	-03
	-03	-01	-12	07	01	10	-12	-10	-12	00	09	-23	01	-11	-09	06	02	-03
	56	46	62	43	-09	07	09	-15	15	20	-12	-17	-15	14	-06	-20	-19	07
		88	-20	-20	-17	-13	-07	-32	15	29	-02	-15	00	27	-01	-20	01	-02
	91		-23	-11	-13	-10	-14	-32	18	18	05	-11	-08	21	-01	-24	-08	05
	-07	-16		74	00	23	09	15	08	05	-21	01	-14	-02	-01	-01	-17	00
	21	13	81		-03	23	-20	-03	10	04	-01	-03	-24	-02	-06	-06	-16	10
	05	08	-31	-22		06	02	-04	-21	06	-01	09	08	-03	05	-26	-04	00
	-04	01	13	03	35		03	00	-13	05	-14	04	13	22	12	-06	13	-27
	-15	-18	03	-07	22	29		30	-14	-07	-10	14	-07	03	23	18	04	-05
	-15	-08	-17	-18	14	-04	01		18	-19	01	20	01	-03	-04	28	-04	-18
	10	14	26	32	-11	01	-11	38		03	14	17	-01	-15	-11	10	-25	10
	-24	-27	09	-12	-22	00	02	02	-04		-52	-32	08	14	10	-22	11	-07
	-06	-04	-27	-38	42	02	11	-03	-07	-09		20	-18	-20	-13	27	-04	03
	-08	-10	-12	-14	-10	-14	-01	05	17	-21	-07		25	01	11	07	-06	-17
	29	24	00	20	-11	-08	04	-07	16	-38	-31	13		-11	03	-08	20	-40
	-12	-22	14	03	-16	-04	-11	00	08	10	00	15	02		19	-22	01	-16
	10	08	13	20	11	09	19	-13	-02	-03	00	-17	04	16		-15	-12	00
	20	13	23	29	13	26	07	-38	-10	-28	07	-08	10	00	28		17	-33
	22	09	03	13	-02	-14	-12	-29	-21	-27	06	09	14	10	-08	12		-57
	-15	-01	-10	-08	-07	-06	-08	15	25	36	-17	-04	-19	-05	-10	-42	-22	

Appendix B-6

Intercorrelations of Major Variables for Low Test Anxious–Low Defensive Males ($N = 30$) and Females ($N = 28$)

Variable	1	2	3	4	5	6	7	8	9	10	11	12	13
1. Choice dilemmas		-42	26	-40	34	-39	-24	41	-17	25	-30	-02	25
2. Chance-max. of gain	-42		-51	96	-82	96	79	-57	74	-68	80	10	-17
3. Chance-min. of loss	30	-54		-27	22	-71	-40	51	-29	25	-42	-04	18
4. Chance-long shot	-40	94	-24		-85	86	76	-49	75	-69	77	14	-13
5. Chance-min. dev. from 1/2	28	-73	27	-72		-72	-62	41	-61	65	-63	-10	15
6. Chance-max. of variance	-45	97	-69	84	-67		76	-60	68	-62	76	13	-16
7. Skill-max. of gain	-41	68	-41	65	-46	67		-51	97	-71	97	19	-19
8. Skill-min. of loss	26	-62	68	-45	11	-68	-65		-33	12	-65	00	08
9. Skill-long shot	-41	59	-34	60	-52	60	95	-44		-79	91	25	-16
10. Skill-min. dev. from 1/2	51	-39	12	-46	42	-39	-78	18	-87		-64	-17	07
11. Skill-max. of variance	-41	69	-51	63	-37	71	97	-77	88	-68		21	-23
12. Number judgments	38	-26	-02	-30	12	-19	-27	21	-21	09	-23		17
13. Clues	26	-15	27	-09	00	-22	-32	37	-32	15	-38	48	
14. Final bet	-38	19	-04	18	-14	18	43	-25	40	-50	35	-09	-01
15. Total winnings	-51	07	-03	05	-02	07	23	-06	26	-28	15	-40	-01
16. Chance-abs. winnings	-45	-04	-11	-12	12	-01	01	-01	01	-16	-04	-37	12
17. Chance-rel. winnings	-25	-43	10	-47	46	-38	-24	14	-26	-01	-26	-13	27
18. Skill-abs. winnings	-38	05	06	09	-11	04	30	-04	37	-32	24	-12	-17
19. Skill-rel. winnings	-41	00	15	08	-05	-02	24	-01	27	-28	14	-28	-03
20. Chance bet dissatisfaction	09	10	-06	15	-23	04	15	-02	20	-25	14	02	-10
21. Skill bet dissatisfaction	28	-35	23	-29	-10	36	-23	52	-05	-08	-30	25	-02
22. Verbal aptitude (SAT)	-10	31	-23	23	-24	33	05	-34	-04	08	11	00	-11
23. Math. aptitude (SAT)	02	-34	19	-33	-07	-35	-25	47	-15	-08	-32	30	26
24. Analytic functioning (EFT)	21	-21	24	-13	02	-24	-36	53	-29	26	-39	12	25
25. Judgmental confidence	-53	04	-15	03	11	12	20	-17	22	-20	25	-10	-31
26. Extremity-high confidence	49	-16	11	-14	02	-23	-04	14	00	09	-04	11	-05
27. Extremity-low confidence	32	-44	37	-34	16	-49	-29	45	-18	15	-29	04	-20
28. Category width	29	-35	-01	-40	33	-28	-29	09	-29	20	-24	22	22
29. Extremity of self-rating	-48	26	-23	24	-23	29	36	-17	38	-38	32	-31	-34
30. Self-sufficiency	-34	06	-25	-03	-19	09	-01	07	05	-06	-03	-27	-20
31. Independence	-54	47	-05	51	-45	43	22	-06	20	-33	20	-24	06
32. Impulsiveness	-02	25	-24	23	00	25	21	-34	13	12	30	-24	-37
33. Rigidity	34	-20	15	-12	05	-25	08	24	17	-20	02	27	25

Appendix B-6 (Continued)

16	17	18	19	20	21	22	23	24	25	26	27	28	29	30	31	32	33
15	29	-07	25	25	12	-17	-22	03	17	-29	00	-08	13	08	-15	-26	36
22	-27	38	-14	-23	-22	45	19	13	-30	28	05	14	-08	-27	11	43	-46
-04	24	-08	16	46	25	-31	05	19	21	-33	-01	-31	-03	18	-12	-36	19
22	-24	37	-14	-14	-20	41	23	18	-26	19	06	05	-15	-28	10	36	-47
-08	34	-44	04	06	24	-50	-23	-23	29	-23	09	-11	-08	03	-23	-21	34
18	-31	31	-16	-31	-25	46	11	04	-32	34	04	24	-10	-29	12	45	-42
11	-33	36	-18	-15	-30	30	24	09	-41	24	11	07	-13	-37	-06	38	-41
00	33	-05	29	01	20	-16	-18	00	03	-22	17	-02	29	19	-17	-29	16
12	-29	38	-14	-14	-29	30	25	11	-44	20	18	04	-12	-39	-10	32	-42
-07	22	-47	-06	30	23	-49	-26	-05	35	-30	-32	-13	-04	29	06	-28	33
10	-33	37	-17	-13	-35	30	27	06	-31	22	04	09	-18	-41	02	38	-44
-09	-29	-17	-16	09	-22	20	20	-35	-35	07	-09	16	-09	-44	12	09	-29
-06	06	-31	-08	30	30	09	01	-21	26	-20	17	-26	19	-04	01	-09	31
36	27	26	19	08	06	-07	31	11	-10	-16	27	-19	12	-14	-57	-23	-16
74	51	82	56	-14	-19	24	17	33	-08	04	19	00	20	-26	-30	-04	-12
	67	26	12	09	23	16	21	21	-06	-08	07	-19	11	-38	-31	04	-11
84		26	42	00	13	-15	09	16	24	-24	15	-11	16	-10	-22	-26	06
25	08		76	-30	-56	26	11	23	-03	10	24	25	15	-12	-19	-11	-15
36	29	83		-23	-53	17	-05	-01	12	03	24	26	19	-01	-18	-31	18
-23	-23	-28	-35		47	-08	12	16	03	-25	-18	-15	16	20	14	-03	03
-21	-11	-14	-32	59		-18	00	10	11	-22	-06	-34	06	14	-03	-02	14
-04	-17	30	21	-27	-29		28	-13	-31	28	17	37	21	-13	09	17	12
09	30	15	22	16	36	-09		13	-43	32	29	04	-02	-32	-16	-22	-07
-31	-20	-31	-24	11	19	-46	33		-05	14	-05	13	09	21	-08	07	13
19	18	32	24	-23	-14	-19	-05	-08		-54	-13	-16	18	22	08	-03	10
-33	-28	-17	-25	35	18	-26	24	18	-51		-05	30	-02	-18	21	34	-02
-28	-12	08	-07	36	67	-16	34	17	-14	45		09	-12	-22	-48	-28	15
-03	25	-38	-39	38	37	-42	19	19	-11	06	13		01	11	10	13	-14
16	00	43	28	11	16	18	-09	-27	15	-28	06	-09		21	16	25	-05
32	16	43	28	-03	11	34	29	-13	06	04	26	-14	56		10	-23	20
35	12	28	20	-15	-18	46	07	-23	01	-29	-14	-39	41	38		43	-17
-16	-27	13	-04	12	-08	-01	-27	-12	-03	35	23	-07	32	13	18		-43
-30	-12	-12	-05	43	34	-38	34	36	-11	35	34	24	-19	00	-46	-31	

Appendix B-7

Intercorrelations of Major Variables for Low Test Anxious–High Defensive Males ($N = 35$) and Females ($N = 22$)

	Variable	1	2	3	4	5	6	7	8	9	10	11	12	13	1
1.	Choice dilemmas		-32	33	-21	21	-33	-22	22	-17	09	-20	-06	-12	2
2.	Chance-max. of gain	-14		-54	95	-80	96	70	-40	65	-65	69	-02	-02	-3
3.	Chance-min. of loss	23	-60		-29	14	-72	-47	77	-31	30	-62	-09	-15	0
4.	Chance-long shot	-10	90	-30		-86	85	60	-20	61	-63	56	-04	-09	-3
5.	Chance-min. dev. from 1/2	17	-69	25	-80		-67	-50	08	-52	64	-44	05	04	2
6.	Chance-max. of variance	-22	93	-81	75	-60		70	-53	63	-62	74	-04	04	-2
7.	Skill-max. of gain	20	78	-54	70	-40	71		-57	96	-84	96	-02	02	-3
8.	Skill-min. of loss	-25	-60	20	-54	34	-42	-66		-34	25	-75	-03	-14	1
9.	Skill-long shot	13	75	-55	68	-40	71	96	-48		-89	86	-05	-03	-3
10.	Skill-min. dev. from 1/2	10	-67	45	-63	53	-68	-77	25	-87		-76	08	16	3
11.	Skill-max. of variance	28	73	-43	66	-35	62	97	-79	89	-67		-01	06	-2
12.	Number judgments	-09	-24	11	-12	-12	-13	-23	37	-18	05	-29		31	2
13.	Clues	23	-05	03	-10	28	-03	02	-16	-08	32	08	34		0
14.	Final bet	-21	-39	51	-25	31	-48	-36	-12	-44	45	-23	13	21	
15.	Total winnings	-14	-10	30	-10	33	-22	-21	-01	-20	31	-17	-22	22	4
16.	Chance-abs. winnings	-16	-35	49	-23	43	-43	-45	27	-41	46	-43	-01	12	5
17.	Chance-rel. winnings	-11	-44	58	-32	48	-54	-53	30	-49	54	-49	01	14	5
18.	Skill-abs. winnings	00	19	-04	06	05	10	14	-21	12	00	15	-17	31	0
19.	Skill-rel. winnings	-06	-24	33	-29	34	-31	-37	19	-37	43	-37	-04	32	2
20.	Chance bet dissatisfaction	-08	-22	-19	-33	04	-05	-19	19	-21	13	-19	08	-07	-0
21.	Skill bet dissatisfaction	-50	-07	-27	-12	-07	10	-18	26	-13	-02	-23	12	-10	-1
22.	Verbal aptitude (SAT)	-21	06	-36	03	-13	19	23	03	25	-22	16	20	-01	-0
23.	Math. aptitude (SAT)	26	10	-23	10	00	23	22	10	23	-16	13	22	20	-3
24.	Analytic functioning (EFT)	-10	-25	13	-24	13	-16	-26	31	-22	15	-34	52	26	1
25.	Judgmental confidence	41	35	-27	31	-25	32	35	-45	28	-12	40	07	01	-1
26.	Extremity-high confidence	11	22	-19	18	-42	24	27	-11	31	-46	24	-11	-57	-2
27.	Extremity-low confidence	-12	07	03	21	-23	12	13	28	25	-40	01	27	16	-1
28.	Category width	-27	-43	26	-42	27	-32	-61	51	-56	44	-62	41	42	3
29.	Extremity of self-rating	12	35	-33	31	-27	36	31	-23	36	-26	27	09	17	-2
30.	Self-sufficiency	-02	-02	18	01	-03	-12	-07	-07	-11	18	-06	10	25	2
31.	Independence	-35	-04	16	-03	11	-15	-07	-03	-11	17	-05	-14	06	2
32.	Impulsiveness	-35	-15	25	-04	06	-25	-37	08	-40	46	-35	-12	-07	4
33.	Rigidity	26	-18	-01	-15	10	-10	-08	-11	-18	25	-05	27	30	0

Appendix B-7 (Continued)

15	16	17	18	19	20	21	22	23	24	25	26	27	28	29	30	31	32	33
06	19	24	-16	09	-25	-14	-30	-21	20	-05	05	-31	-21	-11	-47	12	05	32
45	29	00	30	-21	04	17	28	22	-08	10	-16	-01	03	08	14	-12	-07	03
31	-31	-17	-17	17	20	-06	-23	07	19	-39	36	29	-04	-01	-26	15	08	04
34	22	-08	20	-25	07	17	23	24	-07	-01	-09	10	05	08	09	-07	-02	06
34	-16	13	-23	11	-13	-10	-05	-25	00	08	-03	-16	-12	01	-09	05	09	-13
47	33	06	29	-20	02	14	33	12	-17	16	-18	-06	00	07	19	-17	-08	05
31	11	-06	32	-23	09	08	30	12	-14	00	-05	-08	-02	-17	02	-21	-18	21
30	-23	-12	-20	20	19	01	-25	-09	01	-38	32	35	00	02	-07	13	09	-04
26	05	-11	30	-21	16	12	25	11	-17	-11	03	04	00	-21	-03	-25	-20	26
32	-20	-01	-23	24	-10	-09	-07	-07	14	06	-04	-01	-16	16	-01	19	23	-16
36	17	-01	32	-25	02	08	31	12	-16	09	-14	-18	00	-14	00	-22	-16	18
20	-08	-11	01	-14	-17	27	11	06	-09	-13	-28	18	16	25	16	25	-04	-19
11	04	-03	-14	-06	-02	-01	-04	11	01	-17	04	00	-02	08	-01	-08	14	08
04	-04	03	-04	17	-05	17	-15	-18	-16	-14	-03	-20	-03	-12	-35	15	05	-12
	60	53	68	44	-14	-03	18	02	30	25	-14	-16	-13	22	-02	-27	-24	09
82		93	-12	-16	-32	-07	-06	-16	30	41	-08	-27	-08	31	11	-23	06	-11
79	98		-13	-06	-37	-14	-09	-20	36	39	01	-27	-20	30	10	-18	03	-12
65	14	13		70	03	09	28	20	14	02	-20	03	-08	06	-01	-11	-35	15
79	56	60	72		-01	-03	04	03	23	-01	01	-01	-19	00	-16	-06	-23	20
22	-14	-14	-23	-07		15	16	-01	-37	-04	00	17	20	-01	18	-31	-07	08
22	-14	-13	-22	-18	58		17	10	-08	13	-21	17	27	33	03	-04	21	-37
04	-05	-11	00	-17	54	40		23	-12	-05	-14	33	03	15	17	-04	06	-15
34	-20	-24	-19	-32	-01	-01	-02		01	-23	02	01	12	05	-10	17	-04	-14
06	18	23	07	28	-11	10	-13	43		15	15	07	-02	-10	-08	13	-32	25
40	-34	-35	-26	-50	-31	-33	-15	08	-21		-64	-34	17	22	35	-27	06	-10
47	-39	-39	-35	-51	27	06	12	18	04	15		23	-35	-35	-28	32	-07	20
03	-09	-11	16	01	-22	05	21	29	33	-40	-01		19	12	25	-02	-06	-03
42	56	57	08	41	29	25	25	-09	32	-44	-27	24		-03	13	-11	06	-30
04	-14	-14	04	-16	-31	13	-04	07	17	37	01	22	-12		34	-29	19	-52
13	26	29	-12	14	04	-11	22	-34	-09	08	-20	-04	30	16		-35	-11	-07
46	52	51	07	34	31	17	36	-37	-09	-40	-20	-14	36	-23	54		21	-21
23	27	30	03	25	-11	02	-10	-32	-06	-24	-21	-15	10	-33	-02	11		-54
30	-22	-19	-20	-08	01	14	-19	11	17	30	-26	-23	-19	29	11	-37	-16	

Appendix B-8

INTERCORRELATIONS OF MAJOR VARIABLES FOR HIGH TEST ANXIOUS–LOW DEFENSIVE MALES ($N = 27$) AND FEMALES ($N = 24$)

	Variable	1	2	3	4	5	6	7	8	9	10	11	12	13
1.	Choice dilemmas		03	06	05	-04	01	05	29	17	-07	-04	01	21
2.	Chance-max. of gain	-11		-45	93	-86	95	67	-43	65	-52	67	19	20
3.	Chance-min. of loss	24	-55		-17	13	-68	-60	66	-48	46	-65	-01	01
4.	Chance-long shot	-06	93	-28		-95	80	57	-31	60	-48	56	19	18
5.	Chance-min. dev. from 1/2	-04	-74	-02	-85		-75	-47	23	-52	50	-46	-25	-20
6.	Chance-max. of variance	-15	95	-73	84	-59		75	-58	69	-58	77	19	14
7.	Skill-max. of gain	-17	23	-23	14	-14	33		-65	96	-79	97	-13	10
8.	Skill-min. of loss	28	-46	70	-26	05	-59	-44		-45	28	-78	17	-01
9.	Skill-long shot	-13	10	-06	07	-13	19	96	-22		-86	90	-09	13
10.	Skill-min. dev. from 1/2	29	-13	06	-12	26	-18	-78	28	-80		-73	07	-01
11.	Skill-max. of variance	-22	34	-34	23	-18	44	95	-63	86	-70		-12	09
12.	Number judgments	16	14	-27	00	05	14	-18	-11	-24	36	-09		41
13.	Clues	34	-03	10	-03	-05	-02	-02	21	05	11	-01	44	
14.	Final bet	-21	-27	28	-21	11	-34	-25	12	-24	06	-25	-21	-39
15.	Total winnings	-32	13	-04	20	-08	19	36	-14	41	-37	35	-08	11
16.	Chance-abs. winnings	-32	-07	-01	-03	18	-01	24	-12	24	-21	18	-20	-19
17.	Chance-rel. winnings	-36	-26	03	-25	40	-18	18	-05	18	-12	10	-14	-12
18.	Skill-abs. winnings	-07	21	-09	24	-23	23	09	-06	12	-10	15	24	33
19.	Skill-rel. winnings	01	15	-03	19	-24	15	-08	-02	-09	05	00	34	37
20.	Chance bet dissatisfaction	-18	25	-01	29	-35	17	-39	-07	-49	17	-34	14	-14
21.	Skill bet dissatisfaction	10	-28	38	-25	-02	-41	-18	40	-06	00	-28	-12	-19
22.	Verbal aptitude (SAT)	22	-19	19	-25	02	-26	12	17	11	-07	06	25	27
23.	Math. aptitude (SAT)	34	-53	32	-53	34	-54	-24	56	-10	27	-33	-10	15
24.	Analytic functioning (EFT)	-11	-38	11	-40	53	-35	-17	20	-13	26	-16	11	-02
25.	Judgmental confidence	-34	00	-16	-05	08	05	-11	-09	-19	00	-18	-05	-24
26.	Extremity-high confidence	17	33	06	33	-32	29	44	-29	38	-25	43	11	06
27.	Extremity-low confidence	19	-13	07	-03	09	-06	02	00	05	10	03	28	-10
28.	Category width	-22	06	02	06	-09	06	-17	12	-12	28	-14	36	23
29.	Extremity of self-rating	03	12	21	18	-30	01	-12	22	-10	-09	-15	-34	01
30.	Self-sufficiency	-33	-25	09	-18	25	-19	-24	27	-13	08	-25	09	31
31.	Independence	-59	24	-32	23	-07	31	15	-25	13	-13	25	00	-05
32.	Impulsiveness	-45	12	07	20	-22	10	15	-09	14	-31	16	-30	-18
33.	Rigidity	28	-13	18	-10	-07	-13	06	24	12	03	-02	-23	06

Appendix B-8 (Continued)

	16	17	18	19	20	21	22	23	24	25	26	27	28	29	30	31	32	33
	-50	-46	02	-02	07	16	-06	12	26	-11	10	-07	20	-23	-13	-06	11	08
	36	04	-06	-35	21	-25	-39	03	11	-13	-25	03	10	-20	10	11	-02	21
	08	24	15	23	-11	27	24	-03	-05	-14	10	-23	36	00	-14	-35	-31	34
	37	07	00	-34	21	-14	-38	01	14	-26	-21	-06	30	-30	00	-01	-07	35
	-37	-16	-01	35	-30	-03	36	02	-17	25	17	14	-26	38	-06	-04	02	-26
	29	-03	-13	-42	25	-24	-37	02	15	-07	-22	06	-07	-16	12	21	15	04
	09	-23	-04	-41	23	-37	-37	27	16	-11	-32	-06	00	-20	-15	04	01	12
	-13	05	24	44	00	39	14	05	01	12	-02	-21	13	-03	01	-17	-12	20
	03	-27	05	-37	26	-29	-43	27	21	-16	-37	-14	08	-28	-20	-01	-01	19
	-07	08	-04	35	-30	07	39	-21	-18	08	38	33	00	41	12	-13	-06	-13
	14	-16	-10	-47	17	-40	-31	17	12	-12	-26	-03	-05	-16	-08	08	04	04
	06	02	17	13	12	-02	01	-25	29	15	-11	-13	24	23	01	16	-01	15
	04	-07	32	11	-05	-19	-20	10	02	23	-22	00	05	05	00	-18	-28	07
	41	38	-01	-07	-01	02	04	03	-06	14	-35	-57	-11	-03	09	-24	-19	21
	70	54	39	26	-03	-14	10	08	-22	24	-45	-06	-23	24	34	-37	-16	18
		88	-34	-32	20	03	14	-23	-10	19	-13	-13	-24	05	14	-26	09	17
	93		-37	-28	11	22	31	-34	-16	13	09	-13	-25	08	15	-20	22	03
	-31	-29		78	-22	-14	-04	31	-13	09	-43	08	14	25	29	-02	-31	-01
	-39	-36	94		-23	-06	18	33	-18	38	-29	09	09	34	30	-08	-33	10
	-36	-38	30	46		53	-22	22	59	26	-12	-13	-04	-24	-25	10	30	09
	02	07	-10	-11	-20		09	-08	32	05	03	-32	-01	-29	17	06	45	-10
	-52	-41	31	33	07	15		06	-32	04	35	-05	-26	18	29	00	08	-19
	-33	-27	-28	-24	-32	29	30		03	-02	00	00	-03	-25	-02	-09	-39	13
	21	27	-18	-13	-22	07	-14	28		-11	01	-05	21	07	-41	-18	19	20
	18	26	-33	-30	07	00	-12	-12	02		-51	-20	-28	19	12	05	-02	09
	-11	-18	13	04	11	-33	10	-35	-35	-17		39	-03	-08	-22	11	27	-36
	22	11	-05	01	-08	-15	-31	-03	09	-25	07		-21	36	-18	-11	15	-41
	-18	-16	40	38	24	13	10	07	32	02	-01	01		-04	-41	13	-21	50
	01	06	-19	-19	-04	45	-07	03	-01	30	-28	-50	-07		-03	-04	17	-18
	-15	-05	45	43	13	-07	09	16	23	01	-31	00	54	-15		15	03	-26
	-06	-10	51	40	29	-47	12	-25	02	-11	-02	-02	36	-36	44		26	-43
	-14	-15	28	18	29	-28	12	-39	-14	16	32	-35	11	-14	18	55		-47
	06	09	-31	-32	-21	36	-09	38	-04	-11	-27	-02	-01	53	-25	-37	-57	

Appendix B-9

Intercorrelations of Major Variables for High Test Anxious–High Defensive Males ($N = 22$) and Females ($N = 29$)

	Variable	1	2	3	4	5	6	7	8	9	10	11	12	13
1.	Choice dilemmas		-58	22	-62	49	-53	-55	13	-57	42	-46	-23	-11
2.	Chance-max. of gain	-22		-62	97	-85	97	71	-26	69	-62	62	25	-06
3.	Chance-min. of loss	24	-46		-45	29	-76	-47	51	-35	34	-48	-06	01
4.	Chance-long shot	-15	91	-09		-89	92	69	-16	70	-60	58	24	-06
5.	Chance-min. dev. from 1/2	16	-78	02	-90		-77	-69	27	-68	63	-62	-06	24
6.	Chance-max. of variance	-25	94	-70	74	-59		68	-33	63	-57	61	20	-04
7.	Skill-max. of gain	-14	64	-16	55	-43	53		-60	97	-85	97	-03	-35
8.	Skill-min. of loss	06	-35	58	-07	-02	-44	-36		-44	42	-76	14	31
9.	Skill-long shot	-13	52	06	55	-43	39	92	01		-84	90	-04	-35
10.	Skill-min. dev. from 1/2	12	-42	-12	-47	42	-29	-81	-07	-92		-81	-11	16
11.	Skill-max. of variance	-14	67	-33	51	-39	61	95	-59	78	-69		-06	-34
12.	Number judgments	06	-14	25	01	-14	-18	-26	41	-13	07	-38		56
13.	Clues	38	-60	49	-43	34	-60	-42	58	-20	18	-55	10	
14.	Final bet	46	-62	23	-56	48	-53	-36	44	-18	18	-43	18	60
15.	Total winnings	06	15	-20	06	-09	17	18	-08	15	-14	18	32	00
16.	Chance-abs. winnings	03	-20	-08	-28	19	-15	-11	-14	-17	11	-04	02	12
17.	Chance-rel. winnings	14	-49	05	-54	38	-42	-34	04	-33	26	-29	06	39
18.	Skill-abs. winnings	00	40	-16	38	-36	37	36	01	38	-37	29	48	-19
19.	Skill-rel. winnings	02	35	-16	32	-32	33	23	-01	23	-24	19	53	-23
20.	Chance bet dissatisfaction	11	18	-34	04	-04	24	01	-26	-12	13	06	-38	-09
21.	Skill bet dissatisfaction	-20	35	-37	24	-25	41	10	08	17	-18	09	-07	-21
22.	Verbal aptitude (SAT)	-13	04	-12	-01	-05	05	10	-01	06	03	10	-03	-31
23.	Math. aptitude (SAT)	35	-22	13	-15	03	-19	-06	36	09	-10	-15	-05	30
24.	Analytic functioning (EFT)	25	-03	-04	-03	-11	-01	12	08	13	-16	11	20	10
25.	Judgmental confidence	-19	27	-56	06	09	41	09	-20	00	16	16	02	-42
26.	Extremity-high confidence	04	-05	-12	-08	-02	-05	-17	-34	-35	31	-06	-05	-10
27.	Extremity-low confidence	02	04	-09	06	08	10	-10	-03	-12	19	-10	-14	01
28.	Category width	16	-17	33	-10	20	-20	12	15	24	-36	10	11	10
29.	Extremity of self-rating	22	17	12	23	-12	10	20	-17	14	-26	20	01	-10
30.	Self-sufficiency	-18	43	-11	43	-57	31	37	-10	31	-35	37	03	-20
31.	Independence	-35	31	15	40	-31	23	17	01	20	-26	11	12	-16
32.	Impulsiveness	19	02	14	09	01	01	-04	00	-03	06	-07	14	14
33.	Rigidity	16	-36	-20	-44	43	-20	-44	10	-46	58	-38	13	25

Appendix B-9 (Continued)

16	17	18	19	20	21	22	23	24	25	26	27	28	29	30	31	32	33
14	53	-28	-02	20	07	-15	-05	28	-37	21	-07	-06	-03	23	-43	-12	15
04	-32	24	-17	-24	-35	33	34	17	-09	-09	36	22	-12	-14	43	27	-26
-24	-02	-26	-01	32	11	-11	15	01	07	05	-03	-42	-06	08	00	-21	10
01	-34	24	-16	-16	-33	33	39	19	-06	-07	41	16	-20	-15	49	25	-29
-11	20	-09	33	01	47	-26	-46	-30	07	07	-49	-13	19	24	-57	-16	38
07	-28	28	-11	-25	-31	30	26	16	-06	-04	32	30	-10	-14	37	28	-25
15	-18	01	-46	-12	-41	28	08	07	-07	-28	13	16	15	-34	14	-01	02
-08	10	-08	26	-04	21	21	22	-03	-05	30	10	-27	-23	17	23	-16	03
15	-17	-07	-51	-13	-40	36	12	07	-08	-22	16	14	15	-34	20	-06	03
-05	19	-06	40	18	37	-51	-29	02	12	44	-05	04	-19	24	-26	18	-21
17	-14	-02	-50	-06	-40	18	01	02	-03	-32	10	21	21	-33	03	07	02
-34	-38	58	46	-35	33	27	25	-42	-13	-17	16	-21	09	31	33	17	-16
-20	-17	25	30	-09	53	15	15	-54	29	-04	-02	03	06	13	-01	26	-19
01	-01	-20	02	12	05	-16	-04	-06	24	34	-27	02	-07	23	-16	-06	10
47	37	50	44	06	21	02	-39	-19	08	-05	-19	-18	-09	-08	03	-06	00
	86	-35	-34	19	-29	00	-52	-14	03	18	06	14	13	-17	-07	-01	02
84		-39	-22	24	-12	-08	-41	-04	-13	17	07	07	04	-04	-25	-15	12
-18	-29		80	-07	41	-09	11	-01	11	-27	-01	-19	-17	03	25	08	-21
-12	-24	96		-06	45	-35	-03	-08	10	-01	-06	-24	-12	17	07	-05	-07
13	14	-34	-29		-15	-27	-11	16	34	-07	-11	-12	-06	-28	-15	03	-14
-04	04	26	25	23		-04	-10	-22	-11	03	-18	02	00	36	-01	08	-24
-29	-27	06	06	02	22		33	-17	-11	-10	-13	-26	-01	19	42	-09	18
-05	10	-19	-20	32	04	04		45	-15	-03	46	-14	-10	-01	43	-07	-17
-01	05	39	38	-13	-07	-09	43		-24	12	36	01	-26	-17	05	-14	-12
-08	-16	31	31	-14	33	28	-14	19		-15	-28	-05	-03	-43	-10	24	-05
16	15	-26	-16	49	-12	09	01	-24	-25		12	06	23	21	10	01	-26
-08	-11	-27	-31	-04	-30	-27	-11	01	02	-16		34	-17	-15	27	-06	-37
-02	-07	-06	-09	-41	-35	-27	-08	-04	-31	-39	00		-16	-17	-12	32	-46
-08	-29	20	23	-06	-14	-20	-10	-01	-27	03	08	22		03	03	-20	20
-02	-05	26	24	18	25	17	-07	06	-19	26	-27	-24	15		10	-22	20
-12	-20	33	39	-02	24	-22	-28	-15	-10	10	-05	-12	25	19		04	-44
16	-07	03	10	-03	-26	-16	-22	-35	-28	17	25	19	44	-09	07		-57
-08	12	-05	-07	-14	-22	05	21	33	47	-13	15	-18	-41	-28	-52	-28	

Appendix C

Reliability Data

	Males ($N = 114$) r	Females ($N = 103$) r
Decision-making Variables		
Choice dilemmas	.53[a]	.62[a]
Chance-max. of gain	.94[b]	.91[b]
Chance-min. of loss	.82[b]	.85[b]
Chance-long shot	.94[b]	.91[b]
Chance-min. dev. from 1/2	.88[b]	.84[b]
Chance-max. of variance	.92[b]	.89[b]
Skill-max. of gain	.95[b]	.91[b]
Skill-min. of loss	.79[b]	.79[b]
Skill-long shot	.94[b]	.91[b]
Skill-min. dev. from 1/2	.89[b]	.88[b]
Skill-max. of variance	.92[b]	.89[b]
Number judgments	.63[c]	.68[c]
Clues	.36[c]	.54[c]
Intellective ability variables		
Verbal aptitude (SAT)	.90[d]	.90[d]
Math. aptitude (SAT)	.88[d]	.88[d]
Analytic functioning (EFT)	.48[e]	.76[e]
Cognitive-judgmental variables		
Judgmental confidence	.89[a]	.92[a]
Category width	.75[f]	.69[f]
Extremity of self-rating	.93[a]	.83[a]
Personality variables		
Test anxiety (Alpert-Haber)	.73[b]	.75[b]
Defensiveness (Marlowe-Crowne)	.77[b]	.67[b]
Self-sufficiency	.68[b]	.68[b]
Independence-yielding	.35[b]	.12[b]
Impulsiveness	.66[b]	.52[b]
Rigidity-flexibility	.63[b]	.57[b]

NOTE: Reliability coefficients are not reported for those variables whose nature precluded their computation.

[a] Odd-even coefficients stepped up by Spearman-Brown formula.

[b] Kuder-Richardson Formula 20.

[c] Average inter-item r across the four parts of the measure (a lower-bound estimate).

[d] For a standard reference sample with SD = 100 (College Entrance Examination Board, 1962).

[e] Correlation between chromatic and achromatic portions of test (a lower-bound estimate).

[f] Coefficient alpha (Cronbach, 1951).

Appendix D

JUDGMENT EXTREMITY–CONFIDENCE PROCEDURE

OPINION QUESTIONNAIRE I

Instructions. This questionnaire will help us find out people's opinions about various things. Each item in the questionnaire will describe a specific event. We want your opinion as to how likely each event is. All of the items in the test will be of a form in which you estimate the number of chances out of 100 that a specific event occurs. Thus, if you judge an event to be very likely, you'd write a number close to 100; if you judge an event to be very unlikely, you'd write a number close to 0; and if you judge an event to be about equally likely and unlikely, you'd write a number close to 50.

We also want you to indicate how sure you are of your opinion. So, after you've decided how likely an event is, we want you to indicate how confident you are of this judgment by circling one of the five categories below each question.

Please do not skip any questions.

ALL QUESTIONS CONCERN PEOPLE, THINGS, AND EVENTS IN THE UNITED STATES.

1. The chances that an adult American male will earn at least $5000 a year are about ____ in 100.

Very Sure	Quite Sure	Moderately Sure	Slightly Sure	Not Sure At All

2. The chances that a new car will have white-wall rather than black tires are about ____ in 100.

Very Sure	Quite Sure	Moderately Sure	Slightly Sure	Not Sure At All

3. The chances that a student entering law school will quit before getting his law degree are about ____ in 100.

Very Sure	Quite Sure	Moderately Sure	Slightly Sure	Not Sure At All

4. The chances that a new radio will be an FM/AM combination rather than AM only are about ____ in 100.

Very Sure	Quite Sure	Moderately Sure	Slightly Sure	Not Sure At All

Appendix D

5. The chances that frequent thumbsucking during childhood will make the teeth stick out (cause buck teeth) are about ____ in 100.

| Very | Quite | Moderately | Slightly | Not Sure |
| Sure | Sure | Sure | Sure | At All |

6. The chances that a private home will have a finished basement are about ____ in 100.

| Very | Quite | Moderately | Slightly | Not Sure |
| Sure | Sure | Sure | Sure | At All |

7. The chances that the President of the United States will be a man without a college education are about ____ in 100.

| Very | Quite | Moderately | Slightly | Not Sure |
| Sure | Sure | Sure | Sure | At All |

8. The chances that an airplane will be taking off on an international flight from Idlewild during any minute between noon and 6 p.m. are about ____ in 100.

| Very | Quite | Moderately | Slightly | Not Sure |
| Sure | Sure | Sure | Sure | At All |

9. The chances that a person voted for the same party in all of the presidential elections from 1948 on are about ____ in 100.

| Very | Quite | Moderately | Slightly | Not Sure |
| Sure | Sure | Sure | Sure | At All |

10. The chances that a juvenile delinquent will have a low intelligence (IQ 80 or less) are about ____ in 100.

| Very | Quite | Moderately | Slightly | Not Sure |
| Sure | Sure | Sure | Sure | At All |

11. The chances that a drug salesman will travel more than 20,000 miles per year on business are about ____ in 100.

| Very | Quite | Moderately | Slightly | Not Sure |
| Sure | Sure | Sure | Sure | At All |

12. The chances that a high school graduate will go on to a freshman year in college are about ____ in 100.

| Very | Quite | Moderately | Slightly | Not Sure |
| Sure | Sure | Sure | Sure | At All |

13. The chances that a male smoker will buy filter-tip rather than regular cigarets are about ____ in 100.

| Very | Quite | Moderately | Slightly | Not Sure |
| Sure | Sure | Sure | Sure | At All |

14. The chances that a couple getting married this year will later have a divorce are about ____ in 100.

| Very | Quite | Moderately | Slightly | Not Sure |
| Sure | Sure | Sure | Sure | At All |

15. The chances that a novel published in the United States will sell more than 5000 copies are about ____ in 100.

| Very | Quite | Moderately | Slightly | Not Sure |
| Sure | Sure | Sure | Sure | At All |

16. The chances that an American male now at the age of 40 will live beyond the age of 55 are about ____ in 100.

| Very | Quite | Moderately | Slightly | Not Sure |
| Sure | Sure | Sure | Sure | At All |

17. The chances that an American family will live in a house without a telephone are about ____ in 100.

| Very | Quite | Moderately | Slightly | Not Sure |
| Sure | Sure | Sure | Sure | At All |

18. The chances that an American tourist will fly rather than take a ship to Europe are about ____ in 100.

| Very | Quite | Moderately | Slightly | Not Sure |
| Sure | Sure | Sure | Sure | At All |

19. The chances that an American family will own its own home are about ____ in 100.

| Very | Quite | Moderately | Slightly | Not Sure |
| Sure | Sure | Sure | Sure | At All |

20. The chances that a household will have an extension phone in addition to a regular phone are about ____ in 100.

| Very | Quite | Moderately | Slightly | Not Sure |
| Sure | Sure | Sure | Sure | At All |

21. The chances that a shoe's heel will be made of leather rather than of rubber are about ____ in 100.

| Very | Quite | Moderately | Slightly | Not Sure |
| Sure | Sure | Sure | Sure | At All |

22. The chances that an American citizen will believe in God are about ____ in 100.

| Very | Quite | Moderately | Slightly | Not Sure |
| Sure | Sure | Sure | Sure | At All |

Appendix D

23. The chances that a woman will totally abstain from alcoholic beverages are about ____ in 100.

    | Very Sure | Quite Sure | Moderately Sure | Slightly Sure | Not Sure At All |

24. The chances that a high-school graduate will read at least one book per year are about ____ in 100.

    | Very Sure | Quite Sure | Moderately Sure | Slightly Sure | Not Sure At All |

25. The chances that an American car in the low price range will still be in running order after ten years of use are about ____ in 100.

    | Very Sure | Quite Sure | Moderately Sure | Slightly Sure | Not Sure At All |

26. The chances that an American city of over 50,000 people will have a chapter of the League of Women Voters are about ____ in 100.

    | Very Sure | Quite Sure | Moderately Sure | Slightly Sure | Not Sure At All |

27. The chances that a middle-aged white collar worker and his wife will go to the movies at least once a week are about ____ in 100.

    | Very Sure | Quite Sure | Moderately Sure | Slightly Sure | Not Sure At All |

28. The chances that the average American child is attending the first grade of school in the state in which he was born are about ____ in 100.

    | Very Sure | Quite Sure | Moderately Sure | Slightly Sure | Not Sure At All |

29. The chances that a senator from a state in the northeastern U.S. will be elected for a second term in office are about ____ in 100.

    | Very Sure | Quite Sure | Moderately Sure | Slightly Sure | Not Sure At All |

30. The chances that a 21-year-old male will have spent at least one week in the hospital for accident or illness are about ____ in 100.

    | Very Sure | Quite Sure | Moderately Sure | Slightly Sure | Not Sure At All |

31. The chances that a son will go into the same kind of work as his father are about ____ in 100.

    | Very Sure | Quite Sure | Moderately Sure | Slightly Sure | Not Sure At All |

32. The chances that an American will take a vacation in Europe rather than in Latin America are about _____ in 100.

| Very Sure | Quite Sure | Moderately Sure | Slightly Sure | Not Sure At All |

33. The chances that an American Protestant family will have more than two children are about _____ in 100.

| Very Sure | Quite Sure | Moderately Sure | Slightly Sure | Not Sure At All |

34. The chances that an American-born baby will get a poor and inadequate diet during his first year of life are about _____ in 100.

| Very Sure | Quite Sure | Moderately Sure | Slightly Sure | Not Sure At All |

35. The chances that an adult male will stay home instead of going to church on Sunday are about _____ in 100.

| Very Sure | Quite Sure | Moderately Sure | Slightly Sure | Not Sure At All |

36. The chances that a man 70 years old will need financial help from someone to support himself are about _____ in 100.

| Very Sure | Quite Sure | Moderately Sure | Slightly Sure | Not Sure At All |

37. The chances that a native-born American will travel outside of the United States at some time during his life are about _____ in 100.

| Very Sure | Quite Sure | Moderately Sure | Slightly Sure | Not Sure At All |

38. The chances that a seventh grade teacher in the public schools will be a man are about _____ in 100.

| Very Sure | Quite Sure | Moderately Sure | Slightly Sure | Not Sure At All |

39. The chances that a child whose parents are divorced will need psychiatric treatment are about _____ in 100.

| Very Sure | Quite Sure | Moderately Sure | Slightly Sure | Not Sure At All |

40. The chances that in the United States a girl will be married before the age of 17 are about _____ in 100.

| Very Sure | Quite Sure | Moderately Sure | Slightly Sure | Not Sure At All |

254 | *Appendix D*

41. The chances that the average temperature in August will be higher than in July are about ____ in 100.

| Very | Quite | Moderately | Slightly | Not Sure |
| Sure | Sure | Sure | Sure | At All |

42. The chances that a world's champion prizefighter comes from a poor family (less than $5000 per year income) are about ____ in 100.

| Very | Quite | Moderately | Slightly | Not Sure |
| Sure | Sure | Sure | Sure | At All |

43. The chances that an American citizen will be bilingual (speak two languages) are about ____ in 100.

| Very | Quite | Moderately | Slightly | Not Sure |
| Sure | Sure | Sure | Sure | At All |

44. The chances that a five-card deal will have two cards of the same kind (one pair) are about ____ in 100.

| Very | Quite | Moderately | Slightly | Not Sure |
| Sure | Sure | Sure | Sure | At All |

45. The chances that a male college graduate will stay with his first full-time job more than two years are about ____ in 100.

| Very | Quite | Moderately | Slightly | Not Sure |
| Sure | Sure | Sure | Sure | At All |

46. The chances that the number of auto accidents in a year will be higher than for the year just before are about ____ in 100.

| Very | Quite | Moderately | Slightly | Not Sure |
| Sure | Sure | Sure | Sure | At All |

47. The chances that a small business (for example, a gas station or a motel) will fail within two years after starting are about ____ in 100.

| Very | Quite | Moderately | Slightly | Not Sure |
| Sure | Sure | Sure | Sure | At All |

48. The chances that a crime in the United States will be solved (someone arrested and convicted for it) are about ____ in 100.

| Very | Quite | Moderately | Slightly | Not Sure |
| Sure | Sure | Sure | Sure | At All |

49. The chances that the person one marries will have the same religion are about ____ in 100.

| Very | Quite | Moderately | Slightly | Not Sure |
| Sure | Sure | Sure | Sure | At All |

50. The chances that a major league baseball team will win the pennant if it is in first place July 4th are about ____ in 100.

| Very | Quite | Moderately | Slightly | Not Sure |
| Sure | Sure | Sure | Sure | At All |

Appendix E

Choice Dilemmas Procedure

OPINION QUESTIONNAIRE II

Instructions. On the following pages, you will find a series of situations that are likely to occur in everyday life. The central person in each situation is faced with a choice between two alternative courses of action, which we might call X and Y. Alternative X is more desirable and attractive than alternative Y, but the probability of attaining or achieving X is less than that of attaining or achieving Y.

For each situation on the following pages, you will be asked to indicate the minimum odds of success you would demand before recommending that the more attractive or desirable alternative, X, be chosen.

Read each situation carefully before giving your judgment. Try to place yourself in the position of the central person in each of the situations. There are twelve situations in all. Please do not omit any of them.

1. Mr. A, an electrical engineer, who is married and has one child, has been working for a large electronics corporation since graduating from college five years ago. He is assured of a lifetime job with a modest, though adequate, salary, and liberal pension benefits upon retirement. On the other hand, it is very unlikely that his salary will increase much before he retires. While attending a convention, Mr. A is offered a job with a small, newly founded company which has a highly uncertain future. The new job would pay more to start and would offer the possibility of a share in the ownership if the company survived the competition of the larger firms.

Imagine that you are advising Mr. A. Listed below are several probabilities or odds of the new company's proving financially sound.

Please check the lowest *probability that you would consider acceptable to make it worthwhile for Mr. A to take the new job.*

____ The chances are 1 in 10 that the company will prove financially sound.
____ The chances are 3 in 10 that the company will prove financially sound.
____ The chances are 5 in 10 that the company will prove financially sound.
____ The chances are 7 in 10 that the company will prove financially sound.
____ The chances are 9 in 10 that the company will prove financially sound.
____ Place a check here if you think Mr. A should *not* take the new job no matter what the probabilities.

2. Mr. B, a 45-year-old accountant, has recently been informed by his physician that he has developed a severe heart ailment. The disease would be sufficiently serious to force Mr. B to change many of his strongest life habits — reducing his work load, drastically changing his diet, giving up favorite leisure-time pursuits. The physician suggests that a delicate medical operation could be attempted which, if successful, would completely relieve the heart condition. But its success could not be assured, and in fact, the operation might prove fatal.

Imagine that you are advising Mr. B. Listed below are several probabilities or odds that the operation will prove successful.

Please check the lowest *probability that you would consider acceptable for the operation to be performed.*

____ Place a check here if you think Mr. B should *not* have the operation no matter what the probabilities.
____ The chances are 9 in 10 that the operation will be a success.
____ The chances are 7 in 10 that the operation will be a success.
____ The chances are 5 in 10 that the operation will be a success.
____ The chances are 3 in 10 that the operation will be a success.
____ The chances are 1 in 10 that the operation will be a success.

3. Mr. C, a married man with two children, has a steady job that pays him about $6000 per year. He can easily afford the necessities of life, but few of the luxuries. Mr. C's father, who died recently, carried a $4000 life insurance policy. Mr. C would like to invest this money in stocks. He is well aware of the secure "blue-chip" stocks and bonds that would pay approximately 6% on his investment. On the other hand, Mr. C has heard that the stocks of a relatively unknown Company X might double their present value if a new product currently in production is favorably received by the buying public. However, if the product is unfavorably received, the stocks would decline in value.

Imagine that you are advising Mr. C. Listed below are several probabilities or odds that Company X stocks will double their value.

Please check the lowest *probability that you would consider acceptable for Mr. C to invest in Company X Stocks.*

____ The chances are 1 in 10 that the stocks will double their value.
____ The chances are 3 in 10 that the stocks will double their value.
____ The chances are 5 in 10 that the stocks will double their value.
____ The chances are 7 in 10 that the stocks will double their value.
____ The chances are 9 in 10 that the stocks will double their value.
____ Place a check here if you think Mr. C should *not* invest in Company X stocks, no matter what the probabilities.

4. Mr. D is the captain of College X's football team. College X is playing its traditional rival, College Y, in the final game of the season. The game is in its final seconds, and Mr. D's team, College X, is behind in the score. College X has time to run one more play. Mr. D, the captain, must decide whether it would be best to settle for a tie score with a play which would be almost certain to work or, on the other hand, should he try a more complicated and risky play which could bring victory if it succeeded, but defeat if not.

Imagine that you are advising Mr. D. Listed below are several probabilities or odds that the risky play will work.

Please check the lowest *probability that you would consider acceptable for the risky play to be attempted.*

258 Appendix E

____ Place a check here if you think Mr. D should *not* attempt the risky play no matter what the probabilities.
____ The chances are 9 in 10 that the risky play will work.
____ The chances are 7 in 10 that the risky play will work.
____ The chances are 5 in 10 that the risky play will work.
____ The chances are 3 in 10 that the risky play will work.
____ The chances are 1 in 10 that the risky play will work.

5. Mr. E is president of a light metals corporation in the United States. The corporation is quite prosperous, and has strongly considered the possibilities of business expansion by building an additional plant in a new location. The choice is between building another plant in the U.S., where there would be a moderate return on the initial investment, or building a plant in a foreign country. Lower labor costs and easy access to raw materials in that country would mean a much higher return on the initial investment. On the other hand, there is a history of political instability and revolution in the foreign country under consideration. In fact, the leader of a small minority party is committed to nationalizing, that is, taking over, all foreign investments.

Imagine that you are advising Mr. E. Listed below are several probabilities or odds of continued political stability in the foreign country under consideration.

Please check the lowest *probability that you would consider acceptable for Mr. E's corporation to build a plant in that country.*

____ The chances are 1 in 10 that the foreign country will remain politically stable.
____ The chances are 3 in 10 that the foreign country will remain politically stable.
____ The chances are 5 in 10 that the foreign country will remain politically stable.
____ The chances are 7 in 10 that the foreign country will remain politically stable.
____ The chances are 9 in 10 that the foreign country will remain politically stable.
____ Place a check here if you think Mr. E's corporation should *not* build a plant in the foreign country, no matter what the probabilities.

6. Mr. F is currently a college senior who is very eager to pursue graduate study in chemistry leading to the Doctor of Philosophy degree. He has been accepted by both University X and University Y. University X has a world-wide reputation for excellence in chemistry. While a degree from University X would signify outstanding training in this field, the standards are so very rigorous that only a fraction of the degree candidates actually receive the degree. University Y, on the other hand, has much less of a reputation in chemistry, but almost everyone admitted is awarded the Doctor of Philosophy degree, though the degree has much less prestige than the corresponding degree from University X.

Imagine that you are advising Mr. F. Listed below are several probabilities or odds that Mr. F would be awarded a degree at University X, the one with the greater prestige.

Please check the lowest *probability that you would consider acceptable to make it worthwhile for Mr. F to enroll in University X rather than University Y.*

___ Place a check here if you think Mr. F should *not* enroll in University X, no matter what the probabilities.
___ The chances are 9 in 10 that Mr. F would receive a degree from University X.
___ The chances are 7 in 10 that Mr. F would receive a degree from University X.
___ The chances are 5 in 10 that Mr. F would receive a degree from University X.
___ The chances are 3 in 10 that Mr. F would receive a degree from University X.
___ The chances are 1 in 10 that Mr. F would receive a degree from University X.

7. Mr. G, a competent chess player, is participating in a national chess tournament. In an early match he draws the top-favored player in the tournament as his opponent. Mr. G has been given a relatively low ranking in view of his performance in previous tournaments. During the course of his play with the top-favored man, Mr. G notes the possibility of a deceptive though risky maneuver which might bring him a quick victory. At the same time, if the attempted maneuver should fail, Mr. G would be left in an exposed position and defeat would almost certainly follow.

Imagine that you are advising Mr. G. Listed below are several probabilities or odds that Mr. G's deceptive play would succeed.

Please check the lowest *probability that you would consider acceptable for the risky play in question to be attempted.*

___ The chances are 1 in 10 that the play would succeed.
___ The chances are 3 in 10 that the play would succeed.
___ The chances are 5 in 10 that the play would succeed.
___ The chances are 7 in 10 that the play would succeed.
___ The chances are 9 in 10 that the play would succeed.
___ Place a check here if you think Mr. G should *not* attempt the risky play, no matter what the probabilities.

8. Mr. H, a college senior, has studied the piano since childhood. He has won amateur prizes and given small recitals, suggesting that Mr. H has considerable musical talent. As graduation approaches, Mr. H has the choice of going to medical school to become a physician, a profession which would bring certain prestige and financial rewards; or entering a conservatory of music for advanced training with a well-known pianist. Mr. H realizes that even upon completion of his piano studies, which would take many more years and a lot of money, success as a concert pianist would not be assured.

Imagine that you are advising Mr. H. Listed below are several probabilities or odds that Mr. H would succeed as a concert pianist.

Please check the lowest *probability that you would consider acceptable for Mr. H to continue with his musical training.*

___ Place a check here if you think Mr. H should *not* pursue his musical training, no matter what the probabilities.
___ The chances are 9 in 10 that Mr. H would succeed as a concert pianist.
___ The chances are 7 in 10 that Mr. H would succeed as a concert pianist.

___ The chances are 5 in 10 that Mr. H would succeed as a concert pianist.
___ The chances are 3 in 10 that Mr. H would succeed as a concert pianist.
___ The chances are 1 in 10 that Mr. H would succeed as a concert pianist.

9. Mr. J is an American captured by the enemy in World War II and placed in a prisoner-of-war camp. Conditions in the camp are quite bad, with long hours of hard physical labor and a barely sufficient diet. After spending several months in this camp, Mr. J notes the possibility of escape by concealing himself in a supply truck that shuttles in and out of the camp. Of course, there is no guarantee that the escape would prove successful. Recapture by the enemy could well mean execution.

Imagine that you are advising Mr. J. Listed below are several probabilities or odds of a successful escape from the prisoner-of-war camp.

Please check the lowest *probability that you would consider acceptable for an escape to be attempted.*

___ The chances are 1 in 10 that the escape would succeed.
___ The chances are 3 in 10 that the escape would succeed.
___ The chances are 5 in 10 that the escape would succeed.
___ The chances are 7 in 10 that the escape would succeed.
___ The chances are 9 in 10 that the escape would succeed.
___ Place a check here if you think Mr. J should *not* try to escape no matter what the probabilities.

10. Mr. K is a successful businessman who has participated in a number of civic activities of considerable value to the community. Mr. K has been approached by the leaders of his political party as a possible congressional candidate in the next election. Mr. K's party is a minority party in the district, though the party has won occasional elections in the past. Mr. K would like to hold political office, but to do so would involve a serious financial sacrifice, since the party has insufficient campaign funds. He would also have to endure the attacks of his political opponents in a hot campaign.

Imagine that you are advising Mr. K. Listed below are several probabilities or odds of Mr. K's winning the election in his district.

Please check the lowest *probability that you would consider acceptable to make it worthwhile for Mr. K to run for political office.*

___ Place a check here if you think Mr. K should *not* run for political office no matter what the probabilities.
___ The chances are 9 in 10 that Mr. K would win the election.
___ The chances are 7 in 10 that Mr. K would win the election.
___ The chances are 5 in 10 that Mr. K would win the election.
___ The chances are 3 in 10 that Mr. K would win the election.
___ The chances are 1 in 10 that Mr. K would win the election.

11. Mr. L, a married 30-year-old research physicist, has been given a five-year

appointment by a major university laboratory. As he contemplates the next five years, he realizes that he might work on a difficult, long-term problem which, if a solution could be found, would resolve basic scientific issues in the field and bring high scientific honors. If no solution were found, however, Mr. L would have little to show for his five years in the laboratory, and this would make it hard for him to get a good job afterwards. On the other hand, he could, as most of his professional associates are doing, work on a series of short-term problems where solutions would be easier to find, but where the problems are of lesser scientific importance.

Imagine that you are advising Mr. L. Listed below are several probabilities or odds that a solution would be found to the difficult, long-term problem that Mr. L has in mind.

Please check the lowest probability that you would consider acceptable to make it worthwhile for Mr. L to work on the more difficult long-term problem.

____ The chances are 1 in 10 that Mr. L would solve the long-term problem.
____ The chances are 3 in 10 that Mr. L would solve the long-term problem.
____ The chances are 5 in 10 that Mr. L would solve the long-term problem.
____ The chances are 7 in 10 that Mr. L would solve the long-term problem.
____ The chances are 9 in 10 that Mr. L would solve the long-term problem.
____ Place a check here if you think Mr. L should *not* choose the long-term, difficult problem, no matter what the probabilities.

12. Mr. M is contemplating marriage to Miss T, a girl whom he has known for a little more than a year. Recently, however, a number of arguments have occurred between them, suggesting some sharp differences of opinion in the way each views certain matters. Indeed, they decide to seek professional advice from a marriage counselor as to whether it would be wise for them to marry. On the basis of these meetings with a marriage counselor, they realize that a happy marriage, while possible, would not be assured.

Imagine that you are advising Mr. M and Miss T. Listed below are several probabilities or odds that their marriage would prove to be a happy and successful one.

Please check the lowest probability that you would consider acceptable for Mr. M and Miss T to get married.

____ Place a check here if you think Mr. M and Miss T should *not* marry, no matter what the probabilities.
____ The chances are 9 in 10 that the marriage would be happy and successful.
____ The chances are 7 in 10 that the marriage would be happy and successful.
____ The chances are 5 in 10 that the marriage would be happy and successful.
____ The chances are 3 in 10 that the marriage would be happy and successful.
____ The chances are 1 in 10 that the marriage would be happy and successful.

Appendix F

Chance Bets Instrument

DICE BETS

Instructions. In this task, you will be shown pairs of dice bets that vary in terms of the chances of winning and losing, and the amounts of money that can be won or lost. I would like you to choose, in each pair, the bet that you would prefer to play. Indicate your decision by making a check in the box[1] under the bet that you prefer to play. Consider each pair separately — do not let your decision in one case influence your decision in another. Later you will have the opportunity to actually play the bets that you now choose. You will play them in a dice game for the amounts of money described in the bets. So be sure that you choose now the bets that you actually will want to play, because you will be held to them.

The chances of winning and losing are written as fractions: Thus, 1/4 means 1 chance in 4, 1/2 means 1 chance in 2, 1/9 means 1 chance in 9, etc.

1. 1/9 to win $1.20 vs. 1/2 to win $ .60
   8/9 to lose $ .15   1/2 to lose $ .60

2. 1/4 to win $ .90 vs. 3/4 to win $ .10
   3/4 to lose $ .30   1/4 to lose $ .30

3. 1/4 to win $ .45 vs. 1/9 to win $1.20
   3/4 to lose $ .15   8/9 to lose $ .15

4. 1/9 to win $2.40 vs. 3/4 to win $ .20
   8/9 to lose $ .30   1/4 to lose $ .60

5. 3/4 to win $ .05 vs. 1/2 to win $ .15
   1/4 to lose $ .15   1/2 to lose $ .15

6. 1/2 to win $ .60 vs. 3/4 to win $ .20
   1/2 to lose $ .60   1/4 to lose $ .60

7. 3/4 to win $ .20 vs. 1/9 to win $4.80
   1/4 to lose $ .60   8/9 to lose $ .60

---

[1]The boxes have been omitted here, to save space.

Appendix F | 263

8. 1/9 to win $1.20   vs.   3/4 to win $ .10
   8/9 to lose $ .15   1/4 to lose $ .30

9. 1/2 to win $ .60   vs.   3/4 to win $ .05
   1/2 to lose $ .60   1/4 to lose $ .15

10. 1/9 to win $1.20   vs.   1/2 to win $ .30
    8/9 to lose $ .15   1/2 to lose $ .30

11. 1/2 to win $ .30   vs.   1/9 to win $2.40
    1/2 to lose $ .30   8/9 to lose $ .30

12. 3/4 to win $ .10   vs.   1/9 to win $4.80
    1/4 to lose $ .30   8/9 to lose $ .60

13. 1/4 to win $1.80   vs.   1/9 to win $2.40
    3/4 to lose $ .60   8/9 to lose $ .30

14. 1/2 to win $ .15   vs.   1/9 to win $4.80
    1/2 to lose $ .15   8/9 to lose $ .60

15. 1/4 to win $1.80   vs.   3/4 to win $ .05
    3/4 to lose $ .60   1/4 to lose $ .15

16. 1/2 to win $ .30   vs.   3/4 to win $ .20
    1/2 to lose $ .30   1/4 to lose $ .60

17. 1/2 to win $ .60   vs.   1/4 to win $ .45
    1/2 to lose $ .60   3/4 to lose $ .15

18. 3/4 to win $ .10   vs.   3/4 to win $ .20
    1/4 to lose $ .30   1/4 to lose $ .60

19. 1/4 to win $1.80   vs.   3/4 to win $ .10
    3/4 to lose $ .60   1/4 to lose $ .30

20. 1/9 to win $2.40   vs.   1/4 to win $ .90
    8/9 to lose $ .30   3/4 to lose $ .30

21. 1/2 to win $ .60   vs.   1/9 to win $2.40
    1/2 to lose $ .60   8/9 to lose $ .30

22. 1/9 to win $4.80   vs.   1/2 to win $ .60
    8/9 to lose $ .60   1/2 to lose $ .60

23. 3/4 to win $ .05   vs.   1/4 to win $ .45
    1/4 to lose $ .15   3/4 to lose $ .15

24. 1/4 to win $ .45   vs.   1/9 to win $4.80
    3/4 to lose $ .15   8/9 to lose $ .60

25. 1/4 to win $ .90   vs.   1/2 to win $ .15
    3/4 to lose $ .30   1/2 to lose $ .15

26. 3/4 to win $ .05   vs.   1/9 to win $2.40
    1/4 to lose $ .15   8/9 to lose $ .30

27. 3/4 to win $ .20   vs.   1/2 to win $ .15
    1/4 to lose $ .60   1/2 to lose $ .15

28. 1/9 to win $1.20   vs.   1/9 to win $4.80
    8/9 to lose $ .15   8/9 to lose $ .60

29. 1/4 to win $1.80   vs.   1/2 to win $ .15
    3/4 to lose $ .60   1/2 to lose $ .15

30. 1/4 to win $ .90   vs.   3/4 to win $ .20
    3/4 to lose $ .30   1/4 to lose $ .60

31. 3/4 to win $ .20   vs.   1/9 to win $1.20
    1/4 to lose $ .60   8/9 to lose $ .15

32. 1/2 to win $ .30   vs.   1/4 to win $1.80
    1/2 to lose $ .30   3/4 to lose $ .60

33. 1/9 to win $2.40   vs.   1/2 to win $ .15
    8/9 to lose $ .30   1/2 to lose $ .15

Appendix F | **265**

34. 1/4 to win $ .90   vs.   1/2 to win $ .30
    3/4 to lose $ .30   1/2 to lose $ .30

35. 3/4 to win $ .20   vs.   1/4 to win $ .45
    1/4 to lose $ .60   3/4 to lose $ .15

36. 1/4 to win $1.80   vs.   1/2 to win $ .60
    3/4 to lose $ .60   1/2 to lose $ .60

37. 1/2 to win $ .30   vs.   1/4 to win $ .45
    1/2 to lose $ .30   3/4 to lose $ .15

38. 1/9 to win $1.20   vs.   1/9 to win $2.40
    8/9 to lose $ .15   8/9 to lose $ .30

39. 1/4 to win $ .90   vs.   3/4 to win $ .05
    3/4 to lose $ .30   1/4 to lose $ .15

40. 1/9 to win $2.40   vs.   1/9 to win $4.80
    8/9 to lose $ .30   8/9 to lose $ .60

41. 1/2 to win $ .60   vs.   1/2 to win $ .30
    1/2 to lose $ .60   1/2 to lose $ .30

42. 3/4 to win $ .10   vs.   1/2 to win $ .60
    1/4 to lose $ .30   1/2 to lose $ .60

43. 1/4 to win $1.80   vs.   1/4 to win $ .90
    3/4 to lose $ .60   3/4 to lose $ .30

44. 3/4 to win $ .05   vs.   1/9 to win $4.80
    1/4 to lose $ .15   8/9 to lose $ .60

45. 3/4 to win $ .10   vs.   1/4 to win $ .45
    1/4 to lose $ .30   3/4 to lose $ .15

46. 1/2 to win $ .15   vs.   1/2 to win $ .60
    1/2 to lose $ .15   1/2 to lose $ .60

Appendix F

47. 1/9 to win $4.80   vs.   1/4 to win $ .90
      8/9 to lose $ .60   3/4 to lose $ .30

48. 1/2 to win $ .30   vs.   3/4 to win $ .10
      1/2 to lose $ .30   1/4 to lose $ .30

49. 3/4 to win $ .10   vs.   3/4 to win $ .05
      1/4 to lose $ .30   1/4 to lose $ .15

50. 1/2 to win $ .15   vs.   1/9 to win $4.80
      1/2 to lose $ .15   8/9 to lose $ .60

51. 1/2 to win $ .60   vs.   1/4 to win $ .90
      1/2 to lose $ .60   3/4 to lose $ .30

52. 1/2 to win $ .15   vs.   3/4 to win $ .10
      1/2 to lose $ .15   1/4 to lose $ .30

53. 3/4 to win $ .20   vs.   1/4 to win $1.80
      1/4 to lose $ .60   3/4 to lose $ .60

54. 1/9 to win $1.20   vs.   1/2 to win $ .15
      8/9 to lose $ .15   1/2 to lose $ .15

55. 1/4 to win $1.80   vs.   1/9 to win $4.80
      3/4 to lose $ .60   8/9 to lose $ .60

56. 1/4 to win $ .45   vs.   1/2 to win $ .15
      3/4 to lose $ .15   1/2 to lose $ .15

57. 1/4 to win $ .90   vs.   1/4 to win $ .45
      3/4 to lose $ .30   3/4 to lose $ .15

58. 1/9 to win $2.40   vs.   3/4 to win $ .10
      8/9 to lose $ .30   1/4 to lose $ .30

59. 1/4 to win $ .90   vs.   1/9 to win $1.20
      3/4 to lose $ .30   8/9 to lose $ .15

Appendix F | **267**

60. 1/4 to win $ .45   vs.   1/9 to win $2.40
    3/4 to lose $ .15   8/9 to lose $ .30

61. 1/4 to win $1.80   vs.   1/4 to win $ .45
    3/4 to lose $ .60   3/4 to lose $ .15

62. 3/4 to win $ .05   vs.   1/2 to win $ .30
    1/4 to lose $ .15   1/2 to lose $ .30

63. 3/4 to win $ .05   vs.   1/9 to win $1.20
    1/4 to lose $ .15   8/9 to lose $ .15

64. 3/4 to win $ .20   vs.   3/4 to win $ .05
    1/4 to lose $ .60   1/4 to lose $ .15

65. 1/2 to win $ .30   vs.   1/2 to win $ .15
    1/2 to lose $ .30   1/2 to lose $ .15

66. 1/9 to win $1.20   vs.   1/4 to win $1.80
    8/9 to lose $ .15   3/4 to lose $ .60

Appendix G-1

EXPERIMENTER'S RECORD SHEET FOR SHUFFLEBOARD PRACTICE SERIES

Enter a one for each success, a zero for each failure.

	1	2	3	4	5	6	7	8	9	10	11	12	13	14	15	16	Total
±2½																	5
±1																	2
±3½																	7
±2																	4
±¾																	1½
±1½																	3
±3																	6
±1¼																	2½

Summary: $\frac{1½}{16}$ $\frac{2}{16}$ $\frac{2½}{16}$ $\frac{3}{16}$ $\frac{4}{16}$ $\frac{5}{16}$ $\frac{6}{16}$ $\frac{7}{16}$

Appendix G–2

SUBJECT'S CHART FOR SHUFFLEBOARD BETS

Chances of winning	1/8	1/4	1/2	3/4
Chances of losing	7/8	3/4	1/2	1/4
Post separation	——	——	——	——
15¢ pays	1.05	.45	.15	.05
30¢ pays	2.10	.90	.30	.10
60¢ pays	4.20	1.80	.60	.20

Appendix H

Subject's Chart for Dice Plays

Chances of winning	1/9	1/4	1/2	3/4
Chances of losing	8/9	3/4	1/2	1/4
Wins on	9	5, 6	2, 4, 6, 8, 10, 12	2, 3, 4, 5, 6, 7, 10, 11, 12
15¢ pays	1.20	.45	.15	.05
30¢ pays	2.40	.90	.30	.10
60¢ pays	4.80	1.80	.60	.20

Index

Abilities, intellective, *see* Intellective abilities
Ability and aptitude domain, 11, 14–15, 19–20, 25, 33, 94, 96–101, 107–108, 111, 165, 200–201, 209
Absolute winnings, *see* Winnings, absolute
Accommodation to environment, 206
Acquiescence, 19, 23–24, 160–163, 186
Acting out or counterphobic qualities, 167
Advanced Vocabulary Test, 25
Age, subjective, 13
Age differences, 3–4
Aging, consequences of, 3
Agreement Response Factor, Couch and Keniston's, 24, 163
All-or-none principle, 137, 144, 157, 197–198
ALPERT, R., 23, 120
Alpert-Haber scale, 23, 120
Ambiguity, 136, 147
Analytic functioning, 11, 25, 94, 104, 110–120, 122
Anxiety, 3, 12–13, 23, 40, 47, 63–64, 75–76, 121, 199–200, 212
  manifest, *see* Manifest anxiety
  signals, 17
  stress-induced, 212
  symptoms, 108, 121
  test, *see* Test anxiety
Aptitude, mathematical, *see* Mathematical aptitude
Aptitude, verbal, *see* Verbal aptitude
Aptitude domain, *see* Ability and aptitude domain
ASCH, S. E., 162, 178, 180, 182, 204, 206
Asch-type conformity situation, 162, 179–182, 204
Assimilation of environment, 206
ATKINSON, J. W., 7, 12, 13, 16, 66, 67, 73, 97
Attitude, active, participant, 122
Attitude, passive, spectator, 122
AUSTIN, G. A., 2
Autonomy, 187

Balanced scales, 23–24
BALLACHEY, E. L., 180
BARRATT, E. S., 24, 163
Barratt Impulsiveness Scale, 24, 163, 186
BARRON, F., 24, 178, 182
Barron-Asch-Crutchfield Independence-Yielding Scale, 24, 162, 178–182, 186, 204
BASTIAN, J. R., 7
BEM, D. J., 25
BENDIG, A. W., 24
Bet strategies, *see* Chance strategies *and* Skill strategies
Bets, *see* Chance bets, Dice bets, Final bet, *and* Skill bets
BOOMER, D. S., 11
Breadth of categorization, *see* Categories *and* Categorization
BREHM, J. W., 9, 79, 192
BRIM, O. G., Jr., 4, 6, 10, 22, 128, 134, 140, 205
BRODIE, B., 212
BRUNER, J. S., 2, 3, 10

CARON, A. J., 2, 5, 17
Categories, broad, 2, 4–5, 147–150, 158, 195–196
  narrow, 2–5, 146–149, 158, 195
Categorization, behavior, 2–3, 12, 124, 147–148, 155
  breadth of, 2–5, 146–151, 158, 194–197, 199
Category boundaries, 4–5
Category width, 4, 9, 147–151, 155–158, 194–195, 197
  task, geometric, 6
  test, Pettigrew's, 5–6, 9, 22, 146–148, 150–151, 155
Certainty, desire for, 128–129, 134, 137, 140, 144, 149, 156, 197–198
Certainty levels, subjective, 99
Certainty of class membership, 158
Certainty of occurrence and nonoccurrence, 157

Index

Chance and skill, bet preference booklets, 30
  contexts, 7, 28–30, 36, 48–50, 79–81, 87, 97, 114–115, 122, 129, 142–143, 152, 194–195, 199
    plays, 30–31, 70–72, 81–88
    strategies, 45–49, 66–68, 95, 97, 100, 102, 104, 112, 115, 125, 127, 132, 139, 146–147, 152, 155, 164–165, 174, 185, 187, 194
  Chance bets, 26, 28–31, 49, 57, 83–84, 104, 107, 180
    dissatisfaction, 31, 79–84, 88
  Chance context, 41–42, 49–50, 58–59, 66, 71–74, 79, 84, 87–89, 93, 96, 107, 112, 114–115, 135, 152–153
  Chance plays, 30–31, 70–72, 81–84
  Chance strategies, 38–41, 49–51, 53, 57–59, 61–62, 67, 70–74, 88, 95, 100–101, 104–111, 113–114, 127–133, 135–136, 138, 140, 142, 145, 147–148, 150, 154, 157, 162, 165, 167, 172, 174–175, 177–178, 180–183, 208
    long shot (CLS), 38, 49–50, 57, 71, 88, 159–161
    maximization of gain (CMG), 38, 49–50, 57, 71, 88, 159–161
    maximization of variance (CMV), 38, 49–50, 57, 71, 88, 159–161
    mean differences in, 89
    minimization of deviation from ½ (CMD), 38, 49–50, 57, 71, 88, 159–161
    minimization of loss (CML), 38, 49–50, 57, 71, 88, 159–161
    outcomes, 51, 62, 87
  Chance winnings, 72–73
Choice dilemmas, 6–7, 9, 25–26, 36, 38–47, 57, 95–96, 111–114, 125–127, 152–154, 159–167, 170–171, 174–175, 177, 180, 182–183, 186
Class membership, certainty of, 158
Class of greater value, 147, 195–196
Class of lesser value, 195–196
Classes, inclusion, *see* Inclusion classes
Clues, 30–31, 43–45, 49–57, 62–64, 67–68, 102–104, 115–117, 125, 138–139, 146, 151, 159–161, 194–195, 208–209
  number judgments versus, 68
  reliabilities for, 36
Cognitive and decision domains, 4, 7, 13–14
Cognitive and personality organization, 103, 122
Cognitive control, 17, 116, 207
  of leveling, 207
  and personality, 110–111

Cognitive dissonance, 9, 16, 79, 192
Cognitive-judgmental domain, 3–6, 10, 13–14, 17, 19–21, 32–33, 45–46, 124–125, 127, 135, 139, 142–143, 145, 155–156, 163, 165, 193–194, 199
Cognitive-judgmental forms of risk taking, 5
Cognitive-judgmental indexes, 5, 13, 20, 22, 124, 132–133, 155
Cognitive-judgmental reliabilities, 36
Cognitive organization, personality and, 103, 122
Cognitive steering mechanism, 117–118, 122, 201
Cognitive versus motivational determinants, 191
Cohen, A. R., 9, 192
Cohen, Jacob, 37
Cohen, John, 7
Commitment, 89, 192
Compensatory mechanisms, 140, 157
Concept attainment, 2, 6
Conceptual conservatism, 2–3
Conceptual risk taking, 146
Confidence, 3–4, 19, 22, 124–145, 147–150, 152, 155–158, 194, 196–199
  compensatory relationship with extremity, 139
  extremity under high, *see* Extremity under high confidence
  extremity under low, *see* Extremity under low confidence
  high, 132–139, 141, 143–144, 150, 156
  index, 30, 124–125, 128, 152, 155
  low, 137–145, 148–149, 156–157, 197
  overcompensation for lowered, 134
  self-appraisals of, 194
  self-referent, 152
  sex and age differences in, 3
Conformity, 181, 187
Conservatism, 1, 4, 10–12, 15, 20, 26, 30, 39, 42, 44, 46, 50, 52, 60–62, 64, 69, 71–73, 77–78, 89–90, 93, 97–99, 108–109, 111–112, 114–119, 121–123, 126–127, 134–135, 140, 143–147, 150, 152–153, 156–158, 162, 164–168, 172–173, 175–179, 182–187, 190–195, 197–199, 200–205, 207–213
  conceptual, 2–3
  feminine, 3
  social, 171, 182
Content-style interactions, 151
Conventionality-unconventionality, 162, 178–179, 182, 187
Coombs, C. H., 7, 11, 27
Cost-free conditions, 195

Couch, A., 24, 163
Couch and Keniston's Agreement Response Factor, 24, 163
Counterphobic mechanisms, 133–136, 139, 143, 153–154, 156–157, 166–167, 197–198
Craighill, P. G., 98
Creativity, 205
Cronbach, L. J., 11, 18
Crowne, D. P., 23, 24, 120, 170
Crutchfield, R. S., 11, 24, 178, 180, 182

Decision, correctness of, 30, 84
Decision making, generality of, see Generality of decision making
outcomes, see Outcomes, decision
procedures, 5–9, 19–20, 40, 42–43, 47, 53–54, 64, 68, 94, 111, 155, 174–175, 182, 184, 207–209
rationality and irrationality in, see Rationality-irrationality
Defense mechanisms, 11–12
Defensive inhibition, 14
Defensiveness, 13–17, 19–20, 23–24, 33–36, 39–44, 46–47, 49–69, 73, 75–86, 90–92, 95–97, 99–101, 103, 105–110, 112–116, 118–124, 126–138, 140–145, 147–151, 153–157, 163–190, 193–194, 196, 199–200, 202–206, 209–210, 212–213
Desire for certainty, see Certainty, desire for
Deterrence of failure, 26, 38, 41, 43–46, 126, 170, 177
Deutsch, M., 82, 212, 213
Dice bets, 26, 39, 49–50, 57–59, 83–84, 89, 100–102, 105, 142, 155
Disaffiliation, risks of, 175
Dissatisfaction, chance bets, see Chance bets dissatisfaction
Dissatisfaction, skill bets, see Skill bets dissatisfaction
Drive recruitment, maximal, 207
Drive structures, 207
Dual process conceptualization, 47, 67–68
Duncker, K., 206
Dyk, R. B., 11

Earl, R. W., 7
Edwards, A. L., 24, 151
Edwards, W., 27, 208
Edwards Social Desirability Scale, 24, 151
EFT, see Embedded Figures Test
Ego psychology, 207
Ego-involving conditions, 98
Elliott, R., 11

Embedded Figures Test (EFT), 11–12, 25, 94, 99, 104, 111–112, 114–115, 117–118, 120, 122
Environment, accommodation to, 206
Environment, assimilation of, 206
Error, risk of, 137, 198
tendencies, 189, 195–196
tolerance limits for, 5
Errors of exclusion, 2, 5, 146, 150, 158, 195–196
Errors of inclusion, 2, 4–5, 149–150, 158, 195–196
Estimation Questionnaire, 22
Exclusion, errors of, see Errors of exclusion
Exclusion classes, 147–149, 158, 195–196
Extremity, 3–4, 19, 22, 132–145, 149–150, 155–158, 194, 197–199
of self-rating, 19, 22–23, 25, 151–156, 158
sex and age differences in, 3–4
under high confidence, 132–139, 141–144, 156–157
under low confidence, 139–145, 156–157

Factor analysis, 32–33, 189, 202–203
Failure, deterrence of, see Deterrence of failure
fear of, 12, 16–17, 69
Failure-avoidance motivation, 49–51, 66, 84, 97
Faterson, H. F., 11
Fenichel, O., 206
Festinger, L., 9
Field independence–field dependence, 11–12, 25, 111–120, 122–123, 201–202
Field influences, 201
Fillenbaum, S., 33
Final bet, 31–32, 36, 38, 45–46, 57–69, 117–119, 132, 138, 144–145, 152, 155–156, 160–161, 165, 167, 169, 173–176, 179–181, 183–187, 191, 210
outcomes of, 62, 119
Flexibility, see Rigidity-flexibility
Forehand, G. A., 33
Frank, J. D., 213
French, J. W., 25
French's kit of aptitude and achievement tests, 25
Freud, Anna, 14
Freud, S., 1, 14, 17, 206, 207

Gagné, R. M., 205
Gahm, Ruthellen C., 14
Gain, maximization of, see Maximization of gain
Gain-loss properties, 5, 47, 102, 194, 204

274 Index

Gambling, 12, 39, 45, 62, 64, 69, 109–110, 151, 199–200
  response set, 11, 98, 102–103, 105–106, 108–111, 121–122
GARDNER, R. W., 3, 10, 11, 17, 33, 207
Generality of decision making, 2, 6–7, 9–10, 42–43, 47, 56, 67, 124, 168, 190
Gestalt psychology, 206
GHISELLI, E. E., 13
GLASS, D. C., 4
Global functioning, 111–120, 122
GOODENOUGH, D. R., 11
GOODMAN, N., 4
GOODNOW, JACQUELINE J., 2
GOUGH, H. G., 24, 184
Gough-Sanford Rigidity Scale, 24, 184
GREEN, L. R., 14
GREENBERG, CAROL, 14
Guessing, 11, 25, 98–101, 104, 107–108, 110–111, 121, 200
  penalty for, see Penalty for guessing
GUILFORD, J. P., 205

HABER, R. N., 23, 120
HAMILTON, V., 3
HARTMANN, H., 207
HEIDBREDER, EDNA, 117
HEIDER, F., 8
HERTZMAN, M., 11
HILLS, J., 11
HOFF, D. B., 128, 134, 140
HOLZMAN, P. S., 17, 207
HOMANS, G. C., 204
Hypothetical decision context, 6, 43–45, 47, 94–95, 111–113, 124, 155, 167–168, 180
Hypothetical versus payoff contexts, 38, 42, 44, 47, 67, 158, 186, 193

Identity of opposites, 168
Image, masculine, 66
Image maintenance, 14, 60–61, 64–66, 68, 84, 129, 140, 156, 190, 194, 196, 206
Impulse control, 112–115, 117, 163
Impulse expression, psychodynamic implications of, 118
Impulse inhibition, 122–123, 201
Impulse release, 122
Impulsiveness, 18, 114, 159–161, 163–170, 173, 185–186, 201–203
  scale, 18, 24, 163, 186
Inclusion, errors of, see Errors of inclusion
Inclusion classes, 147, 149, 158, 195–196
Independence-yielding, 18, 36, 139, 159–164, 177–179, 180–182, 185–187, 197, 203–204

Independence-yielding (cont.)
  scale, 18, 24, 162, 178–182, 186, 204
Information-seeking, 7–8, 11, 15, 38, 43–44, 49–57, 62–64, 67, 102, 115–118, 125, 132, 138, 144, 151, 155, 165, 172–174, 182, 195–196
Inhibition, defensive, 14
  impulse, 122–123, 201
Intellective abilities, 2, 10–12, 20, 25, 32–33, 36, 94–122, 163, 199–202
Intelligence, 11, 14–15, 64, 68, 96–100
  test set, 9
Internal-versus-external control, extent of, 12
Interpersonal contexts, 59–60, 87, 173–174, 206
Irrationality, 208–214
IRWIN, F. W., 7, 29

JACKSON, D. N., 10, 11, 19, 25, 120
JOHNSON, L. C., 124
Judgment, 2, 4–5, 19, 61, 68–69, 125, 132, 136–138, 143–144, 148–154, 157, 194, 197–198, 212
  sex differences in, 133
Judgmental confidence, see Confidence
Judgmental extremity, see Extremity
Judgmental extremity-confidence instrument, 22, 29, 124

KAHN, H., 213
KARP, S. A., 11
KELLEY, H. H., 204
KENISTON, K., 24, 163
Kit of aptitude and achievement tests, French's, 25
KLEIN, G. S., 3, 17, 117, 207
KOGAN, N., 3, 4, 6, 9, 10, 13, 14, 17, 22, 25, 36, 125, 133, 146, 198
KÖHLER, W., 206
KRAUSS, R. M., 82
KRECH, D., 180

LAVIN, D. E., 4
LEWIN, K., 189, 194
LEWIS, HELEN B., 11
Lie-scale properties, 23
LIKERT, R., 23, 151
Likert-scale format, 23, 151
Linearity, assumption of, 188
LINTON, HARRIET, 17
LIPSITT, P. D., 14
LITTIG, L. W., 7
LITWIN, G. H., 7, 12
LIVERANT, S., 10, 12
Long shot, 26, 39, 49, 52, 104, 112, 125, 146, 152

Long shot (cont.)
  chance (CLS), see Chance, long shot
  skill (SLS), see Skill, long shot
Loss, minimization of, see Minimization of loss

McClelland, D. C., 66
McGee, R. K., 19
Machover, Karen, 11
Mandler, G., 98
Manifest anxiety, 13, 18, 159–163, 186
Manifest Anxiety Scale (MAS), 18, 24
March, J. C., 208
Marlowe, D., 23, 24, 120, 170
Marlowe-Crowne Scale, 23–24, 120, 170–171
Masculine image, 66
Mathematical aptitude, 11, 22, 25, 94, 102–111, 120, 122, 128, 146
Maximization of gain, 39, 50, 52, 104, 112, 125, 146, 152
  chance (CMG), see Chance, maximization of gain
  skill (SMG), see Skill, maximization of gain
Maximization of variance, 52, 72, 104, 112, 125, 146, 152
  chance (CMV), see Chance, maximization of variance
  skill (SMV), see Skill, maximization of variance
Meehl, P. E., 18
Meissner, Pearl B., 11
Memory, short-term, 207
Menninger Foundation, 207
Messick, S., 3, 10, 11, 19, 24, 25, 146
Methodological consequences, 188
Milholland, J. E., 11
Minas, J. S., 10
Minehart, Jean B., 14
Minimization of deviation from ½, 71–72, 74, 78, 94, 97, 104–105, 112, 125, 141, 146, 152–153, 159–161, 172, 177–178, 183, 185–186
  chance (CMD), see Chance, minimization of deviation from ½
  skill (SMD), see Skill, minimization of deviation from ½
Minimization of loss, 39, 48–50, 72, 89, 104, 108–109, 112, 114, 125, 127, 132, 134–135, 139–140, 146, 152, 154, 162–163, 172
  chance (CML), see Chance, minimization of loss
  skill (SML), see Skill, minimization of loss

MMPI K Scale, 24
Moderator effects, 13–20, 23, 32–35, 39–47, 49–52, 54–56, 58, 61–64, 67–70, 72–78, 81–82, 85–86, 88–90, 93, 95–97, 99–102, 112–113, 115, 117, 119–120, 122, 124–127, 129, 132–133, 135, 138, 144–145, 147, 151–158, 163–167, 170, 172–175, 177, 180, 183–184, 186–189, 193–194, 201–204
Monetary outcomes, 6, 8, 15–17, 27, 38, 40–41, 45, 51, 63–64, 66, 70–88, 90–93, 102, 125, 127, 145, 164, 174, 180, 192–193, 209–210
Monetary risk, 7–8, 15, 27–28, 45–46, 64–66, 81, 119, 125, 135, 155
Motivation, thinking and, 1–2
Motivation-cognition relationship, 116–117, 191, 207, 210
Motivational determinants, cognitive versus, 191
Motivational disturbance, 1–2, 14–15, 41, 43, 47, 51, 54, 59–60, 62, 67–69, 73–77, 79, 92–93, 98–99, 114, 116–119, 122–123, 139, 145, 154, 156, 164, 166–167, 172, 179–180, 186–187, 190, 192–193, 198–200, 202–203, 210
Motor skill, 9, 15, 28, 52–53, 63–64, 67–68, 77–78, 171–172, 192
Myers, C. T., 25

Narrowness of categorization, see Categories and Categorization
Nay-saying response style, 23
Need achievement, 7, 12, 14
Need for social approval, 23, 68, 87, 140, 170–171, 173, 186
Negative outcomes, see Outcomes, negative
Number judgments, 29–31, 36, 43–44, 49–50, 52–53, 55–57, 62–63, 68, 112, 115–117, 124–125, 146, 151, 159–162, 164–165, 172–173, 186, 195, 208
  clues versus, 68

Optimal strategies, 72–74, 173, 186
Osgood, C. E., 211, 212
Outcomes, chance strategies, 51, 62, 87
  control over, 40, 67, 71, 105, 110, 113, 129, 134, 150–151, 167, 172, 178
  decision, 20, 51, 62, 72, 81–83, 87–93, 115, 170–171, 180, 182, 186, 190, 193, 195, 202, 208–210
  of final bet, 62, 119
  monetary, see Monetary outcomes
  negative, 60–61, 79, 82–83, 93, 192
  positive, 79, 83, 128–129

Overcompensation mechanism, 133–136, 157
Overcontrol, 114, 201

Paired comparisons procedure, 47
PALOLA, E. G., 98
Payoff conditions, 6–7, 9, 11, 20, 28, 38, 40–42, 44, 47, 51, 53, 56–57, 67–68, 73, 88, 99, 102, 116, 124–125, 127, 132, 135, 146, 154–156, 167–168, 173, 184, 190, 193–195, 197–198, 204, 208
PEABODY, D., 19, 151
PEARSON, K., 33
Penalty for guessing, 11, 25, 98, 100, 102, 104, 106, 109, 199–200
Permissive testing conditions, 25, 100–102, 106–107, 121–122
Personality, cognitive control and, 110–111
Personality organization, cognitive and, 103, 122
Personality Research Inventory, 24, 151
PETTIGREW, T. F., 3, 5, 6, 22, 146, 147, 148, 149, 150
Pettigrew's Category Width Test, *see* Category Width Test
PIAGET, J., 206
Pleasure principle, 206
Poggles task, 5–6
Policy-making contexts, behavior in, 211, 213
Positive outcomes, 79, 83, 128–129
Postdecision satisfaction, 9, 16, 20, 70, 79, 81, 88–93, 209–210
Predecisional and postdecisional phenomena, 91–92
Press, psychological, 68
Primary-process thought, 207
Prior winnings, *see* Winnings, prior
Probability estimation, 9, 22, 127–131, 133, 136–137, 142, 145, 148–149, 157, 194, 197–198
Problem solving, 1, 5, 51, 53, 57, 98, 102, 200, 205–206
PRUITT, D. G., 7, 27
Psychological press, 68
Psychotherapy, 23–24

QUERESHI, M. Y., 11

Rationality-irrationality, 208–214
RAPAPORT, D., 207
RATOOSH, P., 10
Reaction formation, 168–170
Reality principle, 206
Reflective function, 138–139, 153–154, 157
Relative winnings, *see* Winnings, relative
Reliability of measures, 36

Repression, 14, 207
Response styles, 19, 24, 117, 162, 186
nay-saying, 23
Rigidity-flexibility, 18, 24, 159–164, 182–187, 203
Risk, of error, 137, 198
monetary, *see* Monetary risk
regulation, 47, 49, 51, 54–55, 57, 59, 62–63, 67–69, 190
Risk taking, cognitive-judgmental forms of, 5
conceptual, 146
implicit versus explicit, 4–5, 9, 15, 53–54, 103, 111, 126–127, 134–139, 143–144, 146, 150, 153–154, 164, 193–194, 202
social, 175–179, 182, 187, 204
theory of motivation, 97
threshold, *see* Threshold effects in risk taking
Risks of disaffiliation, 175
ROBERTS, J. S., Jr., 30
ROGERS, C. R., 14
ROSEN, S., 9
ROSENAU, NORAH, 82
RUEBUSH, B. K., 99

Sample sizes, 34
SANFORD, R. N., 24, 184
SARASON, I. G., 23, 24, 98
SARASON, S. B., 98
SAT, *see* Scholastic Aptitude Test
Satisficing, 208
SAUNDERS, D. R., 13, 24
Scales
Alpert-Haber, 23, 120
Barratt Impulsiveness, 24, 163, 186
Barron-Asch-Crutchfield Independence-Yielding, 24, 162, 178–182, 186, 204
Couch-Keniston, 24, 163
Edwards Social Desirability, 24, 151
Gough-Sanford Rigidity, 24, 184
Manifest Anxiety, 18, 24
Marlowe-Crowne, 23–24, 120, 170–171
MMPI K, 24
reliabilities of, 23
Sarason Test Anxiety, 23
Self-sufficiency, 18, 24, 151, 162, 170, 186
Social Desirability, 19, 24, 151
SCHOEN, R. A., 3
Scholastic Aptitude Test (SAT), 25, 98–101, 103–104, 106–109, 111, 121, 199–200, 209
Mathematical section, 25, 104, 106–107, 111
Verbal section, 25, 100, 111, 209

SCODEL, A., 10, 12
Self-evaluation, 66, 130–132, 156, 190, 194
Self-image, 14, 66, 88, 153, 194, 196
Self-sufficiency, 18, 152, 158–164, 170–177, 185–187, 203–204
  scale, 18, 24, 151, 162, 170, 186
Sensorimotor interference, 207
Sex differences, 3–5, 17, 55–56, 67, 71–72, 74, 79, 84, 118, 122, 133, 150, 155–156, 165–166, 174, 180, 187, 191, 202–203, 210
  in confidence, 3
  in extremity, 3–4
  in judgment, 133
SHERIFFS, A. C., 11
Shuffleboard procedure, 27–29, 41, 52–53, 59, 62, 85, 89
SIMON, H. A., 208
Situational influences, 40, 77, 118–119, 129–130, 164–165, 168, 173, 186, 190, 204–205, 207–211
Situational sensitivity, 123, 186, 191
Skill and chance, contexts, see Chance and skill contexts
  plays, see Chance and skill plays
  strategies, see Chance and skill strategies
Skill bets, 27, 30–31, 41, 94, 130–132, 155, 162–163, 191–195
  dissatisfaction, 31, 79–83, 85–86, 89–92, 191–192
  preference booklets, chance and, 30
Skill context, 41–43, 52–53, 67–68, 75–78, 81, 87–89, 91–93, 97, 104, 112–114, 123, 128–129, 135, 152–153, 170–173
Skill strategies, 41–43, 47–50, 52–55, 59–64, 67–68, 75–78, 89–92, 96, 102, 105, 108–110, 112–114, 127, 129–131, 134, 137, 139–143, 147, 149–150, 154, 159, 166, 168, 171–177, 180, 182–184, 186, 192, 208
  long shot (SLS), 41, 52, 59, 89, 160–161
  maximization of gain (SMG), 41, 52, 59, 89, 160–161
  maximization of variance (SMV), 41, 52, 59, 89, 160–161
  minimization of deviation from ½ (SMD), 41, 52, 59, 89, 160–161
  minimization of loss (SML), 41, 52, 59, 89, 160–161
Skilled performance, 75–77, 91–92
SLOVIC, P., 4, 6, 11
SMITH, W. A. S., 7, 29
Social approval, see Need for social approval
Social behaviors, implications for, 182
Social class differences, 12

Social conservatism, 171, 182
Social decision-making phenomena, 204
Social desirability, 152, 160–163, 186
  scales, 19, 24, 151
Social risk taking, 175–179, 182, 187, 204
Socio-economic background of sample, 21
Spatial relations indexes, performance on, 11
SPENCE, D. P., 17
STARKWEATHER, J. A., 11
Statistical test, power of, 37
Strategies, see Chance strategies, Optimal strategies, and Skill strategies
Stress, 66, 100–101, 104, 106, 199–200, 211–213
  of academic examinations, 66, 121–122
STRICKLAND, BONNIE R., 23
Structural task similarities, see Task similarities
Subjective age, 13
Subjective certainty levels, 99
Subjective probability, 2, 4, 7, 9
Subjects of study, 21
Success-failure contexts, 5, 15–17, 47, 190
Sweet femininity syndrome, 152

TAJFEL, H., 2, 3, 10
Task-centeredness, 54, 186, 190, 206–208, 210–211
Task similarities, 54–57, 67, 190–191, 206, 210–211
TAYLOR, D. W., 205
Tension level, 211–212
Test anxiety, 13–17, 19–20, 23, 33–36, 39–44, 46–47, 50–69, 73, 75–86, 90–93, 95–103, 105–110, 112–116, 118–124, 126–138, 140–145, 147–151, 153–157, 163–190, 192–193, 195, 199–200, 202–206, 209–210, 212–213
  Atkinson conceptualization of, 67
  decremental effects of, 102
Test Anxiety Scale, Sarason's, 23
Test-taking performance, 100, 102, 111, 121
Testing context, 102, 121–122
THIBAUT, J. W., 204
Thinking and motivation, 1–2
Thinking processes, 1–2, 205–211
Thirst and perception, 207
Threshold effects in risk taking, 71–73, 99, 105–106, 134
Tolerance limits for error, 5

Uncertainty, 3, 140, 144, 147, 150, 157, 196–200
  reduction, 134, 144, 148–151, 157–158, 197–198

Unconventionality, 152, 158, 162
Utility, 2, 4, 5, 7–8, 16, 27, 208

Value judgments, 211
Variance preferences, 27
Verbal aptitude, 10–11, 25, 67–68, 94–97, 99–109, 111, 120–122, 199–200
Vocabulary test, 100–103, 121

WALLACH, M. A., 2, 3, 4, 5, 6, 9, 13, 14, 17, 22, 25, 36, 125, 133, 147, 149, 195, 198
WAPNER, S., 11
WECHSLER, D., 10, 11
WERTHEIMER, M., 206
WHITE, R. W., 14

Winnings, 8–9, 11, 15–16, 26–27, 30–31, 45–46, 57–78, 81–95, 118, 119, 132, 145, 169, 173–174, 176, 179–181, 183–185, 191–193, 209–210
  absolute, 71–72, 74–76, 78, 81, 83–85, 88–90, 92, 94–95, 192
  prior, 15–16, 45–46, 57–69, 84–86, 118–119, 132, 145, 169, 173–174, 176, 179, 181, 183–185, 191, 210
  relative, 72–74, 76–78, 81–82, 84–89, 193
WITKIN, H. A., 11, 25, 111, 114, 119, 120, 201
WOMER, F. B., 11
WORLEY, D. R., 30

Yielding tendencies, 185–204

ZILLER, R. C., 11